# Australia in the Global Economy

*Continuity and Change*

*For Deborah*
  *D. M.*

*For Mary Ellen*
  *B. D.*

# Australia in the Global Economy

*Continuity and Change*

David Meredith

University of New South Wales

Barrie Dyster

University of New South Wales

PUBLISHED BY THE PRESS SYNDICATE OF THE UNIVERSITY OF CAMBRIDGE
The Pitt Building, Trumpington Street, Cambridge, United Kingdom

CAMBRIDGE UNIVERSITY PRESS
The Edinburgh Building, Cambridge CB2 2RU, UK      www.cup.cam.ac.uk
40 West 20th Street, New York, NY 10011–4211, USA    www.cup.org
10 Stamford Road, Oakleigh 3166, Australia
Ruiz de Alarcón 13, 28014, Madrid, Spain

First published 1999

Printed in Australia by Southwood Press Pty Limited

*Typeface* Berthold Baskerville Book. *System* QuarkXPress®

A catalogue record for this book is available from the British Library

*National Library of Australia Cataloguing in Publication data*
Meredith, David (David George), 1949– .
Australia in the global economy : continuity and change.
Bibliography.
Includes index.
ISBN 0 521 63127 0.
ISBN 0 521 63730 9 (pbk.)
1. International economic relations. 2. Investments,
Foreign – Australia. 3. Australia – Foreign economic
relations. 4. Australia – Economic conditions – 20th
century. 5. Australia – Commerce. I. Dyster, Barrie,
1940– . II. Title.
337.94

ISBN 0 521 63127 0 hardback
ISBN 0 521 63730 9 paperback

# CONTENTS

PART IV

# 1974 TO 1989

PART V

# THE 1990s

# TABLES

# FIGURES

# PREFACE

In writing *Australia in the Global Economy* we have been influenced by the strengths and weaknesses of our previous work, *Australia in the International Economy*. This was published by Cambridge University Press in 1990 and quickly established itself as the leading introductory work on the Australian economy in the twentieth century world economy. The book was widely reviewed, and we have taken into account some of the comments made by reviewers, as well as those of colleagues and students during the 1990s. The present work brings our arguments up to date and reflects the greater interest shown in Australia in questions of 'globalisation' in the late 1990s. Barrie Dyster took chief responsibility for Chapters 3, 5, 6 and 8 and David Meredith for the remainder.

Our thanks go to Katrina Alford for her insightful comments on an earlier draft and to a number of anonymous referees whose views we took on board. Deborah Oxley made valuable comments on various chapters and was an enormous help with the graphics. Expert typing services were provided by Aline Dinel. Phillipa McGuinness, CUP's commissioning editor, was an enthusiastic supporter throughout the process and remained remarkably patient as the deadlines slipped by.

## Overview: how this book is set out

*Australia in the Global Economy* is arranged chronologically. Chapter 1 presents the main themes and historical overview. Chapters 2 and 3 are concerned with Australia in the international economy before the outbreak of the First World War in 1914. Chapter 2 discusses changes in the international economy in the late nineteenth and early twentieth centuries, and how these impacted on Australia. Chapter 3 examines Australia's responses during this period in more detail.

Chapters 4, 5 and 6 deal with the period from the start of the First World War to the outbreak of the Pacific War in 1941. Chapter 4 outlines the relevant changes in the world economy and highlights their significance for Australia. Chapter 5 details Australia's relations with the international economy in the 1920s and Chapter 6, the 1930s.

Chapters 7, 8 and 9 deal with a period in Australian and international economic history known as the Long Boom: from the Second World War to the mid-1970s. Chapter 7 discusses the changes in the world economy during this time of strong economic expansion, and Chapters 8 and 9 contain analyses of how Australia participated in the international Long Boom.

Australia's relations with the global economy in the final quarter of the twentieth century are the subject of Chapters 10, 11, 12 and 13. The upheavals in the world economy in the 1970s and 1980s and their implications for Australia are outlined in Chapter 10. Chapter 11 covers the period of stagflation and economic reform in Australia, from 1975 to 1990. Chapter 12 provides a summary of the international changes that impacted on Australia in the 1990s, the final one of which was the onset of the Asian economic crisis in 1997. Finally, Chapter 13 discusses how the Australian economy performed in its new 'global' setting to 1998, and concludes with a perspective on 'globalisation' at the start of the new century.

A glossary of economic terms has been provided. The terms (including their derivatives, e.g. 'tariff'; 'tariffs') have been marked in bold in all chapters.

# 1

# Introduction, themes and overview

This book is an introduction to Australia's economic history in the twentieth century, taking as its main theme the integration of the Australian economy in the global economy. It focuses on Australian external trade (imports and exports of goods and services), the inflow and outflow of **capital** (**foreign investment**) and the influx of permanent settlers from abroad (immigration). Each of these flows across Australia's borders formed – and continue to form – part of the nation's international integration. Each can be viewed separately in time, but in reality they interacted closely and together defined Australia's relationship with the global economy. This relationship changed and developed in some ways, and remained constant in others, over the first century of Federation. Each of these international economic connections were subjects, both separately and as they interacted, of public policy. And, of course, international flows of trade, capital and people impacted on the performance and development of the domestic economy and ultimately on Australian living standards.

This chapter introduces the nature of these flows and the themes of this book. It begins by examining two fundamental features of the Australian economy in its international context – its size and openness. It then considers how integration with the international economy contributed to Australia's **economic growth**, both through international **demand** for the products that Australian producers could export to the world and through the international supply of two **factors of production**: **capital** and labour. The third part of this chapter introduces the major contours in the history of public policies that shaped the international economic flows: tariff policy, **wages policy** and immigration policy. The chapter concludes with a brief discussion on the development of government management of the Australian economy with particular emphasis on managing Australia's **balance of payments**. The arrangement of subsequent chapters and their themes is given at the end of this chapter.

1

# Features of the Australian economy

## Population growth and urbanisation

Australia at the beginning of the twentieth century was small in population but in an aggregate sense it was not poor. Its **income per head** was below that of the United States, the richest country in the world. But it was above that of Britain, the nation about which more Australians had direct or indirect knowledge than any other foreign country, and the one with which they reasonably compared their standard of living (see Table 1.1). Australia's population did not grow particularly quickly in the twentieth century. Indeed, concerns about its future at the beginning of the century led to the establishment of a Royal Commission into the Decline in the Birth Rate in 1904. The Commissioners reported with alarm that it would take 113 years for Australia to reach 20 million people – a fairly accurate prediction as it turned out (Olds 1993, p. 159).

Although Australia's population grew more quickly than that of Britain from where most nineteenth century settlers had come, it grew noticeably more slowly than some other lands of European settlement – Canada, the United States and Argentina (see Figure 1.1). This outcome was not due to a failure to reduce mortality: death rates in Australia fell significantly over the twentieth century. Rather, it reflected a relatively low birth rate and a restricted inflow of immigration. Table 1.2 shows the contribution of natural increase (the difference between birth rate and death rate) and net immigration (the difference between immigration and emigration) in the growth of Australia's population. Despite the fulmination of the Royal Commission against family planning, significantly raising the birth rate was not a likely outcome: Australia had already achieved the high average material living standards historically associated with smaller family size. Instead, Australia looked to immigration to boost population – at times the phrase 'populate or perish' was used in this connection.

No doubt Australia's population growth would have been faster if immigration had been higher. There were periods when the inflow was relatively large, generally those years of higher economic growth and when Australian governments encouraged immigrants: the half a dozen years before the First World War, the mid-1920s and the 'Long Boom' from the late 1940s to the early 1970s stand out. At other times, net immigration was negligible or negative. In the late 1980s,

**Table 1.1**  GDP per capita in Australia, Britain and USA, 1905–09

| Country | Gross domestic product (average 1905–09) £ millions | Population (average 1905–09) millions | GDP per head £ |
|---|---|---|---|
| Australia | 257.1 | 4.115 | 62.48 |
| United Kingdom | 1975.6 | 34.299 | 57.60 |
| United States | 5979.4 | 83.984 | 71.20 |

Source: Based on Mitchell 1992, pp. 4, 10, 749, 897, 1017.

**Figure 1.1**    Population growth: Australia, Britain, Canada, USA and Argentina, 1901 to 1995

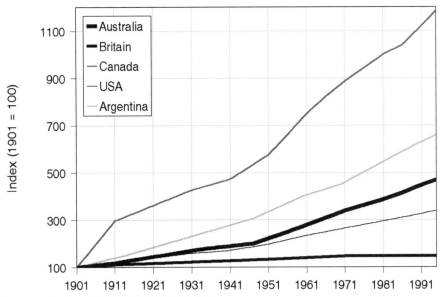

Sources: Based on Mitchell 1992; UN *Yearbook*.

there was a return to higher intakes, but this faded in the 1990s. These ups and downs had less to do with supply than with demand. Comparatively high living standards 'pulled' people in Australia's direction, guaranteeing a constant supply of potential immigrants. But demand varied according to the country's perceived needs for labour, and for another reason. Before the 1970s, immigration was restricted by racism. The White Australia Policy dictated that most of Australia's immigrants should come from Britain and Ireland. When these were not forthcoming in sufficient numbers after the Second World War, Australia turned (somewhat reluctantly) to continental Europe and the Mediterranean. However, it did not turn to Asia or the Pacific until the late 1970s. The White Australia Policy was abandoned in a period when immigration levels were low. When the total intake rose in the 1980s, the proportion coming from Asia certainly increased, but the overall intake did not return to the higher levels of the 1950s and 1960s. Thus the adoption of a non-discriminatory immigration policy did not have much effect on total population growth.

Whether Australia would have been better off had it matched the more rapid population growth of America is uncertain. With more people there would have been more consumers and more labour. The size of the economy would have been larger. This might have attracted more capital **investment** and led to more **land** being released, the two other important factors in the production equation. But even if capital and land were increased in proportion to labour, it is unclear whether this would have translated into a higher *per capita* level of income. Economic growth *per head* requires **productivity** gains. Productivity rises when

**Table 1.2**   Contribution of net migration to Australia's population growth,
1881–1993

| Period (calendar years) | Population at start of period | Population increase during period | Proportion of population increase due to net migration |
|---|---|---|---|
| 1881–1890 | 2 231 531 | 919 824 | 41.6 |
| 1891–1900 | 3 151 355 | 613 984 | 4.1 |
| 1901–1910 | 3 765 339 | 659 744 | 17.9 |
| 1911–1920 | 4 425 083 | 986 214 | 22.5 |
| 1921–1930 | 5 411 297 | 1 089 454 | 27.9 |
| 1931–1940 | 6 500 751 | 576 385 | 5.3 |
| 1941–1945 | 7 077 586 | 352 611 | 2.2 |
| 1946–1950 | 7 430 197 | 877 284 | 40.3 |
| 1951–1955 | 8 307 481 | 1 004 344 | 41.2 |
| 1956–1960 | 9 311 825 | 1 080 095 | 37.5 |
| 1961–1965 | 10 391 920 | 1 072 437 | 37.3 |
| 1966–1970 | 11 505 408 | 1 158 061 | 47.0 |
| 1971–1975 | 12 799 600 | 1 169 300 | 31.5 |
| 1976–1980 | 13 968 900 | 838 500 | 38.0 |
| 1981–1985 | 14 807 400 | 1 093 200 | 39.3 |
| 1986–1990 | 15 900 600 | 1 269 200 | 50.3 |
| 1991–1993 | 17 169 800 | 576 000 | 29.0 |

Source: Based on Bureau of Immigration 1984–95, nos 13–18.

work practices improve or, more typically, when firms purchase new equipment that increases the output of their existing **labour force**. It was quite feasible that faster population growth in the twentieth century may have led to *lower* per capita incomes than were actually achieved, if extra labour was substituted for investment in the new labour-saving technologies. If this were true, it would imply that Australia's immigration program (the element in population growth more easily controlled by the government) was not unduly inadequate. Otherwise, the limits placed on immigration were also limits placed on economic growth.

Despite its geographic size and the importance of the rural economy, Australia was not a rural society. Its degree of urbanisation at the beginning of the century was remarkable, and remarked on by foreign visitors (for example, the American writer Mark Twain). Australia was more urban than the United States or Canada, though less so than Britain which was at that time the most industrialised society in the world (see Table 1.3). Australia's two largest cities, Melbourne and Sydney, between them accounted for 26 per cent of the total population in 1901 and 28 per cent 10 years later. The reasons for this high level of urbanisation lay in the nature of the rural economy and the preferences of Australia's nineteenth-century immigrants. Rural production was land intensive, but it did not absorb the bulk of either capital investment or population increases. As a result, most people lived in the coastal cities and earned their living by working in the

**Table 1.3**   Urbanisation in Australia and USA, 1891–1947

| Year | | Population (persons, 000) | | Percentage of population living in urban centres | |
|---|---|---|---|---|---|
| Australia | USA | Australia | USA | Australia | USA |
| 1891 | 1890 | 3152 | 62 948 | 56.4 | 35.1 |
| 1901 | 1900 | 3744 | 75 995 | 57.1 | 39.7 |
| 1921 | 1920 | 5406 | 105 711 | 62.5 | 51.2 |
| 1933 | 1930 | 6613 | 122 775 | 64.0 | 56.2 |
| 1947 | 1940 | 7561 | 131 669 | 68.9 | 56.5 |

Sources: Based on Vamplew 1987, p. 41; United States, Bureau of the Census, 1960, p. 14.

services sector (including construction and transport) and manufacturing. A great deal of Australia's nineteenth-century population growth was due to immigration from Britain and Ireland, and whatever the background of these migrants in their homeland, most showed a clear preference for city life over rural living once they arrived in Australia. As a consequence, Australia developed a vibrant and relatively prosperous urban economy, linked only partly to the rural economy that supplied the nation's export earnings. Competition between these two economies for resources and tension between them for power formed a permanent theme in Australian domestic politics during the twentieth century.

## Reliance on the world economy

Australia was an open economy at the beginning of the twentieth century in the sense that it depended on the outside world for imports, capital, and, as discussed already, people. It was also open in the sense that there were few restrictions on imports and none on capital. Immigration was open to UK citizens, who could enter Australia at will, though not to other nationalities. Australia was open to ideas and new technology – and sometimes the rest of the world was interested in Australian social experiments. The share of exports in the Australian economy is shown in Figure 1.2. With a very limited manufacturing sector, Australians' high per capita incomes could only be converted to high material living standards through importing **consumer goods** as well as **capital goods** and equipment. Exports were the main means of paying for these, although international lending enabled Australia to live beyond its means for most periods during the twentieth century. The nature of exports was well established by 1900: wool and gold, the staples of the nineteenth century, still predominated, though they were now joined by a limited range of other primary products (wheat, meat, dairy produce and some base metal ores). The **primary products** that were exported were not usually processed in Australia, but entered the global economy as raw foodstuffs and raw materials.

Thus a dual economy had developed by the beginning of the twentieth century. One economy was rural and export orientated; the other was urban and,

**Figure 1.2**    Australia's export ratio, 1900 to 1997–98 (exports of goods as a percentage of GDP)

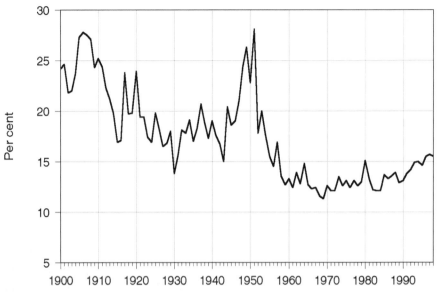

Sources: Based on Pinkstone 1992, p. 393; RBA 1996 p. 4; ABS 1998, pp. 15, 23.

as the century wore on, increasingly protected. Linkages between the two economies existed but were limited. Imports were essential, both to production and consumption. But some at least were also competitive, and seemed to undermine the urban economy. Since this was where the majority lived and worked, and Australia was at least partially democratic, **protection** from imports was a politically popular policy and one that lasted for nearly all of the century. It took the new Commonwealth less than a decade to embark on a protectionist stance that raised barriers to imports constantly for the next 60 years. This encouraged and sustained the growth of the manufacturing industry for most of these years and was an important element in Australia's industrialisation. Protectionism was the major factor that qualified Australia's openness.

Exports not only paid for imports, they also underwrote Australia's ability to attract foreign investment. Ultimately, foreigners who lent to Australian businesses or governments, or directly invested in the Australian economy, expected to be repaid with **interest** and to repatriate their profits. Some of the foreign capital that Australia was able to attract flowed into export industries. Most did not. Rather it consisted of loans to Australian governments (Commonwealth and State) and private investment (of loans or equity) in the manufacturing and services sectors of the economy. Foreign investor confidence in Australia was damaged by the economic crisis in the 1890s (see Chapter 3) but foreign capital inflow returned in the early years of Federation. State governments found that they could once again borrow on the London capital market and private businesses (especially those in the 'new' export industries and in nascent manufacturing) were also recipients of

British funds. State government expended their funds on building **infrastructure**, particularly railways.

The outbreak of the Great War in 1914 produced a series of foreign loans from Britain to the Commonwealth government and the return to peace and expansion of the domestic economy in the 1920s led to a further large capital influx. By the end of the 1920s, Australia had a **foreign debt** problem. Since most of this debt was publicly owed (and therefore could not easily be written off) the international economic **crash** at the beginning of the 1930s exposed Australia's vulnerability. Foreign capital dried up so the foreign debt stabilised, but interest and repayments continued, imposing a heavy burden on Australian living standards in the years before the outbreak of the Second World War.

The Second World War was a watershed in Australia's dependence on foreign capital. Sales of goods and services to the United States during the war enabled most of the existing foreign debt to be repaid. After the war, Australian governments raised the majority of their capital requirements at home, and private foreign borrowing was heavily regulated. Foreign investment flowed into Australia, but now it consisted almost entirely of direct investment by foreign firms, mainly in manufacturing industry. American investment edged ahead of flows from Britain for the first time. Post-war industrialisation depended on foreign investment, foreign technology and foreign workers – a feature that stimulated economic nationalism in the 1960s and led to the imposition of curbs on **direct foreign investment** in the early 1970s. Foreign capital also flowed strongly into the mining sector once the minerals boom of the 1960s was under way, a development that further heightened criticisms of foreign ownership. Financial deregulation in the early 1980s permitted a return to private foreign borrowing. By the end of the decade Australia once again was faced with a high foreign debt, stabilisation of which in the last decade of the century was one of the challenges of 'globalisation'.

Over the twentieth century, then, Australia's openness to **international trade** was qualified by its commitment to protectionist policies, while its dependence on export earnings to pay for both imports and foreign investment remained in place. Its openness to foreign capital was qualified by periods of **slump** when investors

## SUMMARY BOX

In the twentieth century, Australia could be described as a small, open, export-dependent economy that relied on primary production for export earnings to pay for imports and foreign capital. Foreign investment and immigration augmented domestic sources of capital and labour. A dual economy developed between the rural export sector and the urban manufacturing and service sectors, where most Australians lived and worked. These features were qualified by restrictions placed on immigration, import barriers and regulation of capital flows. In the last two decades of the century, globalisation recreated some of the openness lost in the middle part of the century.

lost confidence (for example, the 1890s and 1930s) and by restrictions placed on foreign borrowing in the 1950s and 1960s, and foreign direct investment in the 1970s. Only with deregulation in the early 1980s did Australia return to the openness of international capital markets of the earlier part of the century.

# International economy and economic growth

Australia's economic growth is depicted in Figure 1.3, which shows real output per head rising substantially over the twentieth century (this is the increase in per capita income mentioned earlier). Output per head increased in most years, though faster at some times than others. In a general sense, this increase represents the extent to which material living standards rose during the century. Australia's integration with the international economy played a major role in causing economic growth and shaping its contours. Periods of faster or slower economic growth in Australia coincided with similar patterns in the global economy leading to a close correlation between the pace of expansion internationally and domestically. Australia grew fastest when the world economy grew fastest, and when the world economy was stagnant, Australia's growth rate slowed as well. From this it might be concluded that Australia could not prosper unless the world economy was prosperous and that when this was the case, Australia was usually able to seize the opportunities for growth that the international economy offered. The global economy was Australia's pacemaker.

## Local demand and the international economy

The linkages between the international economy and Australia's economy lay on both the demand and supply sides. Growth of the international economy consisted of expansion of world trade, capital flows and migration of people. Australia was affected by each of these. Faster growth of world trade implied rising demand for Australia's exports of primary products. In some periods of expansion, international demand for primary products was the most dynamic element (for example, before the First World War and just after the Second). The main driving force behind this demand was the rate at which industrialisation occurred.

As discussed in more detail in Chapter 2, industrialisation was fundamental to the growth of the international economy. By the start of the twentieth century, industrialisation was no longer a new phenomenon, having spread in the second half of the nineteenth century from Britain to Western Europe, North America and Japan. As industrialisation spread, and as industrialised economies continued to grow, demand for raw materials needed for the manufacturing industry expanded. Some countries (especially Canada, the United States and Australia later in the twentieth century) were able to supply much of what was required from their own resources, but even they increased their imports of raw materials to some extent. Other countries relied on imports even more, especially those, like Britain and Japan, that were poorly endowed with natural resources for large-scale industry. International demand for raw materials fluctuated with the rate and pattern of

**Figure 1.3**    Australia's real GDP per head, 1901 to 1998

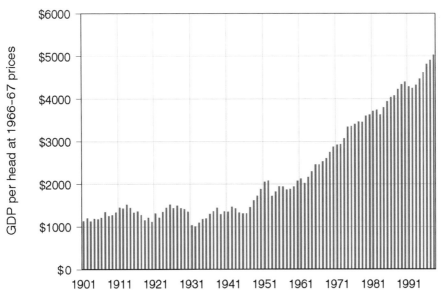

Sources: Based on Butlin 1962, pp. 440–61; RBA 1996; ABS 1998.

these industrial countries' growth. Moreover, in Europe industrialisation had the effect of reducing national self-sufficiency in foodstuffs. Agriculture in industrial countries did not contract absolutely, but in the face of a rapidly rising population, food imports became vital. Industrialisation also led to the solution of the technical problems of developing international trade in perishable foodstuffs through the application of mechanised power to shipping and the invention of refrigeration. By 1900, international demand for raw materials was joined by international demand for food – both resulting from the spread of industrialisation – to produce expansive world demand for primary products.

Australia was hardly the only country able to supply these demands. In fact, some of the supply came from the industrialising countries themselves: Britain was the world's leading exporter of coal, for example, and Japan of raw silk. Moreover, industrialisation in North America did not mean an end to primary exports from the United States and Canada. Indeed, North America was the dominant source of internationally traded temperate foodstuffs. Other countries, yet to be industrialised, entered the world market as suppliers of temperate primary products. All of these suppliers were competitors to Australian farmers and miners. Australia was disadvantaged by its 'tyranny of distance' from Europe, a disability only partly mitigated by improvements in international transport. On the other hand, Australia's **comparative advantage** in certain primary products ensured that if world demand was buoyant, export sales would be made, though prices received fluctuated considerably.

Over the twentieth century, the opportunities for exporting primary products varied. Before the First World War, demand expanded because industrial growth was strong. In the 1920s, however, the growth of industrial nations slowed and the competition to supply primary products increased, leading to weak prices and sluggish world trade. Many industrial countries decided to protect their farming communities from international trade. Population growth in the food-importing countries also slowed. Substitutes for raw materials increased in number and there were significant advances in the efficiency with which raw materials were used. Export-led growth in Australia became less robust as a result. In the 1930s, however, international demand for primary products collapsed completely as the industrial nations went into their worst economic slump – the Great Depression. Australia followed the industrial economies into the **depression** and was unable to recover until they did. Since their recovery was incomplete and had limited impact on the revival of world trade, Australia ended the fourth decade of the century in considerable economic distress.

After the Second World War, the situation changed dramatically. Economic growth in the industrial countries was again strong and temperate foodstuffs in high demand. Some of the highest prices ever paid for Australian primary exports were recorded in the decade following the end of the war. From the mid-1950s, international demand for primary products steadied, but three developments combined to reinforce Australia's dependence on primary exports. First, Japan's economic recovery and industrial expansion. Second, the onset of a minerals and energy resources boom in Australia. Third, the further spread of industrialisation, particularly in East and South-East Asia.

Japan emerged as a significant customer for Australian primary exports in the late 1950s and by the mid-1960s it had replaced Britain as Australia's major export market. The Australian minerals boom began in the 1960s and continued into the 1970s on the back of an extraordinary rise in international energy prices. Industrialisation in Asia, outside of Japan, began in the 1960s in Korea, Singapore, Hong Kong and Taiwan; and in the following decade in China, Malaysia, Indonesia and Thailand. These countries added significantly to world demand for primary products. Australia's own industrialisation after the Second World War eventually led to the growth of exports of manufactured goods, so that primary exports were not so overwhelmingly dominant at the end of the century as they had been for the first six decades. By the late 1990s, services exports also developed and some primary products were exported in a semi-processed form, including those that were genetically engineered. Nevertheless, international demand for primary products remained a fundamental element in Australia's ability to earn export revenue.

## Local supply and the international economy

On the supply side, the expansion of the international economy produced capital and migration flows. Again, it was industrialisation that was the driving force. As industrialisation proceeded, accumulated capital found an outlet in international investment flows. The impact of nineteenth century industrialisation on population growth in the countries undergoing it was complex, but the net effect was to produce the world's first sustained population explosion, part of which became outflows of migration. Australia participated as a recipient in both of these international flows.

## Capital and foreign investment

Before the First World War, the bulk of funds for investment entering the international economy came from private British investors who were mainly interested in secure returns at higher interest rates than on offer at home. Their foreign investments were directed through specialised financial institutions in the City of London. Australia was only one of many countries to which these investors directed their funds, but from Australia's side, all of its imported capital came from Britain. The majority of these inflows were in the form of long-term loans to Colonial (and later State) governments, but there were also British investors who lent to Australian businesses and who purchased shares in Australian firms. Finally, there was some direct investment by British firms that set up subsidiary companies in Australia. British investors regarded Australia as an attractive place to employ their funds. Those who lent to governments were attracted by the relatively high interest rates paid and the absolute security such loans within the British Empire were believed to enjoy. Investors in private Australian ventures were attracted by the possibilities of quick fortunes from wool or mining, while British firms that set up subsidiaries looked to the higher per capita incomes and British orientation of white Australian consumers.

For a number of reasons discussed in more detail in Chapter 3, British investors lost confidence in Australia in the early 1880s, plunging the colonial economies into a damaging financial crisis. British funds began to flow again in the decade prior to the outbreak of the First World War, dominated as before by loans to State governments, but also including portfolio investments in the new mining developments as well as in the growing urban economy. The First World War closed the London money market, but British government loans to the Commonwealth government meant that Australia was more indebted internationally at the end of the war than it had been at its outset. In the 1920s, with the London market reopened, private loans to State governments resumed, augmented by direct British investment. The world financial crisis in 1930 brought chaos and panic to the London market, and Australian borrowers again found themselves cut off from fresh capital inflows. During the rest of the 1930s, very little British capital flowed to Australia, with the result that the net movement was in the opposite direction as Australian **debtors** continued to meet interest commitments and make repayments to their British **creditors**. Australia's foreign debt stabilised, but the cost of servicing remained high at the beginning of the Second World War.

The pattern of capital inflows to Australia in the first half of the twentieth century was similar to that of the nineteenth. Most of the funds were loans to governments that used them to finance a variety of expensive infrastructure projects. These included railways, roads, port facilities, urban transport, social amenities, gas, electricity, water supply and sewerage. These investments improved urban Australians' standard of life, but had very limited linkages to the export sector, with the exception of some railway and port facilities. As the size of the foreign debt grew so did the proportion of export earnings required to service it. This made Australian borrowers vulnerable to changing market sentiment – with dire consequences in 1890 and 1930.

After the Second World War, this pattern was not repeated. Funds for infra-structure were found mainly from domestic sources and neither State governments nor the Commonwealth borrowed heavily abroad. In the 1950s, 1960s and 1970s, capital inflows were dominated by private direct investment and although some of these inflows represented investments by British firms, the bulk now came from United States multinational enterprises. These firms invested heavily in the indus-trial expansion that Australia was undergoing, as well as in the mining boom. Foreign investment crises of the kind that had occurred previously did not recur. Because most of the foreign investment in Australia was direct, Australia's foreign debt remained very low. Foreign firms could repatriate their earnings at will, but the buoyancy of the Australian economy persuaded many of them to reinvest a substantial part of their profits in the local economy, thus avoiding a major nega-tive impact on Australia's balance of payments. Similarly, foreign investors in Australian share markets tended to keep their money in Australia. Foreign owner-ship did, however, become a political issue in Australia in the 1960s and 1970s, often tinged with anti-American paranoia.

In the last two decades of the twentieth century there was a revival of foreign debt for reasons explained in chapters 11 and 13. There was not, however, a repeat of the debt crises of the type experienced by Australia in 1890 and 1930. Partly, this was because even at its height in the early 1990s, Australia's net foreign debt was not so great as at these earlier points, and partly because 'globalisation' made high levels of foreign debt less of a problem. The sources of foreign investment widened: American and British investment still remained important, but by the last

**Figure 1.4**   Australia's foreign investment ratios, 1885–1975 (capital inflow as a % of gross domestic capital formation)

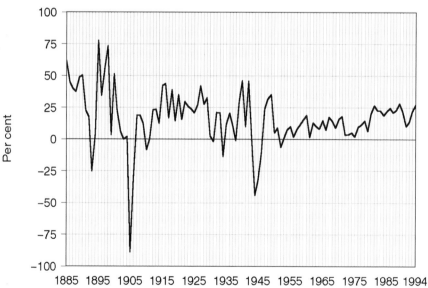

Sources: Based on Butlin 1962, p. 422; Butlin 1977, pp. 78, 108; RBA 1996, pp. 36, 214.

quarter of the century, investors in other countries discovered the attractions of employing surplus funds in the Australian economy, principally the Japanese. The scope of foreign investment also widened. Resources, energy, manufacturing and property continued to attract funds, but so too now did various service industries – financial, business and tourism.

The significance of foreign investment was twofold. First, foreign capital inflows allowed Australia to live beyond its means, an important factor for an economy with so much potential for development. Second, it enhanced structural change by being concentrated in certain sectors. Broadly, these were infrastructure and transport in the first half of the century, manufacturing in the third quarter and services in the final quarter.

The amount of capital investment in Australia was greater than domestic **saving** with the difference being made up by foreign investment. Put another way, foreign investment allowed Australia to import more than it exported. Figure 1.4 and Figure 1.5 indicate the dimensions of the contribution of foreign investment over time. The share of foreign investment in total domestic capital formation (see Figure 1.4) was low (or even negative for a short period) at the beginning of the century, rising to a peak in the 1920s when it represented about 30 per cent. Its wartime and post-war fluctuations gave way to a steadier contribution in the 1950s to 1970s, but at a lower level than in the 1920s. The ratio rose again in the 1980s and 1990s, but still remained below 30 per cent.

The gap between current **foreign income** and foreign expenditure, the **current account** in the balance of payments, shown in Figure 1.5, followed a similar pattern. At the beginning of the century, current account surpluses were more common than

**Figure 1.5**   Australia's current account balance as a percentage of GDP, 1880 to 1997–98

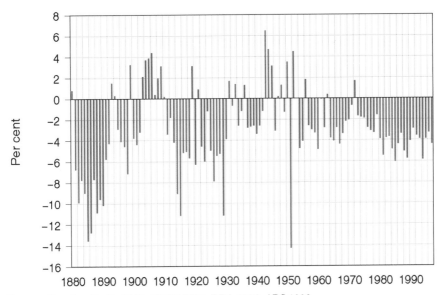

Sources: Based on Butlin 1962; CBCS 1952; RBA 1996; ABS 1998.

**SUMMARY BOX**

Economic growth was faster in Australia as a result of foreign capital inflow than it would have been if it had been less or absent altogether because it increased the rate of domestic investment. In the long run, this was a major benefit to Australia for its integration into the international economy, even if in the short run there were financial crises at various times. Similarly, the advantages of being attractive to foreign investors outweighed the disadvantages of high levels of foreign ownership. Over the century, rising Australian living standards were buttressed by foreign investment. Only in periods when capital could not be attracted and repayments became a burden did Australian living standards decline.

deficits, as Australia was repaying its foreign debt in the wake of the 1890s financial crash. As capital inflows returned, the current account deficit increased to around 5 per cent of **GDP** in the second and third decades of the century. The 1930s and 1940s experienced great instability in Australia's balance of payments, with the largest ever **current account surplus** in 1943–44 followed by its largest ever deficit in 1951–52. Deficits were steadier and smaller in the later 1950s through to the 1970s, followed by a trend to much higher deficits in the era of globalisation at the end of the century.

## Human capital and immigration levels

The first legislative initiative of the newly formed Commonwealth in 1901 was to codify Australia's immigration laws. It did so with the perspective of Australia's nineteenth century immigration experience and fears about the decline in the rate of natural increase. The objective of the policy was to maximise immigration from Britain and Ireland, but to restrict or prohibit immigration from elsewhere. With only minor modifications, this remained the basis of Australia's immigration policy until 1973.

Europe's population more than doubled during the nineteenth century and emigration from Europe was an ever-rising tide until brought to a halt by the First World War. Altogether, about 46 million people left Europe permanently between 1815 and 1915, mostly heading for North and South America. For much of the century, the British Isles provided more intercontinental emigrants than any other country, and about one-third of the total. A very small proportion of the exodus from Europe came to Australia and of these nearly all were from Britain and Ireland. Europe was not the only source of immigration into Australia in the nineteenth century. Significant numbers also arrived from China, India and the Pacific, but their immigration was discouraged and then prohibited by the Australian colonial governments, so that by the end of the century, Australia's population was overwhelmingly descended from British stock.

**Figure 1.6**    Net immigration to Australia, 1880 to 1998

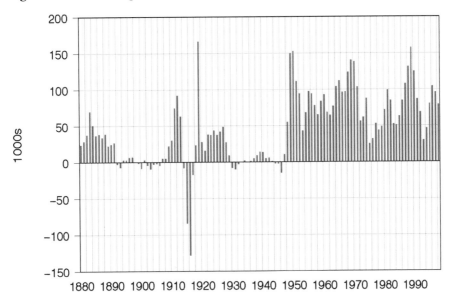

Note: Includes defence personnel 1914–1920. To 1956 includes short-term movements. Calendar years to 1988 and year ended 30 June from 1989.

Sources: Based on Wilcox 1929, p. 947; Australia *Yearbook*, ABS *Arrival and Departures*.

How many migrants entered Australia in the twentieth century was a result of several factors. After the passage of the *Immigration Restriction Act 1901*, two of the major ones were the number of British people wishing to emigrate and the proportion of these willing to come to Australia. The majority always found North America more attractive and there were other destinations within the British Empire with which Australia competed for British migrants. For most of the twentieth century, Australia offered **subsidies** in the form of assisted passages to British emigrants to offset the cost of the greater distance travelling to Australia involved. In periods when the Australian economy was depressed, such inducements were suspended and potential migrants were discouraged by the local conditions. Since there were always some people permanently leaving the country, at these times there could be a net migrant outflow. In periods of economic recovery and expansion, the payments were resumed – Australia appeared to be a relatively more attractive destination and the inflow rose.

At the beginning of the twentieth century, net immigration was very low or negative (see Figure 1.6), a reaction to the economic depression of the 1890s. Only in the five years prior to the outbreak of the First World War did large-scale immigration return, attracted by improved economic conditions and the resumption of assisted passages. Both 1911 and 1912 were record years when arrivals exceeded departures by over 70 000 and 90 000 respectively. Net immigration in the 1920s was only half this level and in the 1930s more people left Australia than arrived, despite some refugee intake at the end of the decade. Immigration revived in the late 1940s and Australia entered its strongest period of sustained intake until the decline seen in the mid-1970s. In this period, however, the share of British immigrants in the total was less, and Australia's immigration program depended on extending entry to other Europeans. In the late 1970s, the first significant numbers of immigrants from Asia since the mid-nineteenth century arrived, spearheaded by refugees from Vietnam. In the 1980s, there was a brief return to the high intake of the 1960s, but in the 1990s the subdued economic conditions were reflected in smaller net immigration levels, though the wide diversity of sources continued.

Immigration over the twentieth century added significantly to Australia's population, as indicated by Table 1.2. By controlling, or at least influencing, the level and nature of immigration, the Australian government exercised a certain degree of power over Australia's demographic structure. The age and gender make-up of the immigrant intake did not necessarily match that of the existing population. Similarly, migrants might have had different skills, qualifications and work experience. These variables affected the impact immigrants had on the Australian economy, both as workers and consumers. Although for much of the century Australian immigration policy was obsessed with the racial origin of potential immigrants, attention was also given to targeting particular migrants who were regarded as having suitable attributes. What these were considered to be varied over time. At the beginning of the century, agricultural workers and domestic servants were sought, in the inter-war years, and even more so in the 1950s and 1960s, workers for manufacturing industry were recruited. In the last two decades of the century, more emphasis was placed on highly skilled and qualified entrants and on business migrants. Throughout the period, however, the attainment of what was considered a desirable mix of ages, skills and gender was a rather impre-

**SUMMARY BOX**

In the absence of immigration, Australia's population would have been smaller. Because migrants generally had bigger families, without them the birth rate and natural population growth would have been lower. Because migrants generally had a higher work **participation rate** than the Australian-born population, their absence would have meant a disproportionate reduction in the size of the labour force and its capacity to grow. Migrants added to the stock of skills in the labour force and, to the degree to which immigrants were more skilled than the Australian born, contributed to a higher level of skill in the workforce. Some migrants brought capital and enterprise that would not have entered the Australian economy otherwise. Immigration enhanced urbanisation and therefore the size of the urban economy. In the last quarter of the century, immigrants considerably extended Australia's cultural diversity, which affected the domestic economy by promoting a greater variety of consumer tastes and demands.

cise affair. The make-up of Australia's actual migrant intake was never exactly what the immigration authorities had in mind, particularly as family reunion came to dominate the inflows at the end of the century.

# The Commonwealth government and economic policy

By the beginning of the twentieth century, governments in Australia had a long history of using the authority of the State to influence the integration of Australia in the international economy. With Federation in 1901, some of the powers of the former colonial (now State) governments were passed to the Commonwealth government, including a number that were significant in regulating Australia's international economic relations. The Commonwealth was now responsible for import taxes and therefore for tariff policy. It was also responsible for immigration policy, though in practice it worked through the States. In the first half of the century, the States retained some access to international capital by being able to borrow on the London market (when it was open) in their own right. This provided them with development funds that they could use as they saw fit. In the second half of the century, however, the Commonwealth significantly increased its power relative to the States, including the power to regulate international capital flows. Despite the shift in political power brought about by Federation, however, the policies pursued for much of the twentieth century owed a great deal to their nineteenth-century antecedents.

## Seeking protection: tariffs, wages and immigration

Policies in these three areas were integrated in a 'protective triangle' that was developed in the first decade of the twentieth century and lasted until the 1970s. The aim was to protect Australian industry and some sections of the Australian workforce from the full impact of international competition.

## Tariff policy

The use of taxes on imported goods in order to protect local manufacturers from the full force of global competition was a hotly debated issue at the time of Federation and was never without its critics during the rest of the century. In the nineteenth century, Australian colonial governments differed in their approach, with Victoria, for example, being more protectionist than New South Wales. Therefore, tariff policy remained to be sorted out by the political process in the early years of the new Commonwealth. By 1907, Australia had adopted a protectionist policy.

The First World War provided Australian manufacturers with an additional degree of protection from imports and they looked to maintain this advantage in the peace that followed. The Commonwealth government was inclined to agree, since it required more revenue to pay for the cost of the war and it supposed that an expanded manufacturing sector would mop up some of the **unemployment** caused by the post-war economic depression. The result was a further extension of the tariff in 1921 to give wider and higher protection from import competition. As discussed in more detail in Chapter 5, the employment-creating aspects of tariff policy remained uppermost in policy-makers' thoughts during the 1920s.

The world depression in 1930 produced a new reason to increase import taxes. The collapse in international demand for Australia's exports created a balance of payments crisis that required a severe curtailment of imports. The tariff increases introduced in 1930 raised **import protection** to even greater heights. Some moderation occurred when Australia concluded a trade pact with Britain in 1932, but generally the degree of import protection given to Australian manufacturers was higher by the end of the 1930s than ever before.

The Second World War demanded total control by the Australian government over its international economic relations. Imports were placed on a licensing system under which the volume of imported goods was decided by an administrative fiat. Such regulation provided the post-war government with unprecedented control over imports and through this the power to grant even greater levels of protection to local producers. Import protection formed an important part of the strategy undertaken in the 1940s and 1950s to stimulate industrialisation in Australia. In 1960 the licensing system was ended, but the subsequent flood of imports led to further tariff increases to provide the same amount of protection as before. Tariff levels drifted upwards throughout the decade, despite a growing feeling among many economists that the policy was building up serious structural problems. Politicians were impressed by the apparent ability of tariff policy to deliver **full employment** and did not respond positively to these criticisms.

It was not until a reformist Labor government took power at the end of 1972 that the policy of high protection was effectively challenged. The tariff was cut by 25 per cent across the board in 1973 as part of the government's attempt to reform industry and fight rising **inflation**. Increasing unemployment and a change of government, however, led to most of these cuts being reinstated in the late 1970s. By the early 1980s, the structural problems of Australian manufacturing that had been identified in the 1960s were more obvious. As part of a general move, both in Australia and internationally, towards deregulation and freer trade (discussed in Chapters 10 and 11) a program of planned tariff reductions and elimination was begun in 1984, again with a Labor government in power.

## Wages policy

If the profits of Australian manufacturers were underpinned by tariff protection, they could afford to pay decent wages. This was the philosophy of the 'New Protection', introduced in the first decade of the century, but built on the industrial relations experiences of the 1880s and 1890s. Tariff protection was tied explicitly to the payment of award wages and enforced by the newly established federal Conciliation and Arbitration Court. The legal ramifications of developing this policy are outlined in Chapter 3, but by the 1920s most Australian workers were paid in accordance with awards set down by either the federal court or one of its counterparts in the States. The policy was grounded in the belief that some of the additional profits resulting from import protection were passed on to workers in the form of wages that were higher than they would have been under **free trade**. Higher wages were also needed to compensate for the higher prices paid for protected consumer goods.

A further form of protection was given to male workers by the new system. Female award wages were set at 54 per cent of the male wage when men and women were doing the same job. This segmented male and female wage rates. Moreover, awards designated employment as being either 'men's work' or 'women's work'. If a man was employed in a 'woman's job' he was paid the female rate and, in theory, vice versa. In practice, few men would offer their labour to do 'women's work' at the lower rate. Employers could employ women in men's jobs and pay them the full rate, but there was no financial incentive for them to do so, unless labour was very scarce, and such a practice was opposed by male-dominated trade unions. This further segmented the Australian labour market, effectively protecting male workers from 'cheap' female labour and obliging employers to pay the highest possible male wages. As the male rate of pay was considered to be a 'family wage', but was paid to single men anyway (to avoid employers giving preference to cheaper unmarried men), the single, white male Australian worker was placed in a relatively privileged position.

This system proved to be highly robust and tended to extend throughout the economy during the twentieth century from its early start in one segment of manufacturing. During the Second World War, labour shortages forced female award rates up: in a few occupations, chiefly those highly strategic for the war effort, female award rates rose to 90 per cent of the male rate, but the average increase was to around 75 per cent. This differential continued after the war, even though the labour market tightened under the post-war conditions of full employment. In 1973, the practice of paying males and females a different award rate for doing the same job was abolished, with a consequent increase in some female wage rates (such as those paid to teachers), although not in all as most women did not work alongside men. In a bid to counter the effect of this 'gendered' labour-market segmentation, a battle continues for 'equal pay for work of equal value'. An attempt was also made in the early 1970s to eliminate some of the grosser wage inequalities faced by Australia's indigenous peoples; in particular, practices of paying Aborigines less, paying in kind (sometimes in alcohol) rather than in money, or of simply not paying at all. During the last quarter of the century there were increasing criticisms of the centralised wage-fixing system, but among the many aspects of deregulation in the Australian economy in the 1980s and 1990s, the wages system survived largely intact.

## Immigration policy

The third side of the 'protection triangle' adopted at the beginning of the century was the White Australia Policy. Again built on nineteenth-century practice, the economic rationale of the policy was to underpin Australian wages by keeping out 'cheap' non-white labour. Whether this reasoning, or virulent racism, was the more important force behind the White Australia Policy was debatable (see

Chapter 3). In any event, the upshot of the adoption of the policy was that immigration before the Second World War was drawn overwhelmingly from Britain, a country where wage rates were relatively high. This made British migrants an expensive increment to the Australian workforce, as they would expect to receive a wage in Australia at least equal to that on offer in Britain. The fact that British migrants required financial assistance to travel to Australia also added to the cost of this particular source of immigration. High wages in the inter-war period were one cause of higher levels of unemployment, and it was doubtful that Australia's high male wages were justified in terms of relative productivity.

The end of the Second World War posed a crisis for the White Australia Policy. It was clear even as the war drew to a close that Britain would not be able to supply all the immigrants the Australian government was planning to bring in. How many would come from non-British sources was unknown, but it was expected to be a substantial proportion. The policy was adjusted, gradually and reluctantly, in the post-war years as Australia recruited immigrants from continental Europe, the Mediterranean and the Middle East. Although Britain remained the single most important source, about half of the migrant intake in the 1950s and 1960s came from countries where average wage rates were lower than in Britain.

Protection of the white Australian-born worker and the British migrant was ensured by further segmentation of the labour force, this time along ethnic boundaries. Non–English-speaking migrants found that their employment opportunities were restricted to the lowest paid and 'dirty' jobs that were expanding under rapid industrialisation and **economic development**. Those who had skills discovered that they were not permitted to use them. As non–English-speaking migrants filled the vacancies on the factory floor, Australian-born and British-born workers moved up the jobs ladder into the bottom and middle rungs of management. Beyond the reach of the award system lay sweated workshops and 'outwork', creating an industrial ghetto of non–English-speaking female workers and their children on the lowest pay of all.

By the early 1970s, the White Australia Policy was non-viable, though its abolition in 1973 was not determined by economic considerations. In the last quarter of the twentieth century, Australia's immigration policy was no longer based on ethnicity but rather on social factors (family reunion and refugees) and economic requirements

## SUMMARY BOX

During the first three-quarters of the twentieth century, Australian economic policy protected the manufacturing industry from import competition and protected Australian and British male workers from 'cheap' labour competition. In the last quarter of the century, the reduction and partial elimination of tariffs and 'de-segmentation' of the labour force modified these forms of protection. As the century ended, however, there were still many features of the Australian economy that reflected the strength of these earlier policies.

(skills, qualifications and enterprise). These changes did not, however, signal the adoption of a policy of importing 'cheap' labour. On the contrary, if the economic requirements had been the sole criteria for entry, then Australia would have only accepted workers who expected remuneration *higher* than the national average.

## Economic management and the balance of payments

The integration of the Australian economy in the world economy meant that the level of economic activity in Australia was strongly influenced by movements in its balance of payments. The balance of payments is the difference between earnings and income from foreigners (received by selling exports of goods and services and receiving interest on loans made by Australians to foreigners, and profits on investments made by Australians abroad) and payments made to foreigners (paid to purchase imports of goods and services, payments to foreigners for interest on loans made to Australians and profits on foreign investments in Australia).

Before the Second World War, economic management policy was largely directed at the balance of payments. Many of the forces that produced fluctuations in Australia's balance of payments lay outside the power (and sometimes outside the cognition) of the Australian government. World prices for Australian exports were occasionally affected by changes in Australian supply, but since Australia was not a sole-seller and because fluctuations in its economy did not have much (or any) impact on the countries that purchased these goods, the prices received for exports were beyond its control.

The aim of policy was for Australia to run a balance of trade surplus and to use this to pay for unavoidable imports of services (such as international shipping costs) and foreign capital investment. The trade surplus underwrote the continued inflow of capital that, as discussed above and throughout this book, was regarded as essential in Australia's long-term economic development. At times, when Australia's **trade surplus** disappeared, financing a trade deficit required more foreign capital than the financial markets were, for very long, prepared to provide. The deleterious consequences of this were made very apparent in the 1890s and 1930s (see Chapters 3 and 6) and remained a constant worry for Australian authorities.

A number of policies were formulated to bolster Australia's international trade position. On the import side, tariffs had a restrictive effect, although the balance of payments argument for import protection was not always explicitly made. On the export side, both state and federal governments took measures intended to expand the volume of exports. These ranged from transport links to agricultural research and included financial concessions to export sectors such as mining. The Commonwealth government had the power to make trade agreements with foreign countries, but its freedom of action in this regard was circumscribed by its belief that Australia's long-term welfare lay in cementing trade links with Britain at the expense of pursuing a more **multilateral** approach. This belief was the basis for the policy 'Men, Money, Markets' that, deconstructed, read 'British men, British money and British markets' (see Chapter 5). In the 1930s, Australia's desire to further its trade links with Britain led to a bungled attempt to substitute British imports for those from the United States and Japan that left the Commonwealth government in some embarrassment (see Chapter 6).

After the Second World War, the measures taken to promote export volumes were widened, for example, by various agricultural subsidy schemes and the use of marketing boards. In foreign relations, the move by Britain in the 1950s to link itself more closely with the European Union led Australia to embark on a more independent line in international trade agreements. In 1957, an historic break-through was made when it concluded its first trade treaty with Japan. At the same time, the nature of economic management was changed by the adoption of Keynesian techniques of macroeconomic policy that allowed the Australian government to influence the pace of economic activity more directly. Policy remained concerned with the maintenance of a trade surplus (and import controls continued to be used for this purpose), but fiscal and monetary policies were now co-ordinated to adjust the domestic economy to the vagaries of the global economy in a more measured way. At least, that was how economic management policy was intended to work. How well it did so in practice is discussed in Chapters 8 and 9.

At the end of the century, policy shifted to emphasise heightened competition as the source of export growth and economic development in contrast to the earlier protectionist stance. All Australian businesses, whether the 'traditional' exporters of food and raw materials or the 'new' exporters of manufactures and services, were expected to perform better if subjected to more intense international competition. Nevertheless, this did not alter the basic aim of ensuring Australia continued to earn export surpluses to pay for capital inflow: in this respect there was complete consistency in economic policy over the century. What changed were the means rather than the aims.

## SUMMARY BOX

Economic management by Australian governments was directed mainly at the balance of payments in the first half of the century, along with immigration policy. The aim was to maximise the excess of export earnings over the cost of imports and to use this surplus to pay for foreign capital inflows. Most of the time this strategy was successful, but if export earnings collapsed an economic crisis ensued. Australia's close ties with Britain prevented it from following an independent foreign policy. In the second half of the century, the aim of achieving an export surplus remained but the means of achieving it changed in the 1980s and 1990s. Keynesian economics and war time economic controls provided Australia's post-1945 governments with a more sophisticated set of economic management tools that were used rather more confidently in the 1950s and 1960s than in the final quarter of the century.

# Suggested further reading

Boehm, E.A. 1993, *Twentieth Century Economic Development in Australia*, 3rd edn, Longman Cheshire, Melbourne.

Butlin, N.G. 1983, 'Trends in Public/Private Relations, 1901–75', in B. W. Head (ed.), *State and Economy in Australia*, Oxford University Press, Melbourne.

Butlin, N.G., Barnard, A. & Pincus, J.J. 1982, *Government and Capitalism: Public and Private Choice in Twentieth Century Australia*, Allen & Unwin, Sydney.

Camm, J.C.R. & McQuilton, J. 1987, *Australians: A Historical Atlas*, Fairfax, Syme & Weldon Associates, Sydney.

Dyster, B. & Meredith, D. 1990, *Australia in the International Economy in the Twentieth Century*, Cambridge University Press, Cambridge.

Jordens, A.-M. 1995, *Redefining Australians: Immigration, Citizenship and National Identity*, Hale and Iremonger, Sydney.

Jupp, J. 1991, *Immigration*, Sydney University Press, Sydney.

Kenwood, A.G. 1995, *Australian Economic Institutions since Federation: an Introduction*, Oxford University Press, Melbourne.

McLean, I. 1989, 'Growth in a small open economy: an historical view', in B. Chapman (ed.), *Australian Economic Growth*, Macmillan, Melbourne.

Pinkstone, B. 1992, *Global Connections: A History of Exports and the Australian Economy*, Australian Government Publishing Service, Canberra.

Pope, D. & Alston, L. J. 1989, *Australia's greatest asset: Human resources in the nineteenth and twentieth centuries*, Federation Press, Sydney.

# PART I

BEFORE 1914

# 2

# International impacts on Australia before 1914

In the 1990s, there was much comment, in Australia and elsewhere, about 'globalisation' and the emergence of a 'global economy' (see H.-P. Martin 1997; Wiseman 1998). Such an economy was characterised by expanding world trade, liberalisation of international flows of money, goods and services, dramatic changes in international transport and communications, massive international flows of **capital** and an increasingly worldwide scale of international business. 'Globalisation' seemed to imply that all national economies were being integrated and linked together so that virtually no part of the planet was economically isolated any longer. The emphasis on 'globalisation' at the end of the twentieth century was not surprising, as the Cold War ended and the information technology revolution gathered pace. However, this description could just as accurately be applied to the growth and development of the international economy in the 40 years prior to the outbreak of the First World War in 1914, a period that should perhaps now be dubbed the 'first global economy'. This chapter explores the causes of the emergence and development of the first global economy and its impact on Australia.

## Industrialisation: transforming agrarian economies

At the heart of the expansion of the international economy in the nineteenth century was the industrial revolution that had started in Britain and by the end of the century had spread to Western Europe, North America and Japan. Industrialisation was a process that fundamentally transformed agrarian economies and created the world's first industrial societies. Over the last 200 years it has spread to many parts of the world and has developed mature and even 'post-industrial' forms in the older industrialised economies. The impact on all aspects of society was profound, perhaps most obviously in the material wealth industrialisation engendered, though the distribution of the material benefits of the revolution was far from equal within the industrial societies. In a global context, industrialisation enhanced enormously the wealth, power and status of those nations whose economies were being transformed, allowing a small number of industrial nations to dominate the world economically and politically in a way that had not been experienced before.[1]

The terms 'industrial revolution' and 'industrialisation' describe the economic transformation these societies experienced. The former term is an attempt to capture the profound nature of the transformation; the latter, the fact that it was a long drawn out process that proceeded in fits and starts, and did not progress at all evenly across the various sectors of the economy. This unevenness and gradual change accounts for the lack of precision as to when the first industrial revolution began – and when it ended. There has also been considerable controversy among economic historians over the causes of the first industrial revolution, a debate that is related partly to the question of dating its starting point.

Central to the transformation was a reorganisation of the processes of production: machine production in factories using inanimate sources of mechanised power, which for much of the nineteenth century meant steam power. Existing industries like textiles were transformed from handicraft or workshop production to factory production; new industries, particularly metallurgical and engineering, were developed. Transport and communications were revolutionised by the invention of railways, steamships and the telegraph. Agriculture was also transformed, becoming more intensive, productive, scientific and commercial. These changes took at least a century to be fully worked out in Britain, and even in the late nineteenth century there remained substantial areas of the pre-industrial economy surviving alongside the industrial.

**SUMMARY BOX**

The first global economy emerged during the nineteenth century in response to an economic transformation, the industrial revolution, that began in Britain and spread to Europe, North America and Japan. Like the global economy at the end of the twentieth century, the first global economy was based on the expansion of world trade, capital flows, migration, communications and business. Together, the industrialising nations of the world created the international flows of trade, capital and people that made up the nineteenth century global economy, drawing foodstuffs and raw materials from the tropical and temperate zones and sending migrants and capital to the Americas, Asia, and Australia and New Zealand. Britain remained at the centre of the world economy, increasingly as a source of international finance and payments, as well as a supplier of manufactured goods and market for primary commodities.

Industrialisation itself was constantly changing. In the last decade of the nineteenth century and in the beginning of the twentieth, as industrial revolutions occurred in a number of countries, the core sectors of the first industrial revolution – cotton and woollen textiles, iron, coal, steam engineering, railways and ship-building – were joined by new industries. These included mass-produced steel, chemicals (dyestuffs, explosives, alkaline, plastics and petroleum), electrical goods, armaments, automobiles and industries based on new materials such as aluminium, rubber and cement. Production in these new industries was more capital intensive and the technology used more advanced and science-based than in the earlier industrial revolutions. As a result, the firms in the new industries tended to be far larger, more vertically integrated and to occupy oligopolistic positions within one or several industries. Firms such as Siemens, Bosch, Krupps, A.G. Farben, Fiat, Ford, Kodak, Standard Oil and Du Pont were established in these new industries around this time (Schmitz 1993; Chandler 1977).

# The impact of industrialisation

## Demographic effects

Two significant effects of industrialisation were population growth and mass emigration (see Figure 2.1 and Table 2.1). The economic expansion associated with industrial revolution allowed the world's first sustained population explosions to occur in the industrialising countries. Europe's population increased threefold between 1800 and 1910, from about 170 million to over 500 million. England and Wales, Germany, The Netherlands, Serbia, Poland, Russia and Greece showed the fastest rates of population increase. The Scandinavian countries, Italy, Spain, Portugal and Austria–Hungary had more modest population increments. France's population grew quite slowly and Ireland was the only country in Europe to experience a population decline (it halved between 1840 and 1910).

The chief cause of the population explosion was a fall in death rates combined with constant or slightly higher birth rates. The falls in the death rates were fairly small, but were particularly significant among infants and children and so had a powerful cumulative effect over a number of years. Improved food supply, both from European agriculture and, after 1870, from imports, meant that the population explosion was not cut short by subsistence crises, as had occurred in earlier times. The age of marriage fell dramatically and the marriage rate increased. Both of these changes were due to greater opportunities for wage employment, especially for women and children, and both contributed to higher birth rates. Death rates fell because of improvements to the environment, especially housing, hygiene and sanitation, and better nutrition. These improvements were slight – and far from uniform, especially in the large industrial cities – but were sufficient to trigger sustained population increase.

As the industrial economy was highly concentrated geographically, much of the rising population was centred in large industrial cities. However, both the struggling urban poor and the dislocated rural population represented a stream of

**Table 2.1** Intercontinental emigration from Europe, 1846–1915

| Country of origin | 1846–1855 | 1856–1865 | 1866–1875 | 1876–1885 | 1886–1895 | 1896–1905 | 1906–1915 | Total 1846–1915 | Percentage of total |
|---|---|---|---|---|---|---|---|---|---|
| British Isles | 2 155 | 1 336 | 1 824 | 2 544 | 2 810 | 2 274 | 3 717 | 16 660 | 37.4 |
| Italy | 5 | 61 | 211 | 465 | 1 422 | 2 432 | 3 573 | 8 169 | 18.4 |
| Austria–Hungary | 28 | 22 | 81 | 232 | 601 | 1 401 | 2 058 | 4 423 | 9.9 |
| Germany | 558 | 465 | 812 | 1 088 | 888 | 266 | 211 | 4 288 | 9.7 |
| Spain | 5 | 18 | 59 | 269 | 771 | 763 | 1 561 | 3 446 | 7.7 |
| Russia | – | 1 | 32 | 92 | 502 | 622 | 911 | 2 161 | 4.9 |
| Poland | – | – | – | – | 52 | 122 | 335 | 509 | 1.1 |
| Portugal | 27 | 81 | 112 | 141 | 258 | 238 | 467 | 1 324 | 3.0 |
| Norway | 32 | 40 | 119 | 146 | 142 | 137 | 133 | 749 | 1.7 |
| Sweden | 22 | 24 | 145 | 209 | 322 | 193 | 157 | 1 072 | 2.4 |
| Other Europe | 162 | 75 | 194 | 218 | 390 | 286 | 356 | 1 681 | 3.8 |
| Total | 2 994 | 2 123 | 3 589 | 5 404 | 8 158 | 8 734 | 13 479 | 44 482 | 100.0 |

Source: Based on Willcox 1929, pp. 230–1.

**Figure 2.1**   Population growth in Europe, 1700 to 1950

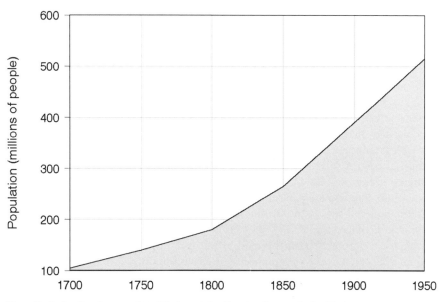

Note: Excludes Russia east of the Urals and the Caspian Sea; excludes Turkey.
Source: Based on McEvedy & Jones 1978, p. 18.

potential and actual emigrants throughout the nineteenth century. Emigration also increased from countries that were not undergoing industrialisation but which had high population densities – southern China and India and some of the Pacific islands. The main movements of intercontinental migration were out of Europe, India, China, Japan and the islands of the Pacific and into North and South America, Australia, New Zealand, South Africa and parts of South-East Asia. These were areas that possessed economic potential, especially for **primary production**, but which lacked **labour**, a shortage that immigration was intended to alleviate. Immigration augmented population growth as well as swelling the immediate **labour force**. It widened (and through forming families, deepened) the size of the domestic market, a dual contribution that was not lost on the governments of the immigrant nations, such as Australia.

About 46 million Europeans emigrated to destinations outside Europe between 1815 and 1915, about one-third of them from the United Kingdom, including Ireland. The number leaving increased over the course of the century and reached a climax in the period just before the First World War, when the exodus averaged one and a half million persons per year. Although British and Irish migration remained important – over a quarter of the emigration immediately pre-war – there was a marked shift in the source of emigration away from north-west Europe and towards south and eastern Europe in the later nineteenth century. Emigrants came from rural and urban backgrounds and ranged from the desperately poor to the modestly well off. They migrated reluctantly or enthusiastically, fleeing from eviction, starvation and persecution, or hoping for work, land

and a higher standard of living. In their new homelands they might become prosperous farmers or exploited sharecroppers, gain employment as skilled workers or end up in the sweatshops of New York, Buenos Aires or Melbourne.

Many factors influenced the exodus from Europe, including employment opportunities and real wages at home, knowledge of other lands, cost of transportation and the intervention of various governmental and other agencies (Williamson & Hatton 1994).

However, two major influences stand out in the nineteenth century: demographic revolution and industrial revolution. These intertwined to create conditions conducive to mass emigration. The population increased but it was also displaced, both geographically and structurally. Expanding employment opportunities in the industrial centres stimulated internal short-distance migration (for example, from southern to northern Italy, or from southern Germany to the Ruhr), some of which spilled into intercontinental emigration. Industrial cities expanded tremendously but also suffered serious **unemployment** and underemployment problems when economic activity slowed and this swelled the number of potential emigrants. People were uprooted from the land in the wake of agricultural revolution and commercialisation and by the impact that cheap imported food had on European farming after 1870, as shown by the case of Norwegian emigration in the 1880s. As the industrial revolution spread its impact east and south in the second half of the nineteenth century, so the major areas of emigration shifted, to Germany, Italy, Russia and the Balkans.

How many of Europe's emigrants would have left in the absence of demand for immigrants in America and Australasia is impossible to know, but it was clearly the need for inflows of people in the immigrant nations that was the dynamic element in the process. Not only were 'pull' factors the dynamic ones in intercontinental migration, but demand for immigrants varied with the state of the economy of the receiving country. Europe was a reservoir of labour for America and Australasia, and the flow increased or diminished largely as economic circumstances altered, which generally allowed the recipient areas to obtain sufficient immigrant labour but to avoid importing labour gluts.

Emigration of Indian workers beyond Asia was stimulated by the demand for manual labour to replace slave labour following the abolition of slavery in the 1840s. Mostly, these workers from southern India laboured on British-owned sugar plantations in Mauritius, South Africa, the West Indies, Guyana and Fiji. Those who went to East Africa laboured on public works and railway construction. Indian labourers also were recruited for work on plantations in Malaysia and Sri Lanka. Attempts to bring them to Australia, however, were thwarted by the nascent White Australia Policy.

Emigration from China was similarly a response to the abolition of slavery, as well as the opening up of Chinese ports by British imperialism in the 1840s and 1850s. Chinese emigrants spread throughout the world, including Australia, though increasingly subjected to racist immigration restrictions in the late nineteenth century. Many found work in agriculture, including market gardening, but many others were located in manufacturing, mining, retail and transportation.

Emigration from Japan did not become significant before the 1890s (and was illegal before 1866). Japanese went to Hawaii, California, Russia, China, Korea and Malaysia, and worked in sugar plantations and fishing, general labouring and personal service. A few came to Australia, but like Chinese immigrants their settlement was greatly restricted by Australia's immigration regulations. About eight million Chinese, four million Indians and a million Japanese emigrated permanently from their home country during the nineteenth and early twentieth centuries. For most, emigration was a matter of survival in the face of rural overcrowding, famine and unemployment. Nevertheless, as with European emigration, it was the demand for their labour, particularly in primary production, that was the vital factor in sustaining the exodus.

About two-thirds of intercontinental migrants went to North America over the period 1850–1920, the vast majority to the United States. More than one-fifth went to the Caribbean and South America, and Asiatic Russia took a little over 10 per cent. Only a small proportion, about 3 per cent, went to Australia and New Zealand. Immigrant nations often drew on a limited range of supplier countries. Canada, for example, took most of its immigrants from Britain and the United States. Brazil relied heavily on Spain, Portugal and Italy. Immigrants to Argentina were mainly from Italy and Spain. Nearly all Australia's immigrants came from Britain or New Zealand. Only the United States was more eclectic, though like Australia, Canada and New Zealand it restricted Asian immigration on racist grounds. More than 30 nations contributed immigrants to the US demographic 'melting pot' in the second half of the nineteenth century.

---

**SUMMARY BOX**

Industrialisation in the nineteenth century led to sustained population growth and mass emigration for the first time in history. Population growth was due to falling death rates and rising birth rates. The population of industrialising economies became far more urbanised, but emigrants came from both urban and rural sectors. Emigration also increased from regions that were not industrialising but which responded to the international demand for labour. The bulk of intercontinental migration went from Britain and Europe to America. Australia received a small proportion of British emigration. Immigration to Australia from other sources was largely ruled out by the White Australia Policy.

---

## International trade

The demographic revolution associated with Britain's industrial revolution also impacted on **international trade**. The United Kingdom had ceased being able to feed itself from its own resources around the middle of the eighteenth century. The remarkable growth of its nineteenth-century population meant that its need for imported foodstuffs expanded, despite the considerable improvements to the productiveness of British agriculture that occurred. After 1860, Britain did not impose any barriers or **tariffs** on its food imports, so that it was generally a buoyant and expanding market for countries that could export foodstuffs, which by the end of the century included Australia.

Britain's industrialisation affected international trade in other ways. The process of industrialisation raised **labour productivity** by combining greater amounts of capital with labour and reorganising production in factories. As a result, factory production of goods greatly increased and to an extent far beyond the capacity (although this was growing too) of the British economy to consume entirely the output of the economy. More and more of Britain's industrial production found its market in exports. The British economy could supply most of the raw material inputs required by industry, particularly iron and coal, but some industrial inputs were only available as imports (cotton, for example) and others were required in such quantities that the domestic British supply was quite inadequate (wool, for example). The need for imports of food and raw materials and the expansion of worldwide markets for British manufactures combined to place Britain at the centre of a growing network of world trade. From the 1850s, Britain promoted international trade liberalisation (the **Free Trade** movement) to enhance its position and, until the 1880s at least, orchestrated a general downward movement in international trade barriers, especially taxes on imports (tariffs).

Industrialisation, although starting in Britain, did not remain confined there. Indeed, the demands that the industrial revolution in Britain placed on the emerging international economy meant that forces for economic transformation were transmitted to other countries. New technologies and new industries could not be kept secret from the world, despite some efforts early in the century by the British government to do so. France and Belgium both began to industrialise soon after Britain, and in the second half of the nineteenth century they were joined by other Western European economies, particularly Germany and Italy. By the end of the nineteenth century, industrialisation was occurring in Russia, Sweden and Poland as well. Moreover, industrialisation was not restricted to Europe: the industrial revolution in the United States began in the first half of the nineteenth century and in Japan during the second half.

All of these industrialising economies followed Britain in demanding more goods from the international economy and seeking foreign markets for their exports (which included food and raw materials, as well as the products of their factories), though none did so to the same extent as Britain.

World trade expanded about threefold in value and volume in the 40 years prior to the outbreak of the First World War, with primary products (food and raw materials) making up two-thirds and manufactured goods one-third. The rate of growth of world trade was approximately the same as the rate of growth of world output. This expansion was based on the continuing **economic growth** of Britain, the spread of industrialisation, particularly to continental Europe, greater international specialisation, the 'opening up' of new areas of primary production and the revolution in international transport. Britain and Europe accounted for almost

**Figure 2.2**    Shares of world trade, 1913

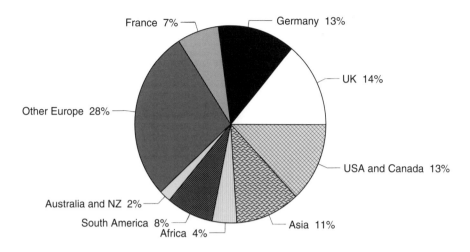

Source: Based on League of Nations 1945, pp. 158–67.

two-thirds of world trade during this period, though Britain's share declined steadily (see Figure 2.2). The European industrialising countries' exports consisted mainly of manufactured goods and their imports of raw materials and food.

On the eve of the First World War, North America was about as important in world trade as Britain, but the contrast between primary and manufactured goods was less striking. The United States and Canada accounted for 11 per cent of world exports of manufactures and 12 per cent of world imports of manufactures; they were responsible for 17 per cent of world exports of primary products and 11 per cent of world imports of primaries. Although the United States was, by this time, the leading industrial economy (with 36 per cent of world output of manufactures) its impact on world trade was muted by the huge size of its own domestic market and sources of supply.

Outside of Britain, Europe and North America, the pattern was the mirror image of the industrialised countries: Asia, Africa, Latin America, and Australia and New Zealand supplied 8 per cent of the manufactures entering world trade in 1913, but purchased 40 per cent of the imports of manufactures. Similarly, their combined exports of primary products accounted for 38 per cent of the total entering world trade but only 14 per cent of the world's imports of primary commodities were purchased by these economies.

By the early twentieth century, then, world trade had experienced a lengthy period of rapid growth and had developed a structure in which the industrialised countries largely exported manufactures and imported primary commodities while the non-industrial ones did the opposite. However, although the non-industrial countries were heavily dependent on the industrial nations for imports of manufactures and markets for their exports (four-fifths of the combined external trade of non-industrial countries was with the industrial nations), the industrial countries traded with each other to a greater extent. In 1913, the industrial countries together sent two-thirds of their exports to other industrial economies and half of their exports of manufactured goods went to other industrial countries. Thus, it was not the case that the manufactures of the industrial economies were simply being traded for the primary products of the non-industrial world: the primary producing countries were certainly dependent on the industrial economies, but the degree of dependence was not equal.

---

**SUMMARY BOX**

Industrialisation greatly increased the scale of world trade. The new industries required raw materials in massive amounts, some of which came from abroad as imports. Industrial output exceeded domestic consumption so that growing volumes of manufactured goods were exported. Population growth led to the need to import foodstuffs in significant quantities. World trade linked together the industrial economies with those that were predominantly primary producing, such as Australia. Manufactured goods dominated the export mix of the industrial countries, while food and raw materials made up the majority of their imports. The opposite was true of the primary producing countries. The United States was in a special position as a significant exporter of both primary and manufactured goods.

---

## Multilateral trade

As a more integrated world trade network replaced earlier regional or localised trading patterns, trading relationships became more complex, and a **multilateral** trading system developed. It was centred on a triangular pattern of international trade between Britain, the newly industrialising countries of Western Europe and the world's primary producing countries (including Australia). Multilateral trade arose because the newly industrialising countries of Western Europe imported primary products (raw materials and foodstuffs) from Latin America, Asia, Africa, and Australia and New Zealand to a much greater value than their exports (chiefly manufactures) to these primary producing countries. Consequently, the Western European countries had trade deficits (imports exceeded exports) with Latin America, Asia, Africa, and Australia and New Zealand. Putting this relationship the other way round, these primary producers had trade surpluses (exports exceeded imports) with the newly industrialising economies.

On the other hand, the newly industrial nations of Western Europe found ready markets for their exports of sophisticated and technologically advanced manufactured goods in the large, high-**income** and open market of the United Kingdom (as did the United States). Since British exporters did not find their industrial rivals in Europe and North America nearly so easy to sell to, the resultant pattern was one of a **trade surplus** between industrialising continental Europe (and the United States) and Britain.

Britain, by contrast, found relatively easy markets in the primary producing countries of the world – many of which were part of the British Empire and all of which were importers of British capital and commercial and financial services. Some, like Australia, were also areas of significant British emigration in the nineteenth century, which enhanced consumer preference for British-made products. By the end of the nineteenth century, Britain's comparative advantage lay in producing just the sort of low-technology manufactured goods that these markets wanted. Nevertheless, while British firms could sell strongly in these markets, Britain did not absorb an equal value of primary produce exports from them. Consequently, Britain had trade surpluses with the primary producing nations (and therefore they had trade deficits with Britain).

This produced an underlying pattern in world trade in the late nineteenth century in which the primary producing countries like Australia used their trade surplus with the newly industrialising countries to pay for their trade deficit with Britain. In turn, Britain used its trade surplus with the primary producing countries to pay for its trade deficit with the newly industrial countries. Finally, the newly industrialising countries of Western Europe used their trade surplus with Britain to cover their trade deficits with the primary producing countries (League of Nations 1942; Saul 1954–55).

Although this pattern can be seen in the trade balances of the various nations making up the international economy, in reality there were many variations and exceptions. The United States, for example, was almost equally an importer and exporter of primary produce and had no need of imported temperate zone foodstuffs. As a result, the United States not only ran a trade surplus with Britain but also with Canada, Argentina and Australia, which took US manufactures but could not sell an equal value of grain and meat in return. On the other hand, the United States ran a large trade deficit with Japan because it required Japanese raw silk but could not export an equal value of manufactures back to the newly industrialising Japanese economy. A large part of the primary produce needs of the newly industrialising economies of continental Europe were financed by sales of manufactures to neighbouring industrialising countries. Germany, for example, had trade surpluses with Switzerland, The Netherlands, Belgium, France, Norway and Denmark, as well as with Britain in the years just before the First World War. Moreover, there was no reason why the actual values of the trade deficits and surpluses should balance each other out at any particular point: Britain, for example, always had a large overall trade deficit, while many primary producers had overall trade surpluses.

The multilateral trading system as it emerged by the end of the nineteenth century was beneficial in a number of ways to the growth of the international economy. It allowed the newly industrialising countries to finance their imports of raw materials from the primary producers. It gave British manufacturing firms looking for export markets a relatively easy entry to primary producer markets. And it permitted the primary producing nations like Australia to buy all they desired from

Britain and finance these purchases by sales of exports to the newly industrialising countries. In each case, trade was greater than it would have been under strict **bilateral** arrangements, where the trade between each pair of countries had to balance exactly (see Kenwood & Lougheed 1983, Chapter 5).

---

**SUMMARY BOX**

World trade became more multilateral in nature as a result of industrialisation and the expansion of trade flows in the second half of the nineteenth century. Under multilateral trade, each nation engaged a number of trading partners and did not need to balance the value of imports from and exports to each partner. The underlying pattern was a triangular one between Britain, the newly industrialising countries of Western Europe and the primary producing nations, including Australia. Variations on the pattern occurred in the case of the United States and Japan. World trade grew faster under conditions of multilateralism than it would have done under bilateralism. Australia, for example, could use its trade surplus with Germany to pay for its trade deficit with Britain.

---

## Multilateral payments

For these multilateral trading networks to operate effectively there had to be a matching multilateral payments system to facilitate them. This was provided by Britain's financial institutions centred in the City of London. Their role was to channel British overseas **investment** and to provide the short-term **credit** necessary to finance world trade. The structure of Britain's **balance of payments** was significant (Eichengreen 1996, pp. 42–3). Britain's balance on merchandise trade was nearly always in deficit. Moreover, the goods that Britain imported were largely the primary products exported by those countries in which British firms and individuals had made investments. These **debtor nations** were thus able to service their international debts by exports to their chief foreign creditor. This mechanism was vital in avoiding the '**transfer problems**' that plagued the international economy after both world wars (Thomas 1967; Nurkse 1954; Salter 1951). Britain's merchandise trade deficit provided the rest of the world with sufficient liquidity to facilitate the expansion of world trade and ensured the position of Britain's currency, the pound sterling, as the world's international trading currency.

Yet, although Britain ran large and increasing deficits on merchandise trade, it had large and increasing surpluses on the total of its current international transactions; that is, on the overall **current account** of its balance of payments. These surpluses arose from the export earnings of commercial and financial services, including a considerable share of world shipping and insurance, and the inward flows of interest payments and dividends earned by British investors on their long-term **foreign investments**. As these **current account surpluses** mounted, they were matched by rising flows of long-term foreign investment. Britain did not build up its **gold and foreign exchange reserves** – in fact the Bank of England kept these **reserves** remarkably low – but rather reinvested its surpluses in other parts of the world. Of course, in the long run this meant ever-rising inflows of interest and dividends and hence current account surpluses, but as long as Britain maintained a trade deficit and directed its current account surplus to long-term investments in the rest of the world, the global economy would function fairly smoothly.

The strength of Britain's balance of payments and the strong outflows of capital from Britain meant that by the end of the nineteenth century, Britain had ceased to occupy its former position as the 'Workshop of the World' (a mid-century boast). Instead it had become dominant in the international economy as the 'Banker of the World'. London's financial and commercial houses provided the world economy with banking, shipping and insurance services, while the London capital market was the world's leading source of short- and long-term international funds. Sterling was used for most international trade transactions with foreign import and export firms maintaining accounts with London banks. For a country like Australia, with both strong commercial and political ties to Britain, this meant that the British commercial banks and the Bank of England largely ran Australia's international financial arrangements before 1914.

World trade and financial transactions were also facilitated by the development of a system of **international currency** convertibility and fixed **exchange rates**. This was ensured by the world's major currencies being freely convertible into gold at fixed prices. The **'gold standard'**, as it was termed, emerged gradually during the nineteenth century as the international economy itself developed. Britain adopted a gold standard for its currency, the pound sterling, in 1816, but other countries took much longer to follow suit. This delay was partly due to the fluctuating supply situation of both gold and silver during the middle part of the century and partly to the fact that the Western European nations were only gradually entering the international economy. During the 1870s, all of the Western European currencies were placed on a gold standard and their silver coinage became tokens. Many other countries followed suit in the 1890s, encouraged to adopt the gold standard by major new gold discoveries that increased the world supply of gold and saw a decline in the price of silver. Austria–Hungary, Russia, India and the United States adopted the gold standard at this time (Eichengreen 1996, pp. 16–18, 20–25; Scammell 1965, pp. 32–45; Drummond 1987).

Adoption of the international gold standard meant that capital flowed unhindered across national boundaries because there were no **exchange controls**. **Fixed exchange rates** and the unimpeded convertibility of currencies one to another produced international monetary stability. However, fixed exchange rates and free convertibility also meant that adjustment of trade deficits and surpluses fell mainly on domestic prices and employment levels (Eichengreen 1996, pp. 43–4). Government policy towards 'economic management' of trade fluctuations was much less well developed than it was to become in the second half of the twentieth century. The damaging effect that fixed exchange rates could have on an economy faced by falling export earnings and reduced capital inflow was dramatically illustrated by the financial crisis in Australia in 1890 (see Chapter 3).

In practice, few countries achieved anything like a balance of payments **equilibrium** in the period before the First World War. The major capital exporting nations – Britain, France, the United States and Germany – ran large current account surpluses. The **developing countries** ran large current account deficits and financed these with inflows of long-term capital. This was particularly so for South America, Canada, Australia, New Zealand and South Africa, and it had been the case for the United States before 1900. Capital outflow cushioned the effects of a trade deficit in the capital-exporting economies – if the deficit increased, capital exports could be reduced – and enabled primary exporting developing economies to finance their **economic development**. In the latter cases, however, the recipient countries had much less control over the inflow of funds than the **creditor nations**, and their balance of payments history was therefore often more unsettled.

> **SUMMARY BOX**
>
> A multilateral payments system developed alongside the world's multilateral trade networks. The payments system was based on Britain's dominant role in the global economy and used the British currency, the pound sterling, as the main international currency. The strength of Britain's international financial institutions meant that Britain acted as the 'World's Banker' before 1914. Fixed exchange rates between currencies and the unhindered convertibility of one currency to another was ensured by the spread throughout the global economy of the 'gold standard' from Britain in 1816 to the United States in 1900. This system produced international monetary stability, but it also transmitted international economic fluctuations directly to domestic price levels and employment conditions. Australia's financial crisis in 1890 illustrated this impact dramatically.

## International investment

A further effect of the industrial revolution in Britain was the accumulation of capital in the hands of a small, but numerically increasing, class of investors. Only a small proportion of these people was super-rich: most were members of the middle or upper middle-class who channelled their relatively modest **savings** through Britain's financial networks and who were looking, above all, for safe investments. Since much of the investment in Britain's new industries came from self-finance and ploughed-back profits, the opportunities for these investors to participate directly in the industrial revolution were slight. Consequently, their funds were channelled by Britain's financial institutions into government bonds and railway stocks. And when the volume of capital seeking such outlets outstripped the investment opportunities in the United Kingdom, these funds were invested in similar forms abroad. In this way, the 'small investor' classes in Britain (and by the end of the nineteenth century in Western Europe as well) helped finance economic development, by loans to governments and the purchase of debenture stock in railway and other utilities, throughout the world.

The export of private long-term capital from Britain, Western Europe and the United States in the years before the First World War was an important effect of the spread of industrialisation and was a vital element in the expansion of the global economy. It performed an essential function in facilitating the opening up and economic growth of world production and trade and the integration of the international economy. It was not possible to expand production of primary products sufficiently to satisfy the rapidly increasing **demand** of the industrial nations, unless large-scale capital investment was made by the leading industrial countries in the primary producing regions themselves, both in production directly and in transport and communications. There was, of course, considerable variation between capital-importing countries as to the importance of foreign capital, the uses to which it was put and the political ties it cemented, but generally these capital flows created debt that had to be serviced by the export of primary commodities.

The outpouring of capital was led and dominated by British investors, especially during the first three-quarters of the nineteenth century (see Table 2.2). British foreign capital stood out in size and character. It was very large and widely distributed both geographically and by types of enterprise. About half of British capital was invested in British Empire countries, around 10 per cent in Australia (see Table 2.3). By 1900, however, investors in France, Germany, The Netherlands and the United States were placing significant amounts of funds outside their national economies. British, French and German investors between them accounted for 80 per cent of total foreign investment by 1914.

Foreign investment took a number of forms. Individual investors bought bonds offered by foreign governments or by foreign railway or other utility companies. They invested in foreign real estate, both directly and by loans to foreign property developers and building societies. Insurance firms and banks also purchased fixed-interest bonds and debentures. Equity in foreign firms could be purchased and consortia of banks often raised loans for foreign clients. Occasionally, governments lent directly to foreign governments. Public joint-stock companies and private firms engaged in foreign direct investment. The bulk of long-term foreign investments before 1914 consisted of fixed-interest bonds and debentures, both private and government, and were owned by individuals. The main exception to this generalisation was the United States where most foreign investment was made by US firms investing abroad directly. Some flows were politically influenced – within the British Empire, for example, and French loans to Russia and German loans to Turkey.

Demand for foreign capital came from governments and public and private firms. Governments raised foreign loans for a variety of purposes including public works, railways, **land** development, currency support and war. Firms raising foreign capital included enterprises in mining, transportation, public utilities such as water supply, urban construction, farming and manufacturing. In many cases, such firms received government backing in one form or another; for example, by being given land grants.

The significance of foreign capital differed between recipient nations. It would be too simplistic to suggest that the demand for capital from abroad was governed

**Table 2.2** Main supplier and recipient countries of international long-term capital, 1885–1914

| | Cumulative totals of capital exported (billions of US $) | | | | | | | |
| Suppliers of capital | 1855 | 1870 | 1885 | 1900 | 1914 | Percentage of total by 1914 | Recipients of capital | Percentage of total by 1914 |
|---|---|---|---|---|---|---|---|---|
| United Kingdom | 2.3 | 4.9 | 7.8 | 12.1 | 19.5 | 44.0 | Australia and New Zealand | 5.0 |
| France | 1.0 | 2.5 | 3.3 | 5.2 | 9.0 | 20.0 | USA | 16.0 |
| Germany | – | – | 1.9 | 4.8 | 6.7 | 15.0 | Canada | 8.0 |
| Netherlands | 0.3 | 0.5 | 1.0 | 1.1 | 1.2 | 2.5 | Central and South America | 19.0 |
| USA | – | 0.1 | 0.4 | 0.5 | 3.5 | 8.0 | Asia | 14.0 |
| Canada | – | – | – | 0.1 | 0.2 | 0.5 | Africa | 11.0 |
| Other countries* | na | na | na | na | 4.3 | 10.0 | Europe | 27.0 |
| Total | 3.6 | 8.0 | 14.4 | 23.8 | 44.4 | 100.0 | | 100.0 |

* Mainly Belgium and Switzerland.
Source: Based on Woodruff 1966, p. 151.

**Table 2.3**   Geographic distribution of British overseas investment in 1913

| Area of investment | Percentage of total British overseas investment in 1913 |
| --- | --- |
| British Empire | 47.0 |
| Canada | 13.5 |
| Australia and New Zealand | 11.0 |
| South Africa | 10.0 |
| India & Ceylon | 10.0 |
| Other British Empire countries | 2.5 |
| | |
| Foreign countries | 53.0 |
| United States | 20.0 |
| Argentina | 8.0 |
| Brazil | 4.0 |
| Other South America | 8.0 |
| Western Europe | 3.0 |
| Russia | 3.0 |
| Other foreign countries | 7.0 |

Source: Based on Saul 1960, p. 67.

only by the desire to expand primary production to meet the demand for raw materials and foodstuffs from the industrial countries. This was, however, a predominant factor in some capital-importing countries in some periods. Similarly, it would be incorrect to assume that foreign capital was always more important than domestically generated capital in the capital-importing countries, though again, it was in some instances. Imported capital added to resources available locally and allowed the country to consume more than it produced or to import more than it exported. This permitted it to sustain a higher rate of capital formation than would otherwise be possible and so opened the possibility of accelerated economic growth. Imported capital might free domestic capital from some of the burden of development projects that were particularly expensive, such as railways. The ratio of capital imports to gross domestic capital formation varied between countries and over time. In the United States, the ratio never exceeded 9 per cent and was usually closer to 3 per cent. In other countries there were periods when the ratio was high; for example, in Australia in the 1880s when it averaged 51 per cent, in New Zealand between 1881 and 1885 when it reached 66 per cent and Canada where the ratio peaked at 46 per cent in the 1911–1913 period. Even when speculative capital flowed in from abroad in response to a mining, plantation or land **boom**, local capital could also have been used. This happened in the Melbourne land boom of the 1880s, in the South African gold and diamonds boom in the 1880s and 1890s, and the Malayan tin boom in the 1880s.

It would be mistaken, also, to attribute all of the economic growth in capital-importing countries to export growth. Inflows of capital, labour and enterprise stimulated domestic economic development in many capital-importing countries. Sometimes this occurred to such an extent that the export industries lost their position as the major engines of growth. This was true particularly of the United States in the nineteenth century, but some element of it could be found in many capital-importing countries.

Although undoubtedly beneficial from an economic development point of view, international flows of capital in the nineteenth and early twentieth centuries could be destabilising forces in the **short term**. Speculative flows of '**hot money**' were not unknown before 1914, though not on the scale they reached later in the century. Capital could take flight in response to localised crises. This happened, for example, to Argentina in 1885 and 1913, to Australia in 1891–93 and to Russia in 1905. Because the international monetary system worked so poorly in the years following the First World War, there was a tendency to look back at the system as it operated in the pre-war years and see it as almost perfect. It was not, but it did work reasonably well most of the time.

> **SUMMARY BOX**
>
> Industrialisation led to the accumulation of capital in the hands of a class of investor who was prepared to lend to foreign governments and public utilities. Other forms of international investment also increased as a result of industrialisation, such as **direct foreign investment** by firms. There was also usually some investor interest in foreign speculative ventures. Overall, secure loans to governments and government-backed agencies dominated pre-1914 international investment flows. British investors remained the most important source of funds. Foreign capital was an essential element in the economic development of primary producing countries like Australia before 1914. At times, foreign investment was a significant proportion of total investment, but domestic sources of saving also developed in many capital-importing countries.

## Economic fluctuations and integration

The development of an integrated international economy in the nineteenth century meant economic fluctuations in one region were more readily transmitted to other areas and economic isolationism was broken down. Small changes in prices in **commodity** markets, for example, could have dramatic effects within a short time in dozens of local economies around the globe. Fluctuations in such activities as foreign investment, international migration, building and construction, transport development (especially railway building) and exports and imports inter-acted in the global economy of the late nineteenth century to produce 'long swings' of accelerating and slower periods of growth. The interaction of business cycles can be seen most clearly in the case of the United States and Britain in the late nineteenth century. By the 1890s, however, business cycles in several of the major economies were moving together in a more co-ordinated way as integration of national economies into the international economy intensified.

**Figure 2.3**    Prices of primary products in world trade, 1881 to 1913

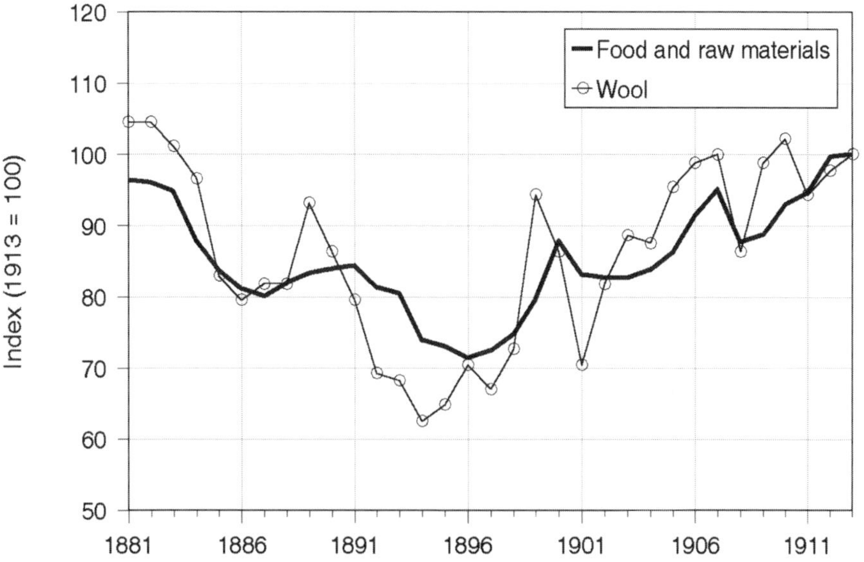

Source: Based on Lewis 1978, p. 280.

In the first half of the 1890s there was a worldwide **recession** that contemporaries termed 'the **depression** of the 1890s', followed by a worldwide expansion from 1896 to 1907. Australia was adversely affected by the international recession but, for reasons explained in the next chapter, was unable to benefit from the subsequent upswing in the global economy. The 'depression' manifested itself in a severe collapse of prices, rising unemployment and falling output. The prices of goods entering world trade fell steeply and the **terms of trade** moved decisively against the primary producing and exporting nations, including Australia (see Figure 2.3). The value and, to a lesser extent, the volume of world trade fell. Foreign investment and international migration declined sharply (see Figure 2.4). This was the first time in which there had been such a co-ordinated worldwide movement in prices, employment and output, and it marked, perhaps, the birth of the international economy in its modern form. Its causes centred on the remarkable increases in output and exports, especially of primary products, since the 1870s, coupled with greatly reduced costs of national and international transport. Contemporaries also linked falling prices to contracting world gold production. Manufactured goods prices fell in response to lower raw materials prices and declining labour costs.

Falling prices alarmed businesses and governments, which acted to increase market power by mergers and the formation of **cartels** and to protect national economies by raising tariff barriers against 'cheap imports'. The price depression also sparked a scramble by the industrial European countries to annex large areas of the tropical world, which they viewed as sources of supply and potential markets.

From 1896, food and raw materials prices rose, turning the terms of trade in favour of primary-exporting countries and bringing to an end the period of rising

**Figure 2.4**   International investment and emigration, 1881 to 1913

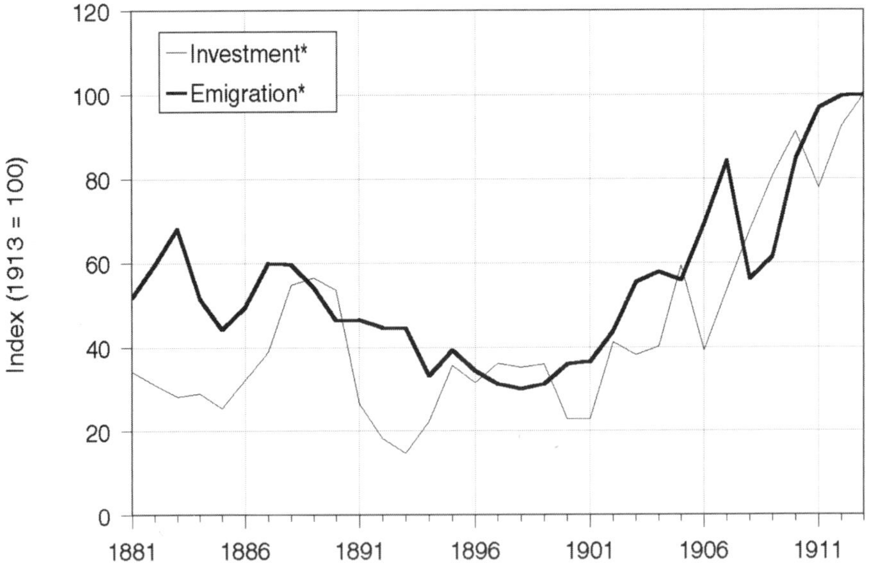

* Indexes of UK foreign investment and emigration.
Sources: Based on Simon 1968, pp. 38–9; Willcox 1929, p. 636.

real wages in Western Europe that had resulted from cheaper food. Recovery from the depression of the 1890s raised employment, but also increased the cost of living, and this led to more intense industrial unrest and social protest (Burnett 1994; Lloyd 1979, Chapters 1 and 2). Higher prices for primary products sparked faster export growth among many primary producing and exporting countries from the end of the 1890s, as well as to more active exploitation of the natural resources of the tropics. The 1890s also represented a watershed in the transfer of world industrial leadership from Britain to Germany, a successful challenge to Britain's industrial supremacy that eventually led to an arms race and the First World War (Porter 1975, Chapter 3; Hoffman 1933).

Of equal significance, the 1890s marked a major economic transition in the United States. From being a primary producing and exporting economy with a growing manufacturing sector, the United States became one in which industrial production predominated and a sizeable export trade in manufactured goods was established. By the end of the century, **economies of scale** and technological advances gave US manufacturing firms a competitive edge whose impact was soon felt by firms in the other industrial countries. As a further sign of its reaching economic maturity, the United States also moved across the line demarcating net debtor countries from net creditor ones, as its current private capital outflow exceeded its current private capital inflow for the first time in 1900.

The impact of Western European industrialisation outside of Europe varied considerably. How any individual country responded to the expansion of the international economy in the late nineteenth and early twentieth centuries was influenced by a multitude of factors. Among these, social and political structure, political status, resource endowment, geographical location and existing 'traditional' agricultural and manufacturing sectors were important.

Many primary-producing countries increased production and export on a sustained basis, but few were able to build on this expansion to develop secondary industry and undergo their own industrial revolution. The only outstanding example of this happening was the United States, which had developed as a major primary producer and exporter in the early nineteenth century, but after the Civil War industrialised and became the largest industrial-manufacturing economy in the world.

A number of 'new areas' were integrated into the international economy by the inflow of foreign capital and labour, including Australia, New Zealand, Argentina, Brazil, parts of Central America, South Africa and Malaysia. Some of these were independent nations, others were tied by political links to European powers. These countries often performed well as exporters of primary produce, but rapid export growth did not always lead to economic development. Linkages between the export sector and the rest of the economy tended to be weak and their economies were structurally unbalanced (Denoon 1983). Other primary-producing economies that were at least partly integrated into the international economy during this period depended mainly on small-scale peasant agricultural production for export earnings. Imported capital was sometimes significant in these cases, but imported labour was not. Some, such as India and China, were countries of emigration. Many – India, Indonesia, Egypt, west and equatorial Africa – were colonial possessions of European countries. Typically, these countries possessed large subsistence sectors that were incompletely linked to the export economy. Peasant producers in the export sector lacked capital and relied heavily on labour-intensive techniques. Such economies often exported only one or two major commodities, and so were highly vulnerable to fluctuations in the world economy (Havinden & Meredith 1993, Chapter 5).

There was one unique case of integration into the world economy before the First World War – Japan. Japan became integrated not as a primary produce exporter – in fact, Japan had to import many of its primary resources such as iron, timber, raw cotton and some foodstuffs – nor as a political vassal of one of the industrial nations. Japan's place in the international economy was as a rapidly growing industrial economy, the first in Asia to undergo an industrial revolution. By 1913, Japan accounted for 2.3 per cent of the world's exports of manufactured goods and 1.2 per cent of world production of manufactures. It had a modern iron and steel industry capable of producing 250 000 tonnes a year. Its military alliance with Britain (1902), its defeat of Russia (1905) and its conquests in Korea after 1905 marked its emergence as a new 'great power', as well as being an important force in the global economy. The emergence of a powerful industrial neighbour in the western Pacific region posed important questions for Australia's political and economic relations within its own region in the new century. As subsequent chapters show, Australia's regional economic integration was hesitant and much delayed.

**SUMMARY BOX**

Greater integration of the global economy produced co-ordinated swings in economic activity (known also as business cycles or **trade cycles**). A worldwide 'depression' occurred in the first half of the 1890s, followed by a strong upswing from 1896. The most obvious signs of the 'depression' were falling prices and rising unemployment. International flows of trade, migration and investment were also affected. Recovery from the depression led to rising prices and improving terms of trade for primary-producing countries. The last decade of the nineteenth century also saw a challenge to Britain's world hegemony from Germany and the United States. Although many primary-producing countries were integrated in the global economy in the years before the First World War, the impact this had on their economic development varied considerably. Of the 'new' countries in the world economy, Japan's integration was of particular significance, especially for Australia.

## The effects of industrialisation

Industrialisation and the growth of the international economy wrought enormous changes in Western society in the century before the First World War. It created the potential for unprecedented improvements in living standards on a mass scale for the first time in human history. Achievements fell short of the maximum possible, but that should not detract from the remarkable benefits that the economic revolutions had brought by 1914. Living standards had improved markedly in many Western countries. Industrial society seemed undoubtedly preferable to pre-industrial society to those who had had the opportunity to experience both, as many had in the industrialising nations. Yet despite the spectacular advances of the nineteenth century, pre-1914 society had hardly solved all of the economic and social problems. It was a period of unique economic and social change, but it was hardly the 'golden age' that some commentators later in the twentieth century pictured it to be. The industrial and demographic revolutions of the nineteenth century and the growth and development of a global economy by the end of the century did nothing to reduce tension and conflict between nation states, though equally, international disputes were no more frequent than in earlier centuries. The diplomatic mechanisms that led from the assassination of an archduke in Sarevejo in June 1914 to the outbreak of the First World War five weeks later owed more to the eighteenth than the nineteenth centuries. What industrialisation did do, however, was make war infinitely more destructive and costly, as the course and aftermath of the 1914–1918 world war was to show.

# Suggested further reading

Denoon, D. 1983, *Settler Capitalism: The Dynamics of Dependent Development in the Southern Hemisphere*, Clarendon Press, Oxford.

Foreman Peck, J. 1983, *A History of the World Economy: International Economic Relations Since 1850*, Wheatsheaf, Brighton.

Hudson, P. 1992, *The Industrial Revolution*, Arnold, London.

Kenwood, A.G. & Lougheed, A.L. 1983, *The Growth of the International Economy 1820–1980*, Allen and Unwin, London.

Lewis, W.A. 1978, *Growth and Fluctuations, 1870–1913*, Allen & Unwin, Boston.

Maddison, A. 1991, *Dynamic Forces in Capitalist Development, a Long Run Comparative View*, Oxford University Press, Oxford.

Rosenberg, N. & Birdzell, L.E. 1986, *How the West Grew Rich: The Economic Transformation of the Industrial World*, Tauris, London.

Woodruff, W. 1966, *The Impact of Western Man: A Study of Europe's Role in the World Economy, 1750–1960*, Macmillan, London.

# End note

[1]  The literature on industrialisation in the nineteenth century is enormous. See P. Hudson 1992.

# 3

# Australia before 1914

When Australia became an independent nation at the beginning of 1901 the United Kingdom of Great Britain and Ireland was, as we have seen, the world's major financial, trading and military power, and the largest exporter of people, goods and **capital**. It was at the centre of the first global economy. Almost one-fifth of the people then in Australia had been born in the United Kingdom, and most of the rest were descended from British or Irish immigrants. A little more than half of Australia's exports went to Britain, and about three-fifths of Australia's imports came from there.[1] Nearly all of the overseas capital was British. And sterling, the world currency, continued as Australia's currency until 1910, while for a further 20 years, until the Great Depression of the 1930s, the Australian pound was held resolutely at par with the pound sterling.

The Commonwealth of Australia did not begin with a unilateral declaration of independence. The Australian Constitution only had legal force once it passed as an Act of the British Parliament in 1900. The British government encouraged the six colonies to federate and to bear greater responsibility for their own management, which would reduce the cost and complexity of Britain's involvement in the South Pacific. The Constitution included a right of appeal from Australian law courts to the Privy Council in London (sections 73 and 74), and clause 5 in its Preamble exempted from Australian laws British shipping when in Australian waters, except when the formal port of clearance and the last port of call were both in Australia. These imperial restrictions on sovereignty ensured that the interests of British investors and traders were not solely at the mercy of Australian decisions. A Coalition government in 1968 and a Labor government in 1975 reduced the scope of appeal outside the country but British extra-territorial rights were extinguished only by the passage of the Australia Act through both the British and Australian parliaments in 1986 (Solomon 1992, pp. 120–32).

Within the new Commonwealth, the States (as the former colonies were now called) retained all their high-spending functions, except for posts and telegraphs. Railways, ports, harbours and other public works, education, health, immigration and police remained state preserves, which (apart from immigration) they are today (*Yearbook*, vol. 4, 1901–1910 (1911), pp. 662–94). But under Section 86 of the Constitution, the States relinquished their traditional source of taxation, drawn from customs and excise, in favour of the Commonwealth. So low were the Commonwealth's expenditures expected to be that, under Section 87, for the first 10 years three-quarters at least of the customs revenue was to be paid back to the States. More than three-quarters was handed back until 1908, when the national government instituted aged pensions and began budgeting for a navy (Solomon 1992, pp. 77–9).

The customs **tariff** soon became another instrument for advancing British interests. Although **free trade** Britain was unable to offer preferential entry to Australian goods, the Australian tariff in and after 1907 set a lesser rate for the entry of goods from the United Kingdom than that imposed on comparable imports from other countries. By 1909, two-thirds of British imports paid duty, but at a rate that on average allowed them to be priced about 5 per cent lower than the competition. Britain's share of imports rose, after a decade of decline (*Yearbook*, vol. 4, 1901–1910 (1911), p. 661; *Yearbook*, vol. 8, 1901–1914 (1915), p. 520). The preferential tariff was, political sentiment aside, an investment in the solvency and goodwill of the British market.

Federation, above all, created a free trade zone inside a customs union. A later generation might have called it the Australian Common Market. Before 1901, each State devised its own tariff regime. Victoria had been staunchly **Protectionist**; manufacturers and farmers voted each other barriers against competitors from elsewhere in Australia and New Zealand. The New South Wales parliament, on the other hand, usually held a free trade majority; there the tariff raised revenue rather than secured special interests and, consistent with being a tax for revenue, it was levied on tobacco, alcohol, sugar, opium and other addictive substances for which **demand** would respond sluggishly to any rise in duty (Patterson 1968, pp. 143–57). Federation demolished the customs houses along state borders. But what would be the ideology at the new national border? Until the election of 1910, the voters returned three roughly equal groupings: Protectionists, Free Traders and Labor. The Labor Party was evenly split between those who believed the tariff preserved jobs and those who believed that free trade brought down the cost of living. The tariff of 1907, explicitly protectionist, depended on the Labor Party being won over in its entirety. In 1901 and 1902, however, the initial customs schedule was less clear cut in its implications. Debate took place on 117 separate sitting days – so diverse were the points of view and interests involved. It was managed by Victorian and South Australian Protectionists who had to manoeuvre around Labor's united resolve to keep the price low of two everyday imports: kerosene for cooking and heating, and tea (Souter 1988, pp. 67–72).

Did the formation of a common market stimulate the economy? Did the mild tariff help or hinder the embryonic nation? The scholarly debate has been brief and inconclusive (Forster 1977). For one thing, whatever processes were at work had little time to evolve. They were interrupted by the First World War. For another thing, Federation occurred during a severe **depression** prolonged by drought, so any subsequent growth might be construed simply as a conventional upswing in the business cycle and in the weather. Before we continue, then, we should look backwards at the strengths and weaknesses of the economy into which this brand-new nation was born.

# The pre-Federation economy: land

**SUMMARY BOX**

Not so long ago it was normal to refer to Australia as 'a **land of recent settlement**', as if any previous inhabitants were neither significant nor permanent. The legal fiction that dignified this assumption was summed up by the Latin term terra nullius, nobody's land, an assumption that ruled until 1992, when the High Court abandoned it in the Mabo decision.

Victorious groups agree, of course, that a completed conquest, however bloody, has the full force of law. As European occupation of North and South America proceeded an international jurisprudence evolved in Europe to justify conquest on the ground that simple economic practices must give way by Divine Providence and by natural law to more complex economic practices (Reynolds 1987; Stephenson & Ratnapala 1993). In parts of North America, and in the North Island of New Zealand, British conquest was assisted by treaties, although it is unlikely that the native signatories intended full surrender. In the South Island of New Zealand and at the founding of Melbourne, Australian-born businessmen struck material bargains with local leaders, who must have seen the payment-in-kind as the first instalment in an annual rental. The businessmen saw no need to renew the rental. On an official level no treaties were signed in Australia, nor was payment made. Australian **land** was an involuntary gift, an export without charge, to the international economy.

Because the British authorities acted as if the continent was empty of ownership, all subsequent claims to property derived from government decisions. Some of the bitterest political conflicts of the nineteenth century were fought over land rights for colonists, whether it was the right to own allotments in Sydney at the beginning of the century, or to secure long leases as graziers in the middle years, or to 'unlock the lands' from alleged grazier monopoly in the second half of the century. Occasionally the Crown (that is, the government) gave away property, sometimes sold at a set price or at auction, or rented on varying forms of tenure. Australia was large and was unevenly exploited. Many enterprises did not want to pay the cost of freehold possession. It has been estimated that by 1900 about 6 per cent of the continent was in freehold, that is to say was privately owned. Tenants of the Crown occupied another 40 per cent of the area (Butlin, Barnard & Pincus 1982, p. 56). The Crown had the reserve power to resume even freehold for a road or a port or some other public purpose. Timber rights and mineral rights complicated the process. The definition of property in Australia in 1900 was recent, shifting and of political origin.

If Australia was a gift that was selectively passed on, it was a gift with value added. There were many different economies before the British arrived (Dingle 1988; Butlin 1993). Each economy involved management of its land, which it modified over the millennia. The earliest colonists admired and coveted in particular the spreading 'parks' they encountered beyond Parramatta, across the Blue Mountains, in the Hunter Valley, and further afield. Regular controlled burning had created vast swathes of pasture fringed and threaded by light bush. The original Australians did it so that animals and birds could feed on fresh open grasses, shelter in or under trees, and be stalked and killed when needed in the open with a minimum of difficulty. The colonists did not domesticate the local fauna. They introduced cattle, sheep and horses, bred for commercial purposes in other parts of the world, and drove them on to the grasslands that Aboriginal Australians had made. A new class of pastoralists displaced the existing pastoralists.

Sheep were the most numerous intruders. The Industrial Revolution in Europe created a vast demand for fibres out of which textiles could be made. Pasture and climate in Australia combined to produce wool that was tough enough to be machine spun and woven but fine enough to earn a profit, despite transport costs, on the other side of the world. For at least half of the nineteenth century wool was the major export. On the eve of the depression of the 1890s it accounted for almost two-thirds of export by value. Cattle were like sheep: hardy, grass-eating beasts. They were slaughtered for their meat close to the domestic markets, with their hides and other by-products joining the export stream. Experiments in refrigeration, many of them done in Australia and New Zealand in response to the challenges of heat and long distance, showed practical results about 1880, allowing the export of deep frozen beef to the growing British market for food. And horses multiplied, too, for riding, haulage, and export as war horses in the British conquest of India (Barnard 1962; Kennedy 1992; Yarwood 1989).

Cultivated crops, like domesticated livestock, developed in specific locations around the world, from where they diffused far and wide, but thousands of years after the seas rose to isolate Australia. The introduced animals ate the native grasses, but the fruit and vegetables eaten by the colonists originated in every other continent. Britain's dietary staple, wheat, had evolved over millennia. Before railways cheapened cartage, wheat was usually grown close to water transport along the Australian coastline, where salt-laden winds and uneven terrain reduced yield and hampered harvest. Only on the level open country beside the sheltered gulfs and peninsulas of South Australia could extensive mechanised farms provide a substantial high-quality surplus for sale overseas (Dunsdorfs 1956). In 1890, once railways ran far inland, wheat was Australia's third most valuable export, mainly to British consumers. Timber, wattle-bark for tanning and other vegetable products had long filled space in the holds of ships, but decisions to grow a surplus of the kinds of food that were perishable had to follow the widespread adoption of refrigeration and canning.

The landmass fortuitously holds a great diversity of minerals, whose presence and variety have been revealed piecemeal over the last 200 years. A succession of Australian gold discoveries throughout the second half of the nineteenth century made gold instantly the major export of the 1850s and 1860s. It was still the second export by value in 1890. The gold rushes drew in population and enlarged the colonial **money supply**. The rushes were also important for the spread of the international **gold standard** (see Chapter 2). Copper, found near Adelaide, also entered the currency, though at a much lower level than gold. It was increasingly used in machinery and cabling on the other side of the world, and in the fashioning of kitchenware. Coal, a plebeian mineral, had been identified north of Sydney early in the colony's history. It was the classic source of energy for mass production and mass transport. Before mines opened in Asia and along the west coast of the Americas, sailing ships from New South Wales carried coal to power factories, steamships, railways, domestic stoves and fireplaces around the Pacific Rim (Pinkstone 1992, pp. 34–6, 40–1, 54–7).

# The pre-Federation economy: Labour

## SUMMARY BOX

People worked hard in Australia before 1788. Given the absence of beasts of burden, of domesticated animals generally, and of cultivated crops, large economic surpluses could not be contrived. The idea of profit was inconceivable in Australia before 1788. Of necessity people collaborated; individual wage **labour** was inconceivable (Dingle 1988; Sahlins 1974). In Britain by 1788, on the other hand, many, although not all, economic relationships had become contractual rather than based on age-old custom. They were negotiated between economic individuals. Property was concentrated in the hands of a minority. The majority had to sell their labour for wages to owners or renters of property in order to survive. Economic relationships in the New World of Australia tended to be even less encumbered than in Britain by customs and traditions. The convicts themselves, at least until 1823, had to be paid a minimum wage in addition to minimum rations and conditions; although the convict wage was made optional in 1823 to mark a clear distinction in rewards with the growing number of non-convict and ex-convict workers in the colonies. As a result, the institution of wage labour became settled policy across Australia.

Although there was an absolute lack of fit between the Aboriginal and the British social structures, recent research has shown that Aborigines regularly entered the colonial workforce across the countryside and in the towns (Reynolds 1990). They might 'come in' out of curiosity or goodwill, and often out of sheer need as their economies were weakened or swamped, and as foreign diseases reduced the size and working capacity of their own communities. Apart from a national reluctance to drudge forever for aliens, most Aborigines tried to live off their own land for as much of the year as the invading livestock and planted fields would allow. In addition, their social, marital and ceremonial obligations stole time away from colonial work, which had been arranged to suit social, marital and ceremonial rhythms customary to Britain and Ireland. This meant that Aborigines appeared to be casual, short-term, unpredictable labour. It reinforced an assumption the newcomers brought with them that non-Europeans everywhere were inferior in their needs as well as their abilities. Employers treated them as a floating reserve, for whose year-round maintenance they were not responsible. Rations and pay were rarely sufficient to support extended families for long, which further deterred Aborigines from committing themselves to permanent wage labour. From the beginning, then, Aborigines occupied a distinct and almost sealed segment of the labour market. Pay-in-kind, or small spasmodic amounts of cash, made it difficult in a cash-based society for Aborigines to rise to become self-employed, let alone owners of freehold property. How were they to escape the segment in which they were trapped?

For the colonies' core workforce, officials and employers preferred people with habits learned in the United Kingdom, which was supposedly the most advanced and productive nation in the world. Recent research has demonstrated that the convicts brought work-experience with them (Nicholas 1988; Oxley 1996). Employers clamoured for convicts with appropriate skills to be assigned to them. Half a century after the convict system began, when the colonial economies were at the peak of a frantic **boom**, employers complained more loudly than before that judges in the United Kingdom did not sentence enough useful people, did not sentence enough people of any kind, and did not send out enough women (five out of six convicts were male) to anchor and reproduce the colonial population. To meet this clamour the proceeds of the sale of Crown lands in the various colonies were, from the early 1830s, converted into passage money for single women and for married couples of child-bearing age. These adults would be available for work the moment they left the ship. Because the gold rushes of the 1850s attracted, on the whole, young unattached men who could leave the country as easily as they entered it, even larger numbers than before of married couples and young women were paid to migrate, largely funded from the proceeds of the sale or lease of public land. More than half of the British migrants between 1788 and 1914 had their passages paid (Sherington 1980; Jupp 1988). Revenue from the public creation of private property thus led directly to the public purchase of the population that would make property ownership profitable. The contours of immigration to Australia in this period are shown in Figure 3.1.

In later decades, the prosperity of south-eastern Australia continued to attract immigrants who found their own fare. The earlier cohort of assisted young women did their duty by enduring many child-births. The non-Aboriginal population rose extraordinarily fast, from 400 000 in 1851 to 3 180 000 in 1891. The electorate now preferred revenue to be spent on railways, roads, schools, hospitals, post-offices and other advanced public works. By the 1880s only the less developed

**Figure 3.1**   Net immigration to Australia, 1870–1913

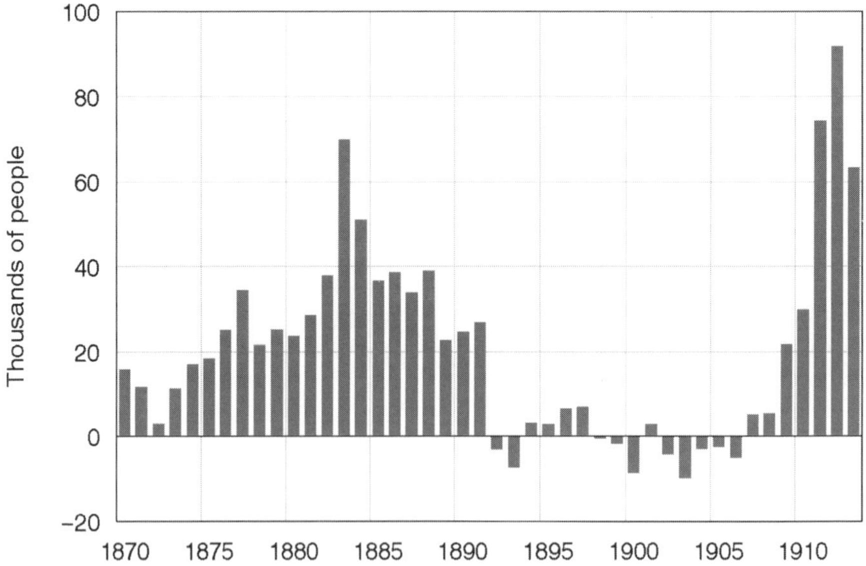

Source: Based on Willcox 1929, p. 947.

colony of Queensland maintained a large assisted passage scheme. That colony was the last stop on the shipping routes from Europe; how else could passengers be persuaded to stay on board beyond the booming cities of Melbourne and Sydney? By the time of Federation, one-quarter of Queensland's non-Aboriginal residents had been born in the United Kingdom, the highest proportion of any state, and nearly another 10 per cent had been born somewhere else overseas – once again the highest proportion (*Yearbook* 1908, vol. I, 1901–07, p. 147). Queensland had recruited village communities and kinship groups in Germany to form instant farming districts. Sugar interests brought men under savage indentures from Vanuatu and the Solomon Islands. Workers from China, Italy, Japan, Java, Scandinavia and other distant places pushed back the tropical frontier.

Queensland's multi-continental workforce dismayed many other Queenslanders, and many colonists further south. The way the international economy had evolved strengthened the tendency to racism that already pervaded the British Empire (Kiernan 1969). Trade theories emphasise the way commerce brings people together, thus reducing conflict. Implicit in such a theory is equality between trading partners and equality of information, as well as bargaining power. This was not the way the international economy developed. The energy that powered production and transport around the north Atlantic Ocean, and that could be harnessed for navies and armies, allowed a handful of nations to draw tribute from the rest of the world, sometimes through conquest (as with Britain over Australia or India) and sometimes through subordination in an 'informal empire' (as with Britain over China or Egypt). Insistence on unequal exchange carried with it a sense of entitlement. Sustained dominance seemed to prove inherent superiority and inferiority. As industrial developments widened gaps in the standards of living between countries and between continents, it became plausible for victorious societies to believe in a detailed hierarchy of ethnic worth, spanning the globe. New scientific orthodoxies, particularly evolutionary biology, spawned stereotypes that justified and dignified sub-division of the human race into numerous separate species, each itself labelled a 'race'. Standards of living – and fortunes of war – became easy to explain, and to explain away.

For the British in Australia, sponsorship of migration from continental Europe was uncommon, and migration on any terms from Asia, Africa or the Pacific was unwelcome. Why accept second-rate or tenth-rate humans when the world's finest, born and nurtured in the United Kingdom, made themselves available? Business people disliked migrants whose market demand (because of apparently different tastes and small **income**) would be closed to them. Working people feared the competition of migrants allegedly willing to accept poorer wages and conditions. Proximity should have brought increasing numbers from Asia instead of from the far side of the globe. By the late 1850s, indeed, during the Gold Rush, about one man in ten in Victoria came from China (Serle 1963, pp. 325, 382). From then on entry from Australia's near neighbourhood became fraught with regulations and levies, until the first Commonwealth Parliament passed an *Immigration Restriction Act 1901*. It was meant to keep out anyone not of European descent. The White Australia Policy, as it was known, would last for the next two-thirds of the century. An official embargo against four humans out of five ran side by side with official assistance to some of the rest. The Australian population, from 1788 onwards, and confirmed in 1901, was the result of conscious manufacture (Price 1974; Markus 1979).

# The pre-Federation economy: Capital

**SUMMARY BOX**

Capital has two main meanings: liquid funds consolidated for **investment** and long-term physical assets, usually produced with the help of invested funds. In the nineteenth century, Britain was the most highly capitalised nation in the world, with by far the largest stock of investments beyond its borders. It was to be the dominant source of overseas finance for Australia until the second half of the twentieth century.

The British taxpayers laid the basis for Australian capitalism. It has been estimated that as late as 1820 almost half of the gross colonial product came from British revenue, spent on the transportation and discipline of the convict **labour force**, on official and military wages, on roads, wharfs, buildings and **infrastructure** generally (Butlin 1986). Farmers and merchant traders made profits within this framework, which they ploughed back into business and consumption. The growth in activity drew **credit** and direct investment from the British home market. Towards the end of the century, domestic and imported capital were concentrated in particular in pastoralism, town building, railways, banking and finance, and mining (Butlin 1964).

Graziers sat at the top of the class structure. Until the middle of the nineteenth century many of them accumulated capital principally through the lambing and calving of their flocks and herds, and they saved money by spreading beyond the surveyed and freehold districts to become what were proudly called squatters on public land. The gold rushes swelled the market for meat. The fleet of ships that brought passengers and merchandise to the gold rushes supplied plentiful and cheap freight back to Europe for the graziers' bales of wool. The woolgrowers were rich enough to spend confidently on land purchases, buildings, fences, water and pasture improvement. An index of the pastoral sector's consolidation is the growth in estimated sheep numbers in eastern Australia from 17 000 000 in 1862 to 89 000 000 in 1892. Specialist financial institutions evolved to serve the sector. These pastoral companies (Dalgetys, Elder Smith, Goldsbrough Mort and others) arranged for the storage, export and sale of the woolclip; they extended credit to graziers for day-to-day expenses, for capital improvements, and to provide bridging finance over the months and years between stocking a station and receiving the proceeds from across the sea. Many of the pastoral companies originated in Australia, and through their specialisation all drew funds into Australia and kept them circulating there to intensify the capitalisation of the sector (Butlin 1964, Chapter 2; Jones 1987).

Australia was not just a huge sheep farm. A century ago a United States scholar pointed out that only little Belgium was a more urbanised place than Australia (Weber 1965). Each colony had started with its sea-port capital, where nearly all people, goods and information entered and left the territory, and where the administration (public and private) of these movements was centred. Immigrants found the streetscape and jobs available in the seaport capitals more familiar than the bush. The population of Sydney grew from 54 000 in 1851 to 400 000, 40 years later, Adelaide from 18 000 to 117 000, and Brisbane from 3000 to 94 000. Marvellous Melbourne was one of the world's most splendid boom-towns, growing from 30 000 to 490 000 over the same period. Building for all these new city-folk swallowed substantial capital. The consequent **fixed capital** of cottages and terraces, schools, post offices, town halls and workplaces continue to dominate the inner suburban areas of those cities today. The construction sector, like the pastoral sector, was capitalised not only through the traditional banks but through very specific and local institutions, including building societies, land and mortgage companies and (for public structures) the colonial governments. Australians managed most of the capital, but the banks received substantial deposits at their London offices, while insurance companies and solicitors' trust funds in Britain transferred lump sums against urban mortgages (Frost 1990).

Railways joined the cities and the countryside, and joined the countryside to the outside world. Without the speedy bulk transport provided by railways (and river steamers) in the last third of the century, in place of bullock drays, it would have been impossible to export the wool of five times as many sheep in 1892 as had existed in 1862. The trunk lines, when close to the city, allowed developers to lay out commuter suburbs, supplemented as they were by rail and tram lines built specifically for suburban development. Private companies planned the first rail projects in most colonies, but these were projects with heavy initial costs and often difficult engineering problems to solve; early or late, boards of directors sold out to the citizenry as a whole, which is to say to the government (Davidson 1982). Governments could mobilise a much larger stock of funds, through taxation, land sales and borrowing, without the pressure to declare a profit, although railway revenue added significantly to state **budgets** until the 1920s. Governments could borrow at cheaper rates than private companies, offering the State's assets and the State's stability as security for government loan issues. This brought down the cost of development and, where the loans were floated in London, increased the stock of capital in Australia at the lowest attainable rate.

Freed from the immediate constraint of profit on each route, let alone each journey, governments could plan either for long distant returns (where farms or suburbs might follow) or for externalities (spin-offs) that would accrue to the wider economy, such as cheap workers' tickets and excess rolling stock for peak hour use to deliver the labour force daily to the workplace, or the laying of a track in regions where crops and therefore freight were narrowly seasonal (Weber 1965, pp. 471–5; Butlin, Barnard & Pincus 1982, pp. 259–69), although a group of speculators might still capture the political process to direct a route through its lands (Davison 1970; Muir 1987). In setting up government workshops and also commissioning railway carriages and parts from local private factories, Australian decision-makers responded to electoral and patriotic pressures by opting for the creation and employment of home-grown skill. This strengthened an engineering culture in Australia, and diffused it to the many smaller towns where steam trains were loaded, fuelled, cleaned and repaired.

# Boom and bust

Unlike many regions that supplied the international economy with **primary products**, Australia moved in the late nineteenth century towards a negative balance of trade. The arrival throughout the 1880s of imports to a greater aggregate value than what exports could pay for was the sign of an affluent society, to which the overseas suppliers extended credit with equal confidence. In the middle years of the 1880s, Australia received one-quarter of all new British overseas investment, and at the end of that decade it still received one-sixth of all new British overseas investment. Many of the imports were **capital goods** (for example, machines) or **producer goods** (for example, metals for heavy industry, textiles for the garment trade) that made an advanced rural sector and a capable manufacturing sector possible. Production of goods and services for domestic consumption outstripped production for overseas markets. Export earnings had accounted for 28 per cent of **GDP** in 1861–65 but only 14 per cent by 1886–90. In the short run, this demonstrated the affluence and expansion of the domestic economy, but in the medium term the capital inflow of the 1880s and the trade deficit had to be serviced. The cost of servicing Australia's international debt rose from 15 per cent of export earnings in 1880 to 40 per cent in 1890 (Butlin 1962, pp. 6, 410–14, 460; Hall 1963, Chapters 5 and 6).

Australian statisticians claimed at the beginning of the 1890s that Australia was the wealthiest place in the world per head of population. International commentators accepted the claim. Pessimists at the end of the twentieth century have sometimes repeated the assertion and looked for some subsequent error in Australia's political and economic history to explain why it has fallen from first place (Coghlan 1886 ff; Thomas 1995).

Australian affluence was acknowledged at that time because its official statisticians led (and instructed) the world in both the theory and practice of their craft (Groenewegen & McFarlane 1990, pp. 92–117). The British earlier in the century needed to keep track of the convicts and to register carefully each transfer of property from Aboriginal to non-Aboriginal ownership. Because Australia and Tasmania were islands, comprehensive knowledge existed of the entry of people and the entry (import) and exit (export) of merchandise. Such information was useful to businessmen as well as to officials, which encouraged people to co-operate with the collectors of economic and social data. T.A. Coghlan, statistician of NSW between 1886 and 1905, produced the world's first example of national accounts, for his own colony and for Australia and New Zealand as a whole (Coghlan 1890). The statisticians wrote eloquent essays interpreting the data. The unique scale of the yearbooks in Australia reflected and served ambitious policies of national development, and in the competition to attract people and capital from overseas they became aggressive marketing tools. To this end, Coghlan renamed his colony's yearbook *Wealth and Progress*. The scope and the propaganda of the colonial yearbooks ensured that Australian wealth and **income** would be more fully recorded and analysed than wealth and income anywhere else.

Comparisons depend also on the date at which they are made. A long and spectacular boom in Australia was ending in 1891. As we have seen in Chapter 1, the dominant economies around the north Atlantic drew the rest of the world into **recession** early in the 1890s. They recovered powerfully in the second half of the decade, but Australia did not. N.G. Butlin calculated that **real** GDP per head in Australia dropped from £66 in 1889 to £48 in 1897. 'It was not until 1904', he wrote, 'that the 1890 aggregate real product was surpassed and only by 1907 that the level of per capita real income attained in 1890 was restored' (Butlin 1962, p.460; 1970, p. 282). It has been argued that Britain's per capita performance probably passed Australia's by 1895, and the gap would have widened for a while thereafter (Thomas 1995, p. 24). The United States and Canadian economies surged from 1896 onwards while Australia continued downwards. If the subdued Federation year of 1901 had been chosen as a benchmark instead of 1890, a year of asset **inflation**, later commentators would be less ready to find fault with Australia's performance relative to other countries in the twentieth century.

Australia, we have seen, was specially vulnerable to a world downturn; the cost of servicing the international debt having risen from 15 per cent of export earnings to 40 per cent through the 1880s. When general panic gripped British financiers after the Baring Crisis at the end of 1890, and world trade contracted, capital inflow dwindled and export receipts dropped. Terms of trade for primary

**Figure 3.2**   Australia's terms of trade, 1870–1913

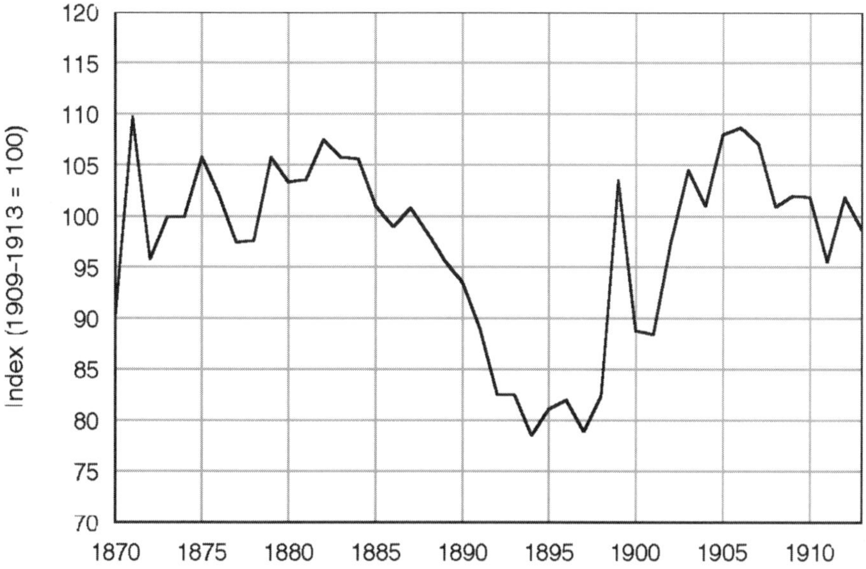

Source: Based on Bambrick 1970, p. 5.

goods around the world had been falling throughout the 1880s (see Figure 2.3 in Chapter 2), making it already more difficult year by year for Australia to service its **foreign debt**, and Australia's **terms of trade** continued to fall until late in the 1890s (see Figure 3.2). Here we find a pattern that was repeated for Australia in the 1920s, the late 1960s and the 1980s. During global booms, Australia was showered with funds, which stimulated swift but heavily indebted growth, so that the world downturn that followed was felt more keenly and repaid more slowly by Australia than by many other economies.

Investors in Australia compounded the problem. As the world's major wool producer the manifold increase in Australian supply pushed prices down, matching the sector's soaring debt with diminishing unit returns to the graziers. The swollen flocks overstocked existing runs, and spilled on to inferior land. Their hard teeth and sharp hooves depleted and degraded the fragile pastures, which were worn out even before drought set in at the end of the 1890s. Ecological as much as economic pressures led to a halving of the number of sheep in Australia within a few seasons. The urban boom burst also. For a while unimproved suburban land in Melbourne had turned over at an annual profit of 75 per cent. This asset bubble was unsustainable. When first local and then international conditions put an end to such speculation, resale prices, business confidence and the solvency of the sector's financial institutions all collapsed. Bankruptcy and **unemployment** affected Melbourne above all, so that its population stagnated throughout the 1890s; in some years there was no net addition to the housing stock, both a reflection and a reinforcement of profound depression. And the railways, which made the rural and urban sprawl possible, lost business – such proceeds were needed to meet the **interest** on current loans (Butlin 1964, pp. 407–50; Boehm 1971; Cannon 1971).

The slowness of Australian recovery has been noted. For 10 out of 15 years more people left Australia than entered it (Willcox 1929, p. 97). Emigrants from Europe preferred the United States, Canada, South Africa, New Zealand and Argentina, and governments, whose revenues had diminished, did not pay passages at a time when jobs were scarce. Migration, assisted and unassisted, did not revive until 1907. Capital inflow revived more tardily still. Overseas funds, in net terms, continued to arrive throughout the 1890s, but there was a net outflow of capital between, and including, 1904 and 1911 (Butlin 1962, pp. 410–14, 436–41). International supplies of people and capital, which characterised the boom before 1890, had nothing to do with Australia's recovery, but resumed only when the economy had recovered completely. Three factors can be identified in bringing the recovery about: booming markets in the world outside, diversification at home in response to world demand, and the creative role of government in the process of reconstruction.

It has been pointed out in Chapter 2 that the industrial economies grew apace in the 20 years before the First World War. Developments in metallurgy, chemicals and energy creation (for example, the conversion of coal into electricity and the use of petroleum) made possible the mass manufacture of new products, and a much more efficient transport of goods from source to market. The enhanced output and trade raised living standards in the richer economies, where people could better afford than before to satisfy their appetite for food. As a result, the terms of trade for Australia's exports turned sharply upwards in the late 1890s (Bambrick 1970, p. 5), and the types of goods sent away became more diverse. Where wool and gold once dominated the cargoes, by the years 1911 to 1913 wool earned less than two-

**Figure 3.3**   Commodity structure of Australia's exports, 1899–1901

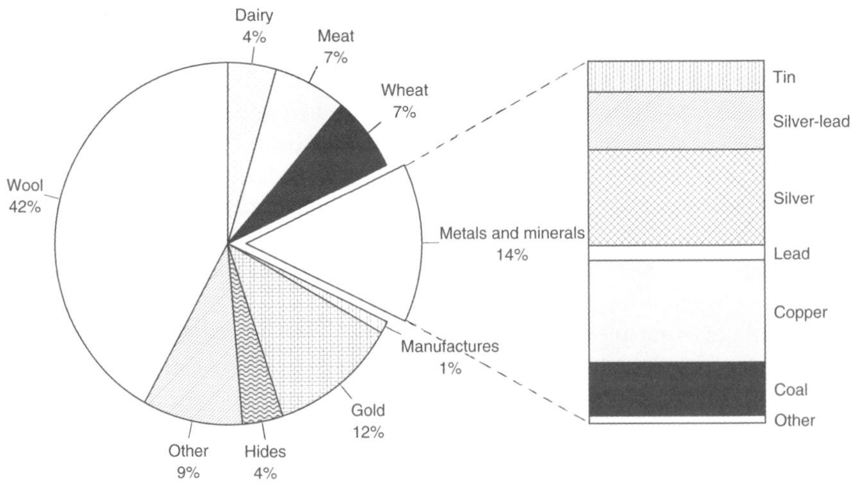

Source: Based on Coghlan 1903.

**Figure 3.4**    Commodity structure of Australia's exports, 1911–1913

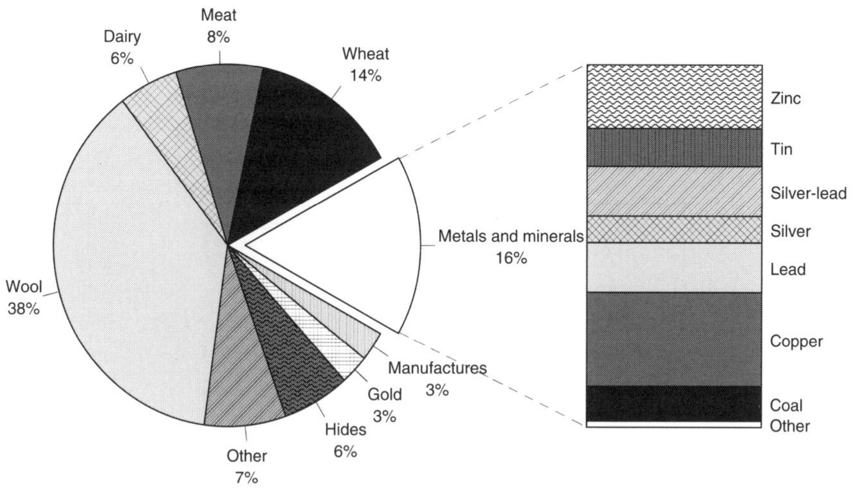

Source: Based on CBCS 1914.

fifths of the total, and of the one-fifth earned by minerals, gold was joined by silver, Queensland copper, lead, zinc and tin. Food accounted for almost 30 per cent of earnings, wheat filling half of that basket and the refrigerated perishables of meat and butter filling the other half (CBCS 1914; see Figures 3.3 and 3.4).

The destination for these commodities became more diverse also, as Table 3.1 indicates. Whereas Britain consumed three-quarters of Australia's exports in 1890, its share had dropped steadily to 44 per cent by 1913. The major shift was to the European mainland where France, Belgium and Germany took 30 per cent of exports in 1913, compared with less than 10 per cent in 1890 (*Yearbook* 1915, vol. 8, 1901–1914, p. 520). Continental Europe, particularly France, now bought more than half the wool and hides; the metallurgical leaders, Belgium and Germany, took most of the zinc and nearly half the copper. Britain consumed most of Australia's food exports, especially the butter and the meat, and was the major market for gold, lead and tin (see Table 3.2). International demand expanded so fast that Australian export earnings in 1913 more than doubled those in 1890, and the surplus in **visible trade** was sufficiently large that it surpassed the combined cost of debt servicing and any net deficit on the **invisible schedule** (shipping, insurance, dividends, and so on) between 1904 and 1911. This favourable **current account** balance provides one explanation of the economy's ability to survive a net outflow of capital during those years (see Table 3.3).

The impressive export performance arose from significant structural change in the Australian countryside or, to put it less abstractly, from a lot of hard work and forward-thinking. When times were good, owners and investors tended to repeat what had been profitable already. Bad times threw land, labour and capital into unemployment. People in search of food and shelter were available for the

Table 3.1 Australia's major trading partners, 1887–1913 (percentage of total)

| Country/region | | 1887–1891 | 1892–1896 | 1897–1901 | 1902–1906 | 1907–1911 | 1913 |
|---|---|---|---|---|---|---|---|
| UK | Imports | 70.0 | 71.0 | 63.0 | 53.0 | 61.0 | 60.0 |
| | Exports | 75.0 | 70.0 | 57.0 | 46.0 | 47.0 | 44.0 |
| W. Europe | Imports | 5.2 | 6.2 | 8.6 | 9.4 | 9.8 | 9.8 |
| | Exports | 8.8 | 15.3 | 14.3 | 18.7 | 27.9 | 30.6 |
| USA | Imports | 6.4 | 6.5 | 12.0 | 12.6 | 11.1 | 11.9 |
| | Exports | 5.6 | 3.8 | 8.9 | 4.7 | 2.9 | 3.4 |
| New Zealand | Imports | 5.2 | 4.3 | 4.2 | 6.2 | 4.4 | 3.2 |
| | Exports | 2.5 | 3.0 | 2.6 | 3.1 | 3.4 | 3.0 |
| India & Ceylon | Imports | 2.5 | 3.3 | 3.6 | 4.4 | 5.0 | 4.9 |
| | Exports | 2.8 | 2.5 | 5.5 | 13.7 | 6.8 | 3.1 |
| South Africa | Imports | – | – | – | – | 0.2 | 0.2 |
| | Exports | 0.6 | 0.5 | 5.7 | 5.8 | 2.6 | 2.5 |
| Other countries | Imports | 10.7 | 8.7 | 8.6 | 14.4 | 8.5 | 10.0 |
| | Exports | 4.7 | 4.9 | 6.0 | 8.0 | 9.4 | 13.4 |

W. Europe: France, Belgium and Germany.
Source: Based on ABS Yearbook, nos 2, 7, 8.

**Table 3.2** Australia's principal export markets by major commodity, 1911–1913 (% of total)

| Commodity | UK | W. Europe | USA | India | China | S. Africa | S.E. Asia | Japan | New Zealand | Chile |
|---|---|---|---|---|---|---|---|---|---|---|
| Wool | 39 | 56 | 2 | | | | | 2 | | |
| Wheat | 59 | 8 | | | | 8 | 7 | | | |
| Meat | 83 | 1 | | | | 3 | 5 | | | |
| Butter | 90 | | | | | 3 | 2 | | | |
| Hides | 40 | 49 | 7 | | | | | | | |
| Copper | 34 | 45 | 19 | 2 | | | | | | |
| Silver | 33 | 15 | 2 | 48 | | | | | | |
| Gold | 53 | | 6 | 38 | | | | | | |
| Tallow | 73 | 15 | | | | 4 | | 4 | | |
| Zinc | 4 | 88 | | | | | | | | |
| Lead | 63 | 9 | | | 9 | | | 15 | 2 | |
| Tin | 51 | 9 | | | | | 33 | | 3 | |
| Coal | | | 9 | 4 | | | 22 | | 18 | 37 |
| Timber | 10 | 4 | 2 | 25 | | 22 | | | 23 | |

W. Europe: France, Germany, Belgium, Italy, Austria–Hungary; USA includes Hawaii; India includes Ceylon; China includes Hong Kong; S.E. Asia includes Singapore, The Netherlands East Indies, The Philippines.
Source: See Table 3.3.

**Table 3.3**   Australia's balance of payments, 1900–1913

| Year | Exports | Imports | Trade balance | Balance of income account | Balance of services and transfers | Current account balance |
|---|---|---|---|---|---|---|
| 1900 | 49.1 | 41.2 | 7.9 | −10.6 | −4.4 | −7.1 |
| 1901 | 49.3 | 41.5 | 7.8 | −11.4 | −0.6 | −4.2 |
| 1902 | 44.1 | 38.9 | 5.2 | −12.0 | −1.9 | −8.7 |
| 1903 | 45.5 | 36.6 | 8.9 | −13.6 | −1.9 | −6.6 |
| 1904 | 55.6 | 35.1 | 20.5 | −15.3 | −0.5 | 4.7 |
| 1905 | 60.6 | 36.3 | 24.3 | −15.6 | −0.1 | 8.6 |
| 1906 | 67.5 | 41.9 | 25.6 | −15.6 | −0.1 | 9.9 |
| 1907 | 76.1 | 49.2 | 26.9 | −15.2 | 0.2 | 11.9 |
| 1908 | 64.3 | 48.1 | 16.2 | −15.2 | 0.1 | 1.1 |
| 1909 | 70.3 | 49.5 | 20.8 | −15.2 | 0.2 | 6.0 |
| 1910 | 82.5 | 58.0 | 24.5 | −14.9 | 0.3 | 9.9 |
| 1911 | 79.2 | 65.0 | 14.2 | −14.9 | 1.5 | 0.8 |
| 1912 | 77.9 | 77.0 | 0.9 | −15.0 | 1.8 | −12.3 |
| 1913 | 85.6 | 78.1 | 7.5 | −15.4 | 0.8 | −7.1 |

Source: Based on Butlin 1962, pp. 410–14, 436–41.

back-breaking tasks of fencing, ploughing, planting and harvest that transformed grazing paddocks into mixed enterprises, and that broke up other large properties into labour-intensive orchards, berry-farms and dairy farms. Idle labour and capital moved to old mining fields, exploiting them intensely, and explored untapped fields; the mines were frequently located in remote and difficult areas, tolerable mainly to men who couldn't, or didn't have to, support families in ordinary town and country jobs.

The processes can be seen most plainly at work in the metamorphosis of Western Australia, a territory of 2.5 million square kilometres with a non-Aboriginal population of 50 000 in 1891 and of 322 000 in 1914. Fixed capital multiplied even faster than labour. At the beginning of the period, farmers fenced, ploughed and sowed 11 000 hectares with wheat; at its end they had sowed 557 000 hectares. At the beginning, one kilometre of railway track had been laid for every 130 non-Aboriginal persons; at the end, despite a magnified population, the number of persons per kilometre of track had dropped to 61 (Glynn 1975).

Government initiative created the conditions to exploit market opportunities. Britain conceded 'responsible government' to Western Australia in 1890, a generation later than it did to the eastern colonies. This gave the colony full control over Crown land, and over most other internal matters. *The Homesteads Act 1893* was passed, its name echoing the measure that opened up the American West. Under the Act, Crown land would be split up into small farms. In 1894, Parliament approved, and in 1895 the government established the Agricultural Bank with capital of £100 000 borrowed from the State Savings Bank. The Agricultural Bank

lent money to homesteaders for ringbarking, clearing and cultivating their holdings. A grid of public railways, built cheaply, tied the wheat, timber, dairying and
mining areas to the capital (Perth grew from 16 000 to 120 000 people) and to the
harbour at Fremantle, which in 1890 had been a dangerous open roadstead on a
lee shore, but which soon changed through public works to a seaport sheltered
from the ocean (Brown 1996, pp. 13–46).

Immigrants arrived from the depressed eastern colonies; from 1907
onwards the State government returned to a program of assisted immigration
from Britain. The government augmented the capital of the Agricultural Bank
regularly until it reached £1 million in 1906, with wider powers to lend against
the range of improvements settlers needed for profitable farming. When
drought hit a section of the wheat belt in 1911 over 6000 farmers were indebted
to the Bank. The government doubled its capital. When a worse drought struck
in 1914, a new Industries Assistance Board supplemented bank finance; producers whose crops failed applied for bridging loans to pay wages, buy seeds and
generally get by.

Coincidentally, gold was discovered in Coolgardie in 1892 and nearby in
Kalgoorlie in 1893. Out-of-work men from the eastern colonies rushed in. More
than one person in five counted in the State's 1901 census had been born in Victoria alone, some of them farmers and miners. British and Australian investors, shy
by now of eastern Australian ventures, paid for the shafts and machinery that, in
1903, extracted the largest amount of ore won from a single Australian goldfield in
a single year. Coolgardie and Kalgoorlie lay many hundreds of kilometres in the
dry interior. A railway and a water pipeline were completed within a few years,
and they in turn could be tapped along their great length by prospective farmers.
The goldfields produced revenue, a consumer market, capital, shipping and sheer
publicity that strengthened the non-mining sectors of the State. A branch of the
Imperial Mint opened in Perth in 1899 to change much of the gold into coins and
bullion. With the mints in Sydney and Melbourne it supplied Australia and to a
lesser degree South Africa and New Zealand with currency.

# National development

The normal bias of public policy favoured rural production, to restore **export
income** and to soak up, and disperse, underemployed citizens. As in Western
Australia, the package included **land tenure**, railways, assisted migration, cheap
public credit and the dissemination of agricultural knowledge. With the onset of
depression, Victoria hastened the laying of long trunk-lines into the Crown land of
the Mallee and Wimmera, where new farms were grubbed from the scrub. Tracks
were laid as well to emerging irrigation schemes. The Victorian and the South
Australian Departments of Agriculture had long provided expert advice; worldwide research improved understanding of the ways in which poor soils lessened
the yield and threatened sustainability. In the years just before 1914, more than
half of the cultivated hectares in both States were brought under fertiliser for the
first time (Powell 1989).

**SUMMARY BOX**

During the Long Boom before 1890 the private sector commanded about three-fifths of investment and the public sector contributed two-fifths. By contrast, during the depression and the recovery, the public sector usually led, accounting for more than half the investment between 1892 and 1901 and between 1909 and 1913 (Butlin 1959; Powell 1988, pp. 41–60). The Western Australian experience of government initiative was exceptional only in detail. Tasmania, for example, committed itself to dam-building so that electric energy could be generated by concentrated water power, which might attract manufacturers to the State and encourage mining companies (including those in Tasmania's western wilderness) to do their processing there (Robson 1990, pp. 294–300).

New South Wales did not fall as deeply into depression as Victoria, the heart of the speculative boom, nor as deeply as South Australia and Tasmania, States with limited resources that were to some extent financial dependants on Victoria. The resource base in New South Wales was diverse, its revenues and railway receipts held up better than in Victoria, and its **credit-rating** remained stronger. The length of track doubled in the quarter century before 1914 (*Yearbook* 1915, vol. 8, 1901–1914, p. 600; *Yearbook* 1955, vol. 40, 1954, p. 115). Routes up and down the coast made it possible for butter, milk and other perishables to fill the market (Todd 1994; Jeans 1972, pp. 201–94). The trunk lines permitted wheat for export to be sown beyond the Great Dividing Range. The crisis in the wool industry now encouraged pastoralists to diversify into cropping, which spread their risks. Freight carried from the mixed farms helped pay for inland branch lines that brought more paddocks close to swift bulk transport. Previously, wheat had grown near the coast, where the damp climate and broken land hampered farming. Crops grew better inland, and the spreading terrain allowed mechanised cultivation. Between 1890 and 1915, the area under wheat in New South Wales increased tenfold, which propelled the State from a distant third behind South Australia and Victoria to clear leadership in national grain production. By 1915, it was estimated, the average bushel travelled 450 kilometres between its paddock and Sydney.

The location and the scale of the harvest had changed spectacularly in a single generation. This was necessarily accompanied by changes in land tenure. The New South Wales government withdrew permission to use ecologically degraded stations in the far west of the State, and split Crown leases into smaller units elsewhere, suitable for small holders running cows or raising crops (Dunsdorfs 1956, pp. 216, 533; Heathcote 1965; Butlin, Barnard & Pincus 1982, pp. 56–9). In that State, perhaps more than elsewhere, there developed an understanding of the counter-cyclical role of the public sector as an engine of investment when the private sector failed, not simply creating conditions for long-term recovery but, through a program of public works on adequate rates of pay, reducing hardship and staving off market stagnation in the short run (Mansfield 1965, pp. 151–211). We shall see its echo in the next great depression.

Queensland, similarly, intensified development over its vast area. Distance encouraged, and the cheapness of narrow-gauge construction allowed, an extension of the railway network by 1914 two and a half times the length in 1890. The cattle frontier, in particular, moved further on to leased Crown land, and Queensland beef became the largest contributor to the new market in Britain for Australian meat. The sugar industry was equally significant, although as a replacement of imports. Queensland cane fields competed in Australia with those of Fiji, Mauritius and Java. Because the Australian palate craved sugar, the various colonies had found it a reliable source of revenue in their customs schedules, as did the Commonwealth after 1901. Federation saw an end to tariffs between the States; they were retained for the nation as a whole and this guaranteed a market for Queensland sugar many times larger than before. A Royal Commission reported in 1912 that the Queensland industry could not be justified on economic grounds, available imports supposedly being cheaper if the tariff were removed, but cane fields occupied land in north-eastern Australia that potential Asian invaders would otherwise covet. The Royal Commission justified Queensland sugar on grounds of national defence and the survival of a White Australia (Graves 1993, pp. 41–4, 58–60).

# Economic forces for Federation

A privileged sugar industry was one of the least ambiguous consequences of Federation. Not every economic interest felt easy with Federation. The No vote in the constitutional referendums of the 1890s was concentrated in cities like Brisbane and Perth because of fears that profits and jobs might be swamped by larger efficient manufacturers elsewhere, and was strong in some rural districts similarly threatened by nation-wide competition (Eastwood & Smith 1964, pp. 152–225; Martin 1969, pp. 137–85; Bennett 1975). Scepticism about Federation might have a broader regional basis. The three economically desperate States, Victoria, Tasmania and South Australia, supported Federation overwhelmingly. The three more prosperous States were uneasy about the constitutional proposals. Queenslanders delayed their ballot, and Western Australia voted after the Constitution Act had already passed the British House of Commons. New South Wales voted twice. The first time 72 000 electors said Yes and 66 000 said No in a low turnout (Bennett 1975, p. 243). The second occasion followed agreement on a couple of constitutional changes (a slightly weaker Senate and the national capital to be inside New South Wales) that elicited a higher Yes and a higher No vote.

The crucial convention had met in 1897–98, at the very trough of the depression. It could be argued generally that the enthusiasts sought a political solution, unity, to an economic crisis, while the sceptics wondered whether tying themselves into a bundle with three conspicuously depressed colonies was the wisest thing to do. Paragraph 6 of the Preamble to the Constitution mentions New Zealand as a possible State of the Commonwealth, but New Zealand had recovered from depression years earlier, and saw no point in joining the failures across the Tasman (Sinclair 1988).

The Western Australian delegation to the convention was won over to Federation by a number of expectations, one of them a hope that the nation would build a railway linking the West to the rest of Australia (this was begun in 1911 and completed in 1917). That delegation, as a bloc, ensured a narrow majority at the Convention in support of Section 51 (xxxv) of the Constitution: 'The Parliament shall ... have power to make laws ... with respect to conciliation and arbitration for the prevention and settlement of industrial disputes extending beyond the limits of any one State'. Strikes tying up ships in the eastern States effectively isolated the West, in the absence of a transcontinental railway, and the business-men who represented the West at the convention were keen that the nation should have the muscle to humble the trade unions (La Nauze 1972, pp. 206–8; Bennett 1975, pp. 212–42).

Conflict between employers and their workforces had escalated at the end of the boom and continued into the early years of the depression. The strikes took place in shearing, mining, shipping and the waterfront, where the largest concen-trations of capital, determined to safeguard increasingly shaky profits, confronted the largest bodies of labour, also suffering the strains of rapid adjustment and resisting the transfer of the full costs of adjustment on to themselves. In the short run, the investors called on governments to use police and armed militias to intim-idate strikers, to pay the fares of labour brought in to break strikes, and in some cases to prosecute and imprison union activists. In the longer run, many citizens, including some of the employers, hoped for solutions that would reduce uncer-tainty in industrial relations. New Zealand pioneered the establishment of a formal conciliation and arbitration court with the ability to negotiate between and impose conditions on contestants. Victoria pioneered the establishment of Wage Boards for specific industries, made up of equal numbers of employer and employee repre-sentatives with a supposedly neutral chair. After several failed attempts, the Commonwealth Parliament passed an Act in 1904 setting up a Conciliation and Arbitration Court, presided over by a judge of the High Court (Patmore 1991, pp. 101–30; Macintyre & Mitchell 1989).

For many supporters of the Commonwealth measure, a stated minimum wage, 'a basic wage', seemed a natural corollary. Questions of equity apart, two hard-headed considerations applied. Given that most urban and many rural producers relied on the domestic market, they had experienced the prolonged depression as a crisis in domestic demand. A universal mechanism that put a floor under the purchasing power of Australians by determining wages, thus stabilising demand, would also remove one matter of dispute from individual workplaces and lessen the ability of their local rivals to gain price advantages by lowering rates of pay. A fixed wage regime would therefore reduce uncertainty for businessmen on several levels. The second consideration involved Australia's competition for population with the United States, Canada and other destinations whose attrac-tions and intakes were stronger than ever before (see Chapter 2). It had long been an Australian axiom that low or fluctuating wages deterred desirable immigrants. Net migration to Australia had been negative for much of the preceding decade and a half. A generous statutory basic wage could send a positive signal in the hectic global competition for people.

Excise Acts, taxing a number of tariff-protected industries, were passed in 1906. The Acts promised a full rebate of excise to a firm if it paid 'fair and reasonable wages'. The Prime Minister, Alfred Deakin, explained what he called the 'New Protection': 'the Old Protection', he said, 'contented itself with making good wages possible. The New Protection seeks to make them actual ... Having put the manufacturer in the position to pay good wages, it goes on to assure the public that he does pay them' (*Commonwealth Parliamentary Papers* 1907–08, vol. 2, pp. 1887–9). By tying industrial reform to the tariff, Deakin won the Labor Party's support for 'the New Protection', and entrenched the practice of actively expanding tariffs for decades to come. Mr Justice Higgins of the Conciliation and Arbitration Court chose the agricultural machine industry for the test case on wages under the Excise Acts. Australian grain lands had been mechanised for generations, much of the invention and manufacture taking place locally. Higgins ruled in the 'Harvester Judgement' in 1907 that the basic wage should supply the needs of a married couple and three children. The leading firm in the industry resented the Court's interference and won a constitutional appeal before the High Court on grounds that it violated the rights of businesses. Three State Parliaments, however, not being bound directly by the Australian Constitution, enacted basic wage legislation for their own jurisdictions just before the First World War. It made these States more attractive to skilled and immigrant labour, and placed pressure on the other tribunals, national and State, to take seriously Higgins' definition of family needs in their wage determinations (Patmore 1991, pp. 115–22; Macintyre 1986, pp. 99–121; Forster 1989, pp. 203–24).

Profits and wages had not been the only casualties of the depression. Financial institutions tottered. The number of banks decreased, and the survivors displayed stifling caution. One justification for establishing the publicly owned Commonwealth Bank in 1912 was to widen competition again in banking. Another was to provide an outlet for the **savings** of people of lesser means, including women and children. This was time-consuming and unprofitable business for private banks. Each State government operated a savings bank, but the Commonwealth claimed it would be able to offer many more branches, plus the post offices, in each State, and in so doing involve the bulk of the population in such capitalist virtues as the practice of thrift and the prospect of accumulation. A nationwide savings bank, moreover, served a national labour market by making it easier for people to move around. One thing the Bank was not, and that was a **central bank**, regulating the banking sector as a whole and acting as a **lender of last resort** in the manner of the Bank of England or of the Federal Reserve System that emerged in the United States in 1913. It did, however, handle business for the Commonwealth Government, at the time on a fairly small scale but soon to balloon once the First World War began (Gollan 1968).

# The eve of the war

The renewed prosperity was spread unevenly. In 1915, G.T. Knibbs, the government statistician, carried out a wealth survey of all men aged between 18 and 60 (Knibbs 1918). He concluded that 90 per cent of the nation's wealth belonged to 20 per cent of the population. It was realistic to survey men only for they usually

**SUMMARY BOX**

The First World War cut short an innovative and (recently) successful period in Australian development. Unemployment was at a lower level, perhaps 4 per cent, than it would reach again until the early 1940s (Barnard, Butlin & Pincus 1977, p. 50). Manufacturing employed one-fifth of the people who were in paid work (Butlin 1962, pp. 460–1). Flour milling, tanning, meat-freezing and ore-smelting added value to primary products for export and domestic consumption. Food and drink processors, leatherworkers, woodworkers, brickmakers and others transformed domestic materials for customers close at hand. Producer goods like metals and textiles comprised over half the imports by value in 1913, the last full year before the war, and machinery accounted for another 15 per cent. Cargoes of consumer goods were therefore in a minority. Australian manufacturers had achieved a significant amount of import-substitution for **consumer goods**, although inputs and technology often came from overseas. For its total trade flows, Australia relied on **multilateral** balance, running a deficit (like other primary exporting countries) with Britain and the United States, and a surplus with the industrial nations of continental Europe (see Table 3.4).

owned the title deeds. Women in paid employment had less chance to save than men. They were barred from most high paid occupations. In factories and service work, the base rate of their wages was about half that of a man, but their average annual earnings fell to 39 per cent of male earnings, because women were conceded smaller or no margins for skill, were less often offered overtime and more often hired part-time. The emerging standard of a basic wage took account of women and children where an adult male was their breadwinner, but it was both the product of, and justification for, the payment of women at a vastly cheaper rate (Alford 1986; Frances 1993). There were at least three tiers of adult income-earners: those who lived off capital, men who worked for wages, and women who worked for wages. Between one-fifth and one-quarter of waged workers were women.

Aborigines occupied a fourth tier. Once they owned the whole country. They were totally absent from Knibbs' wealth survey of 1915. By that stage towns, farms and grazing runs had blanketed the landscape, and each State by legislation herded Aborigines into smaller and smaller reserves, sometimes on the outskirts of towns, sometimes in between grazing properties, and sometimes on islands. This extinguished the kinds of **traditional income** that came from traditional use of ancestral lands. It condemned the reserve-dwellers to marginal jobs. Legislation set contract rates of pay that were a tiny fraction of the basic wage; earnings were often, by law, retained by the non-Aboriginal manager of the reserve and were then available to the nominal recipient only at the discretion of the manager. Communities whose lands were invaded by cattle did a little better. Cattle stations occupied the frontiers

**Table 3.4**    Australia's pattern of multilateral trade, 1913 (£ million)

| Trade surplus with | | Trade deficit with | |
|---|---|---|---|
| France | 9.05 | UK | 12.86 |
| Belgium | 5.21 | Other Europe | 1.33 |
| Germany | 1.91 | USA | 6.89 |
| Austria–Hungary | 0.55 | Canada | 0.99 |
| Italy | 0.44 | India | 1.60 |
| The Netherlands | 0.12 | New Zealand | 0.15 |
| Japan | 0.51 | Total | 23.82 |
| Ceylon | 0.15 | | |
| South Africa | 1.81 | | |
| Other countries | 2.84 | | |
| Total | 22.59 | | |

Source: See Table 3.3.

of the international economy. Their remoteness and severe climate meant that non-Aboriginal labour was scarce. Profits would be low if non-Aborigines had to be coaxed by high wages from jobs elsewhere. Cattle owners depended on Aboriginal men and women, who could carry on some of their old economic and social life on the land they shared with the beasts, but without gaining enough **disposable income** to choose to leave their depleted territory or to buy or rent it back.

---

**SUMMARY BOX**

The international economy and its management in Australia provided an adequate life for people who came, or whose ancestors came, from its European heartland, but each decade deepened the poverty trap it had created for the original Australians (Goodall 1996, pp. 115–48).

---

# Suggested further reading

Buckley, K. & Wheelwright, T. 1988, *No Paradise for Workers: Capitalism and the Common People in Australia, 1788-1914*, Oxford University Press, Melbourne.

Butlin, N.G., Barnard, A. & Pincus, J.J. 1982, *Government and Capitalism: Public and Private Choice in Twentieth Century Australia*, Allen & Unwin, Sydney.

Dingle, T. 1988, *Aboriginal Economy: Patterns of Experience*, McPhee Gribble, Melbourne.

Jupp, J. 1991, *Immigration*, Sydney University Press, Sydney.

Patmore, G. 1991, *Australian Labour History*, Longman Cheshire, Melbourne.

Pinkstone, B. 1992, *Global Connections: A History of Exports and the Australian Economy*, Australian Government Publishing Service, Canberra.

Powell, J.M. 1988, *An Historical Geography of Modern Australia: The Restive Fringe*, Cambridge University Press, Cambridge.

Reynolds, H. 1987, *The Law of the Land*, Penguin, Melbourne.
—— 1990, *With the White People*, Penguin, Melbourne.
White, C. 1992, *Mastering Risk: Environment, Markets and Politics in Australian Economic History*, Oxford University Press, Melbourne.

# End note

[1]    *Yearbook*, vol. 1, 1901–07, Melbourne, pp. 147, 500–8. These calculations have been made from the relevant volumes of the *Official Year Book of the Commonwealth of Australia* (hereafter *Yearbook*), Commonwealth Bureau of Census and Statistics, Melbourne, annual publication.

# PART II

1914 TO 1940

# 4

## International impacts on Australia, 1914–1940

The First World War brought about the virtual cessation of the normal working of the international economy. The disruption to **international trade** was especially serious for countries like Australia that relied on far distant export markets and sources of imports, and on foreign-owned oceanic shipping services. Although the end of the war brought some semblance of normality, in the 1920s the world economy grew sluggishly and was beset by structural problems. Australia found the global economy a much less easy environment in which to prosper. At the end of the decade, the world was shaken by a financial crisis in the United States that quickly plunged most countries into a severe economic contraction. **Primary-producing** countries, Australia included, were hit particularly hard. Recovery from the 'Great Depression' of the 1930s was patchy. Australia's ever-closer ties with Britain proved helpful, but without a full recovery in the industrial countries and the restoration of the mechanisms of the global economy, a return even to the subdued economic conditions of the 1920s was impossible. This chapter sets out the main international forces that impacted on Australia in these years. The next two chapters discuss Australia's plight in more detail.

## War and its aftermath

The Great War of 1914–1918 was the first real crisis the first global economy had had to face and it never fully recovered from it. In some ways, the war merely speeded up economic changes that were already visible, particularly the rise to world economic power of the United States. In other respects, the war led the global economy in completely new directions. The outbreak of the war had not been expected and it occurred during a period of rapid expansion of the world economy: world trade was growing strongly, intercontinental migration had reached record levels and international **capital** movements were at their height. On the eve of the outbreak of the war, British investors, for example, received almost £200 million in returns on **foreign investments**, twice the level 15 years earlier. In 1913, over one million European immigrants arrived to settle in the United States.

The war in Europe brought to an end the free working of the international economy. Trade was impossible between countries that were formerly partners and now enemies. International trade between allies was highly disrupted. For example, Australia's trade with Belgium had been expanding before the war, but during the war virtually disappeared. Belligerents in the war accounted for two-thirds of world trade when the war started, rising to three-quarters by the middle of 1917 when the United States entered. Trade patterns in the global economy generally were distorted and the multilateral structure of world trade broke down. Japan and the United States (both allies, though the United States did not enter the war until April 1917) grew more important in world trade. Oceanic trade was seriously disrupted by the shortage of shipping and loss of ships to enemy action. Submarine warfare in the Atlantic was particularly destructive. For countries like Australia, half the globe away from Europe, shipping of goods to Europe and the Middle East became a nightmare.

Investment flows were brought almost to a standstill. Even if private investors wished to continue to make foreign investments, governments would not permit it. The only significant capital movements were loans and other financial flows between allies for the war effort. The international monetary system, the **gold standard**, was abandoned and nearly all countries imposed **exchange controls** and administrative controls over international capital. Intercontinental migration did not entirely disappear, but compared to 1913 levels, it was reduced to a dribble, supplemented a little by movements of refugees.

The war was disastrous for the European economies because of loss of life, property, capital (including foreign investments), damage to factories and transportation, diversion of production to war materials, the running up of huge national and international debts and political upheavals, including the withdrawal of Russia from the international economy. The war and its aftermath was highly inflationary. To some extent, **inflation** was caused by wartime shortages and the enormous demands that the war imposed on the productive capabilities of the belligerent economies. It was also the result of the way in which the war was financed, with many governments preferring to expand the **money supply** rather than impose higher taxes. Inflation was higher in some of the belligerent economies than in others. In Germany and central Europe, hyperinflation eventually destroyed the value of currencies altogether.

The impact of the war on the economies of the United States and Japan was less severe and in some ways, the war in Europe was advantageous to their economic position. They were not subjected to direct attack and in both countries producers of manufactured goods found business expanded to meet the war **demand** from their own government and those of their allies. American and Japanese exporters also discovered that markets previously dominated by European suppliers were now more open to US and Japanese goods. Australia's imports, for example, greatly expanded from these two sources. Japanese and American trade increased throughout the Asia–Pacific region (and in Latin America in the case of the United States). Consequently, there was a marked shift in world trade in the immediate post-war years towards these two countries. In America's case, this higher profile in world trade was reinforced by its increased global financial power, so that the global balance of economic power shifted as a result of the war towards the United States.

The war ended in September 1918 almost as unexpectedly as it had begun in August 1914. Consideration had been given during the war by the British and French to how Germany and its allies could be forced to pay compensation for the cost of the fighting and to how Germany could be permanently removed from the status of a world economic power. But little or no official attention had been paid to restoring the international economy. Consequently, at the peace conference in Paris in 1919, discussion focused on such matters as financial reparations, commercial sanctions against Germany, and the future status of people formerly subjects of now-defunct empires. However, no plans were put forward for the future working of the international economy. In this respect it was a matter of 'business as usual'.

**SUMMARY BOX**

The First World War brought to a sudden and unanticipated end the expansion and development of the first global economy. It would be half a century before the global economy functioned as well as it had in 1913. The war had enormous direct and indirect economic impacts. International trade was crippled, international investment and migration flows virtually ended. The international payments system that had developed over most of the nineteenth century was abandoned. The relative economic status of the world's leading nations – Britain, France, Germany, the United States and Japan – shifted towards the latter two. The war brought an immense series of economic changes. In the post-war period it would become clear which of these were temporary and which permanent.

# The 1920s: 'business as usual'

As the dust settled and the blood dried after four years of unprecedented mechanised slaughter, the immediate post-war economic problems of shortages and dislocation gave way to more fundamental structural weaknesses in the global economy. These were evident in international trade, international investment flows, migration and the world's monetary system. Failure to solve these problems successfully during the 1920s left the world economy highly vulnerable to economic shocks.

## World trade

After a short post-war **boom** that lasted barely 18 months, it became apparent that world trade was growing much more slowly than before the war (League of Nations 1945a, pp. 157–67). **Demand** by the industrial countries for primary products was adversely affected by a number of problems. Their **economic growth** was slower than before the war and this meant that they did not require as much raw materials, including those that were imported. Their population growth also slowed down, a trend evident before the war but intensified by its impact.

The slower growth of Europe's population was one reason why demand for imported foodstuffs was sluggish, but there were other causes. The war led to a greater degree of self-sufficiency in food and an expansion of domestic agriculture in Europe. After the war, governments were reluctant to see a contraction in domestic food supply, for strategic defence reasons and because of social concerns. Farming was encouraged and supported by the State in most European countries, including Australia's main market, Britain. Additionally, pre-war investments in agriculture in temperate zone primary-producing countries greatly increased the world supply of temperate agricultural products, both of foodstuffs and raw materials such as wool. These investments had brought far more **land** into cultivation and pasture, and had raised the **productivity** of agricultural output through the application of new technology, such as mechanisation and the use of artificial fertiliser. Primary producers throughout the world responded to weak prices by raising output. Although this supported their **incomes** in the short run, in the long run it brought increased supplies on to the international markets and further depressed prices. Primary producers during the 1920s were caught in a vicious circle of global overproduction and falling prices.

As a result of these problems, international prices for primary products were slack during the 1920s, though the impact varied between them. Wheat and other grains were among the worst affected by over-supply, stockpiling and weak prices. The one bright spot in world trade in foodstuffs was rising demand for food of a luxury or semi-luxury nature as living standards continued to rise. For temperate zone suppliers this offered niche markets in meat, dairy produce, fruit, nuts and wine, particularly in the United Kingdom. Australian producers were able to meet some of this demand, though they competed for their place on the British market with suppliers from a number of other countries. Continental Europe and the United States, however, imposed restrictions on many temperate food imports, including these higher value products (League of Nations 1930, p. 30; 1931, pp. 38–104; 1941).

World trade was hampered during the 1920s by increased **protectionism**. Structural changes that had occurred during the war were now cemented in place by protective measures. The proliferation of national borders in Europe as a result of the war also added to the extent of import barriers. **Tariff** levels tended to rise everywhere. Britain, the bastion of **Free Trade** in the nineteenth century, flirted with **import protection**, though it did not introduce a general system of import taxes until the early 1930s. It did, however, offer some import preferences to Empire suppliers in a limited range of niche foodstuffs in the 1920s, which

Australian producers were able to take advantage of. Rising protectionism was discussed in meetings of the League of Nations and at other international gatherings during the 1920s, but the lack of international co-operation evident in all economic negotiations prevented much progress being made towards the liberalisation of world trade.

## International investment

Less capital was invested internationally during the 1920s. To some extent, this was because investment in primary production and the transport systems that needed to move bulk produce offered less attractive prospects to investors. It was also partly because capital was required at home to rebuild the war-shattered European economies. Moreover, the war caused two of the larger pre-war international investor nations, France and Germany, to cease investing any capital abroad at all. Continental Europe declined or disappeared as a source of long-term capital. Britain continued to dominate long-term international capital flows and the London capital market re-opened in 1920 and began lending to its usual clients again, including Australia. Britain remained the world's largest foreign investor by 1938, but increased its investments by only 15 per cent over their level in 1914 (Atkin 1977, pp. 125–64; Woodruff 1966, pp. 156–7). To some extent, US investors stepped into the gap, but their loans were at higher rates and for shorter terms than had been the norm before the war. The New York money market became more important for international capital flows, especially to South America, and more significantly emerged as a source of short- and medium-term loans to Germany and central European countries.

Financial difficulties caused by the war tended to become permanent structural weakness as the 1920s progressed. Inflation and hyperinflation remained a problem until the early 1920s. More intractable was the re-establishment of an international exchange rate system (Moulton & Pasvolsky, 1932, p. 146; Kindleberger 1984, pp. 303–4). All major currencies except the US dollar left the gold standard during the war and became inconvertible. Inflation occurred at different rates in different countries, which meant that pre-war rates of exchange were no longer appropriate even after inflation subsided. The challenge, therefore, was to decide on new exchange rates that reflected the altered relative conditions and an international exchange system that would allow currencies to be convertible at these new rates.

A **Gold Exchange Standard** was agreed to by the League of Nations (of which the United States was not a member) in 1922 that required countries to maintain **fixed exchange rates** and keep their **central bank** reserves in both gold and major currencies (that is, in **foreign exchange**). However, this mechanism relied on there being a strong, accessible, gold-based currency available to fulfil the 'exchange' aspect of the system (League of Nations 1944, pp. 117–42, 162–89; Drummond 1981; Kindleberger 1984, pp. 385–400). Sterling might have fulfilled this role, but Britain's **balance of payments** had been seriously weakened by the cost of the war. Moreover, the underlying weakness of the pound was compounded by the British government deciding to put sterling back on the gold standard in 1925 at its pre-war parity with the US dollar. This decision overvalued sterling by about 10 per cent, harming the competitiveness of British exports and therefore its overall balance of payments (Pollard 1970, pp. 1–26).[1] It also meant that all other currencies that tied their exchange value to sterling – this included the Australian pound – were similarly **overvalued** against the US dollar.

The US dollar was a strong, **gold-based currency**, but it was not accessible. The United States's position as the world's leading industrial economy was not matched by its role in international trade. The US absorbed only 12 per cent of world imports in 1928 (compared to 16 per cent purchased by the United Kingdom and Eire) and provided 16 per cent of the world's exports. The United States ran a large **trade surplus** with the rest of the world and followed high tariff policies, which made the US a difficult economy to export to (US, Bureau of Foreign and Domestic Commerce 1943, pp. 53–4). The trade surplus had the effect of rationing dollars to the global economy, dollars that would have added to **international liquidity**. Many countries (especially Germany) that did borrow from US investors during the 1920s found it difficult to earn sufficient dollars through exports to the United States to service their loans, leading to a '**transfer** problem' that necessitated further borrowing from the New York money market (Falkus 1971; Eichengreen 1992, pp. 390–9). Some of these problems arising from the United States's position in the international economy might have been mitigated if it had not followed an isolationist policy and declined to join the League of Nations. The international community needed the leadership of the United States (it was the largest economy and supplier of capital) through the League, but this was not forthcoming.

The only other currency that could have played an international role was the French franc. However, the French government and its central bank were opposed to such a role. The franc was **undervalued** against most other currencies and France's balance of payments surplus hoarded in gold rather than being made available for international investment. The foreign loans that the French were prepared to make in the 1920s were even more short-term than the Americans' and in 1928 French lenders repatriated these loans and declined to make new ones, a move that sparked a European monetary crisis. The international monetary systems could have been made to work, perhaps, even with these weaknesses, if there had been willingness among the central banks to co-operate. However, the rivalry and tension that made international co-operative action impossible to sustain also marred inter-central bank relations in the 1920s. This left the global economy with a fragile monetary system at the end of the decade.

As if these financial problems were not enough to cope with, the international community was also burdened with war debts and reparation payments, which dogged all attempts to revitalise the world economy. War debts arose from loans made by US private investors to allied governments during the war and amounted to $28 billion by 1919. Reparation payments arose from the decision made at the Paris peace conference in 1919 that Germany and its allies must repay to Britain, France and Belgium the cost of the war. This sum was calculated to be $32 billion dollars. It was far greater than the German economy could be expected to pay, but while there was some prospect of reparation payments from Germany, the United States government insisted that its citizens who had invested in loans to Britain and France must be repaid in full.

**Figure 4.1**    Financial flows in the international economy in the 1920s

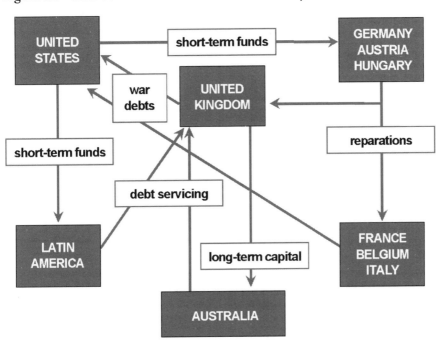

Schedules for German reparation payments were drawn up in 1919 and adjusted downwards in 1924 (the Dawes Plan) and in 1929 (the Young Plan) when it became clear targets could not be met, but some payments were made and these were used to finance the war debt repayments of Britain and France to the United States. Since even the revised amounts of reparation payments scheduled were beyond Germany's capacity to pay, the German government borrowed the funds required from the New York money market. This, of course, created an unstable triangular flow of capital. Loans were made by the New York money market to institutional borrowers in Germany, including the German government. The German government made reparation payments to the governments of France and the United Kingdom. And these governments repaid war debts to US **creditors**. The triangle depended on the continued supply of fresh funds from America. If New York funds to Germany ceased to flow for any reason this entangled web would quickly unravel (see Figure 4.1).

## Intercontinental migration

Intercontinental migration, like world trade and investment, did not return to its pre-war dynamism. Intercontinental emigration from Europe resumed on a smaller scale. One of Europe's major sources of pre-war emigration, Russia, now prohibited its people to leave. The New World remained the preferred destination for Europe's emigrants, but the United States had had a change of heart about its open immigration policy. As part of a general move towards isolationism, engendered partly by the US experience of participating in the war, the US government

imposed tough new restrictions on immigration in 1921. Never again would the
United States accept immigrant settlers in the numbers it did before 1914. Other
primary-producing countries that had taken large numbers of immigrants before
the war seemed less desirable in the eyes of Europe's potential emigrants.

Migrants again left Britain, though in smaller numbers than before the war.
Even with the US restrictions, the bulk of British emigration continued to flow to
North America. British emigration to Australia started again, though more money
was now needed to entice them to come. Higher **unemployment** in Britain made
emigration harder to afford and transport costs had risen considerably. To some
extent this led to Australia being priced out of the emigrant market. Perceptions
that employment opportunities in Australia were less robust than before the war
reduced the attractiveness of Australia to its traditional source of immigrants.
More details of Australian immigration are given in the next chapter.

**SUMMARY BOX**

World trade in the 1920s was hampered by slower European economic
growth and population growth. Demand for imports of primary products
was further restricted by the wartime expansion of agriculture in Europe
and post-war protection for European farmers. World supply of primary
products increased. These factors combined to produce poor international
prices for primary-exporting nations like Australia. International initiatives
to liberalise world trade in the 1920s were undermined by a lack of
international co-operation. Financial arrangements in the global economy
were hampered by two problems: inter-allied debt and reparations, and the
working of the international monetary system. The former created
financial flows that were inherently unstable. The latter depended on a
much greater degree of co-operation between the world's three main
financial centres – London, Paris and New York – than before the war.
Intercontinental migration of people resumed but in smaller numbers.
Emigrants left Britain, mainly destined for Canada and the United States,
but part of the efflux was enticed by financial **subsidies** to Australia. The
implication for Australia of these changes and problems was to draw
Australia even more tightly to the United Kingdom, reinforcing the closer
economic ties that the war itself had brought about.

# The 1930s: economic slump and its aftermath

## The US boom and crash

In contrast to the European economies in the 1920s, the United States economy
enjoyed boom conditions, at least until 1927. This boom took off in the early
1920s. Unemployment was low and **real** incomes on average were rising. This led

to a dramatic expansion of a range of **consumer goods** industries, which in turn stimulated the production of machinery and equipment and transportation. Automobiles, household appliances, electrical goods, radio, financial and commercial services and residential and business construction were the inter-connecting growth nodules of the American economy in the 'roaring twenties'. The United States's share of world manufacturing production peaked in 1929 at over 42 per cent, compared with 36 per cent in 1913.

The New York Stock Exchange also experienced boom conditions from the mid-1920s, fed by higher domestic **savings**, inflow of **short-term** speculative foreign capital and the use of marginal share trading. While the growth of the American economy peaked in 1927 and then slowed as consumer markets were becoming saturated, the stock market kept rising. Eventually the stock market bubble burst, in October 1929, and the ensuing **crash** pushed the US economy from a mild slowdown into a massive economic **depression**. Weaknesses were now revealed in the older US industries such as railroads, cotton textiles, coal mining and agriculture. These sectors had not expanded much during the 1920s boom and now faced a serious decline in demand. Together with the stagnant consumer goods industries, they were major employers in the American economy. As the crisis unfolded, these industries shed **labour**, causing unemployment to rise rapidly, and reducing household incomes and consumer demand. The crash also revealed the way hire purchase and other forms of consumer **credit** had fuelled the 1920s consumer boom, and how sensitive this type of demand was to falls in household incomes (Lee & Passell 1979, pp. 362–72). America entered its worst economic contraction at the beginning of 1930. Over the next four years, unemployment in the United States rose from 3 per cent to 25 per cent, its **national income** fell by half, industrial production fell by one-third and foreign trade declined by two-thirds.

It was ironic, to say the least, that while the American boom of the 1920s had not been transmitted to the rest of the world, the rest of the international community very quickly felt the impact of the American crash. As the New York market fell, capital previously lent abroad was repatriated to the United States as rapidly as possible and fresh loans were not forthcoming. This immediately caused a financial crisis in central Europe and Latin America, areas that had been borrowing heavily from New York in the 1920s.

As the United States economy contracted, its demand for imports declined dramatically, thus sparking a crisis for those countries that normally exported to the United States. In 1930, the US government raised American import barriers by increasing tariffs by between 25 and 50 per cent, an action that further exacerbated the problems of its trading partners and signalled to the rest of the world that the era of trade liberalisation was at an end. Most other countries raised their import barriers in reaction, both by higher tariffs and by the imposition of **import licensing**.

The greatest burden fell on the primary-producing economies that found the international prices for their export commodities plummeting. Primary production and export volumes continued to rise, however, leading to widespread dumping (and retaliatory **import restrictions**) and stockpiling.

As the financial crisis created by the New York market crash spread through central Europe, the structural weaknesses of the European monetary institutions

**Table 4.1**  Depression and recovery in the 1930s

| Economic indicator | Australia | | United States | | United Kingdom | | Germany | | Sweden | |
|---|---|---|---|---|---|---|---|---|---|---|
| | T | P | T | P | T | P | T | P | T | P |
| GDP (1929 = 100) | 69.6 | 105.8 | 48.5 | 86.9 | 87.7 | 118.6 | 59.5 | 100.1 | 83.9 | 112.6 |
| **CPI** (1929 = 100) | 80.6 | 89.3 | 74.8 | 88.4 | 85.4 | 95.1 | 76.6 | 81.6 | 90.6 | 97.8 |
| Unemployment rate % | 21.5 | 8.8 | 25.9 | 13.8 | 22.5 | 11.3 | 30.1 | 2.1 | 23.4 | 10.8 |

T = trough year, P = peak year of the 1930s economic cycle (the trough was usually 1932 or 1933, the peak 1937 or 1938).
Source: Based on Mitchell 1992.

were revealed. In September 1931, the Bank of England took sterling off the gold standard and floated the pound, sparking a round of competitive currency **devaluations** throughout the world. As world trade contracted, so did the economies of both the industrial nations and the primary producers. Unemployment soared to record levels in practically every country, and as incomes fell so did **aggregate demand**, pushing these economies further into depression (see Table 4.1).

> **SUMMARY BOX**
>
> The worldwide economic depression of the 1930s started in the United States in 1929, triggered by the crash of the New York stock market. The economic **slump** in the United States was then transmitted to the rest of the global economy via trade and financial linkages over the next three years. The crisis revealed clearly the weaknesses of the 1920s international economy. The world depression reached its lowest point in 1933, with about one-third to one half of real output having been wiped off the industrial nations' national accounts. From one perspective, the depression can be seen as a 'normal' international **trade cycle** downturn that became unusually severe as a result of the New York stock market crash, but which turned up again as the trade cycle continued. From another perspective, however, the depression wrought structural damage in national and international economies that was not repaired before the onset of the Second World War in 1939.

## Limited recovery

International demand conditions for primary producing and exporting countries like Australia remained problematic. As the economic slump took hold, industrial countries demanded far less primary products than they had before, leading to large price falls, hitting those commodities already depressed (for example, wheat) the most. Until the industrial nations recovered, it was unlikely that commodity prices would rise. As primary product prices fell more than those of manufactured goods, the **terms of trade** turned massively against primary producers. They found that they received fewer and fewer imports of manufactured goods for a given quantity of their exports of primary products. Many producers responded by increasing their output, but, as had occurred in some markets in the 1920s, this had the effect of depressing international prices even more.

As the terms of trade turned against primary producers, they improved from the perspective of the industrial countries. These could now obtain cheaper imports of primary commodities. For some industrial countries, most notably Britain, this set off a limited economic recovery. Unemployment in Britain rose in the depression, as happened in most countries, but from 1934 unemployment levels fell and for those in work in the United Kingdom real income increased. This was part of the explanation of a consumer-led recovery in Britain, but it also produced rising demand for higher quality foodstuffs. This reinforced the niche markets that had emerged in the 1920s for meat, wine, nuts, fruit and dairy produce. Although Britain abandoned its long-held policy of free trade, it did so in a way that gave preference in its home market to imports from the Empire countries, of which Australia was one. This reduced competition in the UK home market and assisted Empire suppliers. However, it did not eliminate competition from home producers, for at the same time that Britain gave import preference to Empire suppliers, it also introduced comprehensive subsidy schemes for British farmers who also looked to supply the growing urban demand for the higher value food items. As a result, the recovery in Britain – Australia's main market for exports of foodstuffs – brought only limited benefits.

Agricultural raw materials remained unaffected by these policy changes. Britain did not impose tariffs on imported agricultural raw materials like wool and cotton and so could not give preferences to the Empire. However, neither did it subsidise British woolgrowers. Once economic recovery was under way in Britain from 1934, and particularly once rearmament was under way from 1936, demand for wool (strategic for uniforms) was strong and Australian woolgrowers faced an improving UK market. Recovery and rearmament affected other countries in Europe, but their imports of primary products were muted by the desire for self-sufficiency and a lack of foreign exchange. There was some impact on wool prices and some metal ores, however.

The United States did not recover or rearm and in any case could well supply practically all the primary products it needed except for tropical ones like rubber. Japan, on the other hand, recovered and expanded militarily in China from 1936, producing a demand for war-related primary products, especially wool and metal ores. This posed a source of international demand that Australia was particularly well positioned to exploit – if it was prepared to seize its opportunities. The extent to which it did so is examined in Chapter 6.

The degree of recovery from the depression varied between the main industrial economies. In some of the European countries, for example Britain, new manufacturing industries such as vehicles and household appliances expanded that, together with increased residential construction, created conditions which resembled in muted form the American economic boom of the 1920s. Industrial countries found the depression turned the terms of trade in their favour and when unemployment subsided from its very high levels and real incomes for those in work increased, a consumer-led recovery was possible. The extent of recovery differed considerably between regions: those that were dependent on the older industries continued to experience very high levels of unemployment and distress; the areas where new industries were located fared rather better.

The two other elements in the recovery were public works and rearmament. In the United States, the Roosevelt 'New Deal' (1934–38) was made up of a series of public works measures and domestic banking reform. These had only limited impact on recovery as federal increases in spending were too modest and in any case were offset by cuts in public expenditure by state and city administrations. Rearmament was not attempted in the United States, but its effect in eliminating unemployment and raising industrial output was dramatically illustrated by the economies of the Fascist countries, particularly Nazi Germany, as well as in Japan. Except in Germany, the recovery by 1937 was incomplete in these nations. After 1937, there was a further downturn in most cases, though rearmament from 1938 prevented this downturn from persisting, except in the United States where rearmament was delayed.

Recovery in the primary-producing countries was even more incomplete. Many of these countries had struggled during the 1920s against sluggish demand and falling prices, but now their export markets were reduced even further, particularly in the case of temperate foodstuffs. Unemployment was generally higher than in the industrial countries; they suffered severe balance of payments difficulties as their export earnings contracted and debt servicing became more burdensome. Devaluations, exchange controls, some debt denunciation and trade protectionism were resorted to more as defensive measures to stave off the worst effects of the depression, rather than as measures taken with any prospect that could lead to a recovery. Since the flow of capital funds from the industrial countries had been severed, primary producers now became net exporters of capital in the form of debt repayment and servicing. Similarly, international migration flows were reversed as some of those who had immigrated at an earlier time returned to their country of origin.

Prices for primary commodities remained low, except for a brief rise in 1937 as rearmament began in some of the industrial countries. This rise was short-lived, and commodity prices fell again in 1938 and 1939. Primary-producing countries in the 1930s experienced high levels of unemployment, falling real living standards and adverse terms of trade. Some attempts were made to raise the international prices of certain commodities, but these either failed to maintain higher prices or benefited only the importing industrial economies (Yates 1943; Rowe 1965, pp. 77–90, 120–54). Many of the countries in this group were colonial possessions of industrial nations, and they found no way out of their economic dependency (Havinden & Meredith 1993, Chapters 7 and 8). Some independent primary-producing countries, however, attempted to restructure their economies away from primary production and towards manufacturing by various State initiatives to encourage industrialisation. Gold-producing countries, including Australia, benefited from the devaluation of the US dollar in 1933 that doubled the dollar price of gold. A few commodities were strategic for waging war and benefited from rearmament demand, but international demand for most primary commodities, especially foodstuffs, remained depressed.

The limited recovery from the depression did not revive the international economy to any great extent. The **multilateral** trade system that had been developing since the mid-nineteenth century went into reverse. In the 1930s, a series of **bilateral** trading arrangements were constructed that isolated groups of countries from each other. Germany became completely autarchic, and tried to avoid international trade altogether, relying instead on domestic production and barter deals (often backed by threats) with its neighbours. Japan, too, increasingly turned for trade to its territorial conquests in Korea, Formosa (Taiwan) and China (Manchuria), converting them into a 'yen bloc'. Both countries complained of a lack of access to raw materials and both, in the end, sought military solutions in south and south-east Europe, and South-East Asia and the Pacific (League of Nations 1942, pp. 61–3; 1946).

Bilateral trading blocs were matched by bilateral payments groups, usually involving the same countries. Britain abandoned a century-long policy of free trade and built a 'sterling group' based on the member countries of the British Empire. France similarly operated a 'franc bloc' based on its overseas empire (League of Nations 1936, pp. 63–9; 1942, pp. 77–8, 91; Alford 1996, pp. 143–51). The only financial flows in the 1930s were reversals of earlier flows: now the developing borrower countries were simply repaying their creditors without any access to fresh investment capital. The London market remained closed throughout the 1930s. The international monetary system collapsed; this drove British Empire countries into the sterling group that tied their exchange rates to the pound during the early 1930s when devaluations were frequent among the world's major currencies. Eventually, with the outbreak of the Second World War, this group became the Sterling Area. Membership of the sterling group in the 1930s kept the exchanges open, guaranteeing **convertibility**, and once the pound had settled its new parities, it produced exchange rate stability. In the absence of a return to long-term capital flows, however, the system could not deliver much more than this.

The League of Nations, which had been active in the 1920s in facilitating international economic and commercial agreements between member states, virtually closed down. Although convertibility of currencies was not entirely abandoned (the pound and the US dollar remained convertible), exchange controls were widely adopted, including by Britain, currencies were frequently devalued in the early 1930s and any semblance of the pre-war gold standard in the world's monetary system disappeared (Brown 1940, pp. 342–6; League of Nations 1944, pp. 27–46). International capital flows continued to a limited extent, but only because most **debtor countries** continued to make payments on capital borrowed earlier and because '**hot money**' scurried around the globe seeking safety and mainly ended up in the US financial system. A handful of debtor countries defaulted on loans raised in the 1920s, most prominent among them being Sweden.[2] By 1935, all of the US government's foreign war loans, as well as about one-third of US private loans, were not paying any **interest**.

International business was understandably highly cautious in these conditions and although foreign direct investment did occur in the 1930s it was at much lower levels than in the 1920s. Some multinationals repatriated foreign assets and profits and pulled out altogether. British and French international firms tended to confine their operations to their respective nation's imperial outposts. US multinationals placed over two-thirds of their investments in their own backyard of Canada and Central and South America. Much of the remainder was invested in Western Europe.

International migration of people was a further element of the global economy that did not survive the Great Depression. In a world of mass unemployment and dislocation, potential emigrants could not afford to move and the immigrant nations no longer wanted them. New emigration dried up as the immigrant nations battled soaring unemployment, and as former migrants returned home the established direction of migrant flows were reversed. Britain, Italy, Spain and Germany became net immigrant nations while Australia, New Zealand, Argentina and the United States became net emigrant ones (ILO 1946, pp. 205–44).

### SUMMARY BOX

Recovery from the 1930s Great Depression occurred to some extent in a number of the industrial economies, but the primary-producing countries failed to recover even to this limited degree. In the industrial nations, economic recovery was often a matter of stimulating the domestic economy through public works, rearmament and improving terms of trade. Australia's main trading partner, Britain, recovered more than some other industrial countries, for example, the United States. This assisted Australian exporters, though it did not lead to a complete recovery in Australia. The global economy was irretrievably damaged. World trade remained subdued and undermined by gross protectionism and bilateralism. Global capital flows were distorted and generally did not represent major new investments. Intercontinental migration of people virtually ceased. The only significant movements in the late 1930s consisted of refugees fleeing Nazism in central Europe and refugees reeling from Japanese invasion forces in China. Very few of the former, and none of the latter, found refuge in Australia.

The history of the first global economy between the mid-nineteenth and mid-twentieth centuries clearly shows the two sides of international economic relations. The world economy, when it was expanding, liberalising, supplying more and more **factors of production**, could act as an engine of growth for long periods. The global economy in decline, 1914–1940, transmitted economic disequilibrium rather than growth and eventually transmitted the economic slump in the United States practically to every other nation. The limited recovery of national economies in the 1930s, and their turning away from international transactions as a source of recovery, showed that the global economy would not revive automatically. After the Second World War, it would have to be rebuilt by intervention and co-operation of the leading national economies.

## Suggested further reading

Aldcroft, D.H. 1977, *From Versailles to Wall Street, 1919–1939*, Allen Lane, London.
Arndt, H.W. 1948, *The Economic Lessons of the 1930s*, Oxford University Press, Oxford.
Eichengreen, B. 1996, *Globalizing Capital: A History of the International Monetary System*, Princeton University Press, Princeton.
Kenwood, A.G. & Lougheed, A.L. 1983, *The Growth of the International Economy 1820–1980*, Allen & Unwin, London.
Kindleberger, C.P. 1973, *The World in Depression, 1929–1939*, University of California Press, Berkeley.
Lewis, A.W. 1949, *Economic Survey 1919–1939*, Allen & Unwin, London.
Woodruff, W. 1966, *The Impact of Western Man: A Study of Europe's Role in the World Economy, 1750–1960*, Macmillan, London.

## End notes

[1]   There is much debate on this point, see: Alford 1996, pp. 131–5.
[2]   Smaller defaulters included Brazil, Chile, Colombia and Mexico; see Lewis 1938, p. 414.

# 5

## Australia 1914–1929: the First World War and post-war reconstruction

When the King of England went to war in 1914, constitutional logic dictated that the King of Australia went to war as well. Although five-sixths of the population was native-born, the majority was descended from migrants from the United Kingdom of Great Britain and Ireland. However ambivalent their feelings about the United Kingdom might be, it stood at the centre of their world, whether expressed through ancestral tales, a derived language and literature, the education system itself, dependence on British wire services for overseas news, sporting contacts, brand names made familiar by direct British investment and by the fact that three-fifths of imports were British. Australian men flocked to fight for King, country and Empire. Nearly one-quarter of the men enlisting in the Australian Army in the early months were British by birth, which testified to the youth, masculinity and size of the stream of immigrants during the preceding seven years. Almost 40 per cent of resident men aged between 18 and 44 enlisted for active service. Of the 330 000 who went abroad, over 60 000 died and 150 000 returned injured or ill, in total about one-quarter of their male age cohort. Death and injury weakened the nation greatly, then and for the future (Beaumont 1995).

The economy faltered in other ways. The war fractured the trading world. The two major trading powers, Britain and Germany, led the opposing alliances. Neutral countries could not ignore the conflict. Producers in the United States, for example, may have wanted to sell impartially to both sides, but the British Navy blockaded the North Sea approaches to Germany and the Mediterranean approaches to Germany's allies. Eventually, the honouring of **credit** extended through American financiers on behalf of American farmers; manufacturers and shipowners depended on victory by Britain and its allies. Australia, whether neutral or aligned, was similarly barred from part of its trading world. The major export **commodity** in particular, wool, lost much of its market, when Germany and Austria–Hungary entered the war, and later as Germany conquered Belgium, and over time as the textile-making region of northern France turned into the stale-mated 'Western Front'. Belgium and Germany, leaders in metallurgy, had consumed much of the zinc, copper and lead from the mines of Broken Hill, western Tasmania and Queensland.

Graziers and mining companies tried to restrict output. Stations, farms and country towns had already shed **labour** to cope with drought. Freight and insurance charges rose swiftly as merchant vessels outside the Atlantic became scarcer, and threatened by warships; the cost of exports and imports rose. Some urban businesses slackened production in response to slowdowns and cost rises. There were fewer housing starts, for the departure of men in uniform meant there were fewer new families in search of shelter, while soldiers' wives and children might go into smaller quarters or move in with relatives to save money. The combined effect was to almost double the **unemployment** figures in a year (Barnard, Butlin & Pincus 1977, p. 50; Haig-Muir & Hay 1996, pp. 97–102). Unemployment caused some men to hurry into the Army.

Once the economy adjusted to the changed conditions, unemployment of its civilian workforce dropped back to a level closer to, but still worse than, the level before the war. The absence of so many men, who were higher earners than women, consistently depressed domestic **demand**. The battles took place far away (which was not to be the case in the second half of the next war). This weakened Australia's ability to supply all the needs of its own forces, let alone those of its allies, for clothing and boots, munitions, vehicles and perishable foodstuffs. Leave from the battle zones was spent in someone else's economy. Australia effectively imported vast quantities of military and **consumer goods** that neither crossed its coastline nor featured in its published balance of trade. The transactions showed up, however, in the **balance of payments**. A **current account** deficit of about £10 million in 1913–14 blew out to an average of £32 million over the next five years (Swan 1968, pp. 91–103; see Table 5.1).

Although export outlets narrowed, Australia's formal alliance with its major market, Britain, softened the impact. Wool had military uses, for uniforms, blankets and other items, especially for winter campaigns, so the Allies' demand for wool increased. Armaments required lead, zinc and copper. Britain agreed in 1916 to take at a fixed price for four years most of Australia's wool, lead and zinc (the last until 1930). In none of these cases did Britain consume each year all that it bought, partly because there was insufficient shipping left on the route from the Pacific to Europe. Payments for the stockpiled commodities kept the producers in business, and the length of the contracts carried them over the turmoil of post-war adjustment. The backlog of wool, after the Armistice, was released into the civilian market in an orderly fashion at rising prices, while the contract for zinc kept incomes higher than they would otherwise have been during the 1920s, when prices for base metals fell (Tsokhas 1990, pp. 18–61; Barnard 1971). The zinc and lead agreements, and the stockpiles, allowed the Broken Hill companies to lock out their workers during a nineteen-month strike in 1919–20 and still deliver dividends to shareholders (Robinson 1967, p. 104).

People in Britain already ate most of Australia's food exports. After a delay of a couple of years, as with wool and metals, the two countries signed marketing

**Table 5.1**   Australia's balance of payments, 1914 to 1930 (£ million)

| Year ended 30 June | Exports | Imports | Trade balance | Balance of income account | Balance of services and transfers | Current account balance |
|---|---|---|---|---|---|---|
| 1914* | 41.2 | 39.2 | 2.0 | −7.8 | 0.4 | −5.4 |
| 1915 | 67.7 | 64.6 | 3.1 | −17.1 | −19.9 | −33.9 |
| 1916 | 73.2 | 79.8 | −6.6 | −18.8 | −21.0 | −46.4 |
| 1917 | 94.2 | 78.0 | 16.2 | −20.7 | −20.2 | −24.7 |
| 1918 | 81.2 | 62.8 | 18.4 | −24.6 | −18.9 | −25.1 |
| 1919 | 111.9 | 98.2 | 13.7 | −24.0 | −19.7 | −30.0 |
| 1920 | 151.1 | 106.4 | 44.7 | −25.0 | −1.7 | 18.0 |
| 1921 | 153.6 | 171.7 | −18.1 | −25.7 | 1.0 | −42.8 |
| 1922 | 137.2 | 103.8 | 33.4 | −28.1 | 0.7 | 6.0 |
| 1923 | 126.9 | 132.1 | −5.2 | −29.0 | 2.1 | −32.1 |
| 1924 | 126.7 | 140.2 | −13.5 | −31.1 | 1.4 | −43.2 |
| 1925 | 164.6 | 143.5 | 21.1 | −31.8 | 1.1 | −9.6 |
| 1926 | 145.0 | 151.5 | −6.5 | −34.4 | 1.9 | −39.0 |
| 1927 | 136.3 | 166.8 | −30.5 | −36.7 | 4.7 | −62.5 |
| 1928 | 140.7 | 148.3 | −7.6 | −39.6 | 3.1 | −44.1 |
| 1929 | 140.9 | 145.4 | −4.5 | −40.7 | 6.7 | −38.5 |
| 1930 | 102.0 | 135.0 | −33.0 | −42.5 | 0.0 | −75.5 |

* 6 months to 30 June
A minus sign indicates that the value of payments made by Australian residents to foreigners exceeded the value of payments made by foreigners to Australian residents.
Source: Based on Butlin 1962, pp. 436–41.

agreements for meat and wheat. The drought in 1914 encouraged slaughter of livestock, increasing the number of carcases for sale, which kept up the meat growers' incomes initially and then reduced the supply of these perishables when refrigerated ships were less available. The wheat was often sent straight to the troops; France and Egypt became important listed destinations. For the first time sugar left the country, the Queensland government buying the crop and the Commonwealth government selling the refined sugar to the British government (Pinkstone 1992, pp. 73–80).

As Britain bought a higher proportion of Australian exports during the war, and imports from there declined, the bilateral balance of trade shifted in Australia's favour.[1] This compensated for the vast reduction in exports to continental Europe, whose previous heavy deficit with Australia had contributed to **multilateral** balance. Advanced German technology was no longer available. Safer routes of supply opened across the Pacific. Imports from the United States had run at about 12 per cent of all imports to Australia for 15 years before the war, but rose to more than a quarter as hostilities continued. The United States had been a minor customer, however, because it was self-sufficient in many **primary products** and raised **tariffs** to protect commodities in which it was not self-sufficient (such as wool). In 1917–18 it entered the war; US military purchases took 15 per cent of Australian exports, still not enough to reverse the perennial deficit in that bilateral relationship. Japan was the other beneficiary of conflict in the Atlantic. In peace-time, modest amounts of Australian wool and tallow produced a surplus in the trade with Japan. The war doubled these sales, and opened a market for zinc concentrates and lead, but Japan's supply of apparel and cotton textiles expanded even faster, bringing about a temporary deficit with that country. The share of Australia's exports to the whole of East and South-East Asia doubled during the war to almost 10 per cent, familiarising a minority of businessmen with customers they tended to despise (Tweedie 1994, pp. 58–61, 71).

# The rise of secondary industry

## SUMMARY BOX

During the war gross **real** output in manufacturing declined by 20 per cent, given the withdrawal of so many men from the market. But the figure disguised two areas of growth, one transitory, the second structural. The transitory development concerned the needs of departing troops. Textile mills, garment workshops, tanneries, boot factories and small arms factories expanded to supply the Army. The structural change arose from the shortage of imports embodying advanced technologies, whose countries of origin bid up their price or formally commandeered them for their own defence efforts. Domestic production as a substitute for these absent imports came about less because of Australia's military role than because the domestic economy relied on advanced and innovative technologies already.

The clearest examples of import substitution arose from the total break with German industry. Pianos had no strategic value whatsoever; once-prized German instruments could not be found, and scarce shipping space restricted import from elsewhere. As a result, piano factories multiplied in Australia. An emerging electri-cal technology had been transferred in an infant company called Amalgamated Wireless of Australasia (AWA), owned largely by Marconi of Britain and Tele-funken of Germany; the Commonwealth government confiscated the German share of the company and parcelled it among the remaining shareholders. AWA consolidated its position in the domestic market in the temporary absence of foreign rivals. The Victorian government had been negotiating with Siemens, a German chemical company, to extract energy from the State's huge brown coal deposits by converting the mineral to gas, which would then be piped from Gipps-land to Melbourne; war postponed these specific plans, but gave breathing space for the establishment of domestic chemical firms. When metal sales to German and Belgian refineries ceased, four Broken Hill companies formed the Electrolytic Zinc Company of Australasia (EZ) in 1916. It refined zinc concentrates at Risdon, near Hobart, using cheap Tasmanian hydro-electricity; the output went into Allied armaments, but the demand existed whether Australia itself was or was not a combatant (Richardson 1987).

An account of the steel industry underlines the assertion that the stimulus to manufacturing was often incidental, not integral, to participation in the conflict (Hughes 1964, pp. 55–79). The largest iron deposits known at the time, in the Middleback Ranges beside Spencer's Gulf, had been leased to the mining company, Broken Hill Proprietary Limited (BHP), by the South Australian government so that the company might locate its ore smelter (iron being essential for the flux) inside the State's boundaries at Port Pirie. The creation of a national market by Federation, and the centrality of iron and steel to industrial development, made conversion of the iron mountains into various grades of metal a very profitable venture. BHP, foreseeing the exhaustion of its mines at Broken Hill, prepared to diversify. It cut dividends, retained profits for **capital**, and in 1911 announced plans for a steelworks.

A common feature of Australian development, from convict settlements to casinos, has been the struggle between States to capture projects – this might be called 'competitive federalism'. At the time it took seven tonnes of black coking coal as fuel to turn one tonne of iron into steel. The sensible place for a furnace was by tidewater at Newcastle, in New South Wales, beside the nation's major coalfield. The New South Wales government already had plans. Its railways and other public works made it Australia's largest customer for iron and steel. A publicly owned steelworks would reap the economies of vertical integration, and be the nucleus of a regional industrial complex. But BHP controlled the iron ore, and talked to other States about sites. Who owned the furnaces mattered less to the State government than their location. The company was promised a regularly dredged harbour at Newcastle, spur lines to the mill, low freights on the railway and a significant margin of preference when tendering for public contracts. The first steel was rolled in April 1915, just as military requirements on the other side of the world began to swallow the world's supply of steel. By 1918, competing imports had fallen to one-tenth of pre-war tonnage and BHP commanded the market.

**SUMMARY BOX**

Because the war isolated Australia a range of heavy industries emerged: iron and steel, chemicals and paints, electrical goods, shipbuilding and ore-refining. They were capital-intensive and often novel technologies where foreign producers would normally hold an advantage through priority and scale. Even under these abnormal conditions, government action often compensated for capital shortage and market uncertainty.

# Financing the war

Commonwealth government debt, which stood at £19.2 million on 30 June 1914, reached £325.8 million on 30 June 1919, one-third payable in London, two-thirds in Australia. Almost half the overseas debt represented credits advanced by the British government for military supplies bought in Europe; formal loans from the British government accounted for another £49.5 million (*Yearbook* 1920, vol. 13, 1919, pp. 782–6, 803). There had been little reliance on the private money market in London. The bond issues floated in Australia, however, drew on private **savings** and turned wealthier citizens into **creditors** of the Commonwealth government. Taxation covered only 15 per cent of expenditure. The decline in imports reduced customs revenue, the traditional source, so **national income** and land taxes were levied side by side with existing state **income** and **land taxes**.

Like other governments in war-time, the Australian government inflated the **money supply**. Between June 1914 and June 1919 the note issue increased by 300 per cent. Some of the note issue was lent to the State governments to ease their credit. The Commonwealth also deposited currency notes with the trading banks, which allowed the banks to expand their lending; bank credit expanded by 70 per cent and the public's cash reserves by 40 per cent. This made it easier for banks, other institutions and cash-rich citizens to subscribe to the bonds and to pay the new taxes. But it also contributed to **inflation**, already fuelled by war-time scarcities and by price rises world-wide, even if inflation was lower than in Britain or the United States. Wholesale prices rose by 80 per cent, and retail prices by 37 per cent between 1914 and 1919 (Bambrick 1968; Haig-Muir & Hay 1996, pp. 108–11).

Wages rose more slowly than prices. The stated basic wage, a benchmark in the courts as much as an enforceable minimum so far, fell by 8 per cent in real terms, and real average weekly earnings in manufacturing fell by 15 per cent (Withers, Endres & Perry 1985, pp. 138, 156). Because there were fewer jobs, and new manufacturing opportunities tended to be in heavy industry, employment for women did not grow, except in the tertiary sector. Their earnings did not rise either. Administration of a war admittedly enlarged the small Commonwealth public service, where the few women in positions held mainly by men (postmasters and clerks) had enjoyed equal pay, but once women joined the clerical staff in numbers their wages, from 1916, were pegged at half that of the man at the next desk. And the labour of men in uniform possessed, quite literally, a sacrificial quality, against which women were represented as passive and dependent. In terms of what the historian Jill Roe has called 'social citizenship', as well as in terms of economic independence, women's standing in Australia in 1919 may well have been weaker than it was in 1914 (Roe 1987, pp. 395–410; McKernan 1980, pp. 65–93).[1]

# Transition to peace

All of the belligerent countries faced immense problems at the end of 1918. Never had civilian populations been so mobilised into uniforms or into production.

Would men, trained to fight, find acceptable and useful jobs on their return? How could factories be retooled to fashion ploughshares again instead of swords? How would the transition to peace be managed so that the surplus capacity of wartime was not dumped on world markets, while inevitable scarcities of peacetime goods drove those prices sky-high?

The problem of world gluts and world scarcities affected the entire system, but it was moderated for Australia by two factors. First, the inter-governmental marketing schemes assured farmers and miners that their incomes would hold up for another season or two; the current holder of the stockpiles, the British government, had both incentive and ability to release the stocks in an orderly way so that markets for these products held firm in the medium-term. And second, the fact that developments in Australian manufacturing involved import-substitution rather than military supply helped smooth the transition too. Because unemployment had been worse, however, during the war than it had been beforehand, the absorption back into the workforce of so many returning soldiers would prove to be very difficult, but any failure to do so would threaten social harmony, as veteran-led revolutions and insurrections in other countries showed clearly.

## Returned soldiers: new concerns

The war damaged Australian lives. Dead men left widows and children. Survivors carried physical and mental scars. Able-bodied veterans lost years of training and work experience. Under the title of Repatriation, a special system of welfare emerged, parallel to the national provision of aged and invalid pensions that dated from 1908 and 1910 respectively. The historian Stephen Garton calculates that in 1938 almost as many people (260 000 men, women and children) still received war pensions as those who received the civilian aged and invalid grants. In that year 23 000 outpatients used the special repatriation hospitals, in addition to 1600 in permanent care. Education assistance went to 20 000 children over the years. The cost of repatriation benefits in 1938 alone, 20 years after the Armistice, amounted to nearly one-fifth of Commonwealth expenditure (Garton 1996, pp. 74–117).

The return of the able-bodied made demands on revenue as well. Training courses for 28 000 men, plus living allowances during training, extended the scope of vocational education. And a greater number, almost 40 000, about one-fifth of the men demobilised in 1918–19, were set up on farms with help from both Commonwealth and State **budgets**. All the Dominions of the Empire – Canada, New Zealand and South Africa as well – embarked on Soldier Settlement schemes. Self-sufficient property ownership seemed to be a fitting reward for the risks and sacrifices undergone (Powell 1981). Each of these Dominions' propaganda campaign for immigrants had traditionally emphasised wide open spaces colonised by independent yeomen. The prime criterion for assisted passages had been rural experience. Australia's destiny within the international economy, according to lessons learned in recent decades, lay with intensive farming and closer settlement. What better way to buy off and disperse potentially unruly veterans than to enlist them in the ranks of self-sustaining producers for overseas markets.

**Figure 5.1**   Australia's terms of trade, 1914–1941

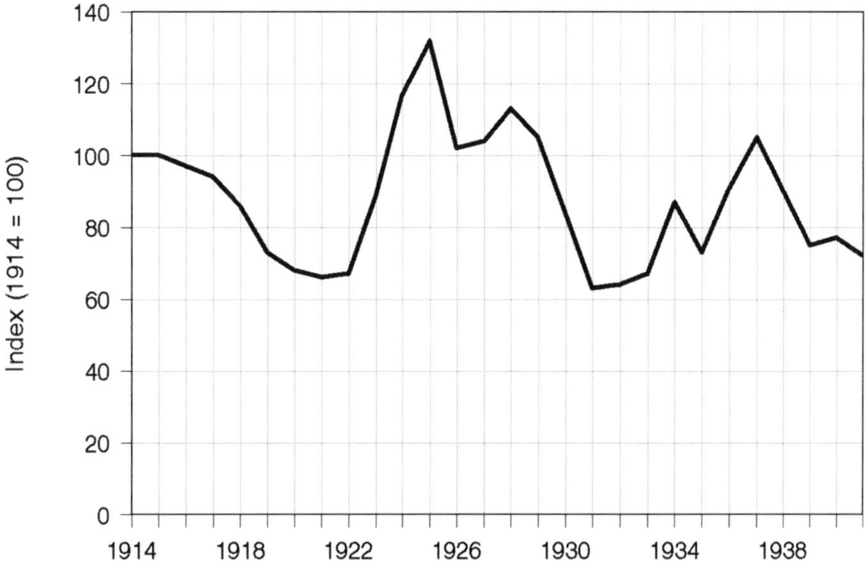

Source: Based on Bambrick 1970, p. 5.

There had been much hardship and failure in the various closer settlement schemes before 1914. Soldier Settlement was no exception. By 1942, according to a government commission of inquiry, less than half the veterans, or their heirs, remained on the allotted farms, those who survived lived Spartan existences and the loss to revenue through failure to repay advances averaged £1200 per farmer (the average award wage was £250). It was pointed out that the farms were often too small and in marginal areas, as a result of the desire to minimise the cost of appropriation to the public and to the veterans. Even where the veteran knew how to farm, his experience might be unsuited to the land allotted (Lake 1987, Fry 1985; Oliver 1995, pp. 132–204).

Generic conditions, moreover, applied. Internationally competitive farming swallowed greater capital than ever before. Use of vehicles, chemicals, oil-driven machinery and other aids distinguished the successful proprietor from the battler. The savings of new entrants, and government loans, often fell short of capital requirements. World prices played their part as well. Prices for farm goods reached a peak in 1924–25, encouraging closer settlement schemes in the years preceding. As prices, and Australia's **terms of trade**, dropped thereafter, the new entrants faced declining terms of trade at their own farm gates (seee Figure 5.1). Debt service and equipment costs became each year more onerous by comparison with the return from their paddocks. The public **subsidy**, nevertheless, increased the scale of Australian export production. Those who did best tended to be men granted property large enough for grazing or mixed farming, where the breeding of livestock and the spread of risks reproduced capital usefully. Also, men placed in publicly irrigated neighbourhoods did well.

# Export development

Soldier Settlement was a special instance of the nation's commitment to export development. Farms assumed an added importance with the decline of the mining sector to a little below 10 per cent of export earnings. World prices for minerals were low, which brought down **aggregate income** and deterred investors, who saw little point in sifting through old tailings or exploring for and opening new mines. This was true of gold as well, at least during the period of world currency instability in the early 1920s. The richest sections of known seams had been exhausted, the cost of boring deeper and of crushing inferior ores inhibited the mine owners, and no important fresh finds had been made (Blainey 1993, pp. 275–85; Pinkstone 1992, pp. 97–100).

On the other hand, demand for wool recovered. By the second half of the decade, the textile mills of France, Germany, Belgium and Italy took almost half the clip, and Britain's share returned to one-third. Australian supply improved as well. By 1930, the national flock was as large as it had been 40 years before, but with two differences: selective breeding strengthened and refined the fleeces, and systematic pasture improvement altered the carrying capacity of the runs (Davidson 1962, p. 81; Barnard 1962, pp. 281–5, 395–400; Pinkstone 1992, pp. 94–5).

The wheat industry also reaped the advantages sown before the war. Mechanisation, fertiliser, trace elements to correct soil deficiencies, and better rail and road transport brought rising yields in the early 1920s. Wheat was harvested from two-thirds as many hectares again in 1929 as in 1920 (Davidson 1962, pp. 76, 78–9; Dunsdorfs 1956, p. 533; Pinkstone 1992, pp. 92–4). The Russian Revolution of 1917 cut off the supply of Ukrainian and Russian grain to outside markets, leaving a vacuum to be filled. Australian grain-growers earned on average through the 1920s about one-fifth of Australia's total **export income**, significantly higher than before the war. The destinations were also far more diverse (see Table 5.2). Britain's share dropped to one-quarter by the end of the decade. For many countries, however, grain imports were extremely **income elastic**, dependent also on the state of their own harvests and on the temporary presence or absence of competing suppliers. In some years, for instance, Egypt and India took large consignments, a short haul across the Indian Ocean from the Western Australian harvest, but the relative poverty of these economies held back the promise of their substantial populations. To an increasing degree, Australian grain left in the form of milled flour; almost by definition this went to markets too poor to have their own mechanised flour mills. Apart from Britain, only three lesser destinations, all with good sea access from Australia, put in consistent orders: Italy (via the Suez Canal), Japan and South Africa.

Sheep-owners sold wool through the traditional private auction system, supported by the pastoral finance companies dating from the previous century; these companies opened retail outlets as stock-and-station agencies, which reflected the diversification of rural life and the maturity of country towns (Tsokhas 1990, pp. 1–15). Grain growers enjoyed a degree of indirect public subsidy, through **infrastructure** development, plant research and agricultural advice. During the war, the States had managed the compulsory pooling of grain, but this reverted to

**Table 5.2** Australia's main trading partners, 1913 to 1938–39 (annual averages as a % of total)

| Country | 1913 | 1919/20–1921/22 | 1922/23–1924/25 | 1925/26–1927/28 | 1928/29–1930/31 | 1931/32–1933/34 | 1934/35–1936/37 | 1937/38–1938/39 |
|---|---|---|---|---|---|---|---|---|
| | | | | **Imports** | | | | |
| UK | 51.8 | 45.9 | 46.8 | 42.4 | 40.1 | 40.4 | 41.0 | 40.1 |
| France | 2.8 | 2.4 | 2.7 | 2.7 | 2.5 | 2.0 | 1.0 | 0.9 |
| Germany | 8.8 | – | 1.0 | 2.5 | 3.2 | 3.2 | 3.5 | 3.7 |
| USA | 13.7 | 21.5 | 22.9 | 24.5 | 23.0 | 14.1 | 15.0 | 15.0 |
| Canada | 1.2 | 2.8 | 3.1 | 2.5 | 2.9 | 4.1 | 6.2 | 7.3 |
| India | 3.9 | 4.3 | 3.6 | 4.1 | 4.4 | 5.6 | 3.3 | 2.8 |
| Japan | 1.2 | 3.6 | 2.7 | 3.0 | 3.4 | 5.9 | 5.4 | 4.4 |
| Netherlands East Indies | 1.3 | 4.2 | 3.4 | 4.0 | 5.2 | 5.8 | 6.2 | 6.8 |
| Papua & New Guinea | – | 0.6 | 0.4 | 0.5 | 0.4 | 1.6 | 2.1 | 1.8 |
| New Zealand | 2.8 | 1.5 | 1.6 | 2.0 | 1.5 | 2.1 | 1.9 | 1.9 |
| Other | 12.5 | 13.2 | 11.8 | 11.8 | 13.4 | 15.2 | 14.4 | 15.3 |
| | | | | **Exports** | | | | |
| UK | 44.0 | 50.3 | 41.7 | 37.6 | 46.2 | 53.6 | 51.6 | 52.0 |
| Belgium | 9.5 | 3.9 | 4.5 | 5.4 | 5.1 | 4.3 | 5.5 | 0.4 |
| France | 12.3 | 5.3 | 11.8 | 11.8 | 8.6 | 4.9 | 4.6 | 6.9 |
| Germany | 8.8 | 1.3 | 4.0 | 6.6 | 5.7 | 5.2 | 2.0 | 2.4 |
| Italy | 1.1 | 3.5 | 5.2 | 3.5 | 1.4 | 3.3 | 1.7 | 1.3 |
| USA | 3.4 | 9.7 | 6.5 | 9.3 | 3.8 | 2.9 | 7.6 | 10.2 |
| Egypt | 0.5 | 3.2 | 1.7 | 2.3 | 1.9 | 0.5 | 0.3 | 0.4 |
| India | 1.7 | 2.8 | 1.6 | 2.2 | 4.7 | 0.7 | 0.7 | 1.0 |
| China | 0.3 | 0.3 | 0.7 | 0.3 | 0.5 | 3.4 | 1.1 | 1.2 |
| Japan | 1.8 | 4.5 | 8.1 | 7.8 | 7.4 | 10.5 | 9.6 | 3.6 |
| New Zealand | 3.0 | 4.9 | 3.8 | 3.1 | 2.9 | 2.4 | 3.3 | 4.6 |
| Other | 13.6 | 10.3 | 10.4 | 10.1 | 11.8 | 8.3 | 12.0 | 16.0 |

Source: Based on CBCS 1914; *Overseas Trade*, nos 19 (1921–22) to 37 (1939–40).

a voluntary arrangement afterwards, with fewer and fewer farmers committing themselves to publicly assisted grower co-operatives, each of which was organised within the borders and policies of a single State (Dunsdorfs 1956, pp. 221–34).

More vulnerable and more recently developed exports – sugar, butter and fruit – readily accepted assistance from federal and state governments. In the case of sugar, a formal agreement in 1924 extended into world markets the war-time conditions whereby the Queensland government bought all the sugar grown in Australia, passed it to the refiners, from whom the Australian government bought a quantity for export – under its regulated marketing scheme the overseas price stood significantly lower than the price paid by Australian consumers. The Australian price held up because overseas sugar, even that controlled by Australian companies in Fiji, could not be imported at all after 1924. In this way taxpayers and domestic consumers subsidised expansion in sugar production and the returns to capital and labour in the industry (Graves 1988, pp. 146–52; Lowndes 1956, pp. 299–301; Pinkstone 1992, pp. 90–1). The subsidy's other justification was its effect on the balance of payments; the marketing scheme added to earnings and the import embargo prevented an outflow of **foreign exchange**.

From 1925 onwards similar marketing schemes applied to dairy products and to dried fruits. Dairy farmers were prohibited, by nationally sanctioned state regulations, from selling to States other than their own. This also effectively barred entry to Australia of New Zealand competitors. The Australian government handled the surplus for sale in Britain in competition with Danish and other European butter and cheese factories. As with sugar, this necessitated a price lower at the end of the voyage than Australians would pay just down the road from the farm (Todd 1994, pp. 101–6; Pinkstone 1992, p. 90). As a result, butter became by the end of the decade Australia's third export by value, bringing in about one-tenth of the economy's overseas income.

## SUMMARY BOX

The developments examined above represented the consolidation of smaller scale farming in Australia, with its moral connotation of virtuous toil by independent property owners, and its material connotation of maximum output from each hectare. Each State negotiated with the national government to secure the right kind of rural resident through immigration, in some cases looking for labour, but Western Australia (the State's wheat area tripled from 1920 to 1930), was also looking for potential proprietors (Roe 1995, pp. 5, 22, 38–42, 220–1; Oliver 1995, pp. 205–37). In political terms it represented the emergence of the Country (now the National) Party at the end of the war. The Country Party entered government in 1923 as junior partner in a coalition, and immediately secured the marketing schemes that rewarded its supporters and that locked them into the international economy (Page 1963, pp. 109–111, 231).

There were two other consequences of this export drive. The Coalition Government drafted a Commonwealth Bank Act, which not only passed control of the Bank to a board of businessmen, but set up a Rural Credits Department inside the Bank whose purpose was to help export producers on better terms than those offered by the private sector. Hence, rural property-owners saw a special role for this publicly owned bank, just as they already did for the banks owned by particular States (Giblin 1951, pp. 57–60; Page 1963, pp. 112–25). Second, because the schemes operated with two-tier pricing (domestic customers paying more than the international rate), there had to be strict controls on imports. These rural interests understood **Protectionist** arguments perfectly, the more so as tariffs in favour of manufacturers strengthened this higher priced domestic market. It was no accident that Jack McEwen, the Country Party Deputy Prime Minister who would bring Protection to its peak in the 1950s and 1960s, was a soldier settler from an irrigation area in Victoria.

# The growing reliance on protection

Agriculturalists, particularly in Victoria, had often welcomed tariff protection in their various colonies before Federation. The revival of smallholder support for protection in the 1920s occurred at a time when the tariff had become the major instrument both for smoothing the transition to peacetime and for engineering national development.

The Greene Tariff, named after the Minister for Trade and Customs, passed Parliament in 1921 and was made retrospective to the day it was presented to Parliament in 1920. The range of protected goods widened to 71 per cent of all imports by value from 57 per cent pre-war. Existing duties rose, on metalwork and machinery in particular, and to a lesser degree on textiles and apparel. Between them these categories accounted for about half of all imports. A Tariff Board was established to field requests for inclusion in or to amend the schedules. The Board, a public servant presiding over three industry representatives, supported protection unreservedly. It encouraged the co-ordination of lobbying through the

**SUMMARY BOX**

The Greene Tariff was popular for many reasons. The capital and labour employed in the industries fostered by the absence of overseas competition in wartime demanded protection from the return of competition. Capital and labour wished to be shielded also from the dumping of other economies' surpluses. Veterans, school-leavers and immigrants expected that jobs awaited them. Public revenue should grow to service public debt, and customs duties were prominent in the federal tax mix. As some of the debt was owed abroad, restraint on spending on imports usefully conserved foreign exchange.

**Figure 5.2**   Index of Australia's tariff levels, 1919–1940

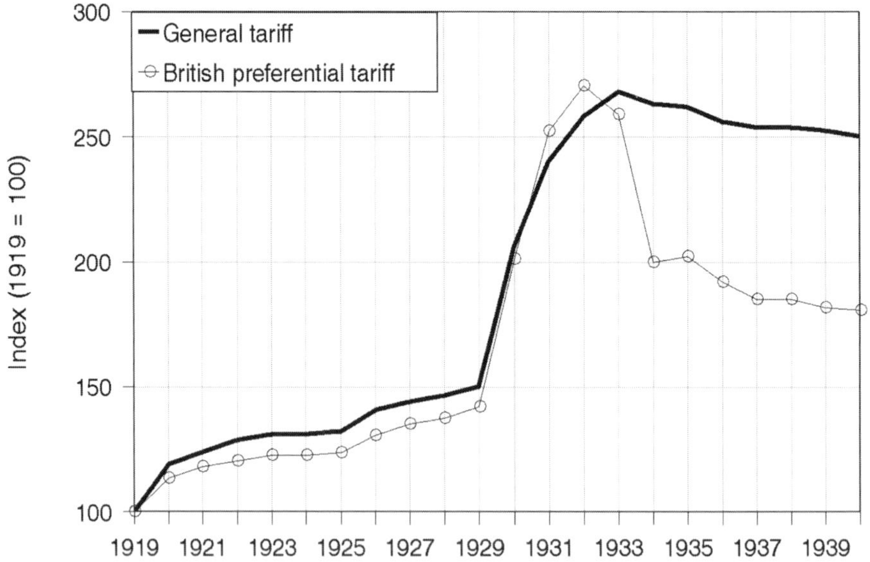

Source: Carmody 1952, p. 63.

Australian Industries' Protection League, a body dominated by the major manufacturing firms. The customs schedule grew, through rate rises and new listings,
during the 1920s (Reitsma 1960, pp. 11–26, 44–52; see Figure 5.2).

Even strict nineteenth-century theorists of **free trade** conceded that 'infant
industries' needed defence before they reached competitive competence and scale,
and before the market came to know them. Steel, refined ore, electrical appliances,
chemicals and paints were undoubtedly infants in Australia. They were also capi-

---

**SUMMARY BOX**

It would be strategic, in a double sense, to hang on to this new level of
manufacturing capability, strategic in its narrow definition because the
infant industries were essential to twentieth-century defence and offence,
and strategic more broadly in that these technologies were integral to a
modern industrial sector. Their presence within the economy would make
the difference between an industrialised nation, one which supplied its
own **capital goods** and **producer goods** in a coherent and mutually
reinforcing way, and a merely industrial nation whose factories depended
on the output of other economies' factories. The war had laid the
foundations for the first time in Australia of an integrated up-to-date
manufacturing economy, which it would take decades more to build, if it
were to be built at all.

tal-intensive procedures, the scale of their capital endowing them with powerful political and financial backers, who could use the argument that significant and brand new capacity would vanish wastefully under peacetime free trade. It would be easy to get the community to agree with this. Australia's recent isolation emphasised how useful a full array of capabilities would be during any future global conflict, whether Australia was neutral or a combatant.

From a short-term perspective, the tariff seemed handy in preserving and creating urban jobs. Once world trading had resumed vigorously by 1920–21, and imports surged into Australia, both male and female unemployment reached the high levels recorded in 1914–15. As women had filled few labour vacancies in wartime, few of them could be sacked (as they would be in the aftermath of the next war) to make way for those veterans who did not go on to farms. A school-leaving age of 13, and a hearty birthrate just before the war, placed extra pressure on the job market. Although many of the assisted immigrants were earmarked for rural work, the migration policy rested on a broader premise, that Australia as a whole had a dangerously small population. It was accepted that some of the newcomers would stay in the cities. Social harmony as well as economic necessity demanded that all of these people find jobs that paid regularly and well.

The Commonwealth government debt increased seventeen-fold between 1914 and 1919. The government's creditors, particularly the banks and wealthy citizens, had a vested interest in an enlarged government revenue. The first Commonwealth income tax was levied in 1915–16. The States taxed income already and continued to do so, but the Commonwealth immediately took more than the States did. A national income tax, although at a lower rate, continued in peacetime because of the bloated debt, but the Commonwealth moved its own emphasis back to indirect taxation. Customs duties were electorally saleable if the earlier arguments, that they advanced national development, were believed. In 1920–21, this rationale was reinforced as pent-up demand by producers and consumers for imports brought about a crisis in the balance of payments; a curb on expenditure for imports would make it easier to service that one-third of the Commonwealth war debt owed in London.

**SUMMARY BOX**

A coalition of disparate interests locked Australia more firmly than before into protection. Although protection had long been the normal policy of all industrial countries except Britain, British economic theory, and the material and emotional ties linking Australia with Britain, qualified Australian commitment to the tariff in two ways. The first was a belated commission of inquiry set up in 1927 by a Prime Minister, educated in England, whose personal fortune came from importing; five leading economists undertook the commission. The second was continuation of a preferential rate of entry for goods from Britain.

The Brigden inquiry, named after the economist who chaired it, reported at the beginning of 1929 that if duties rose further, costs would outweigh benefits; however, until that time the tariff's net effect had been positive. It had raised costs for export industries by 9 per cent, the report estimated, but neither cheaper production in export industries, nor additional **investment** in those industries, would have done much to change Australia's market share. World prices for primary products dropped steadily in the second half of the 1920s, and extra supply (of wool especially) would push prices further down. Australian export production, anyway, had grown fast – this was not a sign of a damaged sector. What the cost of the tariff did, the report acknowledged, was to redistribute some of the exporters' income to owners and workers in secondary industry and, less directly, to urban dwellers in service jobs. As Australia's, and the world's, terms of trade shifted decisively in favour of manufactures, it made sense to diversify activity towards import substitution of manufactures.

The Brigden Report considered employment also. Capital-intensive agriculture, even expanding swiftly as it did in the 1920s, did not absorb large amounts of labour. Manufacturing did need labour. The report concluded that only secondary industry (and labour-intensive protected dairy and fruit farms) could have employed an increase of almost 30 per cent in the workforce over the decade. 'The evidence available does not support the contention that Australia could have maintained its present population at a higher standard of living under free trade' (Cain 1973). The fact that the four other leading economists on the commission of inquiry added their signatures to Brigden's shows how protection had become intellectual orthodoxy in Australia.

Under the Greene Tariff nearly all British goods incurred duty. The margin with equivalent non-British items was wide, however. The average surcharge on British goods in 1921 of 25 per cent compared with an average of 37.5 per cent for competitors, a ratio that persisted during the decade (*Yearbook* 1923, no. 15, 1922, p. 501; *Yearbook* 1931, no. 23, 1930, p. 106). The proportion of imports of British origin had fallen in 1919–20 to its lowest point yet, below two-fifths. Preferential entry, linked to a revival of productive and shipping capacity in Britain, pushed its share of Australia's imports just above the half-way mark in 1921–22 and 1922–23, at the expense of the United States and, to a lesser extent, Japan. But for the rest of the decade, Britain's contribution declined slowly until it fell below two-fifths again in 1928–29. The British cargoes included machines and textiles in great quantities, both categories heavily taxed, and a myriad of consumer items that Australian factories also made.

From 1923–24 onwards the United States and Canada provided between 26 and 28 per cent of imports, much of which avoided duty because they were recognised inputs to industries that otherwise might not exist in Australia. Automobile engines and chassis were the most valuable items of this description. The United States sent electrical and other machinery, a great deal of the oil that powered or lubricated machines and vehicles (an equal amount of oil came from The Netherlands East Indies and present-day Indonesia), unprocessed tobacco and (with Canada) timber. All of these promoted, rather than competed with, Australian production.

Infant industries did well behind the tariff. Iron and steel, for example, doubled in output over the decade, while supplying less than half of domestic demand. Its major customers remained those of the pre-war iron industry. These included governments that gave home producers preference when buying rails, wheels and axles for trains and trams and other kinds of castings for public works, and rural proprietors who used fencing wire, wire netting, water pipes and boilers. Innovative industries like automobiles and electricity looked abroad for most of their iron and steel. Engines and chassis were imported because small engineering workshops could not match North American techniques and **economies of scale**. The car bodies were usually made in Australia, but the sheet steel from which the bodies were made came from the United States and Britain because BHP's Newcastle mill did not yet roll sheet steel. As for electric power generation, some iron castings for dynamos and generators were made locally but the more elaborate forgings, steel blades and alloys had to be imported. Australian iron and steel served secondary industry at the simpler level in the 1920s (Forster 1964, pp. 128–65).

The car industry was set with a complex web of tariffs (Conlon & Perkins 1997, pp. 76–91; Maxcy 1963, pp. 501–4; Forster 1964, pp. 29–57). Car bodies, clumsy and costly to ship, paid high rates. Only a few hundred bodies had been made in Australia at the end of the war, but in the peak year, 1926–27, about 90 000 assembled cars had come off the line. Duties accumulated on many straightforward and generalised accessories like tyres, batteries and shock absorbers, and on the vehicles' leather, timber, paints and glass. New local firms formed to supply components, while paint, glass and other concerns added the business of the automobile industry to their other custom. British makes of car usually reached Australia complete, or at least as a full kit – their exporters were helped by preferential tariffs. The volume of Australian cargoes for Europe, when compared with lesser cargoes for North America, kept many more and cheaper ships available for the return voyage from Europe to Australia, with space for vehicles. The tariff and high freight costs on North American imports, on the other hand, encouraged General Motors and Ford to buy bodies and components in Australia for assembly with chassis and engines from state-of-the-art plants in Canada and the United States. In the absence of a tariff, the evident demand for automobiles would have imposed a heavier charge on the balance of payments, without transferring technology, creating jobs, boosting revenue or retaining a substantial share of the retail price within the economy.

The higgledy-piggledy mass of duties, however, inflated the final price of a car, which was more than twice that of the Canadian or American prototypes. But the industry was necessarily inefficient. A small population of 5 400 000 in 1921 could only support mass production, with economies of scale, if there were a single national plant. Apart from the presence of competing companies, problems of distribution impeded concentration of production. No State, with the partial exception of South Australia, had railways the same gauge as that of its neighbours. Transport interstate and over land of items much smaller than complete vehicles was an awkward and expensive business. Factories for components as well as for assembly, therefore, sprang up in every capital city. All three widths of track used in Australia did pass through South Australia, so it was perhaps no accident that General Motors chose an Adelaide carriage-making firm, Holdens, to be its largest, though not majority, assembler. In any case, development of that State's resources had long ago led to mechanisation in farming and mining, whose products were carried in locally made carts; an advanced engineering, machinery and vehicle-building sector existed in South Australia already, and was reinforced by automobile assembly.

Despite the high cost of cars, Australia ranked with, or just behind, the United States, Canada and New Zealand at the end of the 1920s in the number of vehicles per head of population. This was one index of the economy's relative success in distributing income, at least to higher earners. Another index was the readiness of people on higher incomes to buy electrical appliances, consumer durables that, like automobiles, first entered the market place in quantity during that decade.

A tariff that in many instances added 50 per cent to the price of imports sheltered domestic appliance manufacturers and attracted overseas firms to produce in Australia (Forster 1964, pp. 103–22). The radio was the most glamorous of the electrical appliances – it was a handsome piece of furniture and a medium of entertainment. Radios were dear to start with, but their price dropped swiftly with improved technology and mass assembly. Electric kettles and radiators, mainly made in Australia, were bought in their thousands. Electric stoves and refrigerators, mainly imported, much more slowly replaced the kerosene and wood-burning stoves, and the ice-chests, that the majority of people retained. The shift to electrical appliances, like the purchase of a car, often involved personal debt that became harder to repay as the decade proceeded.

## The effects of demand

Owners of cars and appliances needed, and insisted on, superior infrastructure. State and local governments paved, kerbed and guttered roads and lanes that had previously been muddy and slippery when it rained and dusty and rutted in dry weather. The number, weight and speed of delivery trucks, motor buses and private cars accelerated the deterioration of unsealed roads. Businesses and households alike wished to preserve their expensive wheeled investments against damage. They demanded effective street-lighting for night driving. Motor vehicles allowed people to live greater distances from work, shops and friends; suburban sprawl increased the average length of roadway, power lines, water, sewerage and drainage per head of population. All of these utilities were a charge on state or local government, with the partial exception of the powerlines (Sinclair 1970, pp. 23–40; Spearritt 1978, pp. 11–56).

Electricity was first provided by private enterprise, but these companies usually only served congested and affluent areas, where small outlays earned high returns. Generation and distribution had increasingly become public responsibilities by the 1920s. Investors were content to leave to the taxpayer the capital cost of large power stations, hooked up to a multiplicity of dispersed customers. State and municipal governments supplied the huge but unevenly spread energy load of factories, trams and trains. Only in South Australia did private capital – the

**SUMMARY BOX**

In the early 1920s, only about one-third of all homes had electrical connections. By 1930 over half were plugged in, nearly all of them in cities and towns. This expanded, and set a limit to, the demand for appliances and light-fixtures. Almost all tram routes drew power from overhead wires. In 1923 in Melbourne, and 1926 in Sydney, electric passenger trains took the place of steam trains. Manufacturing, too, had turned to this new energy source. Nearly every factory at the beginning of the century ran off its own furnace and boiler, with a coal pile in the yard and a network of pipes, belts and pulleys. By 1920, electricity generated away from the site perhaps produced as much factory horsepower as steam from a boiler; it accounted for all the net increase of factory power in the decade that followed. The cost of building a fire in the furnace and pressure in the boiler before the day's work got under way, and of running it down in the evening, was transferred to the central power station. Efficient lighting, in addition, made it possible for factories, shops, offices, warehouses, schools and colleges to operate better than before on dark days and at night. Productive potential grew dramatically.

Adelaide Electric Supply Company – continue to dominate its State's output. Tasmania's Hydro Electric Department, from 1914, harnessed its swift rivers. The Victorian State Electricity Commission was formed in 1919 to electrify the suburban railways and to exploit Gippsland's brown coal deposits. Because of Queensland's vast area and unique dispersal of towns, electricity was generated and distributed by scores of different municipalities. In Western Australia and New South Wales, too, governments took over ownership and supply. The public sector generated five times the amount of electric power in 1929 as it had in 1919 (Armstrong & Nelles 1985).

# Public finance

Capital-intensive additions to infrastructure cost a great deal. The federal government extended the post and telegraph system. It paid in full or in part the construction of 170 light airports. It took from the States much of the burden of assisted immigration and of closer rural settlement. It built the nation's capital, Canberra. In some cases these represented aspects of one traditional role of government, which was to prepare for war, to wage war and to cope with its aftermath. **Interest** on the war debt was an unavoidable charge, and in 1923, 1924, 1925 and 1927 the principal of loans fell due (Gilbert 1973, p. 51; Barnard 1987, p. 256). It helped that the money collected from customs duties doubled over the decade.

Fiscal requirements outran revenue. Governments at all levels went into the money markets in competition with each other. Total public debt stood at

> **SUMMARY BOX**
>
> The States continued to be responsible for most development works,
> although the percentage of public capital formation carried by local
> authorities rose across the decade from 10 to 25 per cent (Sinclair 1970,
> p. 39). Capital outlays were large and lumpy because of the size,
> sophistication and novelty of many projects.

£722 million in 1919 and at £1268 million in 1929 (*Yearbook* 1920, no. 13, 1919,
pp. 784, 803; *Yearbook* 1930, no. 23, 1929, pp. 262, 282; see Figure 5.3). During the
war the Commonwealth, at the instigation of the London underwriters, had
handled overseas loans on behalf of the whole public sector and had distributed
agreed amounts to the States. Each government reverted to individual application
in peacetime but fear that competition between them would force up interest rates
and leave issues unfilled brought them together in 1923 in a voluntary Loan Council, an annual consultation between Treasurers that planned and staggered overseas floats. The Loan Council became formal and binding as a result of the
Financial Agreement of 1927. The Agreement was ratified by constitutional refer-
endum in 1928, under Section 105a, and the Council was established as a statutory body on New Year's Day 1929. Chaired by the Commonwealth government,
which stood as guarantor for the loans, the Council approved all loan raisings
(Gilbert 1973, pp. 45–100). The Commonwealth became inexorably implicated in

**Figure 5.3**    Australia's public debt, 1914–1929

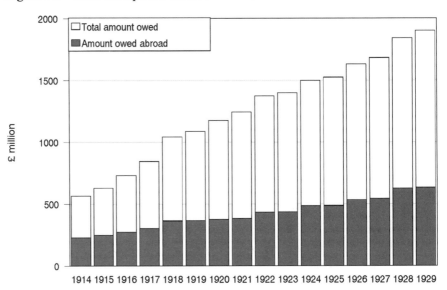

Source: Based on ABS *Yearbook Australia*, nos 13–23.

every transaction, and committed its reputation to all repayments, just as conditions for servicing and renewal of issues would become extremely stringent in the Great Depression during the decade ahead.

Under the voluntary agreement of 1923, the Commonwealth would in future place its own loans overseas, so as not to crowd out the States from the smaller and dearer Australian money market. In this way the Commonwealth added to the pool of savings available to Australians, at a lower rate of interest. It reduced pressure on domestic supplies of savings on which most private investors and the weaker public instrumentalities depended. The States tended to borrow more at home than abroad, particularly in the first half of the 1920s, but they too took advantage of the cheaper rates in London. The amount of public debt owed abroad accounted for exactly half of public debt in 1919; it dropped 4 percentage points by 1923, and rose again to hover around 50 per cent in 1928 and 1929 (see Figure 5.3). At the beginning of the decade, aggregate public debt has been estimated at about 122 per cent of Australian GDP. It fell slightly to about 119 per cent by 1927 and climbed to about 128 per cent in 1929 (*Yearbook* 1920, no. 13, 1919, pp. 784, 803; *Yearbook* 1930, no. 23, 1929, pp. 262, 282; Barnard 1987, p. 256). Government borrowing proceeded in step with the expansion of the economy until (as we shall see) **recession** set in at the end of the decade.

# Men, money and markets

There were still various ways in the 1920s that Australians treated the British relationship differently from any other. British goods alone enjoyed preference in the tariff. Only citizens from the United Kingdom (and a few from the Irish Free State) qualified for assisted passages (Roe 1995, p. 211). The commodity marketing schemes subsidised export solely to the United Kingdom. Even though many Australians were swayed by sentiment, such practices also reflected conscious calculation. Britain had been the moving force in the first global economy, its alliance had won the war and, although war had weakened it, there could be no certainty that Britain had forfeited its eminence in a world where most of its rivals had fared even worse. Shipping lines, financial networks and capital flows continued to tie Australia tightly to Britain's large affluent market and to Britain as a supplier of diverse advanced merchandise. A complex argument lay behind the assertion made by the Australian Prime Minister, echoing his New Zealand counterpart, at the Imperial Economic Conference held in London in 1923: 'The problem of Empire development is dependent upon three things, men, money and markets' (Hancock 1940, pp. 135, 149–230).

This alliterative formula, 'Men, money and markets', encapsulated the traditional imperial division of functions. The metropolitan power dispatched labour (men) and capital (money) to its satellites. Commodities flooded back to the market at the centre, and the immigrant residents out in the satellites spent their solid incomes on finished goods sent from the metropolis. The formula described a mutually reinforcing system. In the insecure post-war world, with nations everywhere strengthening tariff walls, free trade Britain itself made tentative steps

**Figure 5.4**    Net immigration to Australia, 1913–1939

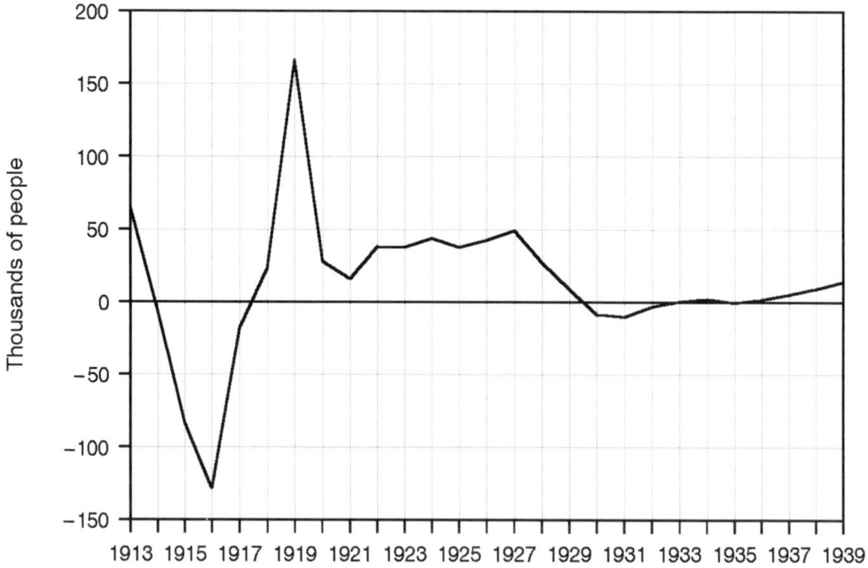

Note: 1914–20 includes expeditionary forces.
Sources: Based on Willcox 1929, pp. 951, 956; ABS *Yearbook Australia*, nos 23, 33.

towards Empire preference; by 1925, Australian government marketing of sugar and dried fruits could take advantage of British discriminatory duties imposed against non-Empire competitors. The British authorities set up an Empire Marketing Board to spread the message to British consumers that their buying goods produced in the Empire allowed people across the Empire to buy more imports from Britain in return (Meredith 1987).

In 1922, the British Parliament passed the Empire Settlement Act, by which £3 million would be paid each year as passage money and farm establishment costs for emigrants to the Dominions, if the receiving territories contributed an equal amount. Only a small part of the annual sum was spent, with the Commonwealth and Western Australia matching the Imperial grants. In 1926, Britain and Australia signed a bilateral arrangement, significantly earmarked for 'Migration and Development', and colloquially known as the Thirty Four Million Pound Agreement after the commitment made at the British end. An even smaller share of this promise was spent before the **depression** of the 1930s ended the experiment (Roe 1995, pp. 38–47, 64–106; Drummond 1964, pp. 110, 114–17; Oliver 1995, pp. 205–37).

The 1926 Migration Agreement went beyond 'rural settlement' in its definition of **economic development**. This was realistic. The net average annual inflow in the 1920s was 35 000 (see Figure 5.4), about 6000 below the average of the years 1907 to 1913 (see Figure 3.1). If none of those who had been assisted to migrate had made the voyage at all, the net annual intake would have been only about 13 000. As emigration from Europe to anywhere else in the world in the

1920s ran at half the pace of the period before the war (see Chapter 4), the Australian (and British) subsidy was significant in coping with the worldwide decline in labour flows. But of those assisted only about one-third were selected because of their self-described farm experience or, if female, for domestic service, and many of these drifted into cities and towns, away from remote and alien rural employment. Two-thirds of assisted passengers had been nominated by companies, relatives and friends; most of whom were urban dwellers (Roe 1995, pp. 3–5, 180–212). Chain migration of this kind minimised the social, financial, occupational and residential shocks of movement, lessening claims on government at a time when public housing and unemployment relief hardly existed. Forty-three per cent of the population lived in the six capital cities at the 1921 census, while 47 per cent were counted there at the next census, in 1933. The migration program did less than expected to promote the **international division of labour** implicit in the slogan 'men, money and markets', whereby Australia should have exchanged primary products for Britain's factory goods.

Migration, in short, mainly filled out the workforce for secondary industry and for the service sector. This was, after all, consistent with the import-substituting intent of the Greene Tariff. Capital, whether borrowed locally or from overseas, whether spent by public or private bodies, built import substituting and urban assets to a greater degree than it served rural and export purposes. This demonstrated a belief by many of Britain's investors that long-term profit relied on Australia replicating Britain's industrial structure rather than strengthening the complementary differences between the two economies.

> **SUMMARY BOX**
>
> The above situation was not a paradox. Trade between industrial countries, historically, was more substantial than trade between complementary countries. Industrial countries provided richer markets for each other, in the first place, and bought the kinds of machines and intermediate goods produced in exportable quantities by countries at a similar stage of development. Two-thirds of Australia's imports before the war had comprised producer and capital goods (see Chapter 3). A significant proportion of those British exporters who were committed already to the Australian market relied on and promoted its industrialisation.

# Heading towards a recession

Overseas markets were partly responsible for subsequent decline in economic performance. Prices for Australia's exports, and the terms of trade, rose to a peak in 1924–25 (see Figure 5.1).[2] Prices then dropped suddenly and steeply. In each of the next four years, Australia's export income stayed about 15 per cent lower than

**SUMMARY BOX**

The economic performance of all the major nations, the United States included, weakened before the Wall Street **crash** of 1929 revealed the radical imperfections in the international economy and hurried the world into the Great Depression. Australia was no exception. We do not have reliable unemployment figures for this period. There seemed no need to collect them comprehensively, as the Australian community made little public provision for the unemployed, leaving their care to families, charities and trade unions. But the diverse estimates that have been attempted, then and since, agree that a higher proportion of job-seekers were in work in 1926–27 than at any other time in the decade, and that conditions deteriorated steadily thereafter (Keating 1973; Butlin, Barnard & Pincus 1982; Butlin 1977).

in 1924–25, despite the annual increase in the volume of Australian commodities sold abroad. The **deflation** of world commodity markets brought about a 20 per cent drop in Australia's terms of trade over those four years. The economy had to work so much harder to buy the same volume of imports. The import bill, however, rose to its peak two years later than the export peak, in 1926–27, when domestic employment and production were at their fullest capacity; employed people swelled the demand for imported consumer goods, and expanded production swelled the demand for imported producer and capital goods. The balance of merchandise trade stayed in deficit, even when importing slackened with deepening unemployment and with cutbacks in domestic production towards the end of the decade. Larger cargoes, inwards and outwards, added to the overseas bill for invisibles like shipping and freight insurance. The economy's international indebtedness worsened as the decade wore on.

The deterioration in the terms of trade seemed to prove the good sense and urgency of a policy of import-substitution, as a tactic to reduce pressure on the balance of payments and as a strategy to shift the economy's structure towards sectors whose world terms of trade were improving. At the time, Australia's **comparative advantage** admittedly did remain with primary products, whose costs of production, according to the Brigden Report, had been inflated by 9 per cent as a result of protective tariffs (tariffs in favour of some rural commodities as well, it will be remembered). Theoretically, primary production became less competitive. It does not seem the case, however, that this surcharge prevented the sale of any of the expanding output. If lower production costs had led to even larger harvests and wool-clips, it might have thrust prices further down, particularly for wool where Australia was the market's prime supplier. Instead of losing Australia customers, the tariff redistributed earnings handily to other sectors.

Exporters, indeed, may have suffered more during the second half of the decade from a shift in the **exchange rate**.[3] The pound sterling and the pound

Australian were technically interchangeable, although the excellent returns in 1924–25 for foods and fibres took the Australian pound uniquely to a small premium. It was at this moment that Britain made its decision to go back to the **gold standard**, overvaluing by 10 per cent against other currencies (see Chapter 4). Both pride and prudence led the Australian authorities to maintain firm parity with the pound sterling when it revalued. Sterling was the economy's natural reserve as a result of its global pre-eminence historically, Britain's supply of nearly all Australia's foreign capital, and Britain's role as the major trading partner. If Australia had not followed the pound sterling upwards, existing loans and credits would have become more expensive to service, and future loans and credits might have been more difficult to secure.

Maintaining parity with sterling had other consequences. In revaluing by 10 per cent against third currencies, imports from those countries became cheaper and more competitive with both domestic goods and with imports from Britain, while exporters earned less once overseas prices were changed back into Australian currency at the revalued level. The latter circumstance did not trouble farmers helped by marketing schemes (butter, sugar and fruit), for these schemes targeted the United Kingdom, but by 1926–27 only one-third of Australia's cargoes went to that destination. This accentuated the gap between international receipts and international payments. It cheapened many overseas inputs to domestic manufacture, but provoked cries for steeper protection from makers of finished goods.

For sellers to third markets (neither Australia nor Britain) the **revaluation** of 1925 speeded the decline of the terms of trade and added to whatever cost burden came from the tariff. Having spent confidently on capital improvements in the first half of the decade, it was hard for primary producers to service business debts against diminishing returns. The drive to expand output exhausted old paddocks and brought inferior **land** into use. There were lower yields per hectare. So in the second half of the decade, primary producers had less **disposable income** to spend in the wider Australian economy or on hiring extra labour. A reverse multiplier came into play.

Redistribution towards the secondary and tertiary sectors sustained demand a little longer there. The greatest number of cars were sold in 1926–27. As there were fewer buyers, farmers among them, in the next year, and fewer the year after that, capital, labour and component makers fell into idleness. The lengthy repayments needed to buy these and other consumer durables held income back from current spending. Housing starts faltered in 1928, throwing workers, sub-contractors and suppliers out of work. The faster that jobs were lost, the faster market demand fell. It is tempting to blame strictly local circumstances. This should be tempered by the fact that the United States, the most successful economy at the time, peaked in automobiles and in house construction in the identical years, and followed a similar path downwards before its stock market crashed. Both countries had reached a limit to their domestic markets.

Research in the United States at the end of the 1920s suggested that almost half of all families lived at or near subsistence, which the study defined as inability to earn beyond immediate needs. Incomes in Australia may have been a little less skewed, but many must still have lived frugally. The basic wage was, admittedly, becoming entrenched in most industrial awards; the High Court, in the *Engineers Case* of 1920, overruled earlier judgements that had restricted Commonwealth action of any kind in state matters (Solomon 1992, pp. 56, 136–41), and so allowed trade unions to shop for the best result by playing Commonwealth and State jurisdictions off against each other.

Many occupations, however, lacked an adequate award, and a judicial decision in 1919 had confirmed the female basic wage at 54 per cent of the male. A federal commission of inquiry that sat and reported in 1920, moreover, found that the basic wage of the day met only 70 per cent of the cost of the family needs defined by the Harvester judgement in 1907 (see Chapter 3), because war-time inflation had risen faster than wages in general (Graham 1995, pp. 79–92). Average male earnings in manufacturing grew by over 20 per cent between 1920 and 1922 as the industrial courts consciously bridged the gap in the awards they set, and as post-war investment demanded labour. But manufacturing wages grew by only about 12 per cent in the next six years (Withers, Endres & Perry 1987, p. 161), despite the flow-on to the cost of living of rising tariffs, high domestic prices for basic foods whose export prices were subsidised (sugar, milk, fruits and their various derivatives), and the allure of expensive new consumer durables. Some later commentators have transferred the phrase 'real wage overhang' from debates in the 1970s to argue that wages rose faster than **productivity** in the 1920s and brought about inefficiency. It might be more pertinent to argue that uneven **distribution of income** in Australia and the United States placed a limit on the ability to buy output, particularly of those industries (automobiles, electricals and construction) that led investment in the 1920s.

Public spending in Australia held up longer than private spending. Some of this was consciously counter-cyclical; the Victorian government, for example, brought forward road-paving and other public works to keep contractors and workers employed. Large unfinished projects, like the Sydney underground railway and the Sydney Harbour Bridge, continued, as they would have been useless if incomplete. And some spending, on electrification above all, represented a long-term commitment to the renovation and restructure of the economy. The tax-base declined with the recession, and private investment dwindled, but governments kept capital and labour employed for a year or two more. Public spending and overseas borrowing cushioned the downturn briefly.

The Great Depression would reach Australia through the crisis in primary product markets and the crisis in world capital markets. The crisis in primary product markets would drag export receipts in 1929–30 down to 62 per cent of the 1924–25 level, although imports held up at 94 per cent of the level five years earlier. The accumulated trading debt exposed Australia sharply to world capital markets. Overseas public debt, which had been 122 per cent of **GDP** in 1920, had fallen (see page 117), as national income grew, partly thanks to new public spending. However, it reached 128 per cent of GDP two years later as national income fell, the deficit on merchandise trade deepened and the economy depended more heavily on government outlays. Even if **foreign debt**, private and

**Figure 5.5**   Burden of Australia's foreign debt, 1914–1940

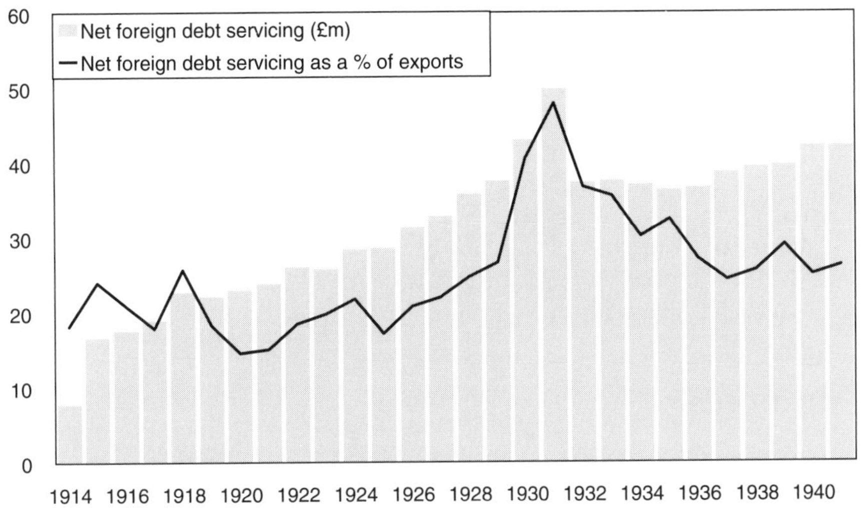

Note: Net foreign servicing = interest and dividends paid to foreigners less interest and dividends received from foreigners.
Sources: Based on Butlin 1962, pp. 436–44; CBCS 1952.

public, might be funded by incurring extra debt, annual export receipts were an indicator for investors of the economy's ability to generate useable foreign exchange to check for annual servicing. In 1924–25, net interest and dividends due overseas equalled 19 per cent of exports, by 1928–29 these had reached 29 per cent. With the collapse of markets for primary products in 1929–30, obligations had blown out to 41 per cent (see Figure 5.5). With the simultaneous collapse of the world capital market, the prospect of funding debt by debt completely vanished.

Australia had entered the 1920s paying the cost of a four-year war, but with an extended industrial base. Thanks to substantial private and public investment the process of diversification and restructuring was well under way, although hampered by an inability to generate economies of scale in production and distribution because of Australia's small domestic market of 6 000 000 and an absence of large affluent markets nearby. Restructuring became more difficult and more necessary as export industries reaped diminished rewards in the second half of the decade. The Australian economy was in a state of transition when the Great Depression overwhelmed it from 1929 onwards. It is not clear that a less active policy of modernisation during the 1920s would have moderated, and certainly it would not have averted, the catastrophe ahead. The price of innovation was debt. Without innovation the Australian economy would have been more backward in 1929, and would have been less resourceful whenever (or if) recovery from depression came about.

## Suggested further reading

Beaumont, J. (ed.) 1995, *Australia's War, 1914–1918*, Allen & Unwin, Sydney.

Butlin, N.G., Barnard, A. & Pincus, J.J. 1982, *Government and Capitalism: Public and Private Choice in Twentieth Century Australia*, Allen & Unwin, Sydney.

Forster, C. 1964, *Industrial Development in Australia, 1920–1930*, Australian National University Press, Canberra.

Jupp, J. 1991, *Immigration*, Sydney University Press, Sydney.

Pinkstone, B. 1992, *Global Connections: A History of Exports and the Australian Economy*, Australian Government Publishing Service, Canberra.

Roe, M. 1995, *Australia, Britain and Migration, 1915–1940: A Study of Desperate Hopes*, Cambridge University Press, Cambridge.

## End notes

[1]   These and subsequent calculations have been made from the relevant volumes of the *Official Year Book of the Commonwealth of Australia* (hereafter *Yearbook*), Commonwealth Bureau of Census and Statistics, Melbourne, annual publication.

[2]   For annual trade figures, see yearbooks; for prices, see Shergold 1987, p. 223; for terms of trade, Bambrick 1970, pp. 1–5.

[3]   For exchange rates, see Pope 1987, 'Private Finance', in W. Vamplew (ed.) p. 245.

# 6

## The Great Depression in Australia, 1929–1940

**SUMMARY BOX**

As the international economy crumpled into depression, the deficit on the Australian **balance of payments** for 1929–30 equalled 11 per cent of a diminished **gross domestic product**. **Credit** had dried up, so this was an immense burden to carry into the future. National income per head fell from £126 in 1928–29 to £82 in 1931–32 (a drop of 35 per cent), although the decline in **real terms** may have been more like 11 per cent, given the sharp **deflation** of prices (Butlin 1962, pp. 442–4, 461).

We have seen that Australia's experience of the **depression** of the 1890s was far more severe and prolonged than that of comparable countries like the United States and Canada, or of trading partners like Great Britain (see Chapter 3). The Great Depression of the 1930s, however, prostrated the entire world. Although Western European industrial economies, such as Britain, weathered the storm better than other countries, they did so because the cheapness of the **primary products** they imported brought down their cost of living, and brought down the costs of manufacture, which subsidised their recovery (see Chapter 4). These same circumstances reduced the likelihood that a primary exporter like Australia could trade its way quickly out of the **slump**. Australia's **terms of trade** deteriorated by 39 per cent between 1928–29 and 1932–33 alone (Bambrick 1970, p. 5; see also Figure 5.1).

For both depressions, Australian **unemployment** remained high 10 years after the crises began; a labour census taken in winter 1939 found that 15 per cent of men aged between 18 and 64 had no jobs (Butlin 1955, pp. 14–19, 227–32). On the earlier occasion, in the 1890s, the United States, already the largest national economy, rebounded quickly, but on the second occasion it, too, suffered persistent unemployment, 15 per cent of its men acknowledged to be still out of work in 1939. At first sight the United States and Australia seem to be poles apart, one a source of **capital** and the other a borrower, although they were both among the few economies sought after by international investors just before 1929, and each would be devastated by the suddenness of the collapse of its capital base. At first sight, also, the United States government acted imaginatively (if almost four years late) through President Roosevelt's New Deal, but in reality both Australia and the United States were federations where power was fairly decentralised before the 1930s. The central governments had few major functions apart from foreign affairs (especially waging and paying for wars), the management of immigration, and the levy of a protective **tariff**. In the United States, the stimulus imparted by the New Deal was countered by the states and cities cutting back their conventional spending, and in Australia, as we shall see, spasmodic state initiatives were muffled by a timid federal government. Both were countries built by immigration, and in both the number of people departing exceeded entries in the early 1930s. Both countries possessed a massive primary sector, whose depressed terms of trade flattened rather than subsidised the overall performance of the domestic economy. Perhaps it was not surprising that the outcome by 1939, expressed in the ability to employ people, was much the same for both places. The fact that the United States had been an international **creditor**, and Australia an international **debtor**, suggests that Australia's indebtedness was not the crux of the matter. The problem was, rather, the drying-up of capital in highly capitalised economies.

# The depression sets in

Everywhere in the world in 1929 investible capital was flowing towards the United States. Between 1925 and 1928, the New South Wales and Commonwealth governments borrowed large sums through New York, but this outlet closed by the end of the latter year. Given the speculative opportunities in the United States and the insecurity in the world economy, loans carried increasingly shorter terms at higher rates, but Australia's cumulative trade deficit and the **interest** due on loans, private and public, had to be covered in some way. After May 1929, the Commonwealth resorted to issuing short-term Treasury bills in London, and not longer term bonds. Australia's credit had become as shaky as any other country's. The London money market looked to its own survival, pulling back from entanglements at the opposite end of the earth, however welcome those entanglements may have been a year or two earlier. The roll-over of current obligations had to be negotiated on more stringent terms, and to be negotiated at shorter and shorter intervals, and fresh obligations were discouraged (Schedvin 1970, pp. 96–116).

## The effects of trade

The **current account** deficit for 1929–30 was about two-thirds greater than the average deficit of the four preceding years (see Table 5.1). The deficit was only half

**Table 6.1**   Australia's balance of payments, 1930–31 to 1940–41

| Year ended 30 June | Exports | Imports | Trade balance | Balance of income account | Balance of services and transfers | Current account balance |
|---|---|---|---|---|---|---|
| 1931 | 104.1 | 82.1 | 22.0 | –49.8 | 4.4 | –23.4 |
| 1932 | 101.7 | 57.8 | 43.9 | –37.3 | 2.9 | 9.5 |
| 1933 | 106.0 | 73.5 | 32.5 | –37.6 | 1.1 | –4.0 |
| 1934 | 122.9 | 76.8 | 46.1 | –37.0 | –0.5 | 8.6 |
| 1935 | 112.2 | 93.7 | 18.5 | –36.3 | 0.7 | –17.1 |
| 1936 | 135.2 | 108.2 | 27.0 | –36.6 | 1.0 | –8.6 |
| 1937 | 159.5 | 103.0 | 56.5 | –38.7 | –7.7 | 10.1 |
| 1938 | 154.1 | 127.2 | 26.9 | –39.4 | –11.3 | –23.8 |
| 1939 | 136.7 | 109.4 | 27.3 | –39.6 | –10.6 | –22.9 |
| 1940 | 169.0 | 123.3 | 45.7 | –42.2 | –29.0 | –25.5 |
| 1941 | 160.7 | 102.1 | 58.6 | –42.1 | –52.8 | –36.3 |

Note: A minus sign indicates that the value of payments made by Australian residents to foreigners exceeded the value of payments made by foreigners to Australian residents.
Source: Based on Butlin 1962, pp. 436–41.

that average in 1930–31, and in the three following years the current account showed, all three years taken together, a modest surplus (see Table 6.1). The deficit had deteriorated in 1929–30 because of a swift decline in **export income**; the subsequent shift towards surplus was achieved by a drastic reduction in imports, dropping in 1930–31 to 56 per cent of the bill from the previous year, while the bill in 1931–32 was only two-fifths of that two years before. At the same time export income held steady between 1929–30 and 1932–33, after which it rose. From 1930–31, until war broke out, **visible trade** would be in substantial surplus.[1]

---

**SUMMARY BOX**

Five circumstances combined to slash the import bill in the early 1930s: vanishing credit, sluggish **demand**, soaring tariffs, falling prices and a **devaluation** of the Australian currency. The falling prices brought down the nominal cost of imports, and might have made them more attractive if the other four factors had not come into play.

---

Australia did not yet have a central or Reserve Bank, so the overseas balances of its trading banks constituted its effective foreign currency reserve. It is true that the government held a stock of gold, but this was backing for the currency that, it was laid down, must never vary from a ratio of 4 to 1 against the value of the gold. The banks traditionally received payments at their London offices on behalf of Australian exporters, putting them in funds in overseas currencies that were then available for use by Australian importers. After peak selling periods, for wool or wheat, for example, the build up through the London branches would be drawn against and would run down until the next selling period. Once the trade deficit widened, and deficit followed deficit, deposits and short-term accommodation at the London branches became insufficient to compensate for the gap, and once the world economy turned sour the deposits and short-term accommodation themselves became scarce. The contraction in the banks' London funds reduced the **foreign exchange** on which importers could draw, and the diminished sum transferred from London back to the domestic economy restricted demand in Australia. In the good times, long-term loans, particularly those raised at lower rates by governments, bolstered the economy against fluctuations and shortfalls, but this support vanished too once governments ceased borrowing (Mills & Walker 1952, Chapter 9).

The government took drastic action. By April 1930, the tariff had been substantially and systematically raised, with revisions upwards every few months afterwards (see Figure 5.2). This was a tactic followed by every nation, countries with trade deficits or **trade surpluses** fearing alike the effect of sacrifice sales from abroad (dumping) on their own shaky industries. Australia prohibited the entry of some types of goods. The incidence of the British preferential tariff almost doubled between 1929 and 1932, while the general tariff was over 70 per cent higher. Taxes on many British goods rose faster because they more often competed directly with Australian products. The British proportion of Australia's imports fell a little, but it remained about two-fifths. The proportions of imports from most other countries changed little too (*Official Year Book of the Commonwealth*, no. 26, 1933, pp. 430–41; Schedvin 1970, pp. 155–68, 278–82).

None of these changes (falling prices, vanishing credit, sluggish demand or soaring tariffs) reversed the accumulated trade deficit quickly enough. Overseas creditors lacked confidence in the Australian currency, and sought payment from banks, merchants and governments in sterling. In January 1931, Australian banks recognised that parity between the Australian pound and sterling was a lost cause and agreed to accept 100 British pounds in return for 130 of their Australian counterparts. The Commonwealth Bank had been given control over gold stocks in December 1929 in order to prevent an exodus of precious metals to meet overseas payments. The devaluation of January 1931 led to a reversal of the official restraint on the outflow of gold. It took a larger number of Australian pounds than before to meet sterling obligations; at the same time precious metals held their international value, and then appreciated after Britain went off the **gold standard** in September 1931, devaluing sterling itself against gold. Any given volume of gold now was worth a much greater number of Australian pounds. It now made sense to use bullion instead of currency. About two-fifths of the cost of imports from Britain in 1931–32 was requited by the transfer to Britain of gold **specie**, bars and dust, and half of the exports by value consigned to the United States and India (both countries perennially in surplus with Australia) comprised gold (plus silver to India) in remittance for past and present advances. This relaxed the strain on the currency, which moved up to a ratio against sterling of 125:100 in December 1931, a ratio that persisted for the next quarter of a century (Mills & Walker 1952, Chapter 10). Because £125 Australian had now to be found to buy an overseas good priced at £100 sterling, which previously needed only £100 Australian to buy, locally made products became more competitive. So devaluation completed the wall against imports.

Despite these many shocks to importing only one of the economies supplying Australia became relatively less important in the Australian market. This was the United States. The loans floated in New York between 1925 and 1928, and the massive disparity favouring the United States in its bilateral trade with Australia, had to be serviced without the benefit of the experienced mediating institutions with long-term involvement in Australian development (branches or partners in Australia of British banks, insurance companies, merchants, brokers and shipping firms) that helped adjust similar imbalances with Great Britain. The United States relationship, above all, was responsive to the trough in demand. The high point of United States' sales had been 1926–27; Australians in 1931–32 spent only one-sixth as many US dollars as they had five years earlier. It will be remembered (see Chapter 5) that 1926–27 was the busiest year for manufacturing, and that the construction sector slackened a year or so later. Fewer and fewer Australians risked getting deeper into debt in order to buy cars, houses or machinery. Automobile parts, machinery and timber comprised much of the cargoes from North America. Before the Great Depression, petroleum came equally from the United States and The Netherlands East Indies (later Indonesia). The shortage of US dollars directed more of this business to the Dutch colony; freight charges too were presumably cheaper on the shorter voyage.

## Trading at a surplus

The **trade schedule** also moved into surplus because export receipts, having plunged in 1929–30, did not fall any further between 1929–30 and 1932–33. Farmers and graziers had expanded production in the second half of the 1920s as **commodity** prices slumped (see Chapter 5). In a declining market, monopolist and **oligopolist** suppliers can cut back output to push prices back up, but in industries with thousands of producers, restraint in output by any individual has no impact on the total supply – it accelerates that individual's loss of income. The rational response to such conditions is to sell larger quantities in the hope of maintaining **income**. The combined effect of each enterprise acting rationally is to flood the market and thrust prices further down. This was still the case in 1930–31. In that year a greater volume than ever before of wool, wheat, flour, hides and skins, meat, butter, sugar and lead (to mention the major commodities) left Australia's shores. Aggregate export receipts did not improve, but at least they did not drop, either. This result took enormous effort to achieve. For example, between 1929 and 1932 wool prices dropped by 49 per cent, while between 1929 and 1933 hides dropped 60 per cent, mutton 43 per cent and beef 24 per cent (Bambrick 1970, p. 5). To earn the same amount each year, farmers worked harder and harder.

## Government intervention

Governments might have stemmed the run on prices if they had used revenues to reward farmers for restraint in production. This was hardly feasible when revenues themselves were constrained and when the number of compensation claims would have been large. It was even less sensible when the output of other national economies continued to expand. The rational response, again, was to encourage maximum export, so as to maintain or raise existing levels of foreign earnings. The Australian government supported a 'Grow More Wheat' campaign in 1930, promising a floor price of 4 shillings a bushel (in the middle of the 1920s wheat nudged 7 shillings). Farmers ploughed a record number of hectares and in an excellent season reaped a bumper harvest. Foreign grain growers excelled themselves, too. The world price plummeted. Indebted Australian farmers, selling at the nearest railway siding for ready cash, got less than 2 shillings a bushel. The government lacked the money to cover the shortfall (Whitwell & Sydenham 1991, pp. 35–36, 48, 50).

Price stabilisation required international action, preferably with producers and consumers both involved. Sugar was a rare example of this. By the beginning of the century, European beet sugar had come to compete powerfully with tropical cane sugar. The Brussels Convention of 1902 attempted to moderate the rivalry. The Chadbourne Agreement of 1931, limiting output, was signed by economies accounting for 50 per cent of world sugar exports, but within a couple of years non-signatories took advantage of their competitors' restraint to capture 75 per cent of the world market. The London Agreement of 1937 brought together 21 countries, including the two major importers, but war two years later interrupted its operation. Australia, however, had already been able to manage its sugar industry through the bilateral marketing deal with Britain (see Chapter 3). Guaranteed access to Australian and British customers allowed the Queensland authorities to limit the extent of cane land from 1925 onwards, and to cap milling quotas after 1929 (Albert & Graves 1988, pp. 1–25, 152–5).

The marketing arrangements with Britain in the 1920s for sugar, dried fruits and butter contributed usefully to national income and kept many small farmers afloat. Butter became by the early 1930s the third most valuable export, after wool and wheat, and the second most valuable export to Britain, after wool. In the peak year of prosperity, 1926–27, Australia had become more independent than before of British custom, only one-third of its goods going to the United Kingdom. As orders and prices for primary products declined across the globe, British custom, under these Empire Preference Schemes, became more important again year by year, until in 1931–32 exactly half of Australia's cargoes by value landed there. By then the devaluation of the Australian pound had so skewed transactions with sterling, making Australian goods cheaper than many of its competitors (including British farm goods), that the traditional trade deficit with Britain became a massive surplus.

Other markets waned alarmingly at the beginning of the 1930s. Only 2 per cent of Australia's receipts were now earned in the United States, whose most important purchases were rabbit skins, wool and sausage casings. Idle European woollen mills halved the share of exports previously bought by France, Belgium and Germany. Egypt and India had recently been substantial buyers of wheat and flour. Egypt's orders were slashed and India's ceased. Many other small economies around the Indian and Pacific Oceans (New Zealand, South Africa and various colonial possessions), that had accounted together for about 10 per cent of Australian sales, now had little money to spare for imports.

The vast but impoverished Chinese market suddenly opened. Demand there for Australian wheat had fluctuated before 1930–31. In that year, sales of wheat and flour soared, and rose steeply in the two succeeding years. China's share of Australia's exports in 1932–33 was, at almost 7 per cent, higher than it had ever been; Australia supplied about 85 per cent of the wheat imported there. In the very next year Australia supplied less than 10 per cent of China's wheat imports, as the United States **subsidised** the disposal of its own large grain surplus. The trade fluctuated around a lower level from then on (Tweedie 1994, pp. 106–11).

Japan was the substance to China's mirage. It was an industrial nation, with a solid domestic market and an effective government that engineered a climb out of depression as early as 1931. From and including 1930–31 the value of exports from Australia to Japan grew year by year, both absolutely and as a proportion of the total. It quickly became Australia's second-best customer, after Britain, taking one-quarter of the exported woolclip and one-sixth of the exported wheat harvest. In the middle of 1932, as we shall see, the Ottawa Agreement would extend Australia's privileged access to the British market, but the strengthening of trade with an economy like Japan, so much nearer and relatively robust, was an encouraging sign (Tweedie 1994, pp. 141–5).

# Unemployment

> **SUMMARY BOX**
>
> In the aftermath of the Depression, during the 1940s, a belated consensus formed around the proposition that **full employment** was a social, political and economic necessity. This was in explicit reaction against the assumption held until then, that unemployment was a natural and even a constructive phenomenon. As Dr H. C. Coombs, Director of Post-War Reconstruction in Australia, observed:
>
>> Any economic system requires some source of elasticity, some buffer against changes in demand. In the normal 'free' economy of pre-war days, this buffer was provided by a body of unemployed. The fluctuations of total demand were reflected in changes in the level of unemployment. And the economic system derived its elasticity from the fact that it rarely, if ever, reached a level of full employment (Coombs 1944, p. 90).

If unemployment was thought to be the economy's safety valve (to vary the metaphor) there was very little pressure on decision-makers to remedy, let alone forestall, the conditions that put people out of work. In normal times, unemployment benefits did not exist. In periods of unusual hardship ad hoc relief measures might be devised. Although unemployment grew quickly towards the end of the 1920s, only New South Wales spent significantly on relief in 1928–29 and 1929–30. The States still had sole responsibility for these matters; responses therefore were uneven and piecemeal across the nation. Queensland, alone among the States, had legislated for unemployment insurance in the early 1920s. The insurance fund was raised by a levy on employers in a number of seasonal industries. The scheme suited a State where seasonal variations in demand for **labour** were extreme; it paid the men who moved between (for example) shearing and harvesting, and loading on the wharves, to stay in Queensland and be ready for work during periods of idleness between the peaks of activity. Even in Queensland aid was not a universal right. Hence, there was no need to collect employment data systematically. Government statisticians relied on quarterly returns submitted by trade unions whose membership, though large, did not cover all types of activity.

Scholars have attempted more recently to make estimates of unemployment in Australia during the 1930s (see Figure 6.1). They agree that 1932 was the worst year and that the figures improved steadily until 1937, after which conditions varied little. But they disagree greatly with each other over the figures themselves, 20 per cent at the trough in 1932 being the lowest estimate, and 35 per cent the highest. The latter calculation builds a substantial margin on to a

**Figure 6.1**   Unemployment in Australia, 1914–1940 (no. of persons unemployed as a % of the civilian workforce)

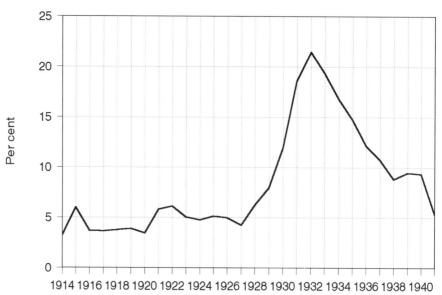

Source: Based on Barnard, Butlin & Pincus 1977, p. 50.

commonly cited estimate of 27 per cent, by taking account of unemployed youth, men labouring on relief projects, and those still in a job whose work week had been significantly shortened to save on the employers' wage bill ('job rationing'). Such an index moves beyond a strict statement of the proportion who were idle and unpaid on a specific day, towards an approximation of those who were idle and unpaid for part of a week or month. It is a measure of underemployment. Relief work and job rationing swelled the number of the underemployed (Keating 1973, Chapters 18, 19; Barnard, Butlin & Pincus 1977; Gregory, Ho & McDermott 1988; Forster 1988).

The extent of underemployment can be deduced from the responses to the census held on 30 June 1933, which included a question on annual income. Between half and two-thirds (depending on city and State) declared an annual income less than the basic wage, which itself had been lowered by 10 per cent in real terms in 1931 (Broomhill 1979, pp. 15–19). Much hard work, admittedly, was being rewarded in kind rather than in cash. Farms provided food and shelter for people in flight from unemployment, but this was not as common as during the previous depression because rural production had become less labour-intensive, and in a sluggish world market there was now little point in diversifying into other kinds of crop or livestock. Men and women also toiled for bed and board in the cities and towns; a greater number than ever before of house servants and gardeners were recorded in the 1930s.

The aggregate unemployment figures can be questioned on another front. They included women as well as men. Fewer low-cost female positions vanished than higher cost male positions, so the adult male rate of joblessness tended to be worse than the rate for all adults. As the basic wage for women was about half that for men, loss or reduction of a man's wage decreased household income markedly. Government and private regulations, as well as social custom, forced women in many occupations to resign on marrying; only about 20 per cent of women in paid work were married. This limited the number of **double-income households**, as well as the possibility that a wife's meagre wage might compensate for a wage lost by the husband. Partly for this reason, the States tended to give priority in their relief provisions to men with dependants.

It has been pointed out that much of the relief budget paid for labour on conventional public **infrastructure** such as roads, water and sewerage. Relief expenditure grew as a proportion of public capital formation from 7 per cent in 1928–29 to 53 per cent in 1933–34. In so doing it reduced the amount of full-time employment afforded by governments, redistributing revenue to the jobless, while still creating or repairing public assets. This may have elicited a larger stock of public funds than would otherwise have been the case, although at the expense of people already in jobs. The severity of the Depression weakened the conventional tax base, while the overhang of debt (made heavier in real terms by price deflation, and then by depreciation of the currency) sapped the political will of governments to borrow and the readiness of institutions and citizens to subscribe to loans. Electoral pressure, on the other hand, to prevent misery, crime, starvation and premature deaths forced governments to expand taxation and to propose bond issues that might not otherwise have been floated (Snooks 1988).

Although the States retained responsibility for allocating relief, the Commonwealth made grants to them for the purpose, helped by the levy of a new sales tax on many domestic manufactures, which raised about one-sixth of its total revenue. The States tried various expedients to maintain revenue, including reduction in the amount of income that could be earned before **income tax** was payable. The Financial Agreement of 1927 that established the Loan Council required every bond issue to be agreed to by all seven governments meeting in the Council. Belatedly, between the end of 1932 and the end of 1935, the Commonwealth floated domestically seven 'national recovery' loans. The Commonwealth passed most of the proceeds on to the States with partial recommendation on how they should be spent.

# New strategies: the battle of the plans

**SUMMARY BOX**

The official responses to the Depression that have been mentioned so far were defensive and piecemeal in their nature. Imports were restricted by higher tariffs and by embargoes on some items. Wheat exports were encouraged by the unfulfilled promise of a floor price. The Commonwealth endorsed the adjusted **exchange rate** only after it was a fait accompli. Direct help to the unemployed stayed in the hands of the States. The States still raised more tax and spent more than the Commonwealth did. The Commonwealth's experience of economic management was brief and shallow.

The stimulus to formulate coherent policy came from Britain. Nearly all of Australia's international debt, public and private, was owed to British creditors. British capitalists owned much of the Foreign Direct Investment in Australia. The British economy was Australia's major supplier of goods and its best customer. Many British institutional and individual investors had a keen concern for the health of the Australian economy, or at least for its ability to meet its obligations to them. The British government habitually found itself protecting and advancing the generalised external interests of its business class and its passive investors, most explicitly (if not always shrewdly or expertly) in its conquest and management of the Empire. Whether it was through the periodic conferences of Imperial Prime Ministers, formal economic missions, constant contact between the British Dominions Office and High Commissioners and Governors General in Australia, messages and judgements about Australia's proper stance towards Britain passed to and fro.

## Bank of England orthodoxy

When it came to debt, however, the arbiter and the **lender of last resort** was the Bank of England, Britain's **central bank** and, at least until 1914, effectively the world's central bank as well. Before the end of 1930, the Bank had presented Australia with a package of reforms, compliance with which seemed to be the Bank's pre-condition for keeping open a line of credit with the economy in general and the Australian Loan Council in particular. Satisfaction of international debt took priority, not the revival of the Australian economy, although only by satisfaction of debt (so the argument went) would investors recover confidence and restore the economy to health. Governments must balance **budgets**, for unbalanced budgets added to debt. Public expenditure must be slashed, so that the unspent revenue would be available for transfer to the governments' creditors. If the arbitration courts cut wages across the board, the Bank of England advised, costs borne by export industries would drop, making exports more competitive internationally. Australian production would be cheaper, too, if tariffs were dismantled. The deflated cost of living would cushion resentment at the decline in wages (Mandle 1978, pp. 73–97; Schedvin 1970, pp. 132–6, 180–4).

This was, on the surface, orthodox advice. It was also what you would expect overseas creditors to insist on, that debtors set domestic obligations aside until international obligations were satisfied. And it was predictable advice from a major trading power, urging an end to Australian tariffs that restricted the importation of British goods, and an end to all practices that might add to the price of Australian goods sold in the British market. As creditors are wont to do, they blamed the debtors for the very trade deficits and borrowing that these same British creditors had encouraged and profited from only a year or two before. The Bank of England's allegedly orthodox remedy contradicted behaviour deemed normal and beneficial until then.

The Bank's remedy ignored a number of empirical factors. The problem faced by the Australian economy in export markets was not caused by expensive production at home but by a collapse in prices abroad. Any attempt to sell below world prices might simply reduce Australia's **aggregate income**, which would reduce the foreign exchange available for the settlement of debts. The failure of the Grow More Wheat campaign showed that sacrificial effort and increased supply could make matters worse. A low tariff reduced customs revenue, and lower wages reduced revenue from other taxes, both of which weakened the ability to repay public borrowings. A lower, let alone an absent, tariff would threaten current production on farms and in factories, throwing owners and workers alike out of work; this would make the large private overseas debt harder to handle, and effective demand would wane for imports, particularly for the capital and producer goods that were used in Australian production and that made up the bulk of the country's overseas purchases. The widening of the Australian market for British exporters of **consumer goods** would be at the expense of the market for British exporters of **capital goods** and **producer goods**.

There was, then, no single British interest, nor a single Australian interest. There was, instead, a tangle of contradictions. Some British financiers and exporters needed cash desperately, even if this drained Australia of ready money, whereas others might be persuaded to hold back so as to keep their Australian clients and customers in business. If Britain as a whole were to trade its own way out of trouble, the Australian economy (which took about one-twentieth of Britain's exports) should order as much British merchandise as possible, yet to safeguard repayment of interest and principal due from Australia to Britain, the bill for imports should be reined in.

## The Australian perspective

The major Australian economists consulted by governments in 1930 and 1931 were the same men who had submitted the Brigden Report on the tariff at the beginning of 1929 (Shann & Copland 1931a; Groenewegen & McFarlane 1990, Chapter 6). They were unlikely to recant their view that **protection** was helpful, although they differed among themselves about the good sense of cranking customs duties even higher. They did agree among themselves that a sudden reversal of protection must weaken whole sectors in the countryside and in the cities, and that the consequent misery and social unrest might tear society apart. Because Australia had long been a society and economy in conscious formation, above all through induced flows of capital and labour, its economists and statisticians saw growth and decline as dominant processes and problems for inquiry. For British economists, located at the centre of a constantly expanding trading world, questions of demand and demand management could almost be taken for granted, until effective demand itself collapsed across the international economy at the end of the 1920s. The immensity of the Great Depression would convert into 'orthodoxy' the evolving ideas about growth, decline, **investment** and the generation of demand being explored by the British scholar J.M. Keynes. But the creation and maintenance of markets had been integral to Australian policy and theory from the earliest days. Appropriately, one of the authors of the Brigden Report may

**SUMMARY BOX**

For Australian politicians, too, an economy existed to be manipulated. Governments were traditional engines of development. The national government, however, was less experienced and, in day-to-day affairs, less important than the States. The creation in the 1920s of the Loan Council, and the constitutional amendment of 1928 (Section 105A of the Constitution) that allowed the Commonwealth to take responsibility for state debts, had recently transferred leadership over fiscal matters to the Commonwealth. When the heads of the national and the six state governments met the Bank of England delegation in Melbourne in August 1930 they bowed before the Bank's prestige as the oldest and most authoritative institution in the international economy. The Melbourne Agreement, signed by all seven governments, endorsed the Bank's reform package. It soon became clear that balanced budgets, the heart of the agreement, imposed burdens and strains on the society. The leading economists advised that governments should continue to play active roles in the economy, rather than retreating from action. One of the participants dubbed what followed 'the Battle of the Plans' (Shann & Copland 1931b).

have been the first analyst of the 'multiplier', calculating the cumulative or acceler-ative consequences of an economic action (Copland 1960), an assumption that Keynes would soon make a commonplace of economic theory. Australian observers had always had to anticipate and explain riskier conditions than those their British masters and teachers hitherto had to grapple with.

## The States: bringing different experiences to bear

Because ministers in the state arena gained more experience of economic manage-ment than did their Commonwealth counterparts, the policy disputes of the time were most fully embodied in three men who had been state premiers in the 1920s: E.G. Theodore of Queensland, J.T. Lang of New South Wales and J.A. Lyons of Tasmania. Theodore became Commonwealth Treasurer at the end of 1929, but stepped aside between July 1930 and January 1931 while fighting a corruption charge arising from his period as premier; he was not a party to the Melbourne Agreement of August 1930. Nor was Lang, who lost office as premier in 1927 but returned at a landslide state election in October 1930, having attacked the Agree-ment in the campaign. Lyons, on the other hand, attended the Melbourne Confer-ence, defended its propositions as Acting Treasurer during Theodore's absence from the Commonwealth Cabinet, and resigned from Cabinet when (and because) Theodore was reinstated. A contemporary journalist pointed out that Tasmania, Lyons' training ground, had a small and simple economy, preoccupied with markets and investors across Bass Strait and over the sea. It was not surprising that Lyons recognised the need for deference to those who bought Australia's products and rationed its credit (Denning 1937, pp. 28–30).

Queensland, on the other hand, covered more area than most nations. The bulk of the useable territory remained Crown **land**, and the government was a busy landlord, not only devising the infrastructure to develop its estate but paying the passages for families and whole farming communities to till the soil. A premier of Queensland like Theodore had to be an **entrepreneur**, and a mediator between rural and urban interests, between substantial Queensland exporters and the local suppliers of a growing Queensland domestic market (Fitzgerald 1994, Chapters 6, 7, 8).

On resuming the federal Treasurership, in January 1931, Theodore announced a policy, drawing on long experience, that he had mulled over during the months of retirement and of public debate. The government should create credit by substantial issue of short-term Treasury bills, using the publicly owned Commonwealth Bank as its partner. The consequent public spending would draw capital and labour out of idleness, so as to lift prices back to but not beyond the level of 1928. Theodore called this **reflation**, an antidote to the downward spiral of deflation. Both capital and labour could be reassured and sustained, as interest rates held steady and wages returned at or near the old standard (earlier in Janu-ary 1931, the Arbitration Court had slashed the basic wage by 20 per cent, half to reflect the drop in prices, half as a cut in real terms).

Theodore welcomed and gave official recognition to the plummeting exchange rate, because it would insulate domestic reflation of prices from the fall in overseas prices by converting foreign currencies into a greater quantity of Australian pounds;

it would translate export earnings into higher **domestic incomes**, and make imports harder to sell in Australia. Theodore took these views to a Premiers' Conference in February 1931. The businessman who chaired the Commonwealth Bank board branded the proposals **inflationary**. Five of the premiers shared his alarm. Lang of New South Wales thought the proposals did not go far enough. The conference decided nothing.

Lang's State, New South Wales, was the most heavily populated, with Australia's largest city as its capital. Its resource base – in farming, grazing, mining, manufacturing and services – was the most diverse of all the States. People in Sydney by the 1920s, if not in the rest of New South Wales, had a strong sense of the interdependence of these various sectors within the domestic economy.

The political education of J.T. Lang had begun in the depression of the 1890s when the New South Wales government attempted a counter-cyclical strategy of public works with a floor under wages in the public sector, and guaranteed the bank deposits of its citizens during the Australia-wide banking crisis of 1893 (Radi & Spearritt 1977; Nairn 1986). The State subsequently pioneered public **transfer payments** and **income supports**: old age pensions in 1900, widows' pensions and child endowment in the 1920s, and half of all the nation's spending on unemployment at the end of the 1920s. The government gave preference in its purchasing policy to locally produced coal, railway rolling stock, steel and other items. A massive and bipartisan schedule of public projects in the 1920s – power stations, railway electrification, the lines under the city, the Harbour Bridge, water and sewerage extensions – supplied or renovated infrastructure, and pumped overseas borrowed capital into the pockets of local contractors and workers.

New South Wales government indebtedness to investors in Australia by 1929 differed little from that of the Victorian government, but the State owed more than two and a half times as much to investors abroad as Victoria did. Although the onset of depression dried up the capital flow, and weakened the ability to service international debt, New South Wales governments on both sides of politics continued throughout the 1930s to provide almost half of the unemployment relief available across Australia (Snooks 1988). They followed the long tradition of keeping money circulating within the State.

J.T. Lang made three demands on the Premiers' Conference in February 1931. First, Australian governments should not pay interest to British bondholders until Britain dealt with the Australian overseas debt as Britain was already negotiating with the United States to revise its own overseas debt. Second, that governments hence should pay Australian bondholders only 3 per cent in interest on existing loans, some of which paid as much as 6 per cent. Finally, Australia should abandon the gold standard, putting in its place a currency based on the country's inherent wealth, which Lang called 'the goods standard'.

On the first matter the other premiers feared that overseas creditors would strip Australia of its credit rating if they bargained too aggressively. Theodore feared the same, from bitter experience. In the early 1920s his government had tried to vary the charges for pastoral and other leases of Crown land in Queensland, which had been static for decades; the State's financial and grazing interests convinced the London money market to boycott Queensland, making it impossible for some years to float new public issues in London (Schedvin 1971). New South Wales nevertheless refused to honour interest due in April, May and June of 1931. The Commonwealth, of which Theodore was Treasurer, paid instead.

On the second matter, that of domestic interest rates, Lang argued that Australian and foreign creditors should share in the deflation of incomes suffered by wage-earners, exporters and, above all, the unemployed. The principle of 'equality of sacrifice' was a persuasive one, but investors preferred the contrary principle of sanctity of contracts.

Concerning the third matter, the gold standard, Lang wondered how money could lose value in a resource-rich country, and was shocked that the State's over-seas debt was now so much heavier (the exchange having reached 130:100 a few days before the Premiers' Conference) than it had been when the Australian and British pounds were worth the same. The gold standard still seemed sacred and safe to many, and Lang's alternative was nebulous and unenforceable, although leading British and American economists were wrestling with the idea of flexible exchange rates expressed in terms of trade flows. Britain itself abandoned the gold standard later in the year, too late to save Lang from being branded a dangerous ignoramus.

In March and April 1931, Theodore piloted a Commonwealth Bank Bill and a Fiduciary Notes Bill through the House of Representatives. The former would have made the Australian note issue legal tender without the **backing of gold**. The latter proposed to add £18 million to the **money supply**, also unbacked by gold, two-thirds of which was earmarked for new public works and one-third to compensate and assist wheat farmers. The chairman of the Commonwealth Bank advised the Senate, where the Opposition held the majority of seats, that the Bills breached the gold standard and were a recipe for runaway inflation. The Senate threw the Bills out. The chairman of the Bank and the Senate had acted similarly a year earlier, in May 1930, stigmatising Theodore's Central Reserve Bank Bill as a gross intrusion on the private sector. This Bill defined a full central bank func-tion, separated from the Commonwealth Bank, that would issue the currency, control discount rates, act as the clearing house, hold statutory deposits from the trading banks and receive their full monthly statements. It would implement the wishes of the international financial conference held at Genoa in 1922, that each advanced economy should have a central bank for regulating matters at home and for dealing with counterpart central banks abroad. In 1930 and 1931, Theodore discovered, as he had earlier in Queensland, the resolve of domestic and foreign investors to thwart any attack on their prerogatives by elected ministries.

It took another Premiers' Conference, stretching over several weeks in May and June 1931, to settle policy by what has become known as the Premiers' Plan. Theodore was mollified by the appendage to the Plan of a small loan for public works and for the wheat industry (to recompense those who responded to the Grow More Wheat campaign). Lang was slightly appeased by an agreement to cut by 22.5 per cent interest paid to Australian bondholders, although not to foreigners, an agreement that each state parliament would pass a law to reduce private mortgage interest by a similar amount, and a promise by the trading banks to bring down the rates they charged. These measures adjusted contracts in favour of middle-class debtors and to the disadvantage of middle-class creditors.

The reduction of payments to Australian bondholders released funds for punctual export to foreign bondholders. The central elements of the Premiers' Plan, indeed, were designed to service the international debt at the expense of the circulation of money within the Australian economy; these central elements were reductions of all adjustable government expenditure by 20 per cent, and a rise in Commonwealth and State taxation. The Plan echoed and reinforced the economy's deflation (Shann & Copland 1931a).

Although New South Wales endorsed the Premiers' Plan, it continued to place domestic obligations, particularly unemployment relief, before foreign obligations. In February 1932, it began to default on monthly overseas payments again. Theodore, ex-premier of Queensland, had lost his seat at the recent federal election, and Lyons, ex-premier of Tasmania, was Prime Minister. Lyons took seriously the Commonwealth's role as guarantor of all public debts, a role sanctioned by the Loan Council and implicit since 1928 in the amendment (section 105A) to the Constitution. The Commonwealth tried to confiscate New South Wales revenue, and the state government shifted its money from place to place. Both jurisdictions passed laws in defiance of the other. A majority on the High Court agreed that the Constitution empowered the Commonwealth in the dispute. Meanwhile two organisations, able to call up tens of thousands of armed men, had formed to overthrow Lang, one (the Old Guard) directed by graziers, generals and the chief executives of major businesses, the other (the New Guard) strong across Sydney's middle-class suburbs. The State Governor, heeding the High Court, and fearing bloodshed, dismissed Lang's ministry, a decision supported by a majority of voters at the subsequent election. The Premier's Plan had prevailed (Moore 1989).

# Reasons for the recovery

**SUMMARY BOX**

There is no doubt that conditions improved in Australia after 1932. Unemployment fell, and national income rose each year until 1937, after which both deteriorated a little again (see Figure 6.2). In 1938 and 1939, the economy, whether expressed in the ability to deliver jobs or in its ability to create income, could not quite match the level of performance of 1928–29, itself a year of **recession**. The recovery had stalled.

Even partial recovery can never be taken for granted. How can the upswing be explained? The trough in Australia's depression, and the upswing, occurred at about the same time in most affluent countries. This created a statistical likelihood, not a certainty, that Australia would rebound into prosperity. Australian cycles did not always synchronise with the rest of the world. In the depression of the 1890s, after all, the worst year in Australia came about while all comparable economies

**Figure 6.2**   Australia, real GDP per head, 1920–1940

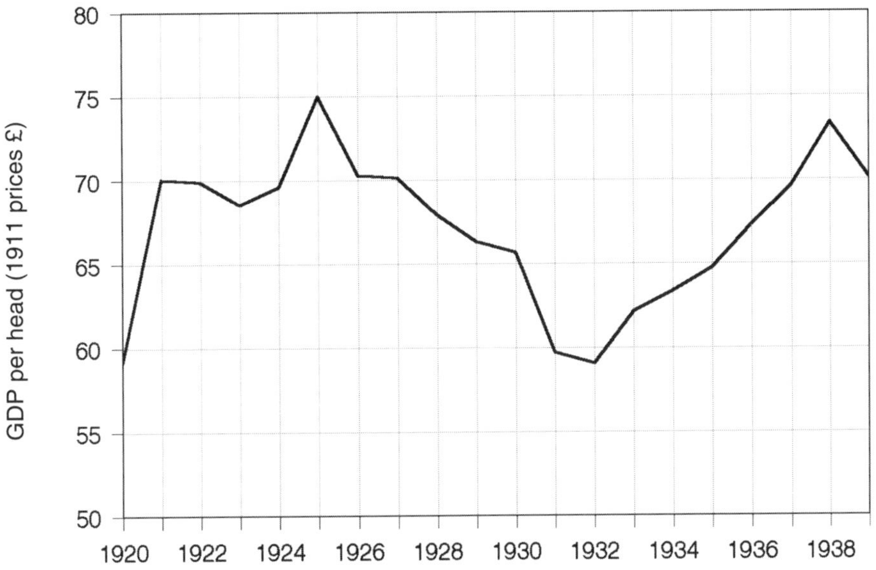

Sources: Based on Butlin 1962, pp. 444–61; ABS *Yearbook Australia*, nos 25, 33.

were booming again. In the depression of the 1930s many economies exporting primary products stayed in the trough until the end of the decade. What distinguished Australia from these perennially poor primary producers was its substantial and up-to-date manufacturing (or secondary) sector, its high level of service industries (tertiary sector), and a population and infrastructure capable of developing these further.

In good times the Australian population was augmented by immigration. The net inflow between 1930 and 1939 (at this time there were 7 000 000 inhabitants) was a mere 10 000. The government assisted only 4610 migrants throughout the decade, three-quarters of them in 1938 and 1939. In 1930, 1931, 1932 and 1935, more people left Australia than entered it (see Figure 5.3). If it had not been for refugees fleeing Nazi Germany and Fascist Italy, there would have been a small net outflow over the decade (Roe 1995, pp. 139–69). As a result of negligible migration and a fall in the birthrate, population growth fell below 1 per cent per annum. Whether viewed as labour, contributing to production, or as consumers, making the market, the effect of population growth was very muted.

Capital inflow stimulated activity a little more. Governments made a point of not borrowing overseas, except to roll over current loans when they fell due. After 1931 they repaid abroad more than they borrowed. At first sight this vindicated J.T. Lang's assumption that Australia need not be hamstrung by concerns about its credit ranking. J.A. Lyons could reply that renewal of the current loans depended on the country's reputation for reliability, and that the lower interest rate at which the loans were renewed proved this. The lower rate, however, also showed that acceptable borrowers were scarce. The Australian economy in the 1930s did perform terribly by comparison with its own experience of the preceding quarter century, but as long as the whole world was depressed, a literate society, with modern primary, secondary and tertiary sectors, remained one of the more attractive places to invest. Despite the vastly diminished supply of funds available internationally, the inflow of capital into privately held Australian assets in the 1930s ran at almost three-quarters of the value of private inflow in the 1920s (Gilbert 1973, pp. 192–4).

## Industrial growth

A significant proportion of the overseas investment went into manufacturing. Record tariff protection, although wound back later in the decade, and a depreciated exchange rate made it harder for imports to undersell local products, particularly as incomes were low. As in the 1920s, British and American corporations set up branch plants behind Australia's tariff walls, winning a share of the market denied to British and American competitors who failed to invest in Australia. Home-grown businesses, of course, also enjoyed these advantages. The import-substitution achieved in the early 1930s, when demand was at its lowest and protection at its highest, was not rolled back later in the decade because cheap raw material prices (coal and coke for energy, mineral, vegetable and animal products) allowed Australia-based businesses to keep input costs down (Thomas 1988). The sector had begun to shed jobs in 1927, and grew in employment from 1932 onwards. More than two-fifths of the new jobs created between 1932 and 1937 were in manufacturing (a workforce perhaps one-quarter larger than the previous peak), but less than one-fifth of the increase in national income came from secondary industry. The men and women in factories took lower wages than before the slump and their purchasing power contributed less to recovery than their labour power (Schedvin 1970, p. 290).

Employment in building and construction, which also peaked in 1926–27, had more than halved by 1931. Revival in construction accounted for about one-quarter of the new jobs in the upswing, but only about 7 per cent of the rise to national income. Output by 1937 ran at two-thirds of capacity at the end of the **boom** 10 years earlier, and the sector's employment was lower too. Population growth had slowed. The companies and individuals who could afford to commission new premises and houses operated in a buyer's market. Contractors and workers had to accept low returns. This sector remained deflated.

## Rural growth

The countryside made the largest addition to national income, about one-third, during the five years after 1932. Only 5 per cent of Australia's new jobs, however, were to be found on stations and farms. Higher incomes in the bush did not lead to much extra work there. The moderately rising prices for farm goods internationally were inflated as income by 25 per cent (or more) when translated after 1931 into devalued Australian pounds. During Australia's previous depression, in the 1890s, world demand had grown fast, and had diversified. This was not the case in the

**Figure 6.3**   Commodity structure of Australia's exports, 1937–1939

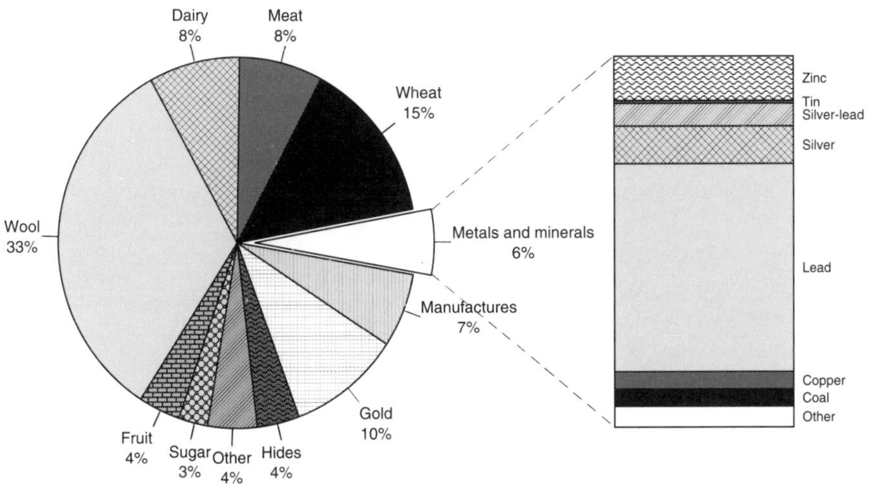

Source: Based on CBCS, *Overseas Trade* no. 36, 1938–39, pp. 601–7.

1930s. Farmers and graziers saw less point in improving performance or shifting to novel crops and livestock. Much of their proceeds, anyway, were committed to paying back loans incurred in happier times, instead of being available for current or future spending, which moderated the flow-on to the rest of economy.

Of all rural commodities, wool was sold most widely, to every European country, to Japan and the United States. In 1933, and 1934, as many industrialised countries emerged from the worst years of depression, the price of wool almost doubled from its lowest point. Wool accounted for between one-third and half of Australia's overseas earnings each year in the 1930s (see Figure 6.3). Australian wheat, second in importance, was a much less reliable export, suffering from a disastrous harvest in 1934, and from wildly fluctuating demand in Italy, China, India, South Africa and the Soviet Union. It was able to count only on Britain and Japan for consistent sales. Wheat farmers (and millers) benefited by the development of markets for flour, at the end of the decade almost equal to the value of exported wheat, in poorly mechanised countries around the Indian and Pacific Oceans. Japan apart, Australia was the most technically sophisticated country in its region, which helps to explain why foreign customers for expensively processed or manufactured goods were few in number (Pinkstone 1992, pp. 110–19).

The existing Australian Marketing Schemes, for transporting and selling sugar, fruits and dairy products to Britain, could immediately take advantage of exemption from the brand new duties imposed on non-Empire consignments. Wheat gained a preference also, and as a result half of Australia's exported harvest was consumed in Britain. Australian meat avoided quotas placed on non-Empire meat; later in the decade, when duties on meat replaced quotas, and when Australia created a Meat Marketing Board, beef and mutton entered duty-free.

> **SUMMARY BOX**
>
> Under the Ottawa Agreement, signed in the middle of 1932, many rural
> exporters gained privileged access to Britain, which undertook to place a
> tariff on a range of items unless the suppliers were those countries of the
> British Commonwealth (the Dominions plus India) in attendance at the
> Ottawa Conference. The Great Depression had ended Britain's 100-year
> commitment to **free trade**. Britain was now able to grant reciprocal tariff
> preference to countries, like Australia, which had long ago conceded
> tariff preference to it. The Ottawa Agreement defined a British trading
> bloc in competition with other trading blocs dominated by France, The
> Netherlands, Germany, Japan and the United States that were
> constructed from colonies (empire) or weaker countries in their
> neighbourhood (informal empire) (Hancock 1940, pp. 190–230; Tweedie
> 1994, pp. 65–9).

Wool was the only major commodity that gained no benefit from the Ottawa
Agreement. Each year after 1932, at least half by value of the goods sent to Britain
avoided the tariffs paid by non-Empire competitors, a margin averaging about 17
per cent under the competitors' prices. The Agreement gave signatories no advantage over other signatories that had similar products to sell – Canadian wheat,
West Indian sugar, South African fruits and New Zealand butter. In the first two
years of its operation, a slightly smaller proportion of Australia's exports went to
Britain than in the preceding year, a circumstance brought about by spectacular
increases in sales to China and Japan. When these two markets contracted equally
spectacularly in the mid 1930s, the certainty of British custom saved Australian
farmers, and the balance of payments, from crisis.

## Growth: mining

The mining sector gained little stimulus from Britain's shift to Empire preference,
with the single and substantial exception of lead, shipped free of duty in massive
quantities. Another British decision in 1932, to leave the gold standard and to
devalue sterling against gold, did have a great impact, however. The price of gold,
now unregulated, almost doubled in terms of the Australian currency. It presented
investors, after a couple of decades of quiescence, with an incentive to extend or
open deep shafts on the Kalgoorlie field, and spurred a gold-rush in the colonial
possession of Papua-New Guinea. The extra quantities, at higher prices, brought
gold up to about 10 per cent of exports by value, equal third with butter in its
contribution to overseas earnings.

## The Trade Diversion Act

Although Australia had given Britain tariff preference 25 years before the gift was
reciprocated, the Lyons government felt that more needed to be done to strengthen

the Ottawa trading bloc. A policy of 'trade diversion' was implemented in May 1936 (Tweedie 1994, pp. 141–7; Hancock 1940, pp. 246–57). The Act aimed to stifle imports from Japan and the United States, in the interests of British and Australian manufacturers. Japanese silk, cotton and rayon goods undersold British textiles in country after country during the 1930s; they comprised the major category of consignments from Japan to Australia. Quotas and embargoes were placed on Japanese textiles, turning around the decline in British supply (and thus, the government argued, safeguarding Britain's ability to import from Australia), and adding to the protection of the local garment industry (while denying it cheaper textiles) that had created new jobs for Australians during the upswing in the economy. The barriers set by trade diversion against products from the United States targeted the automobile industry, helping British firms while pushing American firms to source even more of their imported parts from Canadian branch-plants and to use more Australian steel and components.

Trade diversion was a risky policy, particularly when aimed at Japan. At least in the case of the United States, Australia suffered a perennially huge deficit, which could well be reduced. American car-builders already bought car-parts and assembled the vehicles in Australia, so the policy could be seen as speeding an evolving process. The United States nevertheless withdrew **most favoured nation** status from Australia in retaliation. Woolgrowers had just won record contracts in the United States for delivery and payment in the financial year 1936–37. Receipts from the United States soared in that year, narrowing the deficit perceptibly. The contracts were not renewed. Although Australia revoked Trade Diversion hastily, the United States was slow to restore commercial privileges. The woolgrowers had lost their foothold.

Japanese retaliation was equally swift. Trade with Japan grew greatly in the depressed first half of the 1930s, with Australia always markedly in surplus. Japan had become, after Britain, the second-best customer. Ninety-five per cent of its wool and three-quarters of its wheat came from Australia. For many years, Japan had sought the same kind of commercial treaty with Australia that it had signed already with Britain, Canada, New Zealand and Ireland. Its rulers believed that Australia's failure to negotiate such a treaty sprang from racism, a refusal to modify the White Australia policy so that Japanese nationals could come and go freely on business. Trade diversion seemed to confirm this diagnosis. In reprisal, Japanese wool buyers turned to South Africa, New Zealand and Argentina. There were many alternative suppliers of wheat. When federal Cabinet abandoned trade diversion, the two countries discussed renewal of trade. Each subsequently imposed quotas on their traditional purchases. Japan took only about 40 per cent of its wool from Australia and almost none of its wheat. In 1937–38, 1938–39 and 1939–40 Japan achieved a surplus on trade with Australia. Australia's dependence on the British market necessarily deepened.

In 1938, Japan was the target of another rebuff. Its industrial growth and its militarism generated a hunger for minerals (zinc, lead and iron) mined in Australia. The mineral resources in the tropical north were barely known, let alone exploited. In 1936, a Japanese steel company made an initial investment in iron ore deposits at Yampi Sound on the north coast of Western Australia. The Japanese steel industry hoped that one-fifth of the ore it needed might come from Australia, preferably from mines it owned itself. In March 1938, federal Cabinet prohibited the export of iron ore to anywhere in the world, an embargo that lasted until 1960. In part, this may have been an attempt to preserve what was thought to be a limited resource for domestic ownership and use, but it was widely understood to be a device for excluding Japan specifically without jeopardising the delicate recovery from trade diversion. Japan already waged all-out war in China, a stage on the way to incorporating East Asian assets into its own economic purposes. Iron and steel were strategic metals. Whether intentionally or not, the iron ore embargo was a small act of resistance to Japanese militarism.

Although exporters, ironically, experienced trade diversion as a boomerang, manufacturing did benefit directly. The steel industry, for example, served a reviving local vehicle industry that imported a smaller proportion than before of chassis and sheet metal for bodies. Australian steel output at the end of the 1930s was three times as large as it had been at the beginning. The natural protection and government contracts of the First World War, rising tariffs in the 1920s and import substitution during the depths of the depression, encouraged capital expansion and capital improvement in Australian steel that strengthened all parts of secondary industry that drew on its output. Also, a larger manufacturing complex created an engineering capacity and culture that would be invaluable in the coming war, and in the peacetime that came after.

State governments pursued their traditional role of agents of **economic development**. South Australia had, perhaps, the most to lose during the depression. From its early success as a farming and mining province stemmed notable expertise in agricultural machinery, vehicles and mining science. As mentioned in Chapter 5, it was no accident that General Motors chose an Adelaide vehicle builder, Holden's, as its principal associate and sub-contractor in Australia. Diminishing returns in

**SUMMARY BOX**

The survival of South Australia was, like much else, hard won. Manufacturers nation-wide held on to the share of the domestic market captured during the decline in importing of the early 1930s, but that market was subdued. Rural producers came out of the trough of the depression with the Ottawa arrangements added to the marketing schemes of the 1920s; the higher world prices helped to pay or refinance debt as much as to renew spending on labour and materials. The service sector benefited from debt repayment, and from the pick-up in business, but to an extent the service sector was a conduit to shareholders and creditors overseas. The upward slope of the economy after 1932 reached a plateau of moderate performance in and after 1937, best expressed in the steady state of double-digit male unemployment. When war was declared in September 1939, however, Australia did possess adequate capability in primary, secondary and tertiary industries for coping with the turmoil ahead.

agriculture, poor returns from mining, and a collapse in the market for trucks and cars hit the South Australian economy perilously hard. Even localised consumer industries like food and drink ran the risk of disappearing from Adelaide under the weight of competition from the larger markets of Sydney and Melbourne. To avert de-industrialisation, the State government began to assemble large tracts of land, on which serviced public housing could rise at a price to occupants significantly lower than under piecemeal profit-dependent projects. By deflating the property market, and producing houses ahead of demand, the cost of shelter dropped, and consequently the total cost of living fell visibly below that of other States. With a wage structure and a price structure lower than elsewhere, the South Australian government was able to hold or lure both capital and labour, so as to maintain and expand a large-scale manufacturing base in its State (Mitchell 1962).

# War in Europe

The outbreak of war in 1939 disturbed the Australian economy far less than it had in 1914. Capital inflow and population inflow had both been strong in 1914, but were muted throughout the 1930s. Their interruption called for a smaller adjustment on the second occasion. Australian trade with Germany and its allies was less substantial in 1939 than in 1914, so that loss was easier to bear as well. Before 1914 Australia had been moving away from dependence on bilateral trade with Britain. Between 1927 and 1939, Australia had been moving clearly if erratically back to a bilateral relationship; after 1932 it was part of an explicit British trading bloc (see Table 5.2). A year or more elapsed after 1914 before contracts for British purchase of strategic Australian exports could be confirmed. In 1939, anticipating war, negotiations took place before the outbreak to work out mechanisms for the wartime transport and finance of commodities not covered already by a marketing scheme. By November 1939, a Central Wool Committee, Wheat Board, Barley Board and Hide and Leather Industries Board existed to handle supply. Rural producers could plan confidently for the future. Investment and employment held up, rather than dropping as in 1914.

A Prices Commissioner was appointed in September 1939. Prices were controlled so as to avoid the fluctuation or inflation caused by uncertainty or shortages. Restrictions were placed on the export of about 1000 different goods, in case higher prices overseas led to scarcity at home that could not be remedied if the war dragged on. Many items came off the list when conditions settled. Imports from non-sterling countries were systematically licensed from the earliest weeks, conserving foreign exchange and increasing protection to local manufacturers. The trade-off between export controls and import controls stabilised prices and maintained business confidence and employment. The Commonwealth Bank was given the role of supervising foreign exchange dealings. This involved it in approving or disapproving decisions to import, and in moderating speculative flows of capital into or out of the country. In discounting Treasury bills, the Bank was used to create the deficit finance the government needed to mobilise for war before higher taxes and loans became available. The Bank was more an instrument of public policy than it had been previously, on the way to becoming a full central bank (Butlin 1955, pp. 28–125; Haig-Muir & Hay 1996, pp. 107–22).

Apart from an advance of £12 million from Britain, which was soon repaid, the government maintained the practice of the 1930s in refusing to borrow overseas. All war loans were floated within Australia, insulating the economy from foreign obligations and attracting domestic **savings** into approved channels. But much of the proceeds of the loans left the Australian economy because the troops were fighting in Europe and the Middle East, just as they had in the previous world war. Australia enjoyed a favourable **trade balance** if calculations only took into account imports and exports that crossed the coastline, but it incurred deficits when outlays in the war zones, on food, armaments, services and recreation, were added.

By 1940–41 most of the goods that entered Australia came from five places (Britain, the United States, The Netherlands East Indies (petroleum in particular), Canada and India). The war simplified export patterns even more dramatically. The inter-governmental contracts targeted Britain. The United States provided the only other large market in 1940–41, taking Australian gold, wool, rabbit skins and sheepskins against potential wartime need, which allowed Australia a rare trading surplus in the bilateral relationship.

---

**SUMMARY BOX**

Advance planning and significant management of the economy halved the unemployment rate by the second year of the Second World War; the rate of **unemployment** had doubled on the outbreak of the First World War. The authorities had learned from 25 years of trial and error. By 1941 the proportion of civilians unemployed had dropped to that of a good year in the 1920s, but it was still worse than it had been before the First World War, and than it would be in the 1950s and 1960s. A full-scale war on the other side of the world was not enough to deliver paid work to everyone in Australia who looked for it.

---

# Suggested further reading

Gregory, R.G. & Butlin, N.G. 1988, *Recovery from the Depression: Australia and the World Economy in the 1930s*, Cambridge University Press, Cambridge.

Groenewegen, P. & McFarlane, B. 1990, *A History of Australian Economic Thought*, Routledge, London.

Mackinolty, J. (ed.) 1981, *The Wasted Years? Australia's Great Depression*, Allen & Unwin, Sydney.

McIntyre, S. 1986, *The Succeeding Age*, Oxford University Press, Melbourne.

Pinkstone, B. 1992, *Global Connections: A History of Exports and the Australian Economy*, Australian Government Publishing Service, Canberra.

Schedvin, C.B. 1970, *Australia and the Great Depression: A Study of Economic Development and Policy in the 1920s and 1930s*, Sydney University Press, Sydney.

Tweedie, S.M. 1994, *Trading Partners: Australia and Asia 1790–1993*, UNSW Press, Sydney.

# End notes

[1]   Trade figures in this chapter are drawn from the relevant volumes of *Official Year Book of the Commonwealth of Australia*, Commonwealth Government Printer, Canberra.

# PART III

---

# 1941 TO 1973

# 7

## International impacts on Australia, 1941–1973

The Second World War was far more destructive of the global economy than the First World War had been. At the end of the war in 1945, there was no international economy remaining and in most respects it had to be recreated. Moreover, there was little enthusiasm for putting back the clock, as there had been after the Great War. This led to the creation of new international institutions that were designed to avoid the worst problems of the previous decades. The strength of the international economy, however, rested on the domestic outcomes in the major economies – on how well they would be able to reconstruct and rebuild, and on whether sustained **economic growth**, **full employment** and rising living standards would be delivered as promised. In addition, the world now faced a new division between communist East and capitalist West, and it remained to be seen how the Cold War would impinge on both sides of this ideological divide.

The industrial economies outside North America experienced great shortages of foodstuffs and raw materials at the end of the war, some of which could be supplied by imports, as long as the mechanisms of **international trade** and payments were rebuilt, and there was adequate international shipping available. International prices for **primary products** soared, including those commodities exported by Australia. The international crisis in Korea in 1950 added a further spiral to these prices (for example, wool, shown in Figure 7.1). This created potentially auspicious conditions for countries like Australia that could meet some of this international **demand**. Indeed, in the late 1940s and early 1950s, primary-producing countries faced the most favourable international demand conditions for many decades. How long the high primary produce prices would last and how well primary exporters would be able to take advantage of the **boom** were significant questions in the post-war era.

These broad themes constituted the post-war world economy in which Australia also looked to build a better future. This chapter is concerned with the

**Figure 7.1** Prices paid for Australian wool exports, 1938–39 to 1971–72

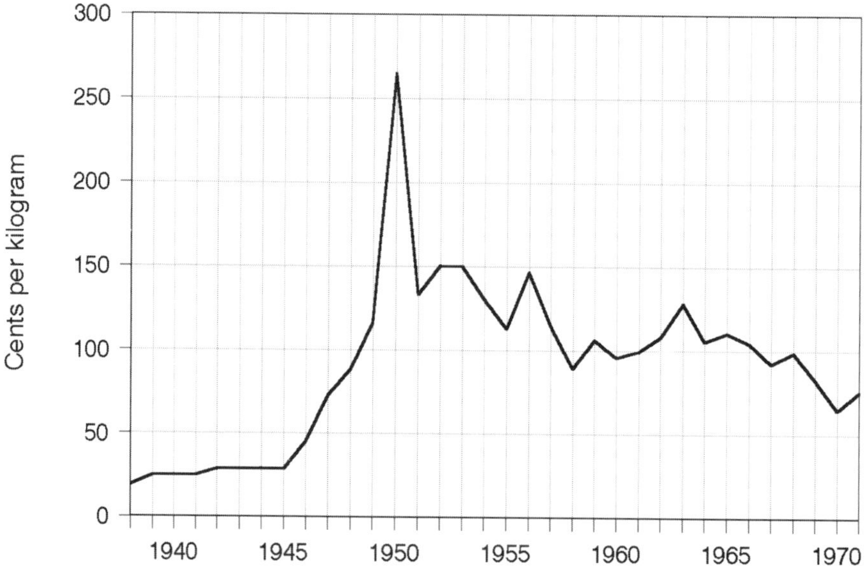

Source: Based on Bureau of Agricultural Economics 1973, Table 81.

chief elements in the post-war boom that impacted on Australia. The next two chapters consider Australia's place in this new world order in more detail.

# Economic effects of the Second World War

## United States

During the 1930s, economists and policy-makers had pondered on what it would take to revive the industrial economies to conditions of full employment (League of Nations 1945a, pp. 87–110). In the Second World War they found out. Government expenditure and government **budget** deficits soared to heights unimaginable in the inter-war years. **Unemployment** ceased to be a problem and **labour** shortages became acute. Industrial output, of course, greatly increased, particularly in manufacturing and transport. **Inflation** was kept in check by administrative controls that wartime emergency powers enabled governments to enforce effectively. The positive economic effects of total war were most obvious in the world's largest and most advanced industrial economy, the United States. There were nearly 15 million Americans unable to find work in 1940 and half a million in the armed forces, but by 1944 there were barely 700 000 registered as unemployed, and almost 12 million in uniform. Manufacturing output doubled in these years, production of machinery rose fourfold and transport equipment by a factor of seven (US Bureau of Commerce 1947). The turn-around in the US economy was as dramatic as the collapse had been in the early 1930s. United States external trade was massively in surplus, the **current account** balance was also in surplus and the American dollar was very strong. By 1944, American economists were wondering what it would take to preserve these economic conditions permanently into the post-war era (Block 1977, pp. 32–69).

## Europe

The effects of the war in Europe were very different. Unemployment certainly disappeared and industrial output increased. Labour shortages brought many people into the paid **labour force** who had not previously sought paid employment. Administrative controls of prices and consumption were wider in their coverage and stricter in their enforcement than in America. Agricultural output, however, declined sharply in all areas except Britain, mainly because of labour shortages. Moreover, the war damaged the European economies through the physical destruction caused by bombing of cities and transport and communications, and by the deaths of 40 million people and injury to millions of others. And even though many factories and farms were left physically unscathed at the end of the fighting, they lacked power, spare parts, raw materials, stock, transport links and a suitable labour force.

Within Europe, Britain was less damaged than most of continental Europe (except those parts that had remained neutral, such as Sweden and Spain). Eastern Europe and parts of the Soviet Union were the worst affected. Industrial production in 1946 was at 1937 levels in Britain, but 25 per cent below 1937 levels in France, Italy, Belgium and the Soviet Union. Agricultural production was well below pre-war levels by 1946, except in Britain where it was slightly higher. Food shortages, whether caused by lack of production or lack of transport, were acute as the war in Europe ended. Europe's external trade was in disarray as exports had been considerably curtailed and international shipping lost. International trade restrictions and exchange controls hampered the revival of international trade after the war. The Europeans had unsustainable **balance of payments** deficits with the United States. Currencies were inconvertible and international **capital** movements had ceased except for inter-allied exchanges under Lend-Lease arrangements, the war-time system by which the United States aided its European allies. For those in Europe, the immediate question was how to reconstruct and repair the damage wrought by five years of fighting. This involved tackling the problems of converting industrial plants to peacetime production, rebuilding bombed **infrastructure** and factories, overcoming labour shortages, especially of skilled labour, ending shortages of food and a wide range of **consumer goods**, and of restoring the health of most inhabitants (Millward 1984, pp. 1–55; Aldcroft 1993, pp. 120–60).

## Asia

In Asia, the war against Japan ended in August 1945 following the atomic bombing of Hiroshima and Nagasaki. The Japanese economy was completely broken and the country occupied by allied forces for the next five years. The defeat of Japan brought the Sino–Japanese war, begun in 1937, to an end, but the civil war in

China between the nationalists and the communists continued. Those parts of South-East Asia that had been overrun by the Japanese were materially damaged by both the occupation and the allied counterattacks. European colonies in Asia were in revolt and a drawn-out and often bloody process of decolonisation was signalled by the defeat of Japan. Before the war, only Japan and a small part of China had been industrialised. The region had been integrated into the international economy in the late nineteenth century as suppliers of primary products, both foodstuffs and raw materials. With the shortages in Europe looming, these economies were poised for an unprecedented price boom for their primary exports. But in order to participate in this bonanza, it would first be necessary to repair and restore farms, plantations and mines and to re-establish international transport links (Tsuru 1993).

## Australia

Each of these regions was important to Australia, and the immediate post-war situation in all three had profound implications for Australia's future economic relations. Britain was the country with which Australia had traditionally the closest economic ties, but continental Europe had in the past also offered some scope for international trade. The industrial reconstruction of Britain and Europe could have led to an expansion in demand for Australia's raw materials and foodstuffs, though **import restrictions** might again have hampered trade in food to the continental countries. Whether Britain would again dominate Australia's inflows of capital and migrants remained uncertain. The United States had emerged as the dominant military power in the world and clearly was the major force in the Pacific. But to what extent would Australia's closer military and political ties with the United States be translated into stronger economic and commercial relations than had existed in the past?

Nor was the defeat of Japan and the civil turmoil in China clear cut in their implications for Australia. The Asia–Pacific was not a region with which Australia had been well integrated economically. As the war came to an end it did not look likely that this situation would change much in the future. For reasons discussed in more detail in the next chapter, Australia continued to look first to Britain and second to the United States for its best opportunities in the global economy for some time after the end of the Second World War.

Apart from its relations with particular parts of the global economy, Australia was, of course, greatly concerned about the restoration of the global economy itself. Primary producing and exporting countries like Australia had been badly affected during the 1920s and 1930s by the failures of the international economy, and there was obviously a great desire to see the world economy working in an unimpeded and expansionary way. The pent-up demand and post-war shortages of primary products boded well for the prices likely to be obtained by Australian producers. But if the reconstruction process faltered because the international economy failed again, then Australia would not be able to reap these potential trade benefits. New international institutions were created at the end of the war in which Australia had a voice. If the expected post-war boom was substantial and

**SUMMARY BOX**

The war had contrasting economic effects on the United States and
Europe, producing different perspectives of the immediate post-war future
on the two sides of the Atlantic. Its devastating effect on Asia was further
complicated by the civil war in China and the beginnings of
decolonisation. The United States escaped physical destruction and
emerged as the world's leading economic as well as military power. At the
end of the war, it was more dominant in the world than any country had
ever been. Europe was physically shattered but to varying degrees. Britain
was the least damaged of the belligerents and the European nation with
the strongest tradition of globalisation. Japan was devastated and much of
China and the rest of Asia was in political and military turmoil. Australia
still looked to Britain, but its relations with the United States were now far
more significant than ever before. World trade was characterised by record
high prices for many primary products, including the major raw materials
and foodstuffs exported by Australia.

persistent, Australia faced its best international prospects for 40 years. The twists
and turns of the immediate post-war history of the international economy,
however, were not always reassuring.

# Restoring the international economy

## Post-war aims

While American and European perceptions differed as the war drew to a close –
the one looking to prolong the wartime boom, the other to reconstruct shattered
economies – both sides of the Atlantic agreed that a return to pre-war conditions
was not desirable. Fear of a post-war **depression** on the scale of the Great Depression of the 1930s haunted policy-makers in all countries. The United States was in
a position at the end of the war, through its military and economic supremacy, to
influence the direction of the international economy into the new era of peace. The
US government's aims were to restore international trade and end trade discrimination against the United States. Such discrimination had been, it felt, an adverse
feature of the world economy in the 1930s. Second, it believed that the international monetary system should be restored, with the US dollar as the world's key
**international currency**, for reserve and transaction purposes, and with the reim-
position of a **gold standard**. Third, it wanted to restore international private
investment flows to the powerful role that they played in the early part of the twentieth century. US firms were not permitted to invest abroad during the war, but at
its end the US administration looked to restore and enhance the global reach of
US multinational corporations. Finally, US policy-makers urged the rapid

economic rehabilitation of Western Europe, including Germany, and, under American guidance, of Japan. The end of the war provided the United States with the opportunity to exercise world economic and political leadership for the first time. In many ways it looked to create a new global economy, rather than simply to repair the damage caused by the Second World War.

European policy-makers shared some of the aims propounded by the United States, but put far more emphasis on national recovery and reconstruction than on the early restoration of the free working of the international economy. Indeed, given the dire state of the European external balances and poor prospects for export earnings, together with their insatiable desire for imported foodstuffs, raw materials, consumer goods and machinery, the Europeans regarded the prospect of an early return to a free working, liberalised international economy with some alarm. In their own economies, they wanted reconstruction to lead to conditions of prosperity with an emphasis on full employment and social welfare. The rise of Fascism in Europe in the 1920s and 1930s was blamed on economic dislocation after the First World War, and high levels of unemployment and falling living standards during the 1930s Great Depression. Permanently banishing these from the European economies would, it was argued, ensure the political stability so ardently desired after seven years of war. Finally, the European countries were not keen to expand military spending. They did not envisage the maintenance of large armed forces or high defence budgets (except in their colonial possessions outside of Europe). There was a natural revulsion against further militarism and it was felt public expenditure could be more usefully directed towards building the Welfare State. This last consideration meant that the front line forces against the further westward expansion of the Soviet Union, as the Cold War in Europe gathered momentum, were more likely to be American than European.

Although the Europeans had some misgivings about American international economic policy, they were not really in a position to dictate terms. US dominance in the post-war period meant that the Europeans went along with initiatives from Washington and made the best of them that they could, dragging their feet on some occasions. Britain, however, regarded itself as separate from continental Europe and closer to the United States than its continental neighbours in many respects. Britain's economic history made it different. It had been the world economic power for a century prior to the First World War and it still had a world-wide territorial Commonwealth Empire that encouraged a more global outlook than was apparent in Europe. London had been an important world financial centre up to the outbreak of the Second World War and the British government was eager to see its position post-war restored and enhanced. Hopes were held that the sterling could be restored to a position as an important world currency. Similarly, British multinational firms had more in common with US multinationals than continental firms. and looked forward to an era of global expansion once controls on private international capital controls could be lifted.

On the other hand, Britain was impoverished by the war, had suffered major war damage, was afflicted by similar shortages as the continental countries and was as concerned as they to make the era of peace one of full employment, rising living standards and comprehensive welfare. Britain's balance of payments at the end of the war was in poor shape, but not as bad as much of continental Europe.

Britain had better prospects of export earnings within its protected Commonwealth Empire, including Australia, and the same group of countries could meet much of its needs for primary produce imports. During the 1930s, Britain had strengthened its trade and financial ties with the Empire. With the outbreak of war, financial controls by the Bank of England over Empire countries that tied their currency to sterling had brought into existence a **currency bloc**, the Sterling Area. This bloc continued after 1945 and provided Britain with a **multilateral** international payments system within the Commonwealth Empire (plus a few non-Commonwealth members of the Area) that financed British foreign trade even though the pound was not convertible to the US dollar. The continental European countries possessed no such trade and payments bloc to enable them to trade internationally as freely as this (Alford 1996, Chapters 6 and 7).

These differences in approach to the restoration of the international economy were displayed at the Monetary and Financial Conference held in July 1944 at Bretton Woods, New Hampshire in the United States. Reflecting the assertion of American leadership, the conference agreed that all major currencies would be made convertible to each other and the US dollar within five years of the end of the war and that **exchange rates** would be fixed by each currency being tied to a gold value and the price of gold fixed and guaranteed by the United States at its pre-war level of $35 per ounce. Only the US dollar, however, would be freely convertible to gold, reflecting the fact that at this point, the United States held about 70 per cent of the world's **monetary gold** stocks. These exchange parities could move up or down by no more than 1 per cent.

In keeping with an American administration still dominated by New Deal ideology, three new international institutions were proposed and agreed to. These comprised, first, the International Monetary Fund, whose function would be to lend to the **central banks** of countries experiencing severe balance of payments deficits. It was felt that if balance of payments crises could be averted, countries would be less likely to engage in autarchic economic policies harmful to the international economy. Second, an International Bank for Reconstruction and Development to channel long-term funds to the European nations that would need assistance with reconstruction when the war ended. And, third, an International Trade Organization that would police international trade barriers and act to eliminate trade discrimination and the more extreme types of restriction, such as **import quotas**, and encourage lower trade barriers generally. The agreements placed more emphasis on the duty of countries with balance of payments deficits to take measures to restore **equilibrium** than on the responsibility of nations with balance of payments surpluses to eliminate these. This bias in favour of surplus nations represented an assertion of US policy over European preferences.

The first post-war international economic crisis occurred in 1947 when the United States attempted to force Britain to restore international **convertibility** of its currency, the pound sterling. The ensuing problems showed that the world economy was not yet in a position to introduce a multilateral payments system. It also indicated that the development of the post-war international monetary system would be determined by the strength of the US dollar and the weakness of the pound sterling. Above all, the convertibility crisis showed that the imbalance between the balance of payments surplus of the United States and the deficits of

Britain and Europe (the so-called 'dollar gap') was a serious structural problem for the international economy. Until it was closed the restoration of the world economy could not be completed (Gardner 1956, pp. 184–223, 348–80).

## European economic integration

The most important initiative by the United States to tackle the dollar gap was the institution of the Marshall Plan following the failure of convertibility in mid-1947. The Marshall Plan set up a European Recovery Program that provided massive **credits** to Britain and Western Europe between 1948 and 1952. It was then superseded by the Mutual Security Act that continued to pump dollars into Western Europe throughout the 1950s. Marshall Aid did more than simply provide balance of payments relief to continental Europe. It also established an administrative structure that the US government hoped would encourage European economic integration.

To administer the recovery program, the recipient European governments and the United States established the Organization for European Economic Co-operation, a body that continued until 1959. In order for intra-European trade to be facilitated, a European Payments Union (EPU) was established in 1950 that acted as a clearing house for the member countries, enabling them to balance credits and debits arising from their trade with each other without full currency convertibility. Further piecemeal moves towards greater integration continued with the establishment in 1951 of the European Coal and Steel Community, which pooled the coal and steel production of six Western European nations. It was a practical measure that gave confidence to proceed to a more comprehensive economic agreement between the six – the Treaty of Rome, which was signed in 1957 between France, West Germany, Luxembourg, Holland, Belgium and Italy, and which brought into being the European Economic Community. The most important aspect of this Treaty was the agreement on a Common Agricultural Policy to protect the farmers of the six countries from external competition by **subsidising** their production and imposing strict import quotas.

Britain remained outside these moves towards European economic integration, though it was a member of the EPU. The failure of convertibility had left the Sterling Area and the trade bloc of the Commonwealth Empire intact and during the 1950s, British governments pursued a quest for a special place for Britain in the world economy and for sterling as a world currency. However, recurrent balance of payments crises prevented this from being realised. A severe balance of payments deficit in 1949 forced Britain to devalue the pound against the dollar by 30 per cent, a **devaluation** that was followed by most of the Sterling Area, including Australia. This devaluation helped to close the dollar gap by revaluing the dollar in terms of most other currencies, but it was the death knell for any real prospect of a return to world currency status for the pound. By the end of the 1950s, it was apparent that Britain was being left behind in the economic boom experienced in Western Europe, and in 1961 Britain reversed its previous stance and applied to join the **EEC**. This was a development that was greeted with dismay and some bitterness by many of Britain's Commonwealth partners, including Australia (Polk 1956, pp. 71–102; Havinden & Meredith 1993, pp. 242–52, 23–43).

In addition to Marshall Aid, the United States tackled the dollar gap by removing restrictions on capital outflow; this allowed US multinationals to invest freely throughout the world. Much of this **investment** was directed at Britain and continental Europe in the case of manufacturing firms and towards resource-rich, less-developed economies in Asia, Africa, the Middle East and Latin America in the case of US food, raw materials and mining companies. US manufacturers in particular found that restrictions placed on dollar imports by European governments meant that they could not sell in these markets. Direct investment provided a way round this problem. American firms providing banking and financial services followed these multinationals and established branches in many of the same countries, as did a number of US hotel chains. American direct private investment helped to close the dollar gap, but a gap of varying size persisted throughout the 1950s, until the European economies had developed sufficient export earnings and import replacement industries to eliminate their chronic imbalance with the United States. This point was reached by most of Western Europe by the end of the decade. At the end of 1958, convertibility at stable rates of exchange to the US dollar was established for all major European currencies (Scammell 1983, pp. 108–16).

---

**SUMMARY BOX**

The United States wanted to build on its strong economic position at the end of the war and restore the free working of the international economy as quickly as possible. European countries were more concerned with domestic outcomes and meeting the aspirations of their people for higher living standards. Britain shared some of the problems of the continental European economies, but was more inclined through its own history of globalisation towards the American stance. The United States imposed its views at the Bretton Woods conference in 1944 that established major new international institutions. An attempt in 1947 to speed up the implementation of the Bretton Woods agreements led to a 'convertibility crisis' that put the process back by another 10 years. Meanwhile, Marshall Aid helped to close the 'dollar gap' and promote European economic integration. By the end of the 1950s, the European Economic Community had been established and the dollar gap had disappeared, paving the way finally for the establishment of the global economy on lines similar to those proposed at Bretton Woods.

# The Long Boom

The international economy entered a prolonged period of expansion from the late 1940s to the early 1970s. This was based on the recovery and expansion of the industrial economies and the restoration and gradual liberalisation of the mechanisms of the global economy. World trade, international investment and intercontinental migration revived and grew more robustly than at any time since before the First World War. The international monetary system was delayed in its full working until the 1960s, but then delivered stable exchange rates and freely convertible currencies until the early 1970s. At the end of the 1960s, inflationary forces gathered strength and at the beginning of the 1970s the rate of price inflation in the major economies threatened the continuance of the Long Boom. Its demise in the crises of 1973 and 1974 is discussed in Chapter 10.

## Economic miracles

Western Europe staged something of an 'economic miracle' during the 1950s and 1960s. Economic growth had been strong in the later 1940s, but hampered by shortages of inputs, which Marshall Aid helped relieve. In the 1950s, growth rates among the Western European nations varied between 3 per cent per annum in Britain (Europe's slowest) and 8 per cent in West Germany (see Table 7.1). High growth rates continued until the second half of the 1970s. Western European economies experienced strong domestic demand as a result of full employment and government spending and gradually improving export demand, particularly among the EEC 'Six'. The rate of capital investment accelerated, boosted by higher domestic **savings**, government investment in nationalised industries and services, and **foreign investment**, most notably from the US multinational corporations that brought new technologies and new products along with their investment. As the Western European economies shifted labour from agriculture to industry, **labour productivity** rose. The quality of labour was enhanced by a strong commitment to education, training and health programs. New technology combined more capital with labour, also resulting in higher productiveness of the labour force.

This process was far from smooth and a number of Western European countries experienced bouts of severe inflation and short-lived economic crises. Nevertheless, the main economic problems challenging their governments were ones caused by strains imposed by rapid economic growth, as opposed to the problems posed by economic **slump** before the war. Western European governments, including Britain, maintained economic regulations and controls during the 1950s and actively intervened in attempts to push market forces in directions they determined. Although these economies in the post-war era were capitalist and market based, they operated in a regulated environment predicated on a belief that unrestrained market forces had been damaging to European economies during the inter-war period.

In Japan, the dislocation brought on the economy by the end of the war and the American occupation hindered an immediate recovery. US policy tended towards reconstructing Japan on more democratic and less industrialised lines than before the war. The victory of the Chinese Communist Party in 1949 and the onset of the Korean War in 1950, however, changed American policy. Japan was the front line against further communist expansion in Asia, and a supply depot and arsenal for the allied war effort in Korea. Japanese reindustrialisation was now promoted and large amounts of civilian and military financial aid flowed to the US's former

**Table 7.1**   Real economic growth, selected countries, 1950–54 to 1975–79 (annual average percentage change)

| Annual average of years | Australia* | Canada | USA | UK | France | Germany | Italy | Japan |
|---|---|---|---|---|---|---|---|---|
| 1950–54 | 6.4 | 4.3 | 3.6 | 4.2 | 4.0 | 8.8 | 5.2 | 6.6 |
| 1955–59 | 4.5 | 5.4 | 3.3 | 2.2 | 4.5 | 7.1 | 5.6 | 7.7 |
| 1960–64 | 5.1 | 5.5 | 4.3 | 3.5 | 6.2 | 4.8 | 5.7 | 11.7 |
| 1965–69 | 5.8 | 5.6 | 4.3 | 2.5 | 5.2 | 4.3 | 5.8 | 11.6 |
| 1970–74 | 5.0 | 5.3 | 2.6 | 2.8 | 5.1 | 3.5 | 4.2 | 6.2 |
| 1975–79 | 2.6 | 3.3 | 3.3 | 2.0 | 3.1 | 2.8 | 2.4 | 4.6 |

* Fiscal year ended June of year shown.
Source: Based on RBA 1986, pp. 206–7.

enemy. From 1952, after the Korean War ended and Japan attained independence, Japan's economic miracle took off, stage-managed, to a considerable extent, by the former Ministry of Munitions now renamed the Ministry of Trade and Industry. Japan's industrial output was well above its pre-war level by 1957 and rates of growth were recorded in the 1960s that were the highest in the developed world at that time (see Table 7.1) (Tsuru 1993, chapters 1–4; Johnson 1982).

By the end of the 1950s, full recovery from the economic effects of the war was complete among the industrial nations and developed primary producers like Australia. Sustained economic growth combined with low inflation and full employment were the conditions that characterised these economies during most of the 1950s and 1960s. Between 1950 and 1967, annual average **real** growth in Britain was 3.5 per cent and this was the lowest rate of the Western European economies. Germany's average rate was 8.3 per cent. During the same period, the United States, the world's largest economy, grew in real terms at an average annual rate of 4.2 per cent and Japan averaged an unprecedented 15.3 per cent rate sustained over these years, the highest growth rate of any industrial economy.

These continuing high rates of growth, together with taxation policies that redistributed income more equitably, the maintenance of full employment, **transfer payments** and welfare provisions, translated into rising real **incomes** for most households and steadily rising average living standards. Often these households had only one member in paid employment. The contrast in economic and social conditions in these nations between the 1950s and 1960s, and the inter-war period, could not have been more striking. They were experienced, of course, by several generations. One had reached adulthood in the 1930s and 1940s and remained very conscious of the past, however rosy the present might appear. The other had grown up in the 1950s and 1960s – the so-called '**baby boomers**', who took material prosperity, rising living standards, full employment and the Welfare State for granted because they had experienced nothing else.

# Growth of the international economy

## World trade

The booming economic conditions in many of the world's economies were reflected in, and enhanced by, growth in the international economy. World trade revived after the war and grew strongly in value and volume through the 1950s and 1960s (see Figure 7.2). The value of world exports was three times higher in 1948 than 10 years earlier. By 1955, the value of world exports were double that reached in 1948 and world exports doubled again in value by 1965. By 1972, their value was twice that of 1966. The strong growth in the value of world trade was matched by its growth in volume up to the mid-1960s. The post-war price boom came to an end in 1952 and from then until 1965 export prices were generally stable (see Figure 7.2). Export volumes continued to rise in the late 1960s and 1970s, but international inflation meant that the value of world exports grew faster. Overall, between the late 1940s and the beginning of the 1970s, world trade grew in volume six fold and in value by eight times (UN, *Yearbook of International Trade Statistics*). This was the longest period of strong growth in world trade in the twentieth century.

The structure of world trade at the end of the 1940s reflected the impact of the Second World War. According to UN yearbook statistics, Europe's share of world exports, for example, declined from 38 per cent in 1938 to 22 per cent in 1948 (excluding the United Kingdom). Japan's share fell from 5 per cent to less than 1 per cent. On the other hand, the share of North America rose from 17 per

**Figure 7.2**   World exports, 1946 to 1975

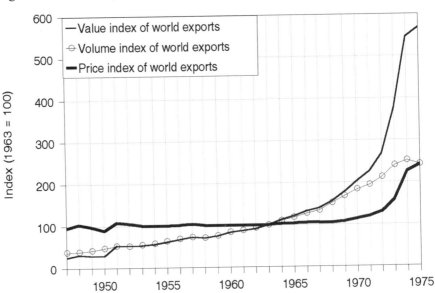

Source: Based on UN *Yearbook of International Trade Statistics*, various years.

**Figure 7.3**    Australia's share of world trade, 1950 to 1980

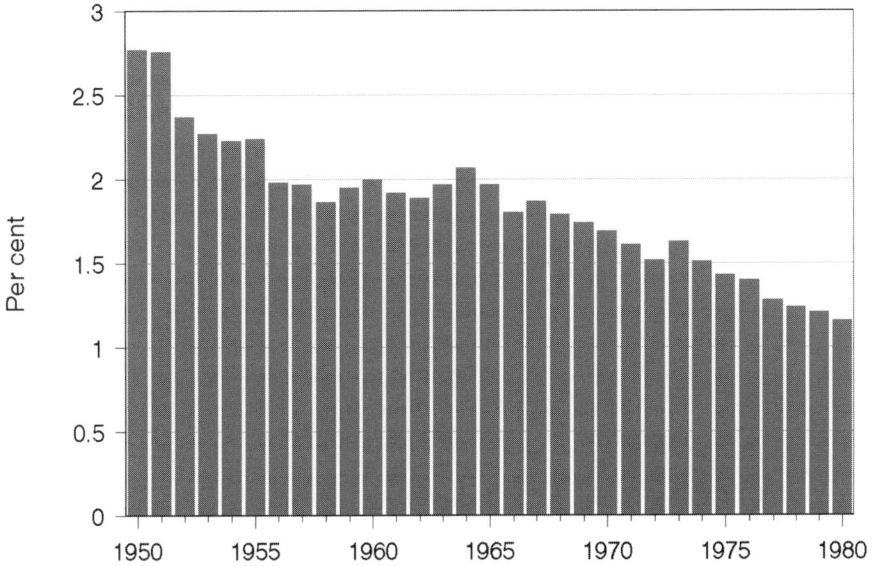

Source: Based on IMF *Yearbook*, various years.

cent to 32 per cent. These changes did not persist once the economic renaissance of Western Europe and Japan blossomed in the 1950s and 1960s. Europe's share of world exports was above its pre-war level by 1958 and accounted for almost half of world trade by the early 1970s. Much of this was due, however, to intra-European trade. Japan's share of world exports were still less than 3 per cent in 1958, but reached 7 per cent by 1972. Conversely, the share of world exports of the United States declined during the 1960s.

Australia's share of world trade declined throughout the Long Boom, from 2.8 per cent in 1950 to 1.5 per cent in 1972 (see Figure 7.3). This was because Australia's exports continued to consist mainly of primary products, but in the 20 years from the early 1950s to the beginning of the 1970s, it was manufactured goods that were the fastest growing sector of world trade. Primary products accounted for 56 per cent of the value of world exports in 1953, but only 34 per cent in 1970. Food and raw materials declined from 46 per cent to 17 per cent. Although Australian exports were boosted in the early 1970s by the dramatic price rise of petroleum oil and other fossil fuels, its export structure consigned it to the slow lane of world trade growth during the Long Boom.

## International investment

International capital flows were also the highest they had been since before the First World War. In contrast to that era, however, in the 1950s and 1960s these flows were dominated by **direct foreign investment** from multinational corporations. Such investments accounted for four-fifths of all long-term capital flows in this period. They began to grow from the late 1940s, but reached their greatest impact following the international freeing up of exchange controls and currency convertibility from 1960 (see below). Most of these corporations were based in the United States and concentrated in manufacturing and the oil industry. These two sectors accounted for over two-thirds of all US direct foreign investment in the 1960s. By the early 1970s, 42 per cent of US foreign investment worldwide was in manufacturing, 30 per cent in oil and 8 per cent in mining. The international expansion of these firms was predicated on strong economic growth in the United States and other industrial countries that made investments in manufacturing and the supply of raw materials and energy highly profitable. Before the Second World War, most of US direct foreign investment had been in Canada and Central and South America. The American continent continued to be important, but in the 1950s and 1960s there was a relative decline in the proportion of US direct invest- ment to other parts of this region. A greater share flowed to Europe, Asia, Africa and the Middle East. By 1972, 45 per cent of US foreign investment was in Canada, Central and South America, 33 per cent in Europe, 7 per cent in Africa and the Middle East, and 6 per cent in Asia. Only a small proportion of US invest- ment stock was in Australia (4 per cent in 1972, half of which was in manufactur- ing) though that was a larger share than in Japan (2.5 per cent) or France (3.7 per cent), and from Australia's point of view its impact was highly significant, as discussed in the next chapter (United States, Department of Commerce 1974).

The governments of recipient countries often sought American foreign invest- ment. Official attitudes towards foreign companies at this time in most areas of the capitalist world put desire for rapid economic – and especially, industrial – expan- sion, access to advanced American technology and the maintenance of full employ- ment ahead of any practical concern about the possible adverse consequences of foreign ownership. These were years when many countries experienced an 'Ameri- can invasion', as US multinationals brought American goods, production tech- niques, management styles and popular culture to a generally receptive world.

In the 1960s and early 1970s, US direct foreign investment accounted for half the world's total. The next most important source of international investment, the United Kingdom, accounted for only 15 per cent and no other single country accounted for more than 6 per cent. Thus the United States dominated interna- tional investment in the third quarter of the twentieth century as Britain had done before the First World War. The trend, however, from the mid-1960s, was for the share of these two sources to decline: by the mid-1970s, the US share was less than half and Britain's barely above 10 per cent. Germany, Japan, Switzerland and France were the fastest growing sources of international investment in the latter stages of the Long Boom (OECD 1981, p. 39). Britain's stock of international investment reflected its imperial past. In 1971, 51 per cent was invested in the Commonwealth – more than one-third of this in Australia, which remained the single most important recipient of overseas investment by British firms (Great Britain, Department of Trade and Industry 1984, p. 423).

Augmenting direct foreign investment were two other forms: official capital flows and loans by private banks. Official flows were associated with economic aid from the United States and Canada to Western Europe in the early 1950s. This was followed by aid given by the governments of developed economies to less developed ones during the later 1950s and the 1960s, and loans made by agencies such as the World Bank (formerly the International Bank for Reconstruction and Development, or IBRD). Private bank loans resulted from the internationalisation of financial services that gathered pace during the 1960s. US and British banks became worldwide lenders, often closely connected with the investments of multi-national corporations. Private capital flows still dominated, but in contrast to the early twentieth century, personal investors were now much less important than corporations and banks.

## Migration

Intercontinental migration of people also revived and expanded as the world economy was revitalised after the war. The level of this migration was about the same as in the 1920s, but lower than the numbers migrating in the pre-1914 era. In the late 1940s and early 1950s, many were refugees and displaced persons for whom migration was a necessity not a choice. Economic prospects attracted migrants to the traditional destinations, though the United States retained strict immigration controls. Improved living conditions in Western Europe together with full employment reduced the number of potential emigrants. Eastern European countries and Russia had figured largely in pre-1914 European emigration but no longer did so, and the bulk of the emigrants to destinations outside of Europe in the 1950s and 1960s came from Britain, Italy, Spain, Portugal, Germany, Belgium, Holland and Scandinavia (in roughly that order). The creation of the European Economic Community in 1956 facilitated the movement of people between the 'six' and this to some extent also damped the desire for intercontinental emigration, though it increased international migration of labour within the EEC. Between 1946 and 1975, approximately 13 million Europeans emigrated to destinations outside Europe (see Table 7.2) and a further 850 000 refugees were resettled outside the continent in the immediate post-war years. Of the emigrants, just under one half went to the New World, chiefly to Canada, the United States, Venezuela, Brazil and Argentina. Almost one-quarter of the outflow went to Australia. This made Australia as important a destination as the United States during the Long Boom. Australia was an important country of settlement for several European emigrant nations, notably Greece, the United Kingdom and Italy. Australia also figured prominently in the settlement of post-war refugees, taking 21 per cent of those who left Europe, second only to the United States (39 per cent) (United Nations, *Demographic Yearbook 1952*, p. 476).

Thus long-established patterns in the European diaspora continued into the third quarter of the twentieth century. The bulk of British emigrants went to Australia, Canada and South Africa, the Germans to the United States, the Italians to North America (with a sizeable number now going to Australia), the Portuguese to North America and Brazil, and the Spanish to South America. Greece became a more significant source of European intercontinental emigration after the Second World War, its emigrants mainly heading to Australia and North America. In many cases, the existence of a community of previous immigrants and their descendants within an immigrant country reinforced the patterns of permanent

**Table 7.2** Emigration from Europe, 1946–1975

| Emigrant nation | No. of emigrants (000s) | Percentage of total emigration | Geographic distribution of emigrants (percentage of total) | | | | | | | |
|---|---|---|---|---|---|---|---|---|---|---|
| | | | Australia | New Zealand | Canada | USA | South America & Caribbean | Asia | Africa | Other |
| UK | 5 141 | 40.6 | 34 | 7 | 16 | 11 | 1 | 6 | 15 | 10 |
| Italy | 2 287 | 18.1 | 22 | – | 29 | 33 | 11 | – | 4 | 1 |
| Germany | 1 571 | 12.4 | 7 | – | 10 | 39 | 8 | 16 | 14 | 6 |
| Spain | 928 | 7.3 | 5 | – | – | 10 | 72 | – | – | 13 |
| Netherlands | 831 | 6.6 | 12 | 3 | 13 | 16 | 18 | 17 | 18 | 3 |
| Portugal | 736 | 5.8 | 1 | – | 26 | 31 | 18 | – | 6 | – |
| Greece | 437 | 3.4 | 40 | – | 18 | 32 | 36 | 3 | 3 | 4 |
| Belgium | 298 | 2.3 | 3 | – | 10 | 24 | – | 13 | 47 | 3 |
| Denmark | 223 | 1.8 | 4 | – | 9 | 24 | 2 | 16 | 8 | 37* |
| Sweden | 123 | 1.0 | 10 | – | 10 | 40 | 7 | 12 | 12 | 9 |
| Norway | 96 | 0.7 | 5 | – | 8 | 54 | 3 | 12 | 14 | 4 |
| Total | 12 671 | 100.0 | 23 | 4 | 16 | 22 | 9 | 7 | 13 | 6 |

* Mainly to Greenland.
Source: Based on United Nations, *Demographic Yearbook*, various years.

migration flows. Certainly the transfer of labour in the form of settler migrants that developed in the nineteenth century continued through the first three-quarters of the twentieth century, though on a smaller scale. This occurred despite forces now acting against intercontinental emigration, such as the rise of short-term contract migration after the Second World War and the much-improved economic and social conditions in Europe during the Long Boom. Australia continued to take the bulk of its immigrants from Britain in the 1950s and 1960s, but, as discussed in the next two chapters, widened the net to include a greater proportion from continental Europe.

Asian emigration in the 1950s and 1960s was greatly curtailed by war and political changes in China, India, Pakistan, Sri Lanka, Korea, Indo-China, Malaysia and Indonesia. Some emigration from the Indian sub-continent occurred to South-East Asia and from Taiwan to Hong Kong, but most potential emigrants sought new destinations in Europe, though more would have gone to Australia had it not been for the White Australia Policy. Compared to Europe, emigration from Asia was not large. Britain, now experiencing conditions of full employment, was the main destination for Asian workers, as well as for migrants from the West Indies and West Africa. Like many migrants, these workers took the lowest paid and least desirable jobs in Britain and formed the basis for the later development of Britain as a multiracial society.

## International monetary system

The international economy was reformed during the later 1950s and 1960s. An international monetary system that bore some resemblance to the Bretton Woods agreements of 1944 emerged in the early 1960s and the General Agreement on Tariffs and Trade (GATT) started to work more effectively in the Dillon and Kennedy Rounds of **tariff**-lowering negotiations that had begun in 1962. Most currencies became fully convertible between 1958 and 1960, and many countries, including Australia, dropped the import quota regimes that had been operating since the war at around the same time. Tariffs on manufactured goods generally moved downward during the 1960s, though this was not an international trend Australia followed.

The international monetary system was based on the US dollar, which remained the only currency convertible to gold. Central banks undertook to maintain **fixed exchange rates** by intervening in **foreign exchange markets**. The IMF, which had had little role to play in the 1950s, became an important lender in the 1960s to countries that experienced balance of payments crises. The system thus rested on the adequacy of the **reserves** of the central banks and the strength of the US dollar. The dollar became a more accessible currency for international transactions in the 1960s as the US balance of payments moved into permanent deficit and US multinational firms invested funds abroad. This ended the dollar gap and provided greater international flows of money, facilitating and stimulating the growth of international trade in the 1960s.

However, although in some ways the US balance of payments deficit was beneficial, it was also inflationary and undermined confidence in the value of the dollar. Frequent adjustments to the international monetary system were found necessary during the 1960s to counter this. The United States government attempted to rein in its balance of payments deficit by restricting the outflow of private capital. As a result, American multinationals raised more of their capital outside of the United States and did not repatriate so much of their profits. This practice led to large amounts of US dollars being retained in the European banking system and by the end of the decade this had given rise to a thriving Eurodollar market that was uncontrolled by any government (Roberts 1995, Chapter 6).

As the US balance of payments deficit increased and more and more dollars were held outside of the country, the United States' **gold reserves** ceased to be adequate cover. When America's balance of payments deficit blew out in 1971, the US administration was faced with two choices: either take measures to reduce the balance of payments deficit or take the dollar off the gold standard. President Nixon chose the latter option in August of that year, though he also imposed a 10 per cent import surcharge designed to reduce America's trade deficit. Attempts to restore fixed exchange rates failed as the US balance of payments continued in deficit. A balance of payments crisis in Britain in 1972 forced the Bank of England to abandon the fixed exchange rate and 'float the pound'. Early in 1973, the US government followed suit and the fixed exchange value of the dollar was ended. These events marked a rapid unravelling of the Bretton Woods system of fixed exchange rates as the basis of the international monetary system.

## Economic consequences of the Cold War

The reconstruction and expansion of the international economy during the quarter century following the end of the Second World War was both a response and a further stimulus to the Long Boom occurring in many Western economies. The international economy, however, was not a global one in this era – it was divided by ideology: the Soviet Union and its Eastern European allies formed a Soviet bloc that remained outside of the international economy. The People's Republic of China, formed in 1949 and an ally of the Soviet Union until the Sino–Soviet split in 1960, also played little or no part in the international economy. A number of smaller communist countries – Cuba, Vietnam, North Korea, Yugoslavia and Albania – also remained economically isolated. These countries missed out on the Long Boom. Their post-war circumstances (including alliance with the Soviet Union) made economic recovery from the war a more daunting task than in Western Europe, and their centrally planned economies proved excessively bureaucratic and inefficient. Industrialisation continued under a series of five-year plans in the Soviet Union and parts of Eastern Europe, but there was little economic progress in China. This division was important, but how these countries might have impacted on the international economy during the post-war period had they been more integrated is a hypothetical question impossible to answer.

What is clear, however, is that there were considerable economic costs associated with the Cold War between the United States and the Soviet Union and their respective allies. The war might have been a 'cold' one, but the expenditure involved in fighting it was still immense as both sides amassed huge arsenals of

nuclear and sub-nuclear weapons that were deployed worldwide. Cold War imperatives provided America's allies with some leverage in negotiations, for example,
over anti-American trade discrimination and the continuation of non-convertibility
of Western European currencies in the 1950s. Some of America's allies were able
to focus their defence expenditure on their colonial possessions outside of Europe
rather than on resisting the Soviet challenge within Europe. Others made material
contributions to the anti-Soviet North Atlantic Treaty Organization (NATO) that
were inconsiderable compared with the defence the organisation provided to them.

The threat of communism in Western Europe smoothed the path of Marshall
Aid through the United States Congress in 1947 and made the American government an enthusiastic supporter of economic integration in Western Europe, despite
the trade **protectionism** of the EEC. The division of Germany into two parts and
the crisis in Berlin in 1949 further cemented American economic support for the
revival of a strong West German economy. On the other hand, the Cold War
prevented the United States from adopting an isolationist position in the world
economy, as it had done after the First World War. Establishing the Bretton Woods
institutions and making them work, lowering tariffs under the GATT and encouraging flows of corporate capital and enterprise from the US to the rest of the world
were projects that were underpinned politically by the Cold War. Even when there
were reversals, as occurred when the US Congress refused to ratify the International Trade Organization, or when the IMF failed to act decisively in the 1950s,
or when the US was forced to impose curbs on private capital outflows in the late
1960s, the ideological struggle against communism kept America firmly in a world
economic leadership role.

The victory of communist forces in China changed American policy towards
Japan and South Korea, both of which were able to use American aid and defence
expenditure to their economic advantage in the 1950s and 1960s. Japanese firms
benefited from access to US markets, an artificially low yen, access to US manufacturing technology and from the dollars spent in Japan by the US defence
forces. Above all, the Cold War led the United States into the Vietnam War,
which had profound effects on the external balance of the United States. The US
balance of payments deficit was greeted with relief when it first appeared in 1958,
but 10 years later it was causing major concern among America's allies. By 1971
it had brought down the Bretton Woods monetary system. The deficit was not
only caused by heavy and increasing defence expenditure outside of the United
States and the enormous cost of fighting the war in Vietnam. Parts of US manufacturing industry proved to be uncompetitive against imports, especially from
Japan and West Germany, in the 1960s, which led to a deterioration in the American **trade balance** and to some US firms moving capital out of the United States
in search of lower labour costs elsewhere. Nevertheless, in 1971 the Nixon administration regarded devaluation of the dollar and ending of the gold standard as the
only viable alternative to curtailment of military operations in Vietnam. Thus the
international economy was revived and expanded in the Long Boom following
the end of the Second World War, but it was also divided and as such could not
be regarded as a completely successful follower of the first global economy of the
pre-1914 era.

**SUMMARY BOX**

The strong economic growth in Western Europe and Japan during the 1950s and 1960s were referred to as 'economic miracles'. Their growth performance was based on high levels of investment, new technology and rising labour productivity. The United States also experienced sustained economic growth. For most of the period, high growth was accompanied by conditions of full employment and low price inflation. Rising living standards were further underpinned by the spread of the Welfare State. World trade boomed, creating favourable conditions for primary producing countries like Australia, though manufactured goods represented the fastest growing sector of international trade. International investment was strong, based on the direct foreign investments of multinational corporations. Intercontinental emigration revived with Australia playing a major role as a recipient country. Australia's relative importance in this regard was greater than ever before. The international monetary system came into full operation from 1960 with fixed exchange rates based on the US dollar. The United States pursued a global leadership role for the first time in its history, driven in part by the imperatives of the Cold War.

# Suggested further reading

Aldcroft, D.H. 1993, *The European Economy 1914–1990*, Routledge, London.
Armstrong, P., Glyn, A. & Harrison, J. 1991, *Capitalism since 1945*, Blackwell, Oxford.
Block, F.L. 1977, *The Origins of International Economic Disorder: a Study of United States International Monetary Policy from World War II to the Present*, University of California Press, Berkeley.
Maddison, A. 1982, *Phases of Capitalist Development*, Oxford University Press, Oxford.
Millward, A.S. 1984, *The Reconstruction of Western Europe, 1945–1951*, Methuen, London.
Scammell, W.M. 1983, *The International Economy since 1945*, Macmillan, London.
Tsuru, S. 1993, *Japan's Capitalism: Creative Defeat and Beyond*, Cambridge University Press, Cambridge.
van Der Wee, H. 1986, *Prosperity and Upheaval: The World Economy 1945–1980*, Pelican, London.

# 8

# War and reconstruction in Australia, 1941–1959

**SUMMARY BOX**

In December 1941, the war waged by Japan in East Asia became a war in the Pacific between Japan and the United States. Australia, already deeply committed to the conflict between the European powers, immediately joined this war also, and gave it priority. The national government strengthened existing powers and assumed new ones, powers that were in some instances not abandoned in peacetime. Federation in 1901 created the institutional framework for a national economy. Each decade had filled in the framework a little more than before. The circumstances of the 1940s fulfilled that potential. The national government took complete control of **income tax**, gained the constitutional right to act in many areas previously reserved to the States, and established a **central bank** with wide regulatory responsibilities. National **fiscal and monetary management** became possible for the first time.

A federal Department of Post-War Reconstruction formed in 1942. Its existence represented a resolve to master economic conditions in peacetime. Its deliberations produced many of the policies and techniques to do so. **Full employment** became both an aim in itself, in a heartfelt reaction against the miseries of **depression**, and the key to fully employing all other resources, in accord with the Keynesian economic assumptions that reaction to the depression had turned into orthodoxy. A federal Department of Immigration existed for the first time in 1945. A revived and vastly enhanced program of immigration became central to a moderate level of labour planning. Activities like housing and vehicle-building that employed many people, and that had strong linkages through their inputs or their outputs with other industries, became central to a kind of industry policy. The federal government expanded its patronage of applied research and began its involvement in both technical and university education. By the end of the 1940s, when European countries were still trying to repair the destruction of war, and **unemployment** in the United States was rising again towards 10 per cent, Australia seemed to be about the most successful economy in the world.

International conditions suited Australia after 1945. Some competitors, exporting rural goods, had been ravaged by war, or had chosen the losing side. Australia's farming and grazing capacity had not been damaged, and wartime contracts had filled the farmers' and graziers' bank accounts. As the industrialised countries' markets revived, a productive and solvent Australia was in an excellent position to supply them. The agreed division of the capitalist world into two separate **currency zones** (one using the US dollar as its international unit and the other the pound sterling) placed Australia in the smaller and weaker sterling pool. This prolonged its privileged position within Britain's trading bloc and gave it access to the substantial US dollar earnings of Britain's subservient colonial empire.

The dual currency regime was one response to the need to regulate affairs, globally and within nations, in the lengthy transition from war to peace. In the 1950s, Australia had to ration sterling as well as US dollars. Explicit public decisions had to be made about which imports could be afforded and in what quantities. The discipline of currency and **import controls** helped, in some ways, to sustain the program of post-war reconstruction through the 1950s, despite the election in December 1949 (and the regular re-election) of a government that distrusted economic planning.

## Full mobilisation

Australia cut off all trade with Japan in July 1941, several months before a state of war existed between the two countries. Trade diversion in 1936 and the embargo on the export of iron ore in 1938 had reversed the swift growth in business between Australia and Japan that had been such a hopeful sign in the first half of the 1930s. By December 1941, when Pearl Harbor was bombed, the shock to the economy of cancelled markets and unobtainable imports had been absorbed already by stages.

In compensation, the United States became an ally-at-arms. In 1941, while it was still neutral, the United States government had made available to the Australian government $US9 million worth of planes and trucks under the Lend-Lease scheme. By the middle of 1942, Lend-Lease transfers reached a monthly average of $US26 million. The massive battles in the South Pacific created an urgent need, met through Lend-Lease, for heavy armaments, ammunition, machine tools, tin plate, petroleum, textiles, agricultural machinery for producing food and a range of other supplies, as well as more planes and trucks. Because US troops were stationed in Australia – more than 100 000 at any one time during 1943 – 'reciprocal aid' from Australia to the US war effort took the form of food, clothing, light arms, military bases and housing, internal transport and a multiplicity of other goods and services.

The battles in 1944 and 1945 were fought further and further offshore; reciprocal aid narrowed in scope, with food the main requirement. It has been estimated that Lend-Lease added about 7 per cent to the goods and services available in Australia, and reciprocal aid used 5 per cent of the goods and services produced there. When the personal spending of the troops is taken into account, it is evident that the United States military alliance gave the Australian economy a powerful boost, with little or no strain on the **balance of payments**. At the end, there may have been a surplus of US dollars in Australia (Butlin & Schedvin 1977, pp. 139, 458–72, 605–12 and Chapter 5).

Sterling **reserves** definitely strengthened in the second half of the war. Expenditure on the opposite side of the world dwindled as the Australian armed forces were recalled to the Pacific. The supply of merchandise under contract to Britain, plus the market opened east of the Suez Canal by the war needs of Britain, India and New Zealand, built up the country's reserves of sterling. Fears that Britain might prevent an outflow of its allies' sterling reserves from the Bank of England once the war was

**Table 8.1**   Growth and unemployment in Australia, 1940–41 to 1959–60

| Year ended 30 June | Real economic growth rate (% change from previous year) | Unemployment rate (number of persons unemployed as a % of civilian workforce) |
|---|---|---|
| 1941 | 7.5 | 5.3 |
| 1942 | 14.7 | 2.3 |
| 1943 | 8.7 | 1.2 |
| 1944 | −2.1 | 1.3 |
| 1945 | −5.8 | 1.5 |
| 1946 | −4.1 | 2.5 |
| 1947 | −3.0 | 3.0 |
| 1948 | 8.1 | 2.0 |
| 1949 | 4.9 | 1.5 |
| 1950 | 8.5 | 1.7 |
| 1951 | 7.2 | 1.1 |
| 1952 | 1.4 | 1.3 |
| 1953 | −0.8 | 2.9 |
| 1954 | 6.3 | 2.0 |
| 1955 | 6.0 | 1.4 |
| 1956 | 5.0 | 1.5 |
| 1957 | 1.9 | 2.1 |
| 1958 | 2.1 | 2.6 |
| 1959 | 7.4 | 2.0 |
| 1960 | 5.4 | 2.4 |

Sources: Based on Barnard, Butlin & Pincus 1977, p. 50; RBA 1996, pp. 92, 117; Butlin 1977, pp. 79, 85.

**Table 8.2**   Australia's balance of payments, 1940–41 to 1959–60 (£ million)

| Year ended 30 June | Exports | Imports | Trade balance | Balance of income account | Balance of services and transfers | Current account balance |
|---|---|---|---|---|---|---|
| 1941 | 160.7 | 102.1 | 58.6 | –42.1 | –52.8 | –36.3 |
| 1942 | 147.6 | 105.1 | 42.5 | –41.2 | –32.9 | –32.3 |
| 1943 | 126.6 | 70.6 | 56.0 | –42.3 | –31.0 | –17.3 |
| 1944 | 143.3 | 69.1 | 74.2 | –44.1 | 63.7 | 93.8 |
| 1945 | 143.4 | 82.9 | 60.5 | –39.3 | 45.7 | 66.9 |
| 1946 | 156.8 | 110.2 | 46.6 | –39.0 | 37.4 | 45.0 |
| 1947 | 273.9 | 208.2 | 65.7 | –40.9 | –72.7 | –47.9 |
| 1948 | 406.0 | 337.8 | 68.2 | –42.2 | –22.4 | 3.6 |
| 1949 | 531.6 | 415.1 | 116.5 | –39.6 | –48.9 | 28.0 |
| 1950 | 592.0 | 524.0 | 68.0 | –51.0 | –52.5 | –35.5 |
| 1951 | 974.0 | 720.5 | 253.5 | –60.5 | –68.5 | 124.5 |
| 1952 | 663.0 | 1 016.5 | –353.5 | –63.0 | –127.5 | –54.4 |
| 1953 | 845.0 | 500.0 | 345.0 | –59.5 | –91.0 | 194.5 |
| 1954 | 811.0 | 661.5 | 149.5 | –79.5 | –72.0 | –2.0 |
| 1955 | 760.0 | 821.0 | –61.0 | –82.0 | –95.5 | –238.5 |
| 1956 | 768.5 | 798.5 | –30.0 | –94.5 | –99.5 | –224.0 |
| 1957 | 977.0 | 690.5 | 268.5 | –94.5 | –83.5 | 108.5 |
| 1958 | 805.0 | 760.5 | 44.5 | –93.5 | –105.5 | –154.5 |
| 1959 | 806.0 | 777.0 | 29.0 | –127.0 | –95.0 | –193.0 |
| 1960 | 930.0 | 907.0 | 23.0 | –146.0 | –111.0 | –234.0 |

Note: A minus sign indicates that the value of payments made by Australian residents to foreigners exceeded the value of payments made by foreigners to Australian residents.
Sources: Based on CBCS 1952; RBA 1996, pp. 1–13.

over, in order to bolster its own economy against a shortage of dollars, prompted the federal government to dip into those reserves and redeem some of the overseas debt before that could happen. The size of the public debt owed outside Australia in 1945 was only, in nominal terms, about eight-ninths of the amount owed in 1939, and was much lower in **real terms** when allowing for **inflation**. This was in contrast with the First World War, which had swollen the overseas debt.

Tables 8.1 and 8.2 show how Australia's external balances improved because of the Asia–Pacific war. Defence expenditure peaked in 1942–43, when commitment to both the European and Asia–Pacific theatres was intense and draining; an outstanding credit result appeared in the following year, 1943–44, because of foreign spending in Australia. When expressed through the nation's total balance of payments, the effect was equally dramatic. Services sold overseas clearly outweighed the purchases of foreign services between 1943 and 1946. **Interest** payments on public **foreign debt** dropped year by year. Throughout the 1940s, as throughout the 1930s, visible exports ran far ahead of visible imports in value.

**Table 8.3** Items on government account in Australia's balance of payments, 1938–39 to 1948–49 (£ million)

| Year ended 30 June | Credits | | | | Debits | | | |
|---|---|---|---|---|---|---|---|---|
| | Payments received from other governments | Expenditure of allied forces in Australia | Other credits | Total credits | Defence expenditure overseas | Other debits | Total debits | Balance on government account |
| 1939 | — | — | 0.6 | 0.6 | 4.0 | 1.0 | 5.0 | -4.4 |
| 1940 | — | — | 0.6 | 0.6 | 12.0 | 1.0 | 13.0 | -12.4 |
| 1941 | 10.9 | — | 0.6 | 11.5 | 48.1 | 0.8 | 48.9 | -37.4 |
| 1942 | 33.8 | 6.5 | 0.5 | 40.8 | 55.1 | 0.9 | 56.0 | -15.2 |
| 1943 | 27.1 | 41.0 | 0.6 | 68.7 | 85.7 | 0.8 | 86.5 | -17.8 |
| 1944 | 56.5 | 76.0 | 0.8 | 133.6 | 58.9 | 1.0 | 59.9 | 73.7 |
| 1945 | 71.7 | 27.0 | 0.9 | 99.6 | 43.7 | 1.1 | 44.8 | 54.8 |
| 1946 | 57.7 | 38.4 | 1.0 | 97.1 | 36.5 | 1.8 | 38.3 | 58.8 |
| 1947 | 20.7 | 6.5 | 1.2 | 28.4 | 34.5 | 4.9 | 39.4 | -11.0 |
| 1948 | 20.3 | — | 1.8 | 22.1 | 9.0 | 7.1 | 16.1 | 6.0 |
| 1949 | 3.3 | — | 1.7 | 5.0 | 6.3 | 10.5 | 16.8 | -11.8 |

Source: Based on CBCS 1952.

Australia was in a much stronger international position in 1945 than it had been in 1939, or at the end of the First World War (CBCS 1952, pp. 51–63; Butlin & Schedvin 1977, pp. 600–1).

The economy was energised further by the fact that, from 1942 onwards, Australia produced the food, clothing, light arms, transport and recreation used by its own fighting forces, to a degree impossible between 1914 and 1918, or in 1940 and 1941, when troops were in Europe and the Middle East. By late 1941, 460 000 men had enlisted. By 1945, almost 1 000 000 men (and about 50 000 women) out of a population of just over 7 000 000 had worn a uniform at some time. This created an enormous **demand** for military goods. Civilian unemployment was greater in the First World War than it had been beforehand, and still stood above 5 per cent in 1941. Unemployment virtually disappeared during the Asia–Pacific phase of the Second World War (Keating 1973, pp. 277–378; *Year Book of the Commonwealth of Australia*, no. 36, 1944–45, pp. 1034–5; see Table 8.3).

## Trends in employment

There was, indeed, a **labour** shortage. So many able-bodied men left farms, factories and offices to join the armed forces. The solution was to fill the vacancies with women. About 570 000 women had earned wages in 1938–39. Many of these shifted into 'essential' (war-related) jobs from 'non-essential' jobs. About 780 000 women (including those in uniform) earned wages in 1943–44, before numbers dropped again. Women did work previously defined as a male preserve. The gender definition of particular tasks was blurred during the labour shortage. Partly to prevent a permanent abandonment of the line separating male from female jobs, and partly to prevent the urgent demand for labour influencing the Arbitration Court to rule in favour of equal pay for men and women, a Women's Employment Board was set up in 1942. It defined wages and conditions for the duration of the emergency. Whereas the female basic wage had been 54 per cent of the male,

**SUMMARY BOX**

As full employment was achieved, with a higher proportion of the population participating in paid work, the public payroll soared and the community's purchasing power grew greatly. How was the war to be paid for? How was inflation to be curbed, or shortage of strategic materials to be averted, as citizens exercised their purchasing power in competition with the vastly increased spending in Australia of the Australian and allied governments? Price control, imposed in 1939, operated fairly well when demand and supply were steady. But as demand rose and Japanese naval action cut the availability of imports, the result would have been bottlenecks, a black market and the inflation of prices. The solution was to ration **consumer and producer goods**, to ration **credit**, and to divert private **savings** into the public sector.

under the Board, women in some essential occupations received 90 per cent. Employers in less essential industries often found they had to raise women's wages to 75 per cent to keep their workforce. Although the wage differential preserved the two-tier or segmented labour market, and held down costs for the government and employers generally, the margin between men's and women's incomes narrowed, more women (still a minority) earned **incomes** than before, and the incomes themselves were larger than before (Darian-Smith 1996, pp. 61–7).

## Rationing and its effects on the economy

A Rationing Commission, set up in May 1942, issued books of coupons that citizens had to present to shopkeepers before they could buy within their annual limit of clothing, footwear, tea, sugar, butter and meat. Quotas of the latter three items were promised under agreements made with the British government; rationing ensured that the quotas were met and that the pressure of consumer demand did not inflate the price to the Australian and British governments. Limits were placed on the quantity of materials allowed to manufacturers (for example, steel to car-makers) and in the range of styles and sizes of products (for example, clothing), so reining in consumer choice and freeing labour and materials for war-related purposes.

The rationing of credit bestowed full central banking status on the Commonwealth Bank. Regulations gazetted in November 1941 required the private banks to make heavy deposits in the Commonwealth Bank – statutory reserves that were increased over time. This reduced the amount that the private banks could lend, and made the reserves available for public purposes. Under the exchange provisions laid down at the outbreak of war, the Commonwealth Bank already supervised international capital flows. Now it managed domestic flows as well (Butlin & Schedvin 1977, Chapter 11 and pp. 310–14, 570–98; Schedvin 1992, Chapters 2, 3).

This bundle of regulations held together because of the way the federal government captured the community's savings through bond issues and taxation. The depression had set the pattern of public borrowing from within Australia. Between September 1939 and the middle of 1941, £78.5 million had been raised for defence and £36 million for civil matters. Then the magnitude and composition of borrowing changed. Two flotations, open between October 1941 and March 1942, brought in £82.5 million for defence and £66 million to convert old loans due for repayment. Before the war ended, a further £801 million was borrowed for military purposes and £118 million for non-military (*Yearbook*, no. 36, 1944–45, pp. 691–701). It soaked up much of the greatly increased liquidity of the fully employed economy and transferred the funds to publicly approved ends, which averted inflation at the same time as it employed people and resources even more securely. Banks, businesses and affluent Australians now became substantial **creditors** of the federal government. For repayment of interest and principal on the War Bonds they would insist on (or at the very least, accept) the continuance into peacetime of a strong national government with a large tax base.

This tax base was also formalised in the Asia–Pacific phase of the war. In 1938–39, Canberra collected only about 8 per cent of **GDP** as revenue. In 1944–45, it collected about 24 per cent. Its traditional **tariffs** were inadequate once trade dwindled and import controls remained. Restraints on domestic production and consumption made it impossible to expand excise and sales taxes. But incomes were rising, and a higher proportion of the population earned income. The States had pioneered income tax. Although the Commonwealth raised an income tax for the First World War in addition to state levies, and had not abandoned the practice in peacetime, even in 1941 the States raised more by income tax than the Commonwealth did. In the middle of 1942, federal parliament passed a law for a national uniform income tax that in practice would have made it impossible (and unpatriotic) for the States to stay in the field while the war lasted. The States were promised grants to make up lost revenue. Responsibility for widows' pensions, unemployment relief and some lesser charges would devolve to the Commonwealth under a National Welfare Fund. The single heightened income tax and the transfer of civilian responsibilities from the regions to the centre were carried over into peacetime, as the financial class and the working class alike preferred a well-funded administration to set uniform standards (Butlin & Schedvin 1977, pp. 331–8, 570–605; Haig-Muir & Hay 1996).

> **SUMMARY BOX**
>
> During the second phase of the war, the Commonwealth directly mobilised about 45 per cent of GDP, maintaining economic stability and dynamism at home and contributing to victory abroad. It showed that economic management was possible, even if under (and despite) desperate conditions. A Department of Post-War Reconstruction was established in December 1942, the portfolio taken by the Treasurer, J.B. Chifley; its administrative head was the Director of Rationing, Dr H.C. Coombs. (Chifley as prime minister and Coombs as head of the central bank remained at the heart of the policy after 1945.) Australians, indeed people all over the globe, were determined that the coming peace should not be as haphazard and unsuccessful as the previous period of peace had been.

# Reconstruction

## The Australian experience

There had never been such full employment in Australia in the twentieth century. The majority of Australian families had experienced unemployment and under-employment at some stage during the depression that had lasted from the late 1920s to the beginning of the 1940s. The electorate insisted that full employment be locked into place in peacetime.

The government issued a White Paper on full employment in the middle of 1945. The sixth paragraph of the document read:

To the worker, it means steady employment, the opportunity to change his employment if he wishes and a secure prospect unmarred by the fear of idleness and the dole. To the business or professional man, the manufacturer, the shopkeeper, it means an expanding scope for his enterprise, free from the fear of periodic **slumps** in spending. To the primary producer it means an expanding home market and – taking a world-wide view – better and more stable export markets. To the people as a whole it means a better opportunity to obtain all the goods and services which their labour, working with necessary knowledge and equipment, is capable of producing …[1]

Implicit in this recital of benefits was a growth model driven by consumer demand, whose predictability and amplitude justified optimistic investment and the full employment of all resources, not only labour, whose full employment justified further **investment**, and so on (Coombs 1971; Whitwell 1986, Chapters 3, 4; Smyth 1994). The problem was how to move from an economy mobilised for warfare and destruction to one programmed for self-sustaining growth. The immediate transition required finesse in dismantling emergency conditions. For the longer term, solutions were sought in trade policy, banking policy, industry policy, population and labour policy, and the renovation of **infrastructure**.

When the war ended, hundreds of thousands of uniformed men and women became redundant to the workforce. Their demobilisation alone could have caused massive unemployment. Some enlisted men had been sent back early from the front to help grow food on short-handed farms; some were kept active into 1946 in captured territories, or in closing bases and disposing of materials. It would have been futile to have resorted to a Soldier Settlement Scheme, as happened in the 1920s, to soak up part of the surplus. That scheme had done badly then, and farming in the 1940s was less labour intensive. Learning from experience, fewer than 9000 **land** titles were passed across to veterans, the veterans themselves chosen for their farming experience, the properties carefully surveyed and endowed with capital and infrastructure. The new farms were to be justified by their **productivity**, rather than as rewards for heroes or as receptacles for the idle energies of returning men. Some space in the workforce could be made by sacking women or by not hiring them, particularly in essential industries. As fewer local and allied troops operated from bases in Australia towards the war's end, there had been a reduction in ancillary activities.

Vacancies for women declined from their peak in 1943–44. Nevertheless, the number of women earning wages at the lowest point of female employment, in 1946–47, stood 10 per cent higher than the number earning wages in 1938–39 (Keating 1973, p. 378). Many of the women returned to what had during wartime been non-essential jobs, which showed that finding work for veterans must be compatible with revival of the conventional economy.

It would take time, however, to return to conventional production. The domestic and international markets for military goods and services disappeared overnight. It would take time to re-tool plants after turning out army trucks or uniforms or soldiers' rations. Most of the owners of production possessed the means. War-time contracts had given them, and their workforce, solid and predictable incomes, which translated into significant savings. The **money supply** was 120 per cent greater at the end of the war than at its beginning (Coombs 1971, p. 11). These were excellent conditions for long-term investment and subsequent consumer spending, but the current shortage of investment and consumer goods on which the savings could be spent created conditions whereby the money reserves might disappear quickly into purchases at sky-high prices. Once the savings drained away, the inflation would be followed by mass unemployment. Rationing and price controls, therefore, carried over into peacetime to rein in spending, and investment controls remained to avert speculative investment.

## International conditions

The external environment was uncertain as well. Would the world as a whole suffer accelerating inflation followed by mass unemployment? There were tendencies that way, but confidence did return to the markets of industrialised countries, where Australia traditionally sold its products, as those countries themselves embarked on 'reconstruction'. Australia's rural exports had been cushioned in wartime by inter-governmental agreements. It was in the interests of both Australia and Britain that their wind-down be gradual and orderly, as they had been after the First World War. The Ottawa Agreement of 1932 was in abeyance during the conflict, but revived afterwards. Britain's farmers, however, were becoming more efficient as a result of public **subsidies**; at the beginning of the 1930s half of Britain's food supplies had been imported, but by the 1950s the proportion had dropped to one-third. Observing this trend, Australian authorities worked hard to reconstruct the international economy in Australia's favour. As early as 1943, Australia endorsed the creation of a Food and Agricultural Organisation (FAO), established two years later under the United Nations, in the expectation that it would open and police markets for food. The Australian Wheat Board, which formed in September 1939 to handle wartime marketing, administered from 1948 a stabilisation scheme that dovetailed with the International Wheat Agreement, signed by 41 nations in 1949 and renewed every three years thereafter. The stabilisation scheme bought all the wheat, set the domestic price, guaranteed the growers a minimum return from exports, took a proportion of the surplus earnings if the achieved export price exceeded the guarantee, and held the proceeds for compensating growers whenever the achieved price fell below the guarantee – the international agreement set quotas at fixed prices for both selling and buying countries. Marketing schemes continued for butter, cheese and fruit, although their weight in the total basket of exports was less after than before the war. Sugar strengthened in significance, helped by a British Commonwealth Sugar Agreement in 1951 and an International Sugar Agreement signed in 1953 (Pinkstone 1992, pp. 137–57; Whitwell & Sydenham 1991, pp. 61–4, 133–64).

The Australian delegation at the founding conference of the United Nations struggled to write middle-power and small-power influence, against great-power dominance, into the UN Charter. Australia wanted the Bretton Woods Conference in 1944 to endorse 'full employment' as a fundamental objective, for the sustenance of a global consumer market; the leading nations refused, on the grounds that it would circumscribe their domestic policy options. Ironically, for similar reasons, the Australian government distrusted the IMF and the World Bank that came out of Bretton Woods, fearing that the great powers, having explicit voting control in both institutions, might use them to weaken the sovereignty of lesser countries over currency and capital flows. The Liberal and Country Parties, in opposition, distrusted the International Trade Organization, which did not come into being, and its weaker replacement, the General Agreement of Tariffs and Trade (GATT); manufacturers feared interference with tariffs and rural producers feared challenges to export subsidies and stabilisation schemes. It was recognised, however, that Australia could not boycott bodies to which the major economies belonged. When Australia joined GATT it exploited a loophole that allowed it to exclude Japan from any concessions made to other trading partners, thus continuing the discrimination practised against Japan from 1936 onwards (Crawford 1968, pp. 30–93).

Australia was not alone in resisting the deregulatory implications of GATT. The United States refused to dismantle the tariffs protecting its primary producers. It made it difficult – in most instances – impossible to export Australian wheat, meat, dairy products, sugar, fruits and metals to the United States. High tariffs limited the entry of wool. For one year, 1946–47, about three-tenths of the Australian clip was exported to the United States, the bilateral balance of trade being in Australia's favour for the first occasion in peacetime. Wool sales then fell away again, as did Australia's ability to claim scarce US dollars with which to buy the advanced technology of North America (Crawford 1968, pp. 30–9, 66–9, 389–411; Pinkstone 1992, pp. 151, 157).

## New opportunities

In compensation, the woollen mills of Western Europe were humming again, dependent on Australia and New Zealand for their fleece. The world price of wool by 1947–48 was two and a half times the price stated in the wartime contracts, and three times that of 1939–40 (see Figure 7.1). Australia's receipts for all exports at the end of the 1940s were four times as large as at the end of the 1930s. The increase can be explained in part by inflation across the entire decade. Greater volumes of some commodities were grown and sold; the quantity of wheat and flour exported, for example, was one-third larger at the end than at the beginning of the 1940s. High export receipts also reflected a fortunate shift in the **terms of trade**; that is to say, there was an improvement of 57 per cent between the beginning and the end of the 1940s in the prices of the primary goods Australia exported relative to the prices of Australia's imports (see Figure 8.1).[2]

These altered conditions provided substantial opportunities to import. Australian industries needed machinery (**capital goods**) and materials or components (**producer goods**) of a standard and cheapness that an economy like Australia could not afford to make, its domestic market being too small, and potential affluent foreign markets being too far away to tempt Australian investors into competing with large-scale and established suppliers in Europe and North America. The natural shortage of US dollars, and the additional constraint on US dollars imposed by membership of the sterling currency bloc, forced importers to

**Figure 8.1**    Net immigration to Australia, 1946–1976

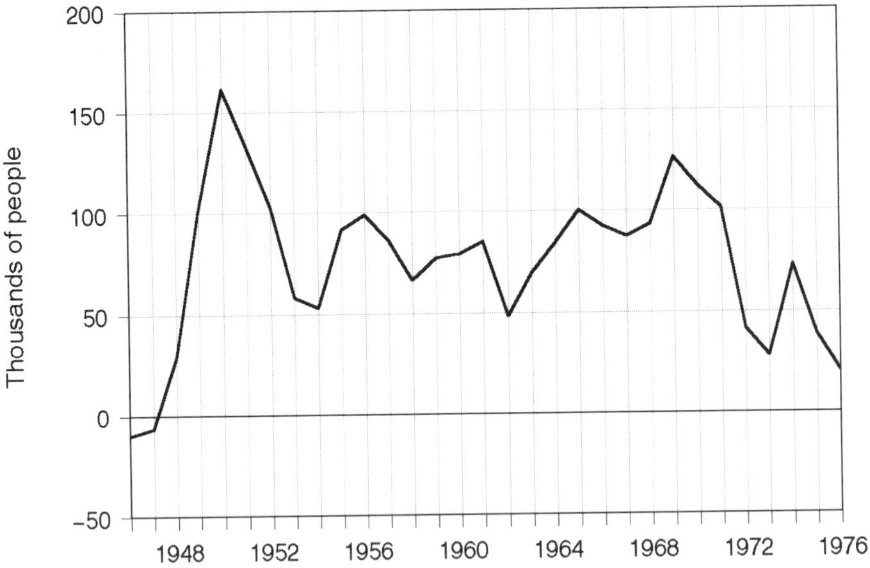

Source: Based on Bureau of Immigration 1984–1995, no. 13.

rely on British manufacturers for cars and car parts, machines and finished metals, electric motors and appliances, chemicals and pharmaceuticals. In some cases, these were second-best. Australia's balance of merchandise trade with Britain, as with the world as a whole, nevertheless remained in surplus until the end of the decade. The **merchandise surplus** was set against the perennial deficit on **invisible trade** (payments for services) and payments of dividends and interest overseas.

Uncertainty about the future, and caution about the balance of payments, held the wartime comprehensive import controls in place until the beginning of 1947. Thereafter goods from the Dollar currency bloc still could enter only with an official licence. Discipline was maintained through exchange controls. These matched, at the national border, the domestic investment controls that deterred speculative production. The powers under which the Commonwealth Bank regulated affairs during the war were entrenched in the *Commonwealth Bank Act 1945*, which created a permanent central bank. The Act enjoined the private banks to lodge monthly balance sheets with the central bank, so that the nation's monetary circumstances were transparent, and to surrender a stated though variable proportion of their assets (say 20 per cent) into Special Accounts (known from 1959 as Statutory Reserve Deposits) with the central bank. Credit was controlled through varying the size of the Special Accounts, which acted as a float within the central bank for adjusting external as well as internal affairs. The Commonwealth Bank's new charter required the board to consult the government; where disagreements occurred, the government's views must prevail.

The Bank's charter laid down three objectives:

a    the stability of the currency of Australia
b    the maintenance of full employment in Australia
c    the economic prosperity and welfare of Australia (Schedvin 1992, p. 63).

## SUMMARY BOX

This could be summarised as 'full employment without inflation'. The charter did not set up an autonomous Reserve Bank; that would occur in 1959. The regulatory functions were added to the Bank's everyday functions of receiving deposits and making loans. The government directed that priority in making loans be given to housing finance, and to municipalities and public utilities. The second set of clients would put in the electricity, roads, water, sewerage and other services for the builders and prospective home-owners, who were the first set of clients. The package spelled 'suburbanisation' (Schedvin 1992, chapters 3, 4).

Housing was singled out because demand, or at least need, had far outrun supply since the late 1920s. A publicly owned lender, without the pressure to maximise profit, could take the inflationary sting out of the high demand for housing by making funds plentiful and cheap. A War Service Homes Scheme helped 300 000 veterans buy houses on easy terms. A Commonwealth–State Housing Agreement made grants to the States to build low-rental dwellings for poorer people, 100 000 of them in the first 10 years. Residential construction was labour-intensive and used local materials that were themselves usually labour-intensive to produce. A proliferation of bungalows, occupied by nuclear families, created demand for furnishings, appliances and many other items manufactured in Australia. In itself, and with all of its spin-offs, the housing industry was an excellent generator of jobs (Stretton 1974).

The suburban sprawl relied heavily on trucks, motor buses and private cars to function properly. It was no accident that the vehicle industry was another object of reconstruction. The companies that assembled vehicles in Australia, Ford and General Motors, were both American. It was evident well before 1945 that US dollars would be scarce and that the operations of American companies would be cramped if they could not import components. As it turned out, easy access to sterling meant that, by 1949, 80 per cent of the cars sold in Australia were either totally or partially made in Britain, although it was widely assumed that British automobile technology was inferior to American and that its smaller vehicles were less well suited to Australian conditions. To secure best practice and to conserve **foreign exchange**, it was decided that the Americans should be encouraged to make the vehicles completely, or almost completely, in Australia. This could have broader advantages. It would give business to iron and steel-making, general engineering, rubber, plastic, electrical and other industries; it would reinforce and diversify secondary industry as a whole and it would consolidate engineering culture in Australia. The government in 1944 invited four American companies to tender for the right to make all-Australian cars and utilities. The successful bidder would receive **import licences** for plant and the minor components unavailable locally, it would not need to pay customs or sales taxes on inputs, and it would gain cheap government-backed loans. General Motors won the tender. The first Holden, GM's Australian badge, came off the line in 1948. By the mid-1950s, half the cars sold in Australia were Holdens (Butlin & Schedvin 1977, pp. 752–62; Maxcy, 1963, pp. 504–7; Bell 1993, pp. 15–30).

State governments had been instruments of **economic development** from the very start. Under post-war reconstruction, the nation shared responsibility for devising necessary infrastructure. The most eye-catching project was the Snowy Mountains Scheme; after years of paralysing drought, the decision was made to divert water from the Snowy River inland through the Great Dividing Range for electricity and irrigation in three states. Aviation and airports had always been regulated nationally; two airlines came into public ownership: Trans Australia Airlines for internal flights and Qantas for international. The Commonwealth Scientific and Industrial Research Organisation (CSIRO) was a more ramified and well-endowed extension of the pre-war Council on Scientific and Industrial Research (CSIR), drawing on a long Australian tradition of State-sponsored agricultural and geological experiments.

Education, too, is part of an economy's infrastructure. It had previously been a state preserve, but the Constitutional amendment passed in 1946 (section 51 (xxiiiA)) that permitted nation-wide pensions, welfare and health-care included the phrase 'benefits to students', which opened the way to Commonwealth university scholarships and to federal grants for universities and schools. Federal funds sent well over 100 000 veterans through technical colleges and 38 000 through university. Because there had been only 12 000 students enrolled in Australian universities in 1938, and fewer during the war, this required federal grants for the extra staff and facilities needed to teach the veterans. The Australian National University was established in Canberra to promote graduate training and research in the natural sciences. The New South Wales University of Technology (later named the University of New South Wales) opened towards the end of the 1940s to turn out a higher breed of researchers and technicians for the industrial State of New South Wales and for a continually modernising Australia.

## SUMMARY BOX

Industrial societies undergo frequent restructuring. The calamities of the Great Depression and the Second World War interrupted normal business so badly, and caused so much suffering, that citizens everywhere, Australia included, demanded that the process of reconstruction be more self-conscious, explicit and comprehensive than ever before.

# Immigration

**SUMMARY BOX**

As part of the program of reconstruction, the federal government turned to a traditional method of stimulating and moulding the economy – assisted immigration. Australian experience associated **economic growth** with population growth, which by widening the domestic market would encourage investors to commit their capital to production in Australia, and by supplying extra labour would make that expanded production possible.

There was a lot of catching up to do after 1945. The birthrate had dropped during the depression and the war and net immigration was static. Population had grown each year by less than 1 per cent between 1930 and 1945. In the next 15 years it grew by more than 2.3 per cent per year; the surplus of births over deaths accounted for three-fifths of the increase, and the surplus of arrivals over departures for the rest. In raw terms, 6.5 million people lived in Australia in 1930, 7.4 million in 1945 and 10.4 million in 1960. As indicated by Figure 8.2, net migration exceeded 100 000 only in 1949, 1950 and 1951, but annual arrivals numbered between 230 000 and 250 000 throughout the 1950s (except for cutbacks in 1953 and 1954). Arrivals were offset by an increase each year in the number of long-term

**Figure 8.2**　Australia's terms of trade, 1939–1960

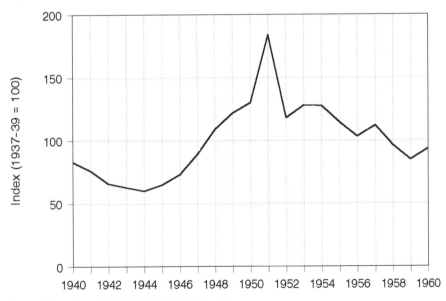

Sources: Based on CBCS 1952; RBA 1986, p. 21.

departures, some of them Australian-born, seeking overseas experience (a reflection of Australia's prosperity and international orientation), some of them immigrants returning home (a reflection of reviving prosperity in their homelands)
(Jupp 1991, Chapters 5, 6; Collins 1988).

In the 1920s, the Commonwealth had consulted the States about their needs,
and consequently had given priority to rural workers and domestic servants,
anachronistic choices even then. After 1945, the Commonwealth recruited for the
cities, for factories and for infrastructure. A United Kingdom Assisted Passage
Scheme began in 1947, ending in 1982. Adults paid a token £10 sterling each for
the five-week voyage while their children travelled free (until February 1955, British
ex-servicemen and their wives migrated free of charge). Family migration typified
the scheme, as it had in previous generations. Skilled tradesmen were preferred.

Britain was targeted out of habit and sheer ethnic prejudice, but also because
the skills of its citizens were highly regarded in Australia, which shared a common
language and customs. The policy-makers, however, were uncertain whether the
supply of immigrants from Britain would be sufficient. They were right. About
one-third of the people arriving between 1945 and 1960 were British. An agreement signed in 1948 with Malta, also a member of the British Commonwealth of
Nations, widened the supply a little. This arrangement split the subsidy to the
migrants between the sending and the receiving governments, a pattern set for
migration treaties signed with other European countries in the 1950s.

An immediate source of settlers was found in the refugee camps set up for
persons displaced by the Nazi conquests in central and eastern Europe, and by
subsequent Soviet conquests. The International Refugee Organisation oversaw the
transfer of 800 000 people from the camps to locations outside Europe, 182 000 of
whom (21 per cent) came to Australia. Australian officials ignored the refugees'
professional and trade qualifications, selecting for health and strength alone. The
refugees' immediate destiny was hard, unskilled labour, in the Snowy Mountains,
for example, or in the steelworks.

As the camps emptied by the beginning of the 1950s, new sources were
tapped. Unemployment was still a problem in Europe. Governments encouraged
emigration as a solution. Through the Inter-Governmental Committee for European Migration, Australia signed agreements with The Netherlands (February
1951), Italy (March 1951), West Germany (August 1952), Austria and Greece (both
in late 1952), committing both the home and the host countries to subsidise the
passages of the persons selected. It was a sign of Australian ethnic bias that almost
two-thirds of the migrants from northern Europe before 1960 received subsidy, but
less than a quarter of those from Italy and about one-third of Greek migrants were
so provided for. One migrant in six between 1945 and 1960 was Italian (second in
importance to the British intake), while The Netherlands, Poland, Germany and
Greece each contributed between 6 and 9 per cent of the total intake.

Professional associations and trade unions made sure that non-British qualifications were not accredited in Australia. Hampered already by having to work in a
language foreign to them, the non-British arrivals in the 1950s were in many cases,
like the refugees from the camps, rendered doubly unskilled by the obligations

incurred in moving. The subsidies often imposed a two-year contract to work in unattractive jobs in unattractive areas, areas where Australian-born workers would have asked high wages to compensate for uprooting their families and leaving their friends. As long as they could not move freely within the workforce, immigrants provided their labour at a discount to the economy. The cost of infrastructure dropped for taxpayers, and the cost of privately owned production dropped for employers. Non-British men were to be found particularly in manufacturing jobs where fluency in English was not a necessary vocational skill, and to a lesser extent in construction, transport and public works. Men from the United Kingdom spread throughout the workforce because they spoke English and had no bar placed on doing what they were qualified to do (Patmore 1991, pp. 199–207; Fox 1991, pp. 149–54, 160–2).

The constantly renewed pool of cheaper labour did not, however, stagnate into a land-locked reservoir. In many countries, what has been described as segmented male labour markets have existed, occupations and incomes being sharply differentiated on ethnic lines. This failed to happen in post-war Australia, at least while full employment lasted. Working Australians and their trade unions agreed to the immigration program as long as it did not weaken the hard-won system of universal wage-fixing (with the basic wage as a floor) and of industrial awards in general; as long, in other words, as it did not erode the wages and conditions of working men. It meant that a man's income, however briefly he had been in the country, however weak his bargaining position, could not fall below the public minimum. It lessened tensions and ethnic stereotyping, within the workforce and within society at large. It allowed every man to support a family with a little dignity, and freed his children to take advantage of universal public education mandated by law, placing both parent and child in Australia's conventional class-structure rather than in a permanent immigrant ghetto. And it meant that immigrant families bid in the same housing and consumer market as did most other residents of Australia, so sustaining the buoyant domestic economy that brought about full employment (Lever-Tracy & Quinlan 1988, Chapters 1, 2; Jordens 1995, pp. 114–36).

The mainstream labour market was sharply segmented, however, into male and female components. The labour shortage during the war had challenged the gendered distinctions, had strengthened women's resolve and capacity to bargain, and had demonstrated their value to employers. Once persistent peacetime full employment set in, the national Arbitration Court, in 1949, amended the female basic wage from 54 per cent to 75 per cent of the male rate. Higher pay drew more women out of wageless work in the home. The **participation rate** of women in paid labour at the beginning of the 1950s was 27.5 per cent and at the end of the decade, 30 per cent. In 1950, about one-third of working women were married; 42 per cent were married in 1960. Of these women, and of these married women, a disproportionate number were immigrants who augmented the savings of families that had just begun to establish themselves in a strange land. This sped up the integration of the immigrants into the economy and society. It also deepened purchasing power generally. And it did away with bottlenecks in producing for that deeper market (Patmore 1991, pp. 172–7; Fox 1991, pp. 144–54).

As Europe's prosperity returned, and the **European Common Market** offered work, not only to its own citizens, but also to the citizens of countries nearby, Australia had to hunt farther afield for population. By 1960, northern Europe (Britain excepted) could no longer be relied on; fewer Italians saw any point in leaving Europe and Australia's best recruiting ground had become south-eastern Europe (Greece and Yugoslavia). The traditional slogan 'populate or perish' carried with it the fear, reinforced by the Second World War, of invasion from Asia. For the White Australia Policy to survive, the authorities had argued in 1945, every corner of Australia must be filled with people from every corner of Europe. This paradoxically diluted the White Australia Policy, which for many Australians had really meant a British Australia Policy. The acceptance of English-speaking professionals from south Asia and South-East Asia was just around the corner. Some of these potential immigrants, indeed, were in Australia already as students. At the University of Sydney in 1960, for example, one-tenth of the student body came from Asia, the Pacific and Africa (Brawley 1995, Chapters 31–3, 38). In migration, as in other aspects, strong subterranean (but not yet surface) currents were taking Australia towards engagement with its Asian neighbourhood.

New South Wales, in 1955, was the first State to legislate that Aboriginal workers must receive pay equal with that of non-Aboriginal workmates, at about the same time as it conceded equal pay to women in the State's public service. The tension in policy-making between the segregation and the assimilation of Aboriginal Australians had as one of its aspects the separation of Aboriginal children from their parents and their placement in orphanages or in foster and adoptive homes. These are known now as 'the Stolen Generations'. Much Aboriginal labour has been done by families rather than by individuals. Once the children were stolen, the family work-unit began to disintegrate, as did the possibilities of inheriting traditional rights and obligations to the land (Fox 1991, pp. 154–8, 162–4; Goodall 1996, Wilson 1997).

### SUMMARY BOX

Although the basic wage and the system of industrial awards eased the entry of newcomers into Australia, they had not extinguished long-standing class and gender distinctions. Nor did they protect most Aborigines. The circumstances described at the end of Chapter 3 persisted throughout much of Australia in the 1950s. In Queensland above all, the law still laid down separate and pitifully low wages for most Aboriginal workers. Their wages were held in an official trust fund and only a fraction of the proceeds were doled out to those who had earned them. Aboriginal labour remained crucial to the cattle industry, as well as being important in seasonal farm work such as fruit-picking. Aborigines were involved disproportionately in producing Australia's **export income** and in putting food on Australian dinner tables. Here, too, they were usually outside the protection of industrial awards.

# Trade and investment in the 1950s

**SUMMARY BOX**

The most significant international Australian initiative in the 1950s was the signature in 1957 of the commercial agreement with Japan. Three years later, the 22-year-old embargo on the export of iron ore was lifted. Just as Japan's hunger for Australian ore had been the unstated reason for the embargo, so the resurgence of Japanese heavy industry offered the best hope for sale of the locked-up minerals. The strict division of the international economy between a dollar and a sterling bloc persisted through the decade; when currencies became fully convertible at the decade's end Australia was freed from the need to negotiate with Britain over access to foreign exchange.

The pattern of trade changed more slowly in the 1950s than it would in the next 10 years. At the end of the 1950s, wool still contributed over two-fifths of the value of exports, various kinds of food about one-third, and minerals and metals hovered about 6 per cent (see Figure 8.3). Britain remained the major destination, although its share of Australian exports dropped over the decade from about 37 per cent to about 28 per cent (see Table 8.4). Western Europe collectively took a steady one-fifth of Australia's exports; south and South-East Asia collectively, one-tenth (sometimes less); and the United States another one-tenth (sometimes less).[3]

The United States continued to be a difficult market. It bought one-fifth of the wool-clip in 1950–51, on the outbreak of the Korean War, stockpiling for uniforms, blankets and other military uses, after which its demand for wool waned dramatically. From 1951–52, the United States, rearming globally, took about half of Australia's then most valuable exported mineral, lead. Cargoes were fewer in and after 1958 – when the United States placed quotas on foreign supplies of lead to protect its own mining companies. Also in 1958, however, the bar against foreign beef imports to the United States disappeared; in 1958–59, Australia's receipts from exported meat rose by a half, a result explained by sustained American demand for hamburger beef (Pinkstone 1992, pp. 151, 157, 182; Crawford 1968, pp. 389–412).

Japan's recovery as a customer compensated for Britain's decline. By 1960 it had returned to the position of second-best market it had occupied a quarter century earlier. The commodities bought, wool and wheat, were the same. Wool-growers and wheat growers pressed their government to confirm this trend by treaty, in case Australia's discrimination against Japanese imports under GATT and discrimination against the entry of Japanese businessmen under the White Australia Policy should jeopardise this burgeoning relationship, as the trade diversion episode did in the 1930s. The Australian authorities had their own fears about

**Figure 8.3**   Commodity structure of Australia's exports, 1958–1960

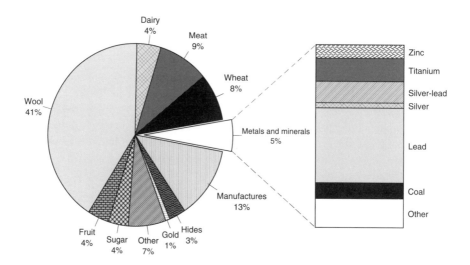

Source: Based on CBCS *Overseas Trade* 1959–60, pp. 517–25.

the future, as renewal of the Ottawa Agreement in the mid-1950s watered down British tariff preferences for Australian commodities, while the movement towards Western European union lessened Australian penetration of European markets and promised competition with Australian exports (in Britain particularly) from subsidised European farmers. The commercial agreement signed with Japan in 1957 was nevertheless a very grudging one on the Australian side. Each party had the right at any time to limit or prohibit imports that it considered might harm domestic producers. In practice, this right would only be invoked by Australia. There were no wool or wheat interests in Japan to be threatened by Australian consignments, but Australian manufacturers resented the textiles that comprised most of Japan's exports. The 1957 agreement worked smoothly, however; the treaty that replaced it in 1963 did not include the proviso for unilateral action (Tweedie 1994, pp. 149–69; Crawford 1968, pp. 357–88; Rix 1986).

The Japanese connection mattered greatly because the amount spent on imports from them lagged far behind the amount earned by exporting to them. The surplus in Australia's favour helped carry the deficit nearly always incurred with the United States. The last time the United States bought more than it sold in Australia was in the Korean War **boom** of 1950–51. The boom was, paradoxically, very disruptive. In Australia's case it was exaggerated by demand for one **commodity**, wool, whose price by March 1951 was five times higher than that of two years earlier. Wool accounted for two-thirds of export receipts for the year; its receipts made up an unprecedented 29 per cent of GDP. The windfall of foreign exchange led to a rush to import. Because the inflation of **primary product** prices flowed on directly and indirectly into the prices of processed goods, the imported goods of the following year, 1951–52, were expensive as well as numerous.

| Country | 1945–47 | 1948–50 | 1951–53 | 1954–56 | 1957–59 | 1960–62 | 1963–65 | 1966–68 |
|---|---|---|---|---|---|---|---|---|
| | | | | Imports | | | | |
| UK | 37.6 | 49.8 | 45.0 | 43.2 | 38.3 | 30.7 | 26.5 | 22.4 |
| EEC | 2.9 | 6.9 | 10.0 | 10.0 | 10.8 | 11.2 | 11.7 | 12.3 |
| Japan | 0.3 | 1.4 | 2.4 | 2.3 | 3.8 | 5.9 | 8.5 | 10.8 |
| China | 0.4 | 0.4 | 0.3 | 0.3 | 0.4 | 0.4 | 0.8 | 0.8 |
| South & South-East Asia | 9.6 | 12.6 | 12.3 | 12.1 | 11.6 | 9.6 | 7.7 | 7.0 |
| New Zealand | 1.6 | 0.7 | 0.8 | 1.2 | 1.6 | 1.6 | 1.7 | 1.9 |
| USA | 21.2 | 9.1 | 11.9 | 12.4 | 14.4 | 20.3 | 23.6 | 25.6 |
| Persian Gulf | 6.0 | 3.4 | 3.1 | 5.3 | 5.9 | 5.8 | 5.1 | 4.2 |
| All others | 20.4 | 15.7 | 14.2 | 13.2 | 13.2 | 14.5 | 14.4 | 15.0 |
| | | | | Exports | | | | |
| UK | 34.6 | 36.9 | 37.0 | 32.2 | 28.5 | 20.5 | 18.5 | 13.3 |
| EEC | 16.0 | 20.8 | 22.4 | 22.5 | 19.5 | 15.8 | 14.7 | 12.4 |
| Japan | 0.3 | 4.1 | 8.0 | 11.1 | 13.3 | 16.7 | 17.3 | 21.8 |
| China | 1.0 | 0.1 | 0.1 | 0.5 | 1.5 | 5.5 | 5.1 | 3.4 |
| South & South-East Asia | 15.3 | 8.7 | 8.8 | 10.4 | 8.6 | 9.4 | 9.6 | 12.8 |
| New Zealand | 3.8 | 2.8 | 4.2 | 5.1 | 6.2 | 6.0 | 5.8 | 5.2 |
| USA | 12.7 | 10.8 | 8.1 | 6.8 | 7.2 | 10.1 | 10.9 | 13.2 |
| All others | 16.3 | 15.8 | 11.4 | 11.0 | 15.2 | 16.0 | 18.1 | 17.9 |

European Economic Community: Belgium, France, West Germany, Italy, Luxembourg and The Netherlands.
South & South-East Asia: Brunei, Burma, Hong Kong, India, Indonesia, Cambodia, Laos, Malaysia, Pakistan, The Philippines, Singapore, Sri Lanka, Taiwan, Thailand and Vietnam.
Persian Gulf: Kuwait, Qatar, Saudi Arabia, Yemen, Iran and Iraq.
Source: Based on CBCS, *Overseas Trade Australia*, Bulletin nos 49 (1951–52), 51 (1953–54), 56 (1958–59), 61 (1963–64), 63 (1965–66), 67 (1969–70).

Domestically, consumer prices by the middle of 1952 were almost 40 per cent higher than they had been two years earlier. But primary product prices fell again, wool by two-thirds in a year, cutting Australia's export income for all commodities by one-third in 1951–52. The **visible trade** deficit for that year exceeded fourfold the visible trade surplus of the year before. The swollen size of the cargoes in both years employed extra shipping and incurred larger insurance premiums, causing record deficits on invisible trade. The **current account** deficit for 1951–52, consequently, was itself a record, at 15 per cent of GDP (RBA 1991, pp. 4–6, 28–9, 209–11, 287–9).

## Domestic concerns with the economy

The government responded belatedly to the balance of payments crisis, and to the problem of inflation. Some of the wool clip's foreign receipts were put into a stabilisation fund ready for dispersal whenever the market fell; it was too late to restrict the explosion of credit that had made importing so easy. There were fewer assisted passages for migrants in 1952–53, dampening consumer demand. The private banks were ordered to increase their deposits in the Special Accounts held with the Commonwealth Bank, squeezing their ability to advance credit. More comprehensively, import controls applied from March 1952 to all foreign purchases, whether from the sterling bloc or the dollar bloc. Imports were slashed by half in 1952–53. Every import had to be justified against the standard of usefulness or of public craving (as in the cases of tea and tobacco, allowed in to the full extent of community demand). Licences were issued to bring in capital goods like turbines and aircraft, as they were for those components not yet made locally by the American and British firms that assembled vehicles in Australia. No payable oil-wells existed yet in Australia; scarce foreign exchange was set aside for petroleum. Import licensing lasted until February 1960, when the separate sterling and dollar blocs had dissolved and the electorate had tired of restrictions. The government, faced by surging consumer demand that came from the full employment of a growing workforce, and by the fear of consequent inflation, did away with the controls so as to fill the marketplace with imports. The result was another balance of payments crisis, in 1960–61, responded to with another official **squeeze on credit** (Whitwell 1985, Chapter 5; Crawford 1968, pp. 490–525).

The licensing system protected domestic manufacturers. It encouraged foreign investors, as tariffs did, to expand existing commitments and to set up new plants rather than bid for scarce licences or to be excluded from Australia's attractive market absolutely. By 1960, perhaps one-third of all Australian manufacturing was foreign-owned, a fraction skewed by overseas dominance in sectors like vehicles, oil-refining and tobacco, where large-scale production used advanced technology and (in many instances) imported plant and materials. As in previous decades, the process of import substitution relied on access to overseas capital goods and producer goods. In 1958–59, half of the capital inflow of that year came from the British money market, although this was the lowest proportion ever for new British investment – the United States' share of 38 per cent was the highest ever. Australia was freeing itself from dependence on just one source of investible funds.

The American capital flowed largely into secondary industry, reflecting United States' world primacy in manufacturing. Because most of the existing overseas ownership in Australia was British, new British capital lodged more widely across the economy, often passing through old institutional channels into rural production, urban mortgages, service industries and trade credits, as well as into manufacturing – the average return to British capital was reliable but lower than the return to American investment, less of which was needed to top up old enterprises and was therefore available to target the growth opportunities of the 1950s (Commonwealth of Australia 1965, vol. I, p. 278, 284, vol. II, pp. 984–6; Perkins 1962, pp. 122–37; Brash 1966).

> **SUMMARY BOX**
>
> Capital inflow constituted about 10 per cent of capital formation in Australia. As a loan to the Australian economy, capital inflow made it possible to run regular current account deficits, part of which comprised payments overseas of interest and dividends on previous inflows of capital. The public sector borrowed little or nothing overseas in the 1950s, consistent with the settled policy of the two preceding decades. The foreign funds flowing into the private sector broadened the Australian productive base and helped employ the inflowing population, at the cost of the outflow of those profits not ploughed back into the business, and of decisions made by some multinational proprietors not to seek export outlets that would compete with their own branch plants in other countries.

# Australia reconstructed

In 1960, partially co-ordinated regulation in Australia through import licensing gave way to incoherent regulation through tariffs, at a time when the European Economic Community and Japan entrenched their own regulatory practices and the United States defended its economy through a mixture of tariffs and subsidies. These import licences had favoured manufacturing and the development of infrastructure (such as electricity and aviation), just as migrant men and women worked, and were meant to work, disproportionately in factories and on public projects. The post-war commitment to modernisation was expensive. Infrastructure costs were high in such an immense country, where population sprawled even in the larger cities. The private sector was happy to leave infrastructure to the taxpayer. Nor could private companies, selling to a domestic market of only 10 000 000 people by 1960, enjoy the **economies of scale** possible in more populous societies. Some smaller industrial countries did find substantial export markets among their larger neighbours, but Australia did not have that luxury. Every Asian and African country was poor in the 1950s, with the exception of Japan, which restricted those imports that might compete with its own factories and farms, and of the white minority in South Africa, who were few in number. New Zealand took about 6 per cent of Australia's exports, but that was insufficient to justify ambitious new investments in Australia in the absence of government assistance and guarantees.

It was not surprising, then, that Australian production in many sectors was concentrated in the hands of a small number of firms. This could give rise to complacency or collusion. There is evidence, however, in vehicle-building, that concentration may have been appropriate to the nation's small population. The unique position bestowed on General Motors Holden's (GMH) had been eroded by 1960. The American and British firms that had operated in Australia before preference was given to GMH in 1944 insisted that their capital investments should not be sacrificed, and their national governments backed them. As a result, they all gained import licences in the 1950s. State governments insisted that plants already open in their State should continue to operate, and in competition with each other they lured other car makers (from Europe and later from Japan) to invest within their borders. Components companies and trade unions insisted that there be as many contracts and jobs as possible. The customers, who were also voters, revelled in the widening choice. The vehicle industry in the 1950s evolved with a multitude of small production runs that were inefficient, costly and out of control. A single company, to whom a monopoly was granted contingent on developing exports, may well have served the country better. It did not seem to be a problem in the short run. A market emerged in the 1950s for Australian-made vehicles (often exported as disassembled kits) among the middle classes and businesses of nearby countries, a market that strengthened in the 1960s. But in the long run these markets grew large and affluent enough to be able to choose from more cost-effective sources than the small-scale Australian car-plants (Brown & Hughes 1970; Capling & Galligan 1992, pp. 197–200; Pinkstone 1992, p. 177).

The Coalition government in the 1950s did not overturn the reconstruction policies of the Labor government of the 1940s, but it did modify them in middle-class ways. More attention was paid to universities, middle-class preserves for professional careers and to airlines, then an expensive form of travel. From 1956, the Commonwealth–State Housing Agreement, previously intended for low-income tenants, earmarked a proportion of the grants as loans to potential purchasers. The central banking functions of the Commonwealth Bank were not repealed, but they were distinguished more clearly in 1953 from the Bank's everyday trading functions and separated completely, as the Reserve Bank, in 1959.

External conditions forced the government to regulate foreign exchange transactions and importing, and farmers and manufacturers encouraged it to maintain marketing schemes and tariff **protection**. The growth of the west European, North American and Japanese economies promised expanding opportunities to sell Australian commodities and to draw on the surplus capital of those regions. But exporters had to work harder as the terms of trade for Australia (the relative prices of exports and imports) declined throughout the 1950s.

**SUMMARY BOX**

The general peacetime objective set down in the 1940s was the maintenance of full employment with stable prices. The Reserve Bank-published estimates show the rate of unemployment fluctuating between 1 per cent and 3 per cent in the 1950s (indeed, not rising above 3 per cent until 1975). The **consumer price index** rose at an average rate of 2.5 per cent a year between 1953–54 and 1959–60, once the severe Korean War inflation had ended. Although the population grew on average by 2.4 per cent a year during the 1950s, the real GDP grew by an average of 4.2 per cent, so real **income per head** rose steadily (RBA 1991, pp. 148–51, 172–5, 188–93, 209–11). By these criteria, the Australian economy had recovered solidly from the tragedies of depression and war.

# Suggested further reading

Beaumont, J. (ed.) 1996, *Australia's War, 1939–1945*, Allen & Unwin, Sydney.

Coombs, H.C. 1971, *Other People's Money: Economic Essays*, Australian National University Press, Canberra.

Crawford, J.G. 1968, *Australian Trade Policy 1942–1966: a Documentary History*, Australian National University Press, Canberra.

Fox, C. 1991, *Working Australia*, Allen & Unwin, Sydney.

Jupp, J. 1991, *Immigration*, Sydney University Press, Sydney.

Patmore, G. 1991, *Australian Labour History*, Longman Cheshire, Melbourne.

Pinkstone, B. 1992, *Global Connections: A History of Exports and the Australian Economy*, Australian Government Publishing Service, Canberra.

Schedvin, C.B. 1992, *In Reserve: central banking in Australia 1945–1975*, Allen & Unwin, Sydney.

Tweedie, S.M. 1994, *Trading Partners: Australia and Asia 1790–1993*, UNSW Press, Sydney.

Whitwell, G. 1986, *The Treasury Line*, Allen & Unwin, Sydney.

# End notes

[1]  'Full employment in Australia', *Parliamentary Paper no. 11, 1945*, reprinted in J.G. Crawford (ed.) 1968, *Australian Trade Policy, 1942–1966: a Documentary History*, Australian National University Press, Canberra., pp. 17–29.

[2]  Calculated from Commonwealth Bureau of Census and Statistics 1952, *The Australian Balance of Payments, 1928–29 to 1948–49*, Government Printer, Canberra, p. 85.

[3]  Trade calculations made from the relevant *Yearbooks*.

# 9

## A booming economy: Australia and the world economy, 1960–1973

By the end of the 1950s, the post-war strategies for **economic growth and development** in Australia seemed to be working. **Full employment** had been achieved and economic growth in the second half of the decade averaged 4 per cent. **Inflation** remained low at 3 per cent and the **current account** deficit remained manageable at around 3 per cent of **GDP** (see Tables 9.1 and 9.2). Home loan **interest** rates were steady at 5 per cent. The industrial **infrastructure** had expanded rapidly during the 1950s, as had manufacturing output and employment. One-quarter of the workforce was now employed in manufacturing. Exports were booming (even if not at the rate of world trade) and the 1957 trade treaty with Japan looked likely to underpin **primary exports** into the future (Pinkstone 1992, pp. 167–8, 188–9). The instability of the late 1940s and early 1950s appeared to have been left behind. Australia was a successful, industrialising economy, that was highly attractive to foreign **capital** and European migrants alike, both of which poured into the country at unprecedented rates. This chapter is concerned with the outcome of post-war strategies for economic development in Australia and the performance of the economy during the latter stages of the 'Long Boom'.

## Strategies for economic development

With the economy booming, some moves towards liberalising Australia's external barriers were made. At the beginning of 1960, the Australian pound became fully **convertible** to the US dollar and **exchange controls** were relaxed. In taking this action, the Australian government was in line with a general movement of currencies to full convertibility in 1959 and 1960. Capital inflows were already mainly unrestricted, and this partial deregulation only affected outflows of capital. It allowed foreign-controlled businesses in Australia to repatriate profits, but the

**Table 9.1**   Economic growth, unemployment and inflation in Australia, 1958–59 to 1973–74

| Year | Real economic growth (percentage change from previous year) | Unemployment (percentage of labour force) | Inflation (percentage change in consumer price index) |
|------|------|------|------|
| 1958–59 | 7.3 | 2.0 | 1.6 |
| 1959–60 | 5.6 | 2.4 | 2.5 |
| 1960–61 | 3.2 | 2.3 | 4.1 |
| 1961–62 | 1.2 | 3.2 | 0.4 |
| 1962–63 | 6.8 | 2.3 | 0.2 |
| 1963–64 | 7.1 | 1.7 | 0.9 |
| 1964–65 | 7.1 | 1.2 | 3.8 |
| 1965–66 | 2.2 | 1.2 | 3.6 |
| 1966–67 | 6.6 | 1.6 | 2.7 |
| 1967–68 | 3.7 | 1.7 | 3.3 |
| 1968–69 | 8.8 | 1.6 | 2.6 |
| 1969–70 | 5.6 | 1.5 | 3.2 |
| 1970–71 | 4.8 | 1.4 | 4.8 |
| 1971–72 | 4.8 | 1.7 | 6.8 |
| 1972–73 | 3.8 | 2.5 | 6.0 |
| 1973–74 | 4.6 | 1.8 | 12.9 |

Source: Based on RBA 1996, pp. 225, 180, 243.

government stopped short of allowing Australian firms and residents a similar free-dom to make **investments** overseas, fearing the impact this would have on the **balance of payments**. Relaxed exchange controls meant that imports were easier to obtain. At the same time, Australia also liberalised foreign trade by abolishing **import quotas and licensing**, again in line with other Western countries and as part of its obligations under the GATT (General Agreement on Tariffs and Trade). The Treasury argued that an increased inflow of imports would soak up some of the excess **demand** in the Australian economy and would encourage manufactur-ing firms to take steps to become more competitive (Whitwell 1986, p. 132).

## The 1961 crisis and the Vernon Report

These actions produced immediate results. Imports surged in the absence of quotas and the freer **foreign exchange** regime. They increased by 17 per cent in 1959–60 and 14 per cent the following financial year. As imports surged, inflation moved up to over 4 per cent and a balance of payments crisis loomed, exacerbated by falling world **commodity** prices. As export prices declined and imports increased, Australia's **trade balance** moved into deficit during 1960, for the first time since 1955, and the current account deficit blew out to over 5 per cent of GDP, its high-est since the Korean War crisis. At the end of the year, the Australian government responded by imposing a **credit squeeze** and raising sales tax on motor vehicles

**Table 9.2** Australia's balance of payments, current account, 1958–59 to 1973–74 ($millions)

| Year | Exports | Imports | Trade balance (exports minus imports) | Balance of transport services | Balance of travel services | Balance of other services | Balance of income account | Net transfers | Balance of services, income & transfers | Current account balance | Current account balance as a % of GDP |
|---|---|---|---|---|---|---|---|---|---|---|---|
| 1958–59 | 1612 | 1554 | 58 | −123 | −39 | 5 | −254 | −33 | −444 | −386 | −3.0 |
| 1959–60 | 1860 | 1814 | 46 | −146 | −50 | 7 | −292 | −33 | −514 | −468 | −3.4 |
| 1960–61 | 1847 | 2056 | −209 | −184 | −52 | 9 | −273 | −37 | −537 | −746 | −5.1 |
| 1961–62 | 2129 | 1701 | 427 | −135 | −46 | 9 | −226 | −42 | −440 | −13 | −0.1 |
| 1962–63 | 2122 | 2065 | 56 | −144 | −55 | 14 | −293 | −49 | −527 | −471 | −2.9 |
| 1963–64 | 2731 | 2237 | 493 | −157 | −59 | 12 | −317 | −35 | −556 | −63 | −0.3 |
| 1964–65 | 2574 | 2739 | −165 | −203 | −60 | −11 | −304 | −46 | −624 | −789 | −4.0 |
| 1965–66 | 2626 | 2822 | −196 | −219 | −64 | −16 | −337 | −65 | −701 | −897 | −4.3 |
| 1966–67 | 2926 | 2837 | 89 | −218 | −69 | −29 | −359 | −78 | −753 | −664 | −2.9 |
| 1967–68 | 2942 | 3159 | −218 | −271 | −59 | −37 | −498 | −64 | −929 | −1147 | −4.7 |
| 1968–69 | 3217 | 3203 | 14 | −282 | −56 | −67 | −556 | −65 | −1026 | −1012 | −3.7 |
| 1969–70 | 3969 | 3553 | 416 | −286 | −72 | −81 | −610 | −89 | −1138 | −772 | −2.4 |
| 1970–71 | 4217 | 3790 | 427 | −317 | −64 | −107 | −626 | −115 | −1229 | −802 | −2.4 |
| 1971–72 | 4722 | 3791 | 931 | −307 | −106 | −129 | −604 | −125 | −1271 | −340 | −0.9 |
| 1972–73 | 5991 | 3808 | 2138 | −288 | −171 | −127 | −674 | −207 | −1467 | 716 | 1.7 |
| 1973–74 | 6709 | 5754 | 956 | −503 | −261 | −156 | −674 | −271 | −1865 | −909 | −1.8 |

Note: A minus sign indicates that the value of payments made by Australian residents to foreigners exceeded the value of payments made by foreigners to Australian residents.

Source: Based on RBA 1986, pp. 2–3, 12–13.

and some other **consumer durables**. Economic growth was slowed by these measures, to under 3 per cent in 1960–61 and to only 1.3 per cent in 1961–62. This produced in 1961 what was, by post-war standards, an economic **recession**. **Unemployment** moved up from 2.3 per cent to 3.2 per cent, its highest level in the entire post-war **boom** of 1950–1974. The Australian electorate indicated its displeasure at these outcomes in an election held in the middle of the **slump**, in December 1961, in which the ruling Coalition parties were returned with a majority of only two seats (as opposed to a majority of 32 seats in the previous parliament).

This hiccup in Australia's post-war boom had a number of repercussions. It led to government concern about strengthening Australia's trade performance. An immediate initiative, taken in December 1960, was to lift the ban, originally imposed in 1938, on the export of iron ore. This raised the prospect of the immense iron deposits of Western Australia being opened up for mining and export. It also signalled that Australia's policy on mining development in general was likely to be an encouraging one and that foreign capital and enterprise would be welcomed in these new mineral endeavours.

This initiative was followed by a decision to raise **tariffs** on imports as an 'emergency' measure to counter the effects of the abolition of import quotas and licensing. The tariff, which had not been of much importance in the 1940s and 1950s because of the direct import controls in place, now assumed considerable significance. Tariffs were set by the Tariff Board, but because the Board was obliged under its rules to investigate all proposals for tariff changes thoroughly, a process that could take up to two years, it could not respond quickly to requests for more assistance. To streamline tariff changes, a new body was created in 1962, the Special Advisory Authority. Its head described his philosophy towards tariffs as, 'You make it, and I'll protect it' (Glezer 1982, p. 71). This attitude set the pattern for much of the 1960s. Tariff **protection** was gradually increased on a wide range of products and in an ad hoc manner in which the only consideration was the needs of the particular producer in each instance. As imports made inroads into various markets, so these producers were given as much extra tariff protection as was considered necessary for them to maintain their market share. When new goods were produced locally and imports of similar goods had been entering duty-free because substitutes were not manufactured in Australia, tariff protection was automatically given under the provisions of the Customs Act, without reference to the Tariff Board at all (Corden 1974, pp. 219–23; Anderson & Garnaut 1986, pp. 158–9).

There was also widespread criticism from elite opinion of the way in which the 1960 crisis had been handled. It was argued that the government's 'stop-go' policies were too disruptive and that more sophisticated and forward-looking economic management policies were required. Eventually, early in 1963, the Prime Minister, Robert Menzies, responded to this pressure by establishing a Committee of Economic Inquiry (the Vernon Committee) that would consider, among other matters, the way in which the ups and downs in the **trade cycle** might be smoothed.

The Vernon Committee reported in May 1965. It recommended that indicative or 'target' planning should be used to permit government economic policy to work ahead of economic change rather than simply react to changes after the event. It envisaged, therefore, the government adopting a longer term view of the economy than had been evident hitherto. To assist in this task, the Committee recommended the establishment of an 'Advisory Council on Economic Growth' whose role would be to take a medium-term perspective and provide advice to Cabinet on future economic policy (Australia, Committee of Economic Enquiry 1965, vol. 1, p. 454; Arndt 1968, pp. 102–18; Corden 1997, pp. 129–48). The Vernon Committee was a wide-ranging inquiry and did not confine itself solely to management of the trade cycle. It also proffered advice on the structural changes that the Australian economy was undergoing in the post-war boom. The stability of Australia's export earnings should be underpinned by a widening of the export base. In particular, new mineral exports should be encouraged, minerals should be processed in Australia rather than being exported in their raw form and the manufacturing industry should export more of its products.

Indeed, manufacturing was criticised generally for being too complacent. The Vernon Committee attributed much of this lack of vigour to the somnolent effect of high tariff protection. It argued that although tariff protection had been necessary in the early stages of building the post-war manufacturing sector, such protection from import competition had become too great and was in danger of damaging the entire industrialisation process. The manufacturing industry, it claimed, was mature enough now to survive a lower tariff regime and to respond positively to greater import competition by lifting efficiency and **productivity**. In particular, it pointed to the additional costs imposed on the whole economy, including manufacturing, of current import barriers and called for more research to be undertaken into the real, or 'effective', as opposed to the nominal, rates of tariff protection. The effective rate of protection for any sector should not, in the Committee's view, be allowed to exceed 30 per cent, a level that it considered to be well below prevailing rates.[1] The Committee foresaw a larger manufacturing sector in Australia and an expanded industrial workforce based on continued large-scale immigration at a net rate of 100 000 migrants per year.

The government largely ignored the Vernon Report. In so far as it recommended the continuation of current policies, such as high immigration rates, full

## SUMMARY BOX

At the beginning of the 1960s, Australia experienced a balance of payments crisis brought about by a booming domestic economy and a relaxation on import controls. Measures taken to counter the crisis caused economic growth to slow and unemployment to rise. In response to electoral discontent with this outcome, the government acted to boost Australia's exports and to restrict imports through higher tariffs. It also set up the first commission of inquiry into the Australian economy since the 1920s. Although many of its recommendations were ignored by the government, the commission's report drew attention to structural problems in Australia's manufacturing sector and was critical of the policy of high tariff protection.

employment, or the expansion of mineral exports, its comments were welcomed. The government gave limited support to the idea that the manufacturing industry should be encouraged to export more, though this was really left up to the individual manufacturing firms themselves. However, where the Committee recommended significant changes in government policies, particularly on tariffs, its proposals fell on deaf ears. The Department of the Treasury did not appreciate the idea of indicative planning and certainly did not wish to see the government establish an alternative source of economic advice to itself. These recommendations were also shelved.

## Manufacturing industry in the Long Boom

In its comments on the growth of the manufacturing industry in Australia, the Vernon Committee reflected the changing role of manufacturing in the Australian economy. The mid-1960s marked a watershed in Australia's post-war industrial history. During the Second World War a hothouse environment for Australian manufacturing had been created. In some ways, there was a kind of 'forced industrialisation' taking place. The war showed how vulnerable Australia was and how much it needed to expand the existing manufacturing industry and develop new ones. The war also showed, however, that Australian firms could enter the high technology end of manufacturing (in building airplane engines and machine tools, for example) and this gave confidence that Australian manufacturing could be world class. The government's post-war aims provided a coherent framework for further industrial expansion and diversification. Between 1945 and 1965, Australian manufacturing had a clear set of aims and rationale and was supported by a range of government initiatives to help achieve these aims. Manufacturing growth was underpinned by four major policies.

## Industry policies

First, 'Populate or Perish!' For various reasons, including a fear of Asian invasion, post-war Australian governments sought to maximise population growth, to be achieved by a mix of natural increase and immigration. As birth rates had been very low in the inter-war years, it was expected that at least half of the growth in population (estimated at 2 per cent per annum) would have to come from immigration. A growing manufacturing sector was necessary to employ this rising population, especially as immigration added to the labour force to a greater extent than it added to the population at large. Immigrants would be factory fodder, or rather, non–English-speaking migrants would be employed in the uncongenial factory work, while native-born workers and English-speaking migrants would fill lower and middle management positions and find jobs in the services sector that depended on manufacturing (Birrell 1988, pp. 882–7). Was industrialisation pursued to absorb mass immigration or was immigration pursued to provide a **labour force** for the rapidly expanding manufacturing sector? This chicken-or-egg question did not require an answer. Both population growth and industrialisation were, in the government's view, desirable outcomes. Each reinforced the other.

Second, even without a populate-or-perish mentality, Australian governments were committed to the achievement of full employment. A return to the conditions of mass unemployment of the pre-war years was not acceptable. But full employment could not be achieved by rural industries alone, however strong was post-war demand for primary products. Only manufacturing could provide sufficient employment growth to achieve sustained full employment, both directly and also indirectly through the impact manufacturing had on the tertiary industry.

Third, there were defence arguments in favour of rapid post-war industrialisation in Australia. The war had revealed how dependent Australia was on imported manufactures and **capital goods**. Only by expanding the manufacturing base could Australia be reasonably assured that in a future world conflict it would not be left without the capacity to supply itself with essential manufactures. This was not an argument about direct defence spending or the build-up of Australia's armed forces: defence spending in the post-war period was not, in fact, very great and Australia continued to rely heavily on its allies for support and equipment (as indicated by the ANZUS treaty). But it was an argument for building up a varied manufacturing industrial base in Australia as a source of import replacement.

Fourth, industrialisation was desired for its expected beneficial effects on Australia's balance of payments. For 20 years after the end of the war, the Australian governments' actions were circumscribed by the state of the balance of payments. Australia was regarded as suffering a chronic and persistent shortage of foreign exchange, particularly of American dollars, that caused shortages of imported consumer and capital goods. In spite of the much higher prices received for commodity exports in the post-war years than before the war, Australia ran successive current account deficits, funded by inflows of foreign capital. Import replacement was viewed as a major factor in keeping the trade balance in surplus (to minimise the current account deficit), and since Australia's imports consisted to a large extent of manufactured goods, import replacement meant expanding, or establishing from scratch in some cases, similar manufacturing industries in Australia.

A further factor in this post-war expansion of industry was the role played by the States. Manufacturing held out considerable benefits to State governments. Increased employment, and therefore population growth, would boost state revenues through taxation, and was seen as a partial counter to the loss of state revenue-raising powers to the Commonwealth. The manufacturing industry would also help diversify state economies that were highly dependent on a few rural products. It was also anticipated that the expansion of manufacturing would generate new regional growth points in the State and that these would stimulate employment and prosperity. For these and other reasons, the States competed with each other to attract manufacturing industry to their region. This had important long-term effects in exacerbating the problem of industrial fragmentation.

These post-war policies for expanding industry put manufacturing at the centre of national strategies for economic development. A number of measures were taken by government to ensure the anticipated expansion did indeed occur. These included **import protection**, public investment in infrastructure, encouragement of **direct foreign investment**, mass immigration programs, macroeconomic settings that emphasised strong economic growth and a laissez faire approach to the pattern of industrial expansion. The Menzies government continued the previous Chifley government's support for industrial growth, though it abandoned Labor's commitment to planning the size, structure and location of Australia's manufacturing industries. Immigration and population policies designed to raise the birth rate provided industry with secure labour force growth. Strong domestic demand was underpinned by increasing **real** wages, growing population and the stimulus to marketing of consumer **credit** and advertising. And foreign direct investment brought the necessary capital (mainly in US dollars), management skills and (almost) up-to-date technology.

These forces shaped Australian manufacturing in the 1950s and 1960s. There was rapid growth in output and employment, especially in motor vehicles, domestic appliances, electrical goods, engineering, iron and steel, rubber products, plastics, petroleum, chemicals, paper, food processing and textiles, footwear and clothing. Motor vehicles, engineering, electrical goods and iron and steel production accounted for two-thirds of the employment growth in manufacturing in the period 1948–49 to 1962–63. There was also expansion of manufacturing through **capital widening**. A more diverse set of industries, many of them new to Australia, existed by the mid-1960s than 20 years earlier. Because import replacement was such a powerful driving force in the growth of Australian manufacturing, the range of products tended to mirror those entering as imports, with a marked emphasis **on consumer goods** and luxury and semi-luxury products. It was for this reason that Australia earned the epithet 'Milk bar economy' in these years. However, it should not be overlooked that heavy industries, especially engineering, chemicals, oil-refining and above all, iron and steel production, also expanded strongly. **Labour productivity** in manufacturing increased, though not at a spectacular rate. The introduction of new technology and more capital-intensive production processes, especially noticeable among foreign-owned firms, yielded average growth in labour productivity of 3.5 per cent to 4.5 per cent per year.

Two drawbacks to this rapid rise of manufacturing became apparent, however, by the 1960s. In the first place, much of it was derivative. Industrialisation in Australia was heavily dependent on foreign capital, foreign workers, foreign technology, foreign management, foreign corporate structures. In fact, everything about it seemed to be in some way foreign – except sales. Exports of manufactures remained low and grew less quickly than total exports, thus reducing the proportion of manufactures in Australia's foreign exchange earnings. Exporting was not a priority for most manufacturing firms, whether Australian or foreign. Overall, the proportion of manufacturing output that was exported between 1950 and 1960 declined from 12 per cent to 6 per cent.

Second, manufacturing industry became highly fragmented. Partly this was due to the States' practice of competing against each other to attract new manufacturing production to their locality and the absence of any control over this competitive behaviour by the failure of the Commonwealth to develop an industry policy. It was caused, partly, by the tariff system that encouraged foreign enterprises to adopt a 'foot-in-the-door' mentality whereby they established a small-scale operation in anticipation of future growth and obtained tariff protection for their products (Corden 1962, pp. 38–46). This led to a proliferation of small concerns that were not always viable in the longer run. Fragmentation was also exacerbated by the geographical realities of Australia. The domestic market was small anyway, but it was also spatially divided between the main cities and poorly served by internal transport. Much of Australia's transport system had been built to connect ports to hinterlands, not to connect major cities to each other. Each main centre of population tended to be somewhat isolated and this encouraged the establishment of duplicate factories in a number of States.

Despite these problems, it could be said that, up to the mid-1960s, the manufacturing industry in Australia fulfilled the role expected of it by the post-war planners quite well. After 20 years of rapid post-war expansion, manufacturing employed around 28 per cent of the labour force, had created many jobs in the services sector and accounted for a steady 26 to 28 per cent of gross domestic product. By international standards, this classified Australia as an industrialised economy. This apparent success meant that up to the early 1960s, criticism of the way in which manufacturing had developed was fairly muted. Academics criticised some aspects of manufacturing growth, but did not question at this time the basic post-war aims. They were critical, for example, of the manufacturing industry's failure to develop exports, but assumed that this was a result of the 'infant industry' stage it was still in, and assumed manufactures exports would increase naturally over the next 20 years as this stage receded. Similarly, the Vernon Report, for all its complaints about Australian manufacturing, retained a general mood of optimism about its future. It still cast its analysis in terms of Australia having a fundamentally weak balance of payments and the role of manufacturing in import replacement.

Critics agreed that the Australian manufacturing industry was not internationally competitive, but this was not seen as the central problem at this time. Rather, analysis focused on the small size of the Australian domestic market, which made it difficult for manufacturers to obtain scale economies, or on 'fragmentation', which caused firms to operate with less than optimal-sized plants, but also caused over-capacity problems. Attention was also drawn to high transport and electrical power costs; and on insufficient investment in Australian research and development. On this last problem, the Vernon Report recommended the creation of a National Science Council to stimulate industrial research and development in Australia. This body, it was hoped, would be to manufacturing what the CSIRO was to agriculture. The Menzies government rejected this proposal. It was argued that Australia had successfully attracted some of the world's leading manufacturing corporations and these had brought with them the benefits of their extensive research and development (R&D) investment. It would be difficult and expensive, it was claimed, for Australian firms, or the government or universities, to match the R&D efforts of these multinationals. The question was raised about whether more needed to be spent on research and development in Australia when new technology arrived from overseas with a time delay of only one or two years. As far as the government was concerned, the answer was no.

From an economic point of view, the late 1960s was a period that was highly conducive to the adoption of a less protectionist policy towards Australian manufacturing. The economy exhibited high rates of economic growth. The balance of trade was stronger as a result of the minerals boom and could thus withstand an initial increase in imports if tariffs were reduced. Full employment and labour force growth, together with controllable inflows of migrant workers who tended to be more mobile, could help to cushion the immediate employment consequences of reduced tariff protection. If Australia had followed a liberalisation path it would have been acting in a similar way to most industrial countries that were reducing trade barriers in manufactures at this time. **International trade** in manufactured goods was the most dynamic sector of world trade and one that was becoming increasingly competitive. A country that did not develop its manufacturing industry in line with world trends could expect to be left behind.

Australia's manufacturing sector was certainly larger and more integrated than in earlier decades, but its future growth could not be taken for granted. If it stagnated behind high tariff walls there would eventually be a decline in its share of GDP and employment. The rate of growth of labour productivity in Australian manufacturing was not particularly high by world standards and not likely to improve without a more competitive environment. The costs to the rest of the economy of the misallocation of resources that was caused by overprotection were rising and becoming more noticed. Australia's share of world trade was declining. This could not be arrested simply by the minerals boom. A reorientation of manufacturing towards export markets was required, but this was less likely to occur if tariff barriers remained excessively high. As inflation became a more significant economic problem towards the end of the 1960s, the impact of high tariffs on price levels was noted. Inflation was also fuelled by wage rises that were set for the whole economy by the rates paid in one of the most sheltered manufacturing sectors, the metalworking industry (Gregory & Pincus 1982, pp. 1309–31; Corden 1962, pp. 174–214).

## Crisis in Australian manufacturing

From around 1965, the economic environment for Australian manufacturing changed. The mineral export boom that took off in the second half of the decade considerably strengthened Australia's balance of payments. This development removed a major post-war rationale for the expansion of manufacturing – the building up of manufacturing to replace imports at any price and without any overall planning. At the same time, in the late 1960s some of the post-war consensus on industrialisation began to crumble (Glezer 1982, p. 68; Snape 1973, pp. 37–8). In 1967, the Tariff Board, under its new chairman, Alf Rattigan, announced that it intended to pursue a policy of reducing tariff protection in order to improve the competitiveness of the manufacturing sector (Rattigan 1986, p. 27).

It intended to use the concept of 'effective rates of protection' developed earlier by the economist Max Corden. This took into account the cumulative effects of tariffs on various stages of production to measure the true amount of assistance being given. Using this concept, the Board aimed to divide Australian manufacturers into three categories – high, medium and low cost, corresponding to effective protection above 50 per cent, between 25 per cent and 50 per cent, and below 25 per cent. High-cost industries would be investigated immediately with a view to discouraging investment in them unless it could be shown that they were likely to become more efficient in a reasonable length of time. Medium-cost firms would be monitored closely to see in which direction they were developing, and low-cost producers would be encouraged to expand. The Board also announced that it intended to carry out the first comprehensive survey ever undertaken of the impact of the entire tariff regime on the economy as a whole. The manufacturers' lobby groups, the trade unions involved and the government fiercely resisted these proposals. Employers feared loss of profits and market share, unions feared job losses and the government objected to the Board's 'political interference'. Even the publication of effective assistance rates was contested as falling outside the Board's jurisdiction. It was not until 1971 that the Board was allowed to begin its comprehensive review. Meanwhile tariffs continued to rise (Rattigan 1986, p. 85–6; Glezer 1982, p. 108).

The new approach of the Tariff Board marked a shift in its orientation away from a role in which it had acted as a compliant servant of manufacturing interests and towards one where it eventually became the manufacturing industry's most strident critic. Its estimates of effective rates of protection clearly showed the high cost burden that was being placed on all parts of manufacturing and consumers by the policy of heavy protection for certain broad sectors. Moreover, the post-war imperative to 'populate or perish' was no longer seen as urgent or even necessary. High immigration rates coupled with the post-war **'baby boom'** were beginning to cause strains on services such as health and education, as well as on the infrastructure of towns and cities. By the end of the 1960s, there appeared to be a backlog of investment required for the provision of a number of basic services because of population pressure. The post-war expansion of manufacturing was seen as a major driving force in Australia's immigration policy. In addition, arguments that Australia needed to industrialise to supply itself in time of war seemed less pressing now that a large manufacturing sector had developed. Questions were also being asked by this time about the role of foreign ownership in the manufacturing sector. Australia had industrialised successfully, it was asserted, but at the price of foreign domination of key parts of the economy (Fitzpatrick & Wheelwright 1965). However irrational such sentiments were, they undermined the earlier confidence in the role of foreign capital in Australia's industrial modernisation.

The decline in the credibility of the post-war rationale for manufacturing expansion, together with increasingly strident criticism of foreign investment, immigration and the tariff, exposed the lack of competitiveness of Australian industry to greater scrutiny. In the 1950s, the lack of competitiveness had been acknowledged, but had not been regarded as a vital problem because manufacturing growth was seen as fulfilling other important tasks. Now its functions were less clear and its international competitiveness was called into question. Ironically, the fact that manufactures exports rose as a proportion of all exports between 1963 and 1969 only served to attract further criticism. It drew attention to the narrow range of manufactured exports and focused attention on those sectors in manufacturing that had not been able successfully to enter international trade. The surge in exports of manufactures as a share of total exports occurred between 1963–64 when the share was 12.5 per cent and 1968–69 when it reached 19.1 per cent. Thereafter the share remained static at around 20 per cent. A large part of manufactures exports consisted of processed foodstuffs and semi-manufactures such as alumina. Basic metal products and foodstuffs accounted for over 70 per cent of all exports of manufactured goods in the early 1970s, and six subdivisions accounted for 95 per cent. Exports were not important for most industries. Only four sectors exported more than 10 per cent of their output (foodstuffs, textiles, basic metal products and transport equipment). The two sectors that exported most – food-stuffs and basic metals – between them employed less than one-quarter of the manufacturing workforce and made up only a little over one-quarter of the value added in manufacturing (Pinkstone 1992, pp. 175–8).

As a result of these changes, by the early 1970s new demands were being placed on Australia's manufacturing firms. They must, it was argued, become internationally competitive. Industrialisation was rapidly expanding in other parts of the world, including South-East Asia, and in the long run it would be impossible to resist imports. If Australian business could not compete, many jobs would be placed in jeopardy. Australian manufacturing must become more Australian. It was strongly suggested at this time that the sector was too dependent on foreign capital and enterprise, foreign technology and migrant labour. Manufacturing firms in Australia had to become more export oriented and make a greater contri-bution to Australia's export earnings. The reasoning here was not so much that Australia's exports needed a boost (the mineral boom was seeing to that) but that manufacturers needed export markets to provide the economies of scale that the small, fragmented, domestic market denied them.

Finally, it was no longer sufficient for manufacturing to provide employment at increasing real wages and to underpin full employment. After 20 years of the Long Boom these were taken for granted. What was emphasised now was the quality of the employment provided by manufacturing. In particular, it was claimed that manufacturing firms had an obligation to the community to provide clean, safe and pleasant working conditions; to recognise the special needs of migrants from non–English-speaking backgrounds who made up such a large part of their workforce; to cater to the particular concerns of female workers, including equal pay, but also extending to working conditions; and to give more job satisfac-tion to workers by allowing more participation in decision-making. In short, the quality of manufacturing employment, and not just its quantity and material bene-fits, was being emphasised. Since most manufacturing firms in Australia found these demands difficult or impossible to meet, or declined to make any effort to meet them, manufacturing industry was, by the beginning of the 1970s, increas-ingly castigated as 'failing' (Davidson &. Stewardson 1974).

Apart from unfulfilled expectations, the manufacturing industry was regarded as being in crisis as a result of its economic failings. In the period between 1965 and 1973, its productivity growth was slight and compared unfavourably with other industrial countries. Critics identified a run-down of equipment, a lack of fresh investment in new plant and new technology, a lack of scale economies, poor management and poor industrial relations as some of the causes. The scope for large-scale import replacement that had sustained manufac-turing between 1945 and 1965 was less now. Manufacturing was less profitable than before and corporate tax rates were higher. Investors, both domestic and foreign, now saw other sectors, especially minerals and services, of the Australian economy as more attractive. As **per capita incomes** rose, Australian consumers spent a declining proportion of their disposable incomes on manufactures and a greater proportion on services.

In 1974, another committee of inquiry sat in judgement on Australian manufacturing. The Jackson Committee found a 'deep-seated malaise' in the sector. Partly this was due to the recession that had begun in 1974, but it went far deeper than any particular short-term problems. 'Factories opened proudly in the early post-war years,' the Committee noted, '[and] have become today's structural problems in terms of efficient use of resources … For manufacturing in general, a period of expansion gave way to consolidation and then to stagnation' (Australia, Committee to Advise on Policies for Manufacturing Industry 1975). By the time the Jackson Committee reported, in August 1975, manufacturing firms in Australia were under attack from all sides. Nationalists complained of too much foreign ownership and control. The labour movement was critical of poor work conditions and practices, rising unemployment and a failure to deliver on previous promises. Academic economists criticised tariff protection that was, in their view, too high and indiscriminate, and complained that too little was being done to boost Australia's research and development effort. Environmentalists accused manufacturers of causing pollution and by attracting immigrants of adding to overcrowding and all the problems of urban services. The government, faced with an economic recession, lamented the failure of manufacturing to continue to be Australia's engine of growth. And the manufacturing businesses themselves were not slow to highlight their falling profits, higher tax burden and increasing rate of bankruptcy. As the Long Boom came to an end in Australia, the manufacturing industry in particular was faced with a long and painful process of structural readjustment that did not get under way until the mid-1980s.

**SUMMARY BOX**

In the 20 years after the end of the Second World War, Australian industrialisation was underpinned by policies of mass immigration, foreign investment and public investment in infrastructure. The growth of manufacturing was encouraged by both federal and state governments. Industrialisation was seen as essential to Australia's economic development, its national independence and the maintenance of full employment. Industrialisation and population growth were regarded as desirable and mutually reinforcing. From the mid-1960s, however, the manufacturing sector was increasingly criticised for inefficiencies and lack of international competitiveness. In the late 1960s, attempts were made to reform the highly protectionist regime that was regarded as causing many of the problems of the manufacturing sector, but with little practical success before 1973. By the early 1970s, Australian manufacturing was in serious crisis and in the less buoyant economic conditions from the mid-1970s, it was in urgent need of structural renewal.

# The Long Boom

The Long Boom in Australia, 1950–1974, was characterised by an economic performance that seemed unprecedented to the generation that had experienced the Great Depression and something of a golden age to the generation that grew up in Australia after its end. Only the 'baby boomers' – those born between 1945 and 1955 – could take it for granted. Not only was real growth strong and sustained, averaging over 5 per cent per year over a quarter of a century, but from the mid-1950s, real GDP per head grew more rapidly than at any other time, reflecting rising material living standards (see Chapter 1, Figure 1.3).

Chief among the sources of this economic growth was market demand for goods and services underpinned by full employment. Investment in new plants, especially in manufacturing, and rising labour productivity, again particularly in manufacturing, at least until the late 1960s, added to total output. A 'consumer age' dawned in Australia, where rising consumption of goods and services was enhanced by advertising, hire-purchase, built-in obsolescence and fashion. Home construction had its longest boom since the Federation era, and new houses were filled with new consumer durables. Unemployment remained below 2.5 per cent (an official definition of full employment) despite a considerable rise in the size in the labour force and in the **participation rate**. Controlling the inflationary effects of the boom conditions was the main problem facing the Treasury and the Reserve Bank, but inflation was usually low and kept under control by fiscal and monetary measures until the late 1960s (Whitwell 1986, p. 119; Schedvin 1992). Although the economy was responsive to measures taken every few years to slow down the inflation rate, underlying inflation quickly re-emerged and each time took off again from a slightly higher level, producing a sort of ratchet effect in the long term. From the late 1960s, inflationary forces gathered pace and economic management proved less effective.

Australia's experience of the Long Boom was not out of line with that in the other developed economies. It was an international boom and internationally transmitted. Australia's ability to attract international **factors of production** and to participate in the strong growth of world trade underpinned the Long Boom's continuation. Not all countries participated. The centrally planned communist countries did not experience these conditions nor did large parts of the 'developing' world. Even some older economies, including ones that had once been the equal of Australia, missed out on the Long Boom, as the case of Argentina in these years illustrates.

## Foreign investment

Capital inflow to Australia reached a peak in the 1960s and early 1970s (Figure 9.1), but there were important differences compared to earlier periods when foreign capital had flowed in heavily, such as the 1920s and 1880s. A much greater proportion of the capital in the 1960s was private direct investment by multinational firms as opposed to the public borrowing from abroad by Australian governments that had characterised the earlier flows. A greater proportion of the investment in the 1960s

**Figure 9.1**   Foreign investment in Australia, 1952–53 to 1973–74 (annual inflow)

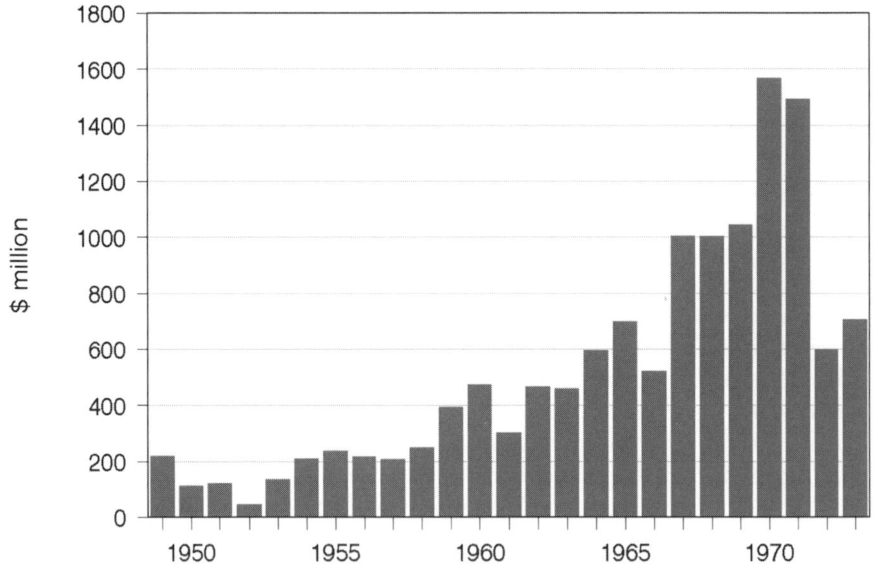

Source: Based on RBA 1996, p. 38.

was by United States companies, whereas the earlier capital inflows had been predominantly from Britain. The ratio of foreign investment to gross domestic capital formation was lower than in the earlier periods, though it rose during the 1960s to a high point of 20 per cent in 1971. Australian governments in the post-war era welcomed such foreign investment. Before 1972, there were virtually no restrictions on capital inflows, with the exception that foreign investment was not permitted in banking, aviation, media or some kinds of real estate (Sexton & Adamovich 1981, pp. 13–14). The role of foreign investment in post-war strategies for economic development was fairly obvious. Foreign firms, it was hoped, would provide employment, transfer technology and know-how, ensure the continued expansion of manufacturing and protect Australia's balance of payments.

American companies, it was believed, provided these attributes better than firms from any other country, even after the end of the dollar gap. Before the resources boom of the late 1960s, most of these firms were located in manufacturing and services. Why did they want to establish operations in Australia? It was Australia's booming domestic market and demand for consumer goods that made Australia seem a profitable place to invest (Brash 1966, p. 36). Australia's Consumer Age beckoned. Tariff protection also helped. On the one hand, import barriers made it difficult for foreign firms to supply the growing Australian market simply through imports (though many that ended up investing in Australia started off by supplying imports), and on the other it gave these firms protection from imports after they had set up production in Australia. During the 1960s, direct foreign investment and rising tariff barriers went hand in hand. Australia was, perhaps, an unfamiliar place at first to the executives from the US corporations, but they soon discovered that it was a stable country with a well-established commercial legal system. Their investments were secure, they could repatriate profits without hindrance and after 1960 the Australian pound was freely convertible to the US dollar. These were attributes of investment in Australia that had long been appreciated by British firms that had established themselves in the country. They were attractive incentives to weigh against the relatively high cost of Australian labour, the poorly articulated domestic market, the small size of Australia's population, the inconveniences of different state laws and administrations, and the powerful position of Australian trade unions. For many foreign firms, the balance was tipped towards investment by an array of customised concessions offered by state governments competing against each other.

Earlier periods of strong capital inflow had ended in **foreign debt** and balance of payments crises (as discussed in Chapters 3 and 4). By contrast, capital inflow during the 1960s had benign balance of payments effects in that repatriation of profits was not great and the direct investment reduced dependence on imports. Yet by the early 1970s there was a crisis in foreign investment that led to restrictions being put in place. This was a crisis of **equity** rather than a debt crisis. It was a reaction to the rising share of foreign ownership in the Australian economy that resulted from the expansion in foreign investment (Wheelwright 1963, pp. 141–73). For manufacturing as a whole, foreign ownership rose from 25 per cent in 1962 to 29 per cent in 1966 and to 34 per cent in 1972 (ABS 1976, pp. 2–4). Some parts of manufacturing had much higher rates: 60 per cent in tobacco products, over 60 per cent in chemicals, 91 per cent in petroleum refining and 75 per cent in motor vehicles and parts. In addition, the mining boom was dependent on foreign capital. Foreign ownership in the entire Australian mining industry reached 45 per cent in 1966 and 52 per cent in 1972 (Anderson 1983, p. 76).

Such high levels of foreign ownership raised the ire of nationalists, economic xenophobes and left-wing critics who regarded the United States as the home of international capitalism and US multinationals as their chief agents. Some concerns were legitimate. Foreign-owned subsidiaries in Australia could reduce their tax liability by selling products to their parent company at a loss. This practice of 'transfer pricing' was subject to regulation by the Australian Taxation Office, but it remained a problem, especially in the mining industry (Anderson 1983; Loveday 1982, pp. 147–58). A study carried out in 1974 concluded that firms (Australian and foreign) in the mining industry paid less in taxes than they received back in tax concessions, bounties and so forth (Fitzgerald 1974, p. 16). Some Australian subsidiaries were not permitted by their parent to produce the full range of products or were not permitted to export to certain markets that were reserved for another subsidiary elsewhere. A survey conducted by the Department of Trade in the late 1950s into this practice found it to be fairly widespread, particularly among British-owned firms (Arndt & Sherk 1959, pp. 239–42). This kind of global decision-making by multinationals was generally beyond the control of Australian authorities and remained a disadvantage seized on by the critics of foreign investment.

By the early 1970s, political opinion in Australia was running strongly in favour of curbing the role of foreign direct investment. During the first two years of the decade, foreign capital flowed into Australia at twice the average rate of the previous decade. In November 1972, just prior to a general election, the government passed the *Foreign Companies (Takeovers) Act*. This was the first occasion in peacetime that the Australian government had taken powers to restrict foreign direct investment across all sectors. It gave the government the right to block a takeover if a foreigner would, as a result, obtain more than 15 per cent of the voting rights in the target company, or a foreign company more than 40 per cent, and such ownership was deemed by the government to be against the 'national interest'. This action was followed up by the new Labor government, which introduced restrictions on foreign investment in real estate in March 1974, and in September created the Foreign Investment Advisory Committee to vet all foreign investment proposals. Special provisions were enacted to ensure higher minimum levels of Australian ownership in mining, non-bank finance, insurance and real estate.

---

**SUMMARY BOX**

Australia's participation in the Long Boom enjoyed by the world's developed economies depended on its ability to attract international resources and to pay for these by expanding exports. Once again, Australia tapped heavily into international sources of capital, but in this period most of the foreign funding comprised direct investment by overseas firms. American and British companies invested in Australian manufacturing and resources, attracted by the strongly growing home market for manufactures and the minerals boom. This form of capital inflow prevented the external debt crises that Australia had experienced in the past, but it also led to a high degree of foreign ownership. By the end of the 1960s there were growing concerns expressed about this and in the early 1970s Australian governments took measures to restrict foreign investment.

---

## Immigration

The restrictions imposed on foreign investment by both sides of politics in the early 1970s was an indication that the Australian electorate was not willing to tolerate a degree of internationalisation that was regarded as excessive. Similar sentiments led to curbs on immigration levels at the same time, marking the beginning of the end of the era of post-war mass immigration. Such expressions of economic nationalism revealed a continuing unease in Australia about its relationship with the world economy. In spite of, or perhaps because of, the successful employment of international factors of production and booming Australian exports, there remained a lack of complete commitment to globalisation. This hesitancy was evident in the increase in tariff protection during the 1960s and early 1970s. The Australian government's reluctance to join the OECD for a decade after it was formed in 1960, for fear that membership might increase foreign influence over Australian economic policy, was another example of the same phenomenon.

**Table 9.3**   Immigration to Australia, 1958–1973 (thousands of persons)

| Year | Arrivals | Departures | Net immigration |
|------|----------|------------|-----------------|
| 1958 | 110 | 45  | 65  |
| 1959 | 124 | 40  | 84  |
| 1960 | 139 | 47  | 92  |
| 1961 | 128 | 59  | 69  |
| 1962 | 125 | 60  | 65  |
| 1963 | 144 | 67  | 77  |
| 1964 | 173 | 69  | 104 |
| 1965 | 191 | 80  | 111 |
| 1966 | 189 | 93  | 96  |
| 1967 | 192 | 96  | 96  |
| 1968 | 219 | 96  | 123 |
| 1969 | 249 | 108 | 141 |
| 1970 | 259 | 120 | 139 |
| 1971 | 234 | 130 | 104 |
| 1972 | 193 | 137 | 56  |
| 1973 | 170 | 108 | 62  |

Note: Arrivals and departures refer to 'permanent and long-term arrivals and departures'.
Source: Based on ABS *Arrivals and Departures* (Cat. no. 3404.0).

Mass immigration did, however, continue almost to the end of the Long Boom. Australia's population increased from 8.3 million in 1951 to just over 13 million in 1971, an average annual rate of growth of 2.9 per cent. This was not particularly high by world standards, but was the highest rate of growth in Australia since the nineteenth century. About one-third of the increase was due to net migration, though the proportion rose to over 40 per cent between 1964 and 1971, the period of heaviest immigration (see Table 9.3). These eight years alone accounted for 41 per cent of the total net migration of 2.2 million that occurred between 1950 and 1973, the period of highest net immigration to Australia in the twentieth century (see Fig 1.6 in Chapter 1). Immigration was closely controlled by government regulation, so these high influxes of people reflected consistent government policy and practice.

Why was mass immigration pursued? One reason was concern about the level of population in such a geographically large country. Partly, this was an argument about defence and partly a counter to international comment that pointed to what seemed to be small numbers of Australians selfishly reserving vast resources and **land** area to themselves. Immigration was also a major tactic in the strategy for post-war economic growth and industrialisation. Immigrants were required as an immediate and controllable addition to the labour force. In the period of post-war reconstruction, discussed in Chapter 8, 'displaced persons' were directly recruited for public works schemes such as the Snowy Mountains Hydro Electric Project. The role of immigrants as workers continued to be emphasised during the 1950s and 1960s, particularly in the manufacturing and construction industries. In the 1950s, immigrants comprised more than two-thirds of the net increase to the manufacturing workforce. In the 1960s, there was an absolute decline in the number of native-born workers in manufacturing and so factories became even more dependent on immigrants as workers (Collins 1975).

Migrants, as long as some members of their family could find work, also made excellent consumers, since they often arrived with little in the way of personal possessions. Migrants joined native-born Australians in pursuing the Australian dream of home ownership, with its prerequisite accumulation of durable goods and motor vehicles. Maintaining high levels of **aggregate demand** was an essential part of the economic growth strategy of the post-war years and immigration was regarded as important in achieving this and overcoming the disadvantage of the small domestic market. Immigration was also linked to capital inflow. This was not so much through funds brought in by migrants. In fact, immigration had a small negative effect on the balance of payments through remittances by migrants to their families back home. Rather it reflected the belief that mass immigration encouraged foreign multinational firms to establish operations in Australia. A strong commitment to large-scale immigration, it was felt, gave foreign investors confidence in the future growth of the Australian economy.

How was mass immigration ensured in these years? As discussed in the last chapter, initial plans to bring British migrants failed and the bulk of immigrants during the late 1940s were displaced persons and other refugees who were selected for immigration by the Australian authorities. This source dried up by the early 1950s, however, and from then on the Australian government recruited immigrants by means of assisted passages and sponsorship. Offering assisted passages allowed the Australian government both to attract potential migrants and select those they wanted. Sponsorship schemes were used to boost British migration in the face of rising numbers of non–English-speaking migrants. Assisted passages, however, were not made available to all migrants. Those from the UK generally came on programs such as the '£10 fare', but many of the non–English-speaking migrants financed their own immigration costs or had these paid for by Australian firms recruiting them as workers.

Who came? The *Immigration Restriction Act of 1901* that consolidated the White Australia Policy was not abolished until 1973, so that for nearly all of the Long Boom period there was a prohibition on non-white immigration. This was based on race and racial appearance rather than on nationality. Thus a UK citizen of West Indian, Indian, Pakistani, Sri Lankan or West African origin or parents was not allowed to enter Australia as a permanent settler, whereas a South African, Kenyan or Rhodesian of British (or Dutch) origin, might. Jews were also discriminated against until 1953, though the Australian government was less frank about this aspect of the policy (Morgan 1992; Rutland 1988). US citizens were welcomed, unless they happened to be Afro-Americans, in which case they were refused settlement. None of these restrictions were stated in the Act of 1901 and nor was the term 'White Australia Policy' used officially. Rather, immigration officials with the co-operation of shipping companies enforced the policy during the twentieth century (Palfreeman 1967; Yarwood 1964). This meant that there was some room for flexibility in the definitions of the White Australia Policy. This was exercised after the Second World War so that all Europeans and some migrants from the

**Figure 9.2**   Sources of settler arrivals to Australia, 1959 to 1971

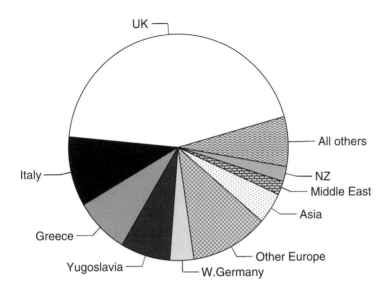

Source: Based on ABS *Overseas Arrivals and Departures* (Cat. no. 3404.0).

Middle East were included. The official definition of Australia's immigration policy, however, was explicit about Asians: 'In pursuance of the established policy, the general practice is not to permit Asiatics or other coloured persons to enter Australia for the purpose of settling permanently' (Australia 1954, p. 372). Through a series of agreements between Australia and continental European governments in the 1950s, the net was cast wider than ever before. The result is shown in Figure 9.2. The UK provided 44 per cent of Australian immigration in 1959–1971 and Europe 40 per cent. The remaining 16 per cent was drawn from a variety of sources, particularly New Zealand, the Middle East, the United States and Asia.

Although the net was cast wider in the 1950s and 1960s, it was not cast over Asia in any real sense. In 1957, 'highly qualified and distinguished' non-whites were allowed to settle and this category was widened in 1966 to include highly skilled technicians (Kunz 1988, p. 105). By this time the Asian population of Australia, descendants of the nineteenth century Asian inflows, was very small and in decline. Asian migrants were considered not to assimilate well to Australia's predominantly European culture and society and to be too 'different' to be acceptable to the bulk of the electorate.

This created a racially driven immigration policy that allowed Europeans in and kept Asians out irrespective of skills, language, educational qualifications and other such criteria. It also meant that Australia was prepared to take some refugees from communism in Hungary or Czechoslovakia, but not those fleeing from communist regimes in China or South-East Asia. From the late 1960s, domestic and international critics pressed the Australian government to make concessions. Their appeal was made largely on moral and political grounds, but Australia's growing trading relations with Asia (or at least, Japan) were used as additional leverage. From 1966, a trickle of highly educated Asians, mainly from the Indian sub-continent, were permitted to settle, though they remained subject to regulations that were not imposed on other migrant citizens (Rivett 1975, p. 51; Yarwood & Knowling 1982, pp. 282–90). The racial basis of immigration policy was not basically altered, however, until the introduction of new legislation in 1973. This introduced an immigration regime in which selection was non-discriminatory on grounds of race, colour, ethnicity, country of birth, religion or gender. Instead, migrants were chosen for skills and family connections with existing Australian residents. By this time, mass immigration had ended and it was considered unlikely that the number of immigrants from Asia would be very high since there was not a large Asian population already in Australia to provide the basis for family reunion. Indeed, this proved to be correct, until the refugee crisis in the late 1970s changed the situation.

Immigration restrictions during the 1950s and 1960s determined who was not allowed to settle in Australia, but there were important differences between the experiences of the English and non–English-speaking immigrants who were allowed in. The former made up the largest group and came overwhelmingly from the United Kingdom. They tended to have educational qualifications and work experience that were more readily recognised in the Australian economy. They found employment in the better paid jobs in manufacturing, including much of lower and middle management, and in services, including large numbers in the public service, health and education. They were more likely to be part of a family migrating than single persons and the proportion of females was higher than among those from continental Europe.

Immigrants from a non–English-speaking background came from a variety of countries among which Italy, Greece, Yugoslavia and West Germany figured strongly at different times. Immigrants from the Middle East were chiefly from Lebanon. These migrants were more likely to experience periods of unemployment and obtain jobs at the bottom of the pay structure. Such jobs were likely to be the least desirable and safe in Australia's burgeoning factory system (Collins 1975). Non–English-speaking households were more likely to have more than one adult in employment or seeking employment. Family members were more likely to engage in 'outwork' in the home, a group that was the most exploited class of workers of all (McAllister & Kelley 1984, pp. 53–68; Storer & Hargreaves 1976, pp. 39–103). Income per head among non–English-speaking migrants in Australia was below that of English-speaking settlers (Birrell 1988, p. 885; Collins 1988; Lever-Tracy & Quinlan 1988, chapters 1 and 5). Denied access to the better paid jobs and professions and unable to build a career in the public service, non–English-speaking migrants were over represented in business. Most of these were small businesses, chiefly urban and predominantly in retailing and construction, though there were some in agriculture and viticulture. Some became successful large business owners in property, construction, transport, engineering and retailing, and here too they were a disproportionate group among Australia's richest and most successful **entrepreneurs** (Ostrow 1987; Glezer 1988, pp. 860–4).

It seems likely that migration led to an improvement in material living conditions for most migrants who came to settle in Australia during the Long Boom, though their happiness and spiritual well-being are impossible to quantify. Relatively few returned to their homeland permanently and of those who did there were a disproportionate number from the UK. For these disappointed migrants, perhaps Australia was *too* much like Britain to make a 'new life' and in any case, returning to Britain was easier than repatriation in the case of non–English-speakers. Whatever the balance sheet of each individual migrant experience, there is no doubt that as a group, migrants made a vital contribution to achieving the strategies of growth, development and modernisation pursued by the post-war planners. Whether their vision for Australia as an industrial country with a larger and more diverse population was appropriate is a matter of opinion. The role of migrants in the Long Boom, on the other hand, is a matter of fact.

**SUMMARY BOX**

Australia pursued a post-war policy of high immigration to expand the size of the labour force and the domestic market. It also hoped to allay international criticisms of Australia's small population in such a large country. Immigrant labour for manufacturing industry was an integral part of the post-war strategy of economic development through industrialisation. Immigration was encouraged by the use of financial inducements to potential migrants, at first from Britain and then from Europe and the Middle East. The White Australia Policy continued to operate, however, to prevent immigration from Asia and Africa. The advent of large numbers of non–English-speaking settlers in Australia led to further segmentation of the Australian workforce, with the lower paid and less agreeable jobs being disproportionately taken by the non–English-speaking migrants. Their exclusion from the better paid white-collar jobs also encouraged a move into business enterprise by non–English-speakers.

## Exports and the balance of payments

The growth strategies of the Australian governments in the 1950s and 1960s depended on capital inflow being matched as far as possible by foreign exchange earnings. If the current account balance moved too far into deficit the capital inflow might decline and a balance of payments crisis occur. As a rule of thumb, a deficit greater than 4 per cent of GDP was a matter for concern, above 5 per cent and it demanded the kind of action taken in 1961. The current account deficit could be managed by restricting imports, and in the short run this is what happened in balance of payments crises. But in the longer term, it undermined Australia's economic development to hold down imports too much for too long. The Australian economy ran a deficit on **net services**, **unrequited transfers** and **net income** throughout the twentieth century.

During the Long Boom these deficits tended to rise (see Table 9.2). International transport costs paid to foreigners increased as foreign trade grew; the net deficit on international travel items increased as Australian residents discovered the pleasures of international tourism at a time when in-bound tourism was in its infancy. Unrequited transfers rose because immigrants sent more money out of the country than they brought in and because Australia made foreign aid donations. Net income (chiefly interest and dividends) was a deficit item as a result of foreign investment in Australia exceeding by a huge margin Australian investment abroad in these years. To keep the current account manageable and not to unduly restrict Australian access to imports, the economy must maximise its exports. Until 1968–69, efforts to achieve this were not met with great success. In the 10 years 1950–51 to 1959–60, exports exceeded imports in all but three years. In the next 10 years, exports exceeded imports in only five years. Putting this comparison another way, in the 1950s the value of imports was 92 per cent on average of the value of exports, but in the 1960s they were 98 per cent. Yet a merchandise **trade surplus** (exports greater than imports) was essential if the rest of the balance of payments was to remain viable.

## Searching for new markets

By the early 1960s, Australia was looking for new export markets and new commodities. Britain's move to join the European Economic Community adversely affected food exports from Australia to Britain. Wool prices were low and declining. The treaty signed in 1957 between Australia and Japan and the decision taken three years later to allow iron ore exports addressed both problems: Japan would replace Britain and iron ore would replace wool. In fact, Japan proved to be an important customer for a range of products beyond minerals, wool in particular. Mineral exports proved to comprise a much wider range than simply iron ore: bauxite, coal, copper, lead, manganese, nickel, tin, titanium, tungsten, zinc and zirconium were also new exports, or old ones that received a new lease of life in the minerals boom (Pinkstone 1992, pp. 178–90). Minerals began to be more significant in Australia's exports from 1968. They increased as a proportion of all merchandise exports, from 5.5 per cent in the first half of the 1960s to 11.4 per cent in the second half. In the early 1970s, mineral and fuel exports accounted for over 18 per cent of Australia's exports, making them the second largest export earner, just ahead of wool. Iron ore made up two-thirds of these mineral exports by this time.

Japanese demand was vital to the success of the boom in mineral exports. Japan had purchased the bulk of Australia's smaller iron ore output in the 1930s until such exports were banned in 1938. Now Japanese firms resumed as Australian iron ore mining companies' major customers. Around four-fifths of all iron ore exported from Australia in the late 1960s and early 1970s went to Japan. Coal also headed north with almost all of the much-enlarged production of coal being sold to Japanese industrial users by the mid-1960s. Foreign investment was also an essential element in making the minerals boom work. Australian firms did not have the expertise or capital resources to exploit the newly prospected finds, though there were one or two exceptions, such as the Western Mining Corporation in Western Australia (McKern 1976, pp. 36–47; Bambrick 1970, p. 21; Tsokhas 1986). By the early 1970s, about 52 per cent of the value added by the mining industry came from firms that were foreign owned. The mining companies normally paid for infrastructure and development costs, but both Australian and foreign mining enterprises were able to write these costs off against tax and royalty payments. Such tax incentives were criticised in the early 1970s as arguments about the role of foreign investment in Australia gathered force and in the Whit-lam era tax concessions to foreign and domestic mining firms were reduced.

## Manufactures exports

The second area where Australian exports strengthened in the 1960s was manu-factures. This was perhaps surprising in view of the criticisms that had been made about manufacturing firms in Australia being unwilling or unable to export. Yet manufactures as a share of total merchandise exports increased from 12 per cent at the beginning of the 1950s to 20 per cent in the mid-1960s and to 26 per cent in the early 1970s. By the end of the Long Boom, manufactures were the largest export earner, well ahead of both minerals and fuels and wool (Pinkstone 1992, pp. 175–8, 379–80). Even more surprising was that export of both simply trans-formed and elaborately transformed manufactured goods increased at about the same pace during these years. Manufactures exports were quite varied and included sophisticated products, such as motor vehicles, electrical equipment, machinery and scientific instruments, as well as the more basic textiles, iron and steel products, chemicals and non-ferrous metal manufactures.

Markets for these exports were also diverse, in contrast to Australia's 'tradi-tional' exports that tended to go to one major trading partner. By 1970, three-quar-ters of manufactures sales went to 12 countries: New Zealand, the United Kingdom, Japan, the United States, South Africa, Papua New Guinea, Singapore, Indonesia, West Germany, Hong Kong, The Philippines and Malaysia. By this time, 55 per cent of manufactures exports went to Asia–Pacific countries and to this extent they played a pioneering role in Australia's closer trading ties with the neighbouring region. Most of the more sophisticated manufactures went to the less industrialised markets, whereas the industrial countries, especially Japan, the United Kingdom and the United States, purchased mainly semi-manufactures and simply transformed metal products from Australian producers.

The rise of manufactures exports reflected the growth of manufacturing output in Australia generally in the Long Boom and, in the 1960s, rapidly growing world trade in manufactured goods. Trade liberalisation in the 1960s focused on reducing trade barriers to the international exchange of manufactures and Australian firms benefited from this, though Australian tariff policy did not contribute to world trade liberalisation itself. Manufactures was certainly the dynamic sector of world trade in these years, and perhaps if manufacturing firms in Australia had pursued export growth with more vigour, the results would have been even more dramatic. Not only did foreign ownership and Australian tariff protection encourage manufacturing firms to concentrate on the home market, but it was noticeable that the Australian government gave far more support and encouragement to other 'traditional' export industries, including mining, than they did to manufacturing. As most manufactur-ing firms continued to make good profits from the domestic market, and the government did nothing to stimulate a more outward looking perspective, there was little incentive to make more than a minimal effort to export.

Nevertheless, the rise in the proportion of manufactures in Australia's export mix did represent an important structural change and did show what could be achieved in the absence of an export-oriented industry policy. By the early 1970s, when manufactures accounted for one-quarter of the value of all merchandise exports, a stage had been reached that might have seen Australian manufactures become the dominant force in export growth. In fact, manufacturing moved into a long-term decline and the level manufactures reached in the share of total merchandise exports at the beginning of the 1970s was not surpassed for many years.

## Traditional exports

Apart from minerals, fuels and manufactures, Australian exports were not dynamic. Wool exports experienced a secular decline in prices caused by competition from synthetic fibres and large increases in output from other suppliers to the world market. Wool was exported in greater volumes during the 1960s, but this did not offset falling prices, so by the early 1970s foreign exchange earnings from wool-growers had declined by one-quarter. Inevitably, wool became less important in the total export mix. From dominating Australia's merchandise exports in the mid-1950s, wool's share declined to less than one-fifth by 1972. Australian wool producers needed to find new markets as it was their traditional ones of Britain and Western Europe that were switching most heavily to synthetics. The Soviet Union and China were novel destinations for Australian wool bales, but the saviour of the wool farmers was Japan. As Japan's dazzling industrial expansion continued, its woollen mills took more and more of their raw product from Australia, so that by the early 1970s, nearly 40 per cent of wool sales were to Japanese buyers, which was significantly more than sales to Britain and Western Europe put together. Government assistance to the wool-growing industry was undertaken by the Australian Wool Board established in 1962 and by the introduction of a floor price scheme in 1970. But although such action might have been helpful in the short run, it could not offset market forces and declining prices in the longer term.

Wheat exports suffered similarly to wool. Australian wheat production and export increased considerably between 1950 and 1970, as more land was brought under cultivation and more intensive methods of farming were adopted. But world prices declined and the value of wheat exports did not keep up with the rises in volumes. Declining world prices were a reflection of agricultural protectionism, especially in Australia's 'traditional' wheat markets of the United Kingdom, Egypt, India, West Germany and Italy. Large sales were made to the Soviet Union and China in some years, but these markets, although potentially great, were unreliable and subject to short-term fluctuations. Japan was a more reliable new customer and sales also increased to South-East Asia. Australia was a signatory to the International Wheat Agreements (extended to other grains in 1968) from 1949 onwards. These attempted to balance world supply and demand through stockpiling and, until 1971, by the importing nations agreeing to minimum and maximum prices. The most useful contribution of the international agreements was co-ordination of the disposal of US surplus wheat to **less developed countries**, but the agreements could not counter the underlying downward movement of wheat prices that continued until the early 1970s. By that time, wheat had declined to less than 10 per cent of Australia's export earnings.

The only agricultural exports to show dynamic growth during the Long Boom were beef and sugar. Beef benefited from rising world prices that were a reflection of rising real **incomes** in many importing countries, but increases in output from Queensland and the Northern Territory were more important than the price rises in raising export values. Beef was also one of the few primary products Australian producers could sell to the United States, which took between two-thirds and three-quarters of exports during the 1960s. Japan also emerged as a significant market for Australian beef in the late 1960s. These two countries also accounted for the relative success of sugar exports in the 1960s, despite declining world prices. Much progress was made with the mechanisation of sugar production, but nevertheless, growers still relied heavily on the high domestic price of sugar ensured by the complete protection of the home market.

Overall, agricultural and pastoral exports declined in importance in Australia's export mix during the 1960s as manufactures and minerals increased their shares. It was these 'new' exports that helped lift Australia's trade balance into a stronger position by the beginning of the 1970s. Manufactures exports in particular gave rise to the hope that a more mature stage of economic development had been reached. Exports to the United Kingdom and the original six EEC countries declined and Japan moved into first position as an export market from 1966 on (see Table 8.4). The United States also became a more significant source of export demand, particularly for beef, alumina and some other manufactures. Sales to Japan were varied, but iron-ore, coal and wool dominated. Market opportunities in Asia, outside of Japan, were not realised during the Long Boom. Exports to China were only important for wheat in certain years and had declined to less than 1 per cent by 1972. South-East Asian nations took about 10 per cent of Australia's exports by value in the early 1970s, due more to sales of foodstuffs to the expatriate populations of Hong Kong and Singapore than to sales of manufactures or industrial raw materials. The two East Asian countries that were industrialising rapidly in this period, South Korea and Taiwan, bought virtually nothing from Australia. Apart from the rise of Japan as a significant trading partner, Australia's exports to Asia, like its attitude generally to Asia, remained in the mould of the nineteenth century.

## Protectionism

Despite the strong growth of world trade in the 1960s and the liberalisation of international trade barriers for manufactures, protectionism remained stubbornly high in trade in agricultural commodities. Often these barriers were non-tariff ones, principally various forms of quotas and other devices that restricted the volume of these imports. The United States was a major force in reducing tariffs on manufactures, but proved lukewarm when it came to agricultural protectionism. American farmers remained a powerful political lobby. The establishment of the **EEC** in 1957, with the Common Agricultural Policy as its centrepiece, marked a further intensification of protectionism against agricultural goods coming into the 'six'. In 1973, the United Kingdom, Ireland and Denmark also joined the EEC, further reducing the prospects of sales of agricultural commodities to the **Common Market** by the rest of the world. In the 1960s, Australia refused to join in the liberalisation of international trade in manufactures and was unable to make any progress in persuading the international community to extend trade liberalisation to agricultural produce (Curzon 1965, pp. 34–53). Partly as a result of this protectionism, world trade in agricultural products remained sluggish and this was a major reason why Australia's export position remained precarious until the advent of the minerals export boom at the end of the decade.

## Bilateral trade agreements

In the absence of progress within GATT towards areas of trade liberalisation that would benefit Australia, the government turned its attention to its bilateral trade relationships. Britain's economic realignment with nearby Europe forced Australia to re-think its commercial relations with the former Mother Country. Negotiations for a trade treaty with Japan immediately followed the disappointing trade talks with Britain in 1956 (Crawford 1968, pp. 128–9, 351–6; Rix 1986, pp. 135–62, 185–210). Britain announced its intention to join the 'six' in 1961, but the preferential tariff that British imports enjoyed in the Australian market, dating from the 1920s, continued until Britain actually joined the EEC in 1973 (Gelber 1966, pp. 23–43). Meanwhile, Japan overtook Britain as Australia's main export market in 1966 and was the chief market for mineral exports as these developed at the end of the 1960s.

The Trade Treaty with Japan, signed in 1957 and revised in 1963, was the only important such treaty entered into by Australia during the Long Boom. Trade relations with China were hampered by the Australian government's refusal diplomatically to recognise the government of the People's Republic. The Vietnam War and the intensification of the Cold War in Asia meant that Australia's position as an uncritical follower of US policy in Asia was a further obstacle to good relations with the region. Bilateral trade talks with members of the EEC were pointless, and so this left Australia's wartime ally, the United States, as the only country with whom a bilateral trade agreement might be possible (Crawford 1968, p. 618). However, although Australia was closer politically to the United States than at any former time, it could not translate political goodwill into greater penetration of the US market.

After 1960, Australia no longer discriminated against US imports as the dollar gap had closed and the world moved on to the dollar-**gold standard**. But US goods reached Australian consumers not so much by import as via the direct foreign investment in Australia of American multinationals. Consequently, its high tariff on imports of manufactures was not a strong bargaining weapon for Australia. From its perspective, the US government did not feel that the additional sales of manufactured goods to Australia that might result from a reduction in Australia's tariff were worth the political opposition that would be provoked by an increase in imports of

Australian agricultural produce to the US market. The United States did not participate in Australia's minerals export boom as a market, even though American mining multinationals held a strong position in the industry. As for other primary produce Australia exported, the United States was either self-sufficient or, in the case of wool, beef, lead and zinc, imposed high tariffs or quotas against their entry. In the early 1960s, the Australian government held out some hopes that a trade treaty with the United States might be negotiated, but as the decade progressed, these hopes faded and were not brought to fruition.

## SUMMARY BOX

Export expansion was essential to maintaining the momentum of the Long Boom in Australia, but until the late 1960s Australia's exports were beset with difficulties. Britain, Australia's traditional trading partner, decided in 1961 to join the European Economic Community, and although it did not actually do so until 1973, its decision highlighted the problem of finding new export markets and new export commodities. Japan provided an alternative market to Britain, particularly for the rapidly expanding minerals exports at the end of the 1960s. Attempts to forge closer export ties with the United States, however, failed and Australia's closer ties with Japan were not part of a general integration with the Asia–Pacific area. The expansion of Australian manufacturing output and the buoyancy of world trade in manufactures also led to a rise in importance of manufactured goods in Australia's export mix, though the criticism that Australian manufacturers should be more export-orientated continued to be made. With the rise of minerals and energy exports, Australia was still highly dependent on world demand for primary products at the end of the Long Boom.

## Missed opportunities

The lack of complete success in forging new trading partnerships meant that Australia remained less than fully committed to the international economy during the Long Boom, despite the emphasis placed on international trade and international inflows of capital and people as being vital for its economic development. The Australian government delayed for 10 years joining the OECD. Australia increased its tariff barriers during the 1960s, maintained the White Australia Policy more or less intact to 1973, and by the early 1970s was beginning to question the wisdom of unrestricted capital inflow. Economic nationalism had become an election winner by 1972. These were years when Australia's economic prosperity depended on the continuing boom in the international economy, but they did not represent a period of 'globalisation'. Australia's exports did not grow as fast as world trade increased and Australia's share of world trade declined (see Figure

**Figure 9.3** Australia's terms of trade, 1949–50 to 1974–75

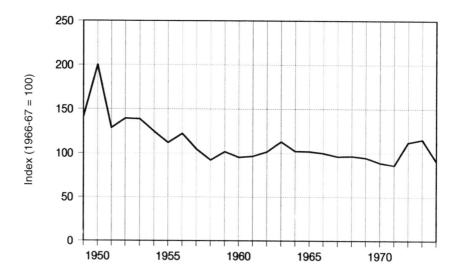

Source: Based on RBA 1996, p. 30.

9.3). The growth of world trade and the widening of Australia's exports to include significant shares to manufactures and minerals and fuels kept Australia's terms of trade fairly stable during the Long Boom. The balance of payments crises that occurred periodically up to the end of the 1960s were the result of domestic surges of growth that pulled in too many imports, rather than caused by a collapse of export prices as had occurred in earlier times.

But the absence of any such external shock, together with full employment, rising living standards and industrialisation, created complacency. Despite many warnings that there were structural deficiencies in the Australian economy, governments looked only at the superficial economic outcomes and concluded that there was no need for economic reform. Complacency led governments to accede to the demands of vested interests on all sides: unions, foreign multinationals, farmers and mining companies. Rather than embark on economic restructuring, governments in the Long Boom (until 1973) were ideologically opposed to reform and the actions they did take only entrenched the structural problems ever more deeply. These were, ironically, the ideal years for implementing economic structural changes that would dislocate labour and capital in the short run. Gender equity in pay scales, for example, could have been brought in gradually over the 1960s without causing the disruption their sudden introduction led to after 1973. Similarly, cutting tariffs would have caused some **structural unemployment**, but given the strength of the labour market, adjustment costs would have been minimal. A later generation would look back on this period as a 'golden age', but it was also one of missed opportunities.

# Suggested further reading

Bell, S. 1993, *Australian Manufacturing and the State: the Politics of Industry Policy in the Post-war Era*, Cambridge University Press, Cambridge.

Boehm, E.A. 1993, *Twentieth Century Economic Development in Australia*, 3rd edn, Longman Cheshire, Melbourne.

Capling, A. & Galligan, B. 1992, *Beyond the Protective State*, Cambridge University Press, Cambridge.

Catley, B. 1996, *Globalising Australian Capitalism*, Cambridge University Press, Cambridge.

Crawford, J.G. 1968, *Australian Trade Policy 1942–1966: a Documentary History*, Australian National University Press, Canberra.

Davidson, F.G. 1969, *The Industrialization of Australia*, 4th edn, Melbourne University Press, Melbourne.

Glezer, L. 1982, *Tariff Politics: Australian Policy-making 1960–1980*, Melbourne University Press, Melbourne.

Pinkstone, B. 1992, *Global Connections: A History of Exports and the Australian Economy*, Australian Government Publishing Service, Canberra.

Rattigan, A. 1986, *Industry Assistance: the Inside Story*, Melbourne University Press, Melbourne.

Whitwell, G. 1986, *The Treasury Line*, Allen & Unwin, Sydney.

# End note

[1]  *Economic Enquiry*, vol. I, pp. 373–5, vol. II, p. 1073. The theoretical work for determining effective rates of protection had already been done: W. Max Corden 1957, pp. 29–51, reprinted in Corden 1997, pp. 8–30; in Hunter 1963, pp. 174–214.

# PART IV

1974 TO 1989

# 10

# International impacts on Australia, 1974–1989

Australia's position in the global economy appeared to improve significantly in the early 1970s. Strong **economic growth** in the industrial nations drove up international **demand** for **primary products**, pushing their prices to record levels and Australia's exports boomed. The world economy was shaken by dramatic oil price rises in 1972 and 1973, but Australia seemed better placed than most of the OECD in that it was more or less self-sufficient in crude oil and its coal exports made it a net energy exporter. Australia's export earnings were so great in 1972 and 1973 that they produced an overall **current account balance of payments** surplus, a rare occurrence. However, inflationary forces from the late 1960s undermined the sustainability of economic growth in the industrial countries. When such nations slowed their growth in response to the oil price rises, an international recession brought the post-war Long Boom to an end.

Australia was not insulated from these impacts and indeed, **inflation** in Australia was higher than in most of the rest of the OECD in the 1970s. In 1974 and 1975, economic growth in Australia slowed to under 2 per cent and **unemployment** began to rise. From the mid-1970s, the global economy entered a more turbulent period characterised by slower growth of world trade and great volatility in the world's financial system. This created international conditions that were much less favourable to Australia than those of the 1960s. This chapter outlines the main changes that brought about the end of the Long Boom internationally and the weaker economic conditions that replaced it. Chapter 11 looks at Australia's struggle to cope with these adverse international forces in more detail.

## The end of the Long Boom

The Long Boom came to an end in 1974 when the industrial economies entered a severe recession that impacted one on the other. The economic indicators of the

**Figure 10.1**    Inflation in Australia and the OECD, 1970 to 1989

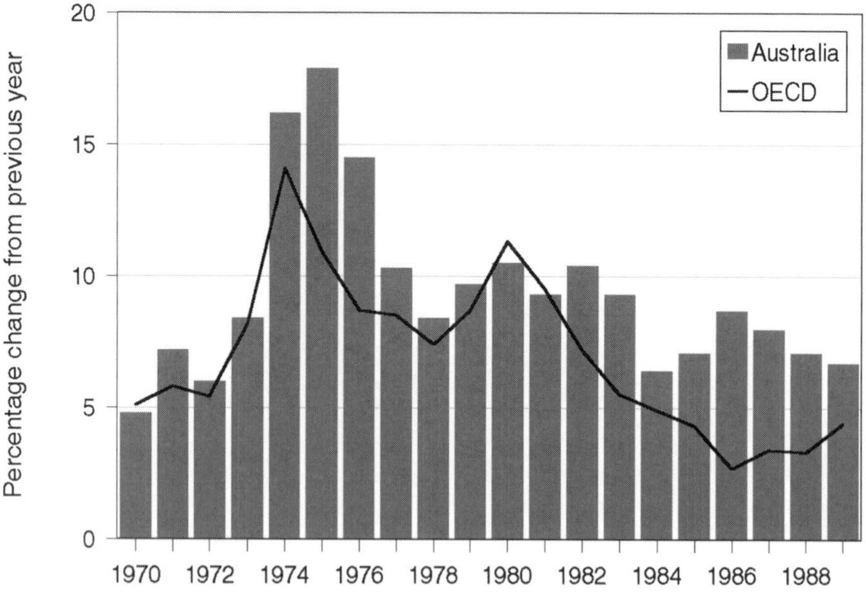

Source: Based on OECD 1990, no. 48, p. 185.

previous period were reversed: inflation soared, economic growth declined and unemployment increased. The principal cause of this crisis was inflation, though the forces causing inflation were varied.

## The effects of inflation

Inflation rates began to rise in the major industrial economies in the late 1960s. The average rate for OECD member countries was 3 per cent per annum in the mid-1960s but 5 per cent in the years 1968–1972, rising swiftly thereafter to average 11 per cent between 1973 and 1975. Inflation rates varied among OECD members: Australia's rate was one of the highest (see Figure 10.1). Inflation began as a domestic phenomenon, but soon became an international one as well. Inflation was always part and parcel of the post-war recovery and 'economic miracles' of the industrial nations. In the late 1940s and early 1950s, inflationary crises in a number of industrial countries had required drastic action. The Korean War Boom in 1950–1951 also forced prices to spiral upwards and led to tough deflationary countermeasures. In the mid-1950s, inflationary forces were kept under control by government intervention. Governments punctuated the growth cycle with short periods of **deflation**, which usually involved a combination of **wage and price freezes**, tax increases and monetary squeezes.

From the mid-1960s, however, these measures became more difficult to impose in the industrial democracies. Trade unions exercised strong bargaining power after two decades of **full employment**. **Oligopolistic** firms that passed on wage increases in the form of price rises dominated many industries. Nationalised industries and services were, by their nature, monopolies, and were also more inclined to meet wage demands quickly and pass on the costs to their customers. Short periods of deflation were not so acceptable to an electorate for whom the major economic crises of the 1930s and 1940s now seemed a distant memory. Faster economic growth implied more inflationary pressures, but these pressures were not contained in the late 1960s as effectively as they had been earlier (van Cleveland & Brittain 1976, pp. 31–6).

In the United States, increased government spending in the mid-1960s, both on the Vietnam War and on domestic welfare measures, led to federal **budget** deficits that were financed chiefly by borrowing. The effect was inflationary. The US Federal Reserve Board alternately adopted policies of monetary expansion and contraction, but overall **monetary policy** was expansionary, especially in 1971 and 1972 in the run-up to the presidential election, and prices moved up sharply in 1973, producing an inflation rate of over 6 per cent. A number of other countries ran expansionary monetary policies during the early 1970s, among them Britain, France, Italy and Japan. In these four countries, the average inflation rate rose from 6.5 per cent in 1971 to 10 per cent in 1973. Even in Germany, the European nation with a reputation for low inflation in the Long Boom, the rate jumped from 1.9 per cent in 1969 to 6.9 per cent in 1973. By that year a number of OECD countries were experiencing double-digit inflation rates, including Japan, Italy and Spain. Overall, the level of price inflation in the OECD doubled between 1968 and 1973.

Inflation also gathered pace internationally. By the end of the 1960s, the international monetary system was based virtually on a dollar standard. The run-down of American **gold reserves** and US balance of payments deficits meant that **convertibility** of the US dollar to gold was, for all practical purposes, suspended. Foreign **central banks** recognised this fact and accumulated dollars in their reserves without demanding the US Federal Reserve convert them to gold. Such restraint, especially by the large holders of official dollars, Japan and West Germany, helped support the international monetary system, but the build-up of these dollar reserves was also inflationary. Some countries, for example, West Germany, sterilised the inflow by cutting the growth of their own **money supply** and **revaluing** their currency against the US dollar. Others, however, accepted the imported inflation in addition to their own domestically driven price increases. When dollar–gold convertibility was formally ended, in August 1971, the gold reserves of central banks were unlocked and, as gold prices rose, these reserves also increased in value. Some of this increased liquidity expanded domestic money supply and added to inflation (Eichengreen 1996, pp. 128–38).

The international economy was also hit by a series of supply-side shocks in the early 1970s. The prices of primary commodities had risen dramatically in the late 1940s and early 1950s, but had subsided thereafter as supplies increased. By the late 1960s, however, supplies of both internationally traded foodstuffs and raw materials were running behind demand as the industrial countries stepped on the accelerator of economic growth. Substantial price rises were recorded in a broad range of primary products in world trade in 1971 and 1972. The greatest inflationary pressure, however, was felt in energy prices, especially the price of crude oil (see Figure 10.2).

**Figure 10.2**    International oil prices, 1960 to 1995

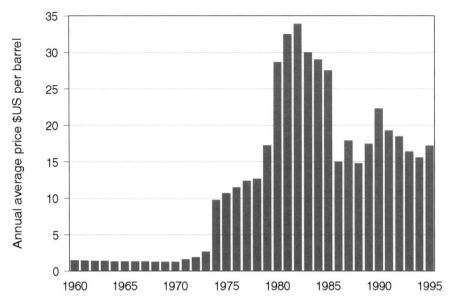

Source: Based on OECD 1997, p. A20.

The dominance in world oil production and distribution of a handful of American and European multinationals, together with the relative political weakness of the oil producing and exporting nations, had kept the price of oil artificially low throughout the 1950s and 1960s. In the early 1970s, however, the oil companies combined with governments of the oil-exporting nations to impose sudden and enormous price rises. The price of crude oil rose from $1.30 a barrel in 1970 to $9.76 a barrel by the end of 1973 – a rise of 650 per cent in three years. The price rises exposed the dependence of the industrial countries, including those that produced some oil themselves, such as the United States, on international supplies of energy for the continuation of the Long Boom. The steep rise in oil prices was inflationary in that it increased costs of production and transportation as well as the pump-price of petrol. Some governments took the opportunity of rising oil prices to raise the level of sales tax on petroleum products. Since the volume of oil consumed did not fall, and there were no significant gains made in the efficiency with which petroleum energy was used, the oil price rise distorted demand patterns as firms and households had to spend more on fuel and less on everything else. This dampened demand for some **consumer goods**, which fed into the gathering economic slowdown (Cooper & Lawrence 1975; OECD 1980, pp. 114–31).

## Economic recession and 'stagflation'

The oil price rise that was announced by the Organisation of Petroleum Exporting Countries (OPEC) in Vienna on Christmas Day 1973 was a trigger that sent all of the industrial countries into a deflationary policy panic. During the first half of

**Table 10.1**  Real economic growth in the OECD area, 1970–1989 (percentage change from previous year)

| Year | Australia | G7 | OECD |
|------|-----------|-----|------|
| 1970 | 5.5 | 3.9 | 4.1 |
| 1971 | 5.0 | 3.3 | 3.5 |
| 1972 | 2.8 | 5.4 | 5.4 |
| 1973 | 6.2 | 6.1 | 6.0 |
| 1974 | 1.9 | 0.2 | 0.6 |
| 1975 | 1.7 | −0.2 | −0.2 |
| 1976 | 3.7 | 4.9 | 4.7 |
| 1977 | 1.0 | 4.2 | 3.9 |
| 1978 | 3.5 | 4.7 | 4.3 |
| 1979 | 3.8 | 3.6 | 3.5 |
| 1980 | 2.4 | 1.4 | 1.5 |
| 1981 | 3.2 | 1.9 | 1.7 |
| 1982 | −0.3 | −0.3 | −0.1 |
| 1983 | 0.5 | 2.9 | 2.7 |
| 1984 | 7.5 | 5.0 | 4.8 |
| 1985 | 5.3 | 3.5 | 3.4 |
| 1986 | 1.6 | 2.7 | 2.7 |
| 1987 | 4.1 | 3.5 | 3.4 |
| 1988 | 3.8 | 4.4 | 4.4 |
| 1989 | 4.2 | 3.6 | 3.7 |

Note: G7 = USA, Japan, Germany, France, Italy, United Kingdom and Canada.
Source: Based on OECD 1990, p. 175.

1974, they all took measures to slow down the economic growth of their economies, imposing more severe measures in many cases than had been seen since the Korean War crisis 23 years earlier. The effect of such ubiquitous economic deceleration was to reduce economic growth to negative levels, and for the first time since the end of the war, the industrial economies moved into an economic recession (see Table 10.1). Inflationary forces, however, proved far more intractable than had been antici-pated. The actions of governments in 1974 and 1975 certainly slowed economic growth substantially, but only gradually and incompletely reduced the underlying rate of inflation. These economies thus experienced a new phenomenon, termed 'stagflation', where economies were stagnant, yet price inflation was still rampant. The slow-down in economic growth in the industrial nations caused a deceleration in the growth of world trade and many countries experienced, or feared they would soon experience, balance of payments difficulties. They therefore took measures to protect their external balances, for example, by restricting imports, that collectively further slowed the pace of world trade (Black 1985; *The Economist* 1979).

As long as inflationary forces remained entrenched in the industrial economies, it was difficult for recovery to take place and economic growth to be restored to previous levels. By the mid-1970s, inflationary expectations were becom-ing embedded in the Western economies. Workers demanded wage rises that

**Table 10.2**   Unemployment in the OECD area, 1970–1989 (per cent of total labour force)

| Year | Australia | G7 | OECD |
|------|-----------|-----|------|
| 1970 | 1.6 | 3.2 | 3.1 |
| 1971 | 1.9 | 3.7 | 3.6 |
| 1972 | 2.6 | 3.8 | 3.7 |
| 1973 | 2.3 | 3.4 | 3.3 |
| 1974 | 2.6 | 3.7 | 3.5 |
| 1975 | 4.8 | 5.4 | 5.2 |
| 1976 | 4.7 | 5.4 | 5.3 |
| 1977 | 5.6 | 5.4 | 5.3 |
| 1978 | 6.2 | 5.1 | 5.2 |
| 1979 | 6.2 | 4.9 | 5.1 |
| 1980 | 6.0 | 5.5 | 5.8 |
| 1981 | 5.7 | 6.2 | 6.3 |
| 1982 | 7.1 | 7.6 | 7.6 |
| 1983 | 9.9 | 8.0 | 8.1 |
| 1984 | 8.9 | 7.4 | 7.7 |
| 1985 | 8.1 | 7.3 | 7.6 |
| 1986 | 8.0 | 7.3 | 7.6 |
| 1987 | 8.0 | 6.8 | 7.2 |
| 1988 | 7.1 | 6.2 | 6.5 |
| 1989 | 6.1 | 5.7 | 6.0 |

Source and notes: see Table 10.1

allowed for expected rises in the cost of living as well as recent or current rises. When governments took fiscal and monetary steps to stimulate growth, inflation accelerated again, usually faster than output could rise or unemployment could fall. This resulted in further bouts of 'stagflation' where relatively high levels of inflation were combined with rising unemployment and sluggish economic growth (World Bank 1984).

It proved impossible to restore full employment conditions, though it was some time before it was generally recognised that the Long Boom was indeed over. **Unemployment rates** rose to record post-war levels in all of the OECD countries (see Table 10.2). Unemployment averaged 3 per cent in the OECD during the 1960s and early 1970s, but jumped to over 5 per cent in 1975, then rose more slowly to 6.5 per cent in 1980. Unemployment rates in Australia also rose in line with the OECD trend, though the levels recorded in Australia were below the average of the OECD until 1977. Australia reached 6 per cent unemployment levels (twice the Long Boom average) in 1978, slightly earlier than the major OECD countries (see Chapter 11). Industries adjusted to lower growth conditions and new jobs were not created as fast as the **labour force** itself grew. Unemployment became structural rather than simply cyclical. **Investment** made in labour-conserving technology in the era of full employment now became a source of 'technological unemployment', as firms continued to shed labour to become more competitive. Moreover, some manufacturing capacity moved from industrial countries to less developed economies in search of cheaper labour, and so these jobs in the industrial nations were lost permanently, though gained elsewhere in the world. Unemployed persons, however, were not perfectly mobile and consequently unemployment in industrial countries tended to be geographically concentrated. Because of the disappearance of relatively less skilled, lower paid jobs in the manufacturing industry, unemployment in these countries tended to be age, gender and skill specific; that is, it was higher among the young, female and less skilled.

Weak recovery from the 1974–1975 world recession occurred from 1976 and continued to 1980. Oil prices stabilised, which meant they declined in **real terms**. Inflation subsided in one or two countries ( Japan and West Germany), but continued to rise in the United States and most of Western Europe, and accelerated in 1979 and 1980 elsewhere. Unemployment was higher in the second half of the 1970s in all OECD countries. Economic growth improved in 1978 and 1979, but higher rates of economic growth in some of the industrial countries in 1979 triggered another oil crisis. As demand for oil rose (the Japanese economy, for example, was growing at over 5 per cent) OPEC's bargaining position strengthened and higher oil prices were posted. The price of crude oil rose by 34 per cent in 1979 and 66 per cent in 1980. By 1980, most governments in the industrial nations were imposing deflationary measures again in order to reduce inflation. As before, the result was a co-ordinated downturn that became a prolonged period of low or negative growth lasting until

## SUMMARY BOX

Inflationary forces in the major industrial economies and internationally grew much stronger at the beginning of the 1970s. During 1972 and 1973, the prices of a range of primary products increased significantly, but in particular there was a dramatic rise in the price of petroleum oil. Governments in the developed economies took measures to counter inflation that resulted in a slowing down in their economic growth and eventually to economic contraction. As inflation continued at high levels, this gave rise to a phenomenon dubbed 'stagflation'. The combination of rampant inflation and economic stagnation in 1974 and 1975 brought to an end the Long Boom of the post-1945 era, though it took several years for this fact to be widely recognised. With slower economic growth, unemployment rose to significant levels for the first time in two decades. At the end of the 1970s, a second oil price rise again caused an international reaction that slowed the major economies and caused another bout of 'stagflation' in 1980–82. Economic growth resumed in the mid-1980s and oil prices fell. By the end of the decade, inflation was low again in most OECD countries (though not in Australia), but unemployment was permanently higher. In 1990, the major economies again slowed, this time in reaction to over-heated asset markets, and another period of economic recession ensued.

1983 or 1984. Unemployment reached record levels, peaking in 1983 at 8.5 per cent average in OECD countries and over 10 per cent in the EEC.

In the next cycle, 1984 to 1989, economic growth recovered, but remained below the levels of the late 1970s recovery. For the OECD as a whole, economic growth averaged 3.7 per cent between 1984 and 1989, compared to 4.1 per cent between 1976 and 1979. It faltered in 1986 and 1989. The years 1984 and 1988 were outstanding for economic growth in the 1980s when rates approached 5 per cent, but higher economic growth could not be sustained. Unemployment fell from 1983 to 1989, but remained higher than in the period 1976–1982. Most OECD countries experienced unemployment rates of around 10 per cent. Inflation, however, did fall substantially. From high points of over 14 per cent in 1974 and 11.3 per cent in 1980, inflation fell to less than 5 per cent in 1984 and to 2.7 per cent in 1986. Inflation in Australia, however, remained well above this. Energy prices fell dramatically in 1986 in response to the more modest economic growth in the industrial nations, and increased world output of crude oil. Other primary commodities also experienced weaker price levels in the mid-1980s. By contrast, share markets and other asset prices (commercial property, for example) boomed in the late 1980s, leading eventually to widespread recessions at the beginning of the 1990s.

# World trade and structural imbalances

## United States–Japan trade relations

International trade conditions deteriorated for Australia from the mid-1970s as the Long Boom unwound. The emergence of the United States as the world's largest debtor nation and Japan as the world's largest creditor created tensions between the two that inhibited the achievement of freer trade. Protectionism increased in the 1970s and 1980s, making it harder for Australian exporters. The oil price rises worsened the US trade deficit although it had been losing trade competitiveness before the first oil shock, and had recorded trade deficits for the first time in the post-war years in 1971 and 1972. In the later 1970s and into the 1980s, the US trade deficit became much larger, partly with the oil-exporting countries, of course, but also with Japan. The United States also experienced rising trade deficits with a number of industrialising countries that 'invaded' the US market with low-cost manufactures. China, Taiwan and Korea were particularly strong exporters to the United States in the late 1970s and 1980s.

The large trade deficits of the United States in the 1980s resulted in rising current account balance of payments deficits and a dramatic expansion of the US **foreign debt**. The foreign debt also increased because of budget deficits caused by US defence expenditure as Cold War tensions escalated. Both the balance of payments deficits and the budget deficits were funded mainly by **capital** inflow from Japan. As the US balance of payments deficits rose, the surpluses of its major trading partners increased (see Figure 10.3). Japan, East Asia and the European Community found the US market an open and expanding one.

**Figure 10.3**   Current account balances of USA, Japan and Germany, 1974 to 1989

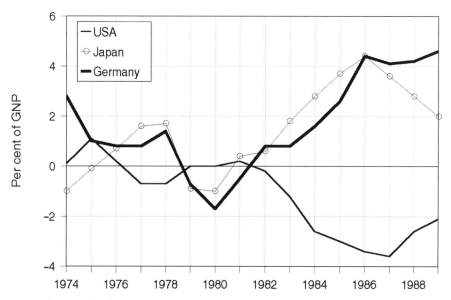

Source: Based on OECD 1990, no. 48, p. 195.

Tensions between the United States government and the Japanese government increased, aggravated by both the huge trade deficit between the United States and Japan, and the indebtedness of the US government to private Japanese lenders to fund the budget deficits. US manufacturers complained of 'unfair competition' from Japanese imports, especially in electronics and motor vehicles, but restrictions on Japanese imports to the US market only stimulated direct investment by Japanese firms in the United States. By the end of the 1980s, the American auto manufacturers, for example, found that US-produced Japanese cars and motor cycles were a more potent form of competition than imports had previously been. Financial deregulation in the major economies in the 1980s made it difficult for the US firms to argue that Japanese firms should not be permitted to set up in the United States. Entry of US goods into the Japanese market, however, remained a sore point, and trade tensions between the two continued into the 1990s (Encarnation 1992).

Competition from Japan was a foretaste of the future for American business. By the end of the 1980s, imports from South-East Asia and imports and direct investment from Korea were affecting American producers. Some of the firms producing in Korea and other parts of South-East Asia were Japanese, but many others were local enterprises that found the United States an attractive market, as the Japanese exporters had done since the 1960s. Imports of goods from China, Taiwan and Hong Kong also entered the US market by the end of the decade, heightening trade tensions between America and Asia (Nester 1990).

Trade tensions also intensified between the United States and Western Europe, and between Japan and Western Europe in the 1980s. The European Community (as the EEC had now become) expanded in size with the addition of new members and adopted further measures for internal economic integration.[1] As the EC grew it also became more **protectionist** in its relations with the rest of the world. Japanese manufactured goods were restricted and in some member countries, Japanese direct investment was curtailed. Like their US counterparts, some European firms complained of lack of fair access to the Japanese domestic market. Japan for its part pointed to the rising exchange rate of the yen as evidence that its firms were simply more efficient than their American and European rivals and argued that it would be unfair to penalise them for that. Despite exhortations to open up the Japanese market, little progress was made in reducing trade imbalances between Japan and the other industrial countries before the end of the growth cycle in 1989 (Murphy 1996, Chaps 6 and 7).

## Protectionism and slowdown of world trade

Protectionism increased generally during the 1980s, much of it taking a non-**tariff** form. Mostly it affected commodities in which the industrial countries had previously had a clear **comparative advantage**, but which were now growing areas for export from the **developing countries**. These goods included textiles, clothing and footwear, metalware, low-price plastic manufactures, steel, motor vehicle parts, and electrical and electronic goods. But additionally, **international trade** in foodstuffs came under increasing protectionist pressure as the United States and the European Community expanded food exports that were heavily **subsidised** and protected their home markets from foreign foodstuffs. This form of protectionism also hurt the developing countries, though some developed temperate food exporters (including Australia) were also adversely affected. Another sector of world trade that was heavily subsidised and protected by the industrial nations was the area of services; for example, insurance, banking, construction, shipping and data-processing. Like foodstuffs, international trade in services effectively lay outside the reach of the GATT and was an area where some developing countries were attempting to expand their exports or at least develop their own service industries for their home market.

By the mid-1980s, the GATT was almost 40 years old and in sore need of reform. A widening of scope was achieved in the Eighth Round of **multilateral** trade negotiations begun at Punta del Este in Uruguay in 1986. For the first time international trade in services and agricultural commodities were included, the latter due to Australia and others. Progress was painfully slow, however, and any liberalisation of world trade that was achieved in the economic cycle which ended in 1989 tended to be the result of bilateral rather than multinational negotiations (the Uruguay Round ended in 1994 at the Marrakesh Conference that brought the World Trade Organisation into being).

World trade appeared to grow rapidly in the early 1970s, but this was largely caused by inflationary forces that pushed world trade values up. By 1974, for example, the value of world exports was 70 per cent above its 1970 level, but in volume terms only 37 per cent above. This was the peak of the world trade **boom** of the post-war era. In 1975, for the first time since the end of the Second World War, the volume of world trade declined. It recovered in **quantum** terms in the late 1970s and by 1979 was 23 per cent up on its 1975 level, but this represented a slower annual growth rate than in the Long Boom. Over the next four years, world trade stagnated and by 1982 it was below its level of 1979 in volume and value terms. Between 1975 and 1982, the volume of world exports grew at an average annual rate of only 3.7 per cent, compared to 11.4 per cent per year at the height of the Long Boom (1965–1972). As discussed in earlier chapters, sluggish or even stationary world trade impacted adversely on the Australian economy leading to a slow-down in growth. The failure of world trade to continue to act as an engine of growth led to calls in the 1980s for new initiatives to revitalise international trade by reducing tariffs, though little was achieved before the end of the decade.

The oil price rises created major distortions in world trade. Despite the oil price rises, most industrial countries increased the volume of their oil imports. For example, the United States, although an oil producer itself, imported almost twice as much mineral fuel and related products in 1980 than in 1970. In the United

## SUMMARY BOX

The rise in the US balance of payments deficit and external debt caused major problems for the international economy. The balance of payments deficit was due to the oil crisis and rising trade deficits with Japan, and the newly industrialising Asian economies. The United States financed its deficit by borrowing from international capital markets, chiefly those of Japan and Germany. The US dollar fell sharply against the yen, leading to a flow of **direct foreign investment** from Japan to the United States. United States–Japan relations deteriorated as trade tensions between the two increased during the 1980s. Trade disputes also arose between the United States and the European Community, and between the European Community and Japan. These imbalances exacerbated trade protectionism, which became more of a problem in world trade in the 1980s. Attempts to curb protectionism through the Uruguay Round of the GATT were stalled by trade tensions between the major economies. World trade contracted in 1975, the first time it had done so since the end of the Second World War. In the late 1970s and 1980s, world trade failed to return to the growth levels of the Long Boom. World trade patterns were distorted by the 'oil shocks' of 1973 and 1979. In the 1980s, the most dynamic sector in world trade was the export of manufactured goods from east and South-East Asia. These developments created difficulties for Australia's trade with its 'traditional' partners, while at the same time it made trade with Asia more attractive and profitable. As a result, in the 1980s and 1990s there was a major shift in Australia's external trade towards its own region.

States, oil imports took up less than 8 per cent of the import bill in 1970, but 31 per cent 11 years later. Fuel accounted for 9 per cent of Germany's import costs in 1970, but 24 per cent in 1981. The impact of this extra cost of fuel in the industrial countries' international trade meant that they had proportionally less to spend on other types of imports, including all other primary products and manufactures. This adversely affected Australia's exports to the major industrial nations.

In the 1960s, the industrial countries traded more and more with each other, with the consequence that their share of world trade increased while the share of the less developed countries declined. In the 1970s, this trend was reversed as oil-exporting **less developed countries** increased their share of world trade. Moreover, from the 1960s, some of the less developed nations began to industrialise rapidly and developed new export markets for manufactures and pulled in more raw materials (and in some instances foodstuffs). This reversal meant that by 1980 the share of world trade of developed and less developed nations was about the same as it had been in 1960: three-quarters from the developed and one-quarter from the less developed. Similarly, by 1980 the dependence of the industrial countries on other industrial countries for international trade was about the same as two decades before (75 per cent). International trade in manufactured goods remained the most buoyant sector of world trade in the 1970s and 1980s, allowing for the distorting impact of the oil price rises. In addition to international trade in manufactures between the older industrial economies, in the 1980s exports of manufactured goods rose rapidly from the newly industrialising economies of east and South-East Asia. Such a development made this region – in which Australia increasingly figured itself to belong – the most dynamic in the global economy.

# International financial flows

## International debt

The oil price shock at the end of 1973 created problems for an international financial system that was still reeling from the move by the major currencies to **floating exchange rates** during the previous two years. Members of the Organisation of Petroleum Exporting Countries (OPEC) found themselves with enormously inflated balance of payments surpluses as the price of their exports soared. As the volume of internationally traded oil continued to rise, the additional export earnings flowing to the OPEC countries from the price rises were not, in the medium term at least, offset by lower physical shipments of oil. What were the OPEC countries going to do with their new-found wealth? And which international institutions would they turn to for assistance? Although some of the 'petrodollars' were spent on increased imports of consumer and **capital goods**, and the governments of some OPEC countries invested in major Western industrial firms, the bulk of the export earnings were deposited with international banks. This produced a considerable increase in the liquidity of such banks over a very short period (Wachtel 1990, Chapter 5).

These banks were well established by the 1970s. After the Second World War, US multinational banks like Chase Manhattan were prominent in managing the financial flows from the United States to Europe under the Marshall Plan, and they provided financial services to many of the American multinational corporations expanding in the world during the 1950s and 1960s. British banks, such as Barclays and National Westminster, and some European ones also expanded international operations during the Long Boom. International banks had become more prominent in the years just before the oil price rise through the rise of the Eurodollar market. Eurodollars were US dollars held in the European banking system and lent to governments and other official institutions. The international banks had developed the techniques necessary to facilitate these loans, particularly the use of syndication, in which a group of banks lent to a government. **Interest** rates on these loans were flexible, being adjusted every six months in accordance with the prevailing inter-bank interest rate in London. As the system expanded, more of these loans were made to the larger less developed countries in the late 1960s and early 1970s. Mexico, Brazil, Argentina, Peru, South Korea and The Philippines were major borrowers. Eurocurrency loans by private international banks were also made to Eastern European governments anxious to cash in on the growing prosperity of the West.

Thus, by the time the oil-exporting countries were experiencing huge balance of payments surpluses, the international banking system was well established and had some experience in recycling funds that had arisen from unforeseen circumstances. The oil crisis of 1973 provided the international banks with a great deal more money to lend and at the same time created an urgent need for loans by many oil-importing nations, especially those in the Third World. Petrodollars were now added to Eurodollars in a massive expansion of the international money supply, as the **export surpluses** of the member nations of OPEC were recycled through the major banks. The recession in 1974 and 1975 in the industrial countries reduced the scope for bank lending, and so it was that the non–oil-exporting less developed countries became the chief targets of the international banks' activities.

In contrast to loans made by official agencies like the World Bank, loans from international banks were not made for any particular project and thus could be used by the borrowing government for a variety of purposes. This aspect of the lending led to gross overborrowing by developing countries and many were plunged into a severe debt crisis by the beginning of the 1980s. Total external debt of the less developed countries rose from $93 billion in 1972 to $501 billion in 1981, and the proportion owed to private **creditors** increased from one-third to one-half (World Bank 1984b, p. 2). Bank loans accounted for 48 per cent of the increase in external indebtedness of these nations during this period. Loans from aid agencies and government-to-government loans made up the rest. These were generally on much longer terms than loans from banks and often at concessional interest rates, but they took much longer to arrange and their use was carefully monitored or controlled, which made them less popular with many governments seeking loans. Thus, although not all of the money owed by the Third World was owed to banks, it was the international bank lending of the 1970s that drove indebtedness up.

By 1983, the extent of the debt crisis was apparent. On average, servicing international debt absorbed one-fifth of the exports of the less developed countries, but in the case of a number of large borrowers, the debt burden was much greater.

Mexico's debt equalled 43 per cent of its **GNP** in 1983, and servicing this debt took 47 per cent of its export earnings. Brazil's debt servicing absorbed 59 per cent of its export earnings, and Argentina's 39 per cent (World Bank 1984a). The rate of growth of Third World indebtedness slowed in the early 1980s as lower world interest rates eased the servicing burden somewhat and many of the debts could not be met and were 'rescheduled', sometimes a polite term for repudiation. The international banks refused to make any fresh loans, however, and throughout the 1980s the indebted less-developed nations were forced to accept International Monetary Fund (IMF) intervention if they wanted any more money.

The IMF had been somewhat sidelined during the late 1960s and 1970s. The Eurocurrency market lay outside its jurisdiction. The international monetary system was fundamentally changed by the US government in 1971 without consultation with the IMF. And it was the international banks, not the IMF, that the OPEC members turned to when they needed to recycle their export surpluses. The rise of Third Word indebtedness had been driven by the banks in the 1970s, not the IMF or the World Bank, but in the mid-1980s it was the IMF that organised 'rescue programs' to ease the burden of indebtedness and provide some new money in return for government spending cuts and fiscal and monetary reform. The price of IMF support was not popular, but in the end all indebted Third World nations accepted the international body's terms (George 1990).

In the mid-1980s, the international banks looked for new customers to replace the profits they had previously made from lending to the Third World countries. Financial deregulation among the OECD countries provided opportunities to lend to firms seeking capital for expansion by mergers and takeovers. Many major firms were restructured during the mid-1980s using funds borrowed from the international banks. The intense activity in corporate takeovers and mergers in an environment of loose monetary policy was reflected in a rising stock market. This too was fuelled by funds provided by the international banks. By 1987, the main stock markets were very overheated and in need of a correction that came in the form of the '**crash**' of 1987. This was the worst contraction of share prices since the Wall Street Crash of 1929, but it was not as severe as that crash and it did not signify a sudden contraction of the industrial economies. It led, however, to a spate of business failures and corporate crashes that left most international banks with bad debts. After their roller-coaster ride since the late 1960s, by the beginning of the 1990s, with much of the industrial world in recession, the international banks entered a prolonged period of consolidation during which they were less prepared to lend to business (Wood 1988).

## Floating exchange rates, financial deregulation and economic reform

As a system that ensured stable and predictable exchange rates, the international monetary system had completely collapsed by the early 1980s. Although viewed by many at first as a temporary expedient, floating exchange rates became permanent. Towards the end of the 1970s, members of the IMF agreed that a system of 'managed floating exchange rates' should prevail and rules for such management

**Figure 10.4** US dollar/Japanese yen exchange rate, 1970 to 1996

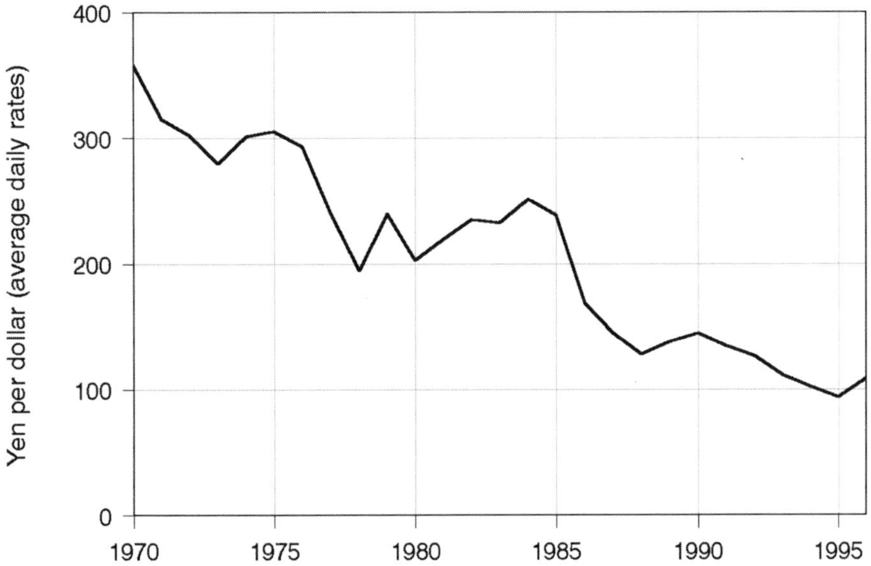

Source: Based on OECD 1997a, p. A40.

were enacted in 1978. The European Community attempted to operate its own monetary system as a kind of 'regional Bretton Woods' from 1979. Both the European Community's system and the set of rules adopted by the IMF envisaged government intervention in the financial markets to regulate or manage floating exchange rates. Experience with such intervention, however, clearly showed that in practice exchange rates were no longer controlled by governments but by the world's financial markets. Many smaller currencies attached themselves to the US dollar or the French franc, or to some other floating currency, but this did not of itself produce stability or predictability.

Exchange rates proved highly unstable. Figure 10.4 shows the volatility between the currencies of the world's two largest economies, culminating in the second half of the 1980s in the 'high yen' crisis. Governments that attempted to influence rates either by direct intervention in the financial market or by taking domestic measures of expansion or contraction often found that their efforts did not produce the exchange rate outcomes they desired. With financial deregulation and the growth of computerised currency trading, an international financial market emerged early in the 1980s that was open nearly all the time. Currency transactions in this market amounted to billions of dollars a day and nearly all these transactions were speculative. No central bank had the resources to defend its currency against the market, though a number tried and failed rather spectacularly.

By the early 1980s, the impact of two international recessions had led to a substantial shift in economic policy directions. It took some time for the realisation of the end of the Long Boom to sink in, but by the beginning of the 1980s it was more widely accepted that a return to the conditions of the 1960s was not a likely occurrence in the near future. This changed perspective led to a more reformist approach in economic policy. Keynesianism, a term that was used fairly loosely by this time, was regarded as having failed or indeed as having caused the overheating of the Long Boom and hence its end in the early 1970s. 'Monetarism', an even looser term, became fashionable as an antidote to what were now viewed as the excesses of government spending in the 1950s and 1960s. Controlling the growth of the money supply (however defined) became the aim of many Western governments during the early 1980s in the hope that such restriction would slow down the pace of inflation and break the 'stagflation' cycle.

Cutting government spending, reducing taxation and balancing budgets were also regarded as the way forward for the industrial countries, even if in practice balanced budgets proved elusive. Above all, the new paradigm called for deregulation and the winding back of the role of the State in capitalist economies so that market forces, not government intervention, would allocate resources. These prescriptions were not really new, but their dominance over the previous practices of managing economies through government controls and intervention did mark a substantial change in emphasis.

The sector that most Western governments deregulated first and to the greatest extent was the financial system: removing controls over capital flows, exchange rates and the activities of banks and other financial institutions. These changes certainly facilitated the growth of a global money market from the early 1980s. The extent of economic reform differed between countries. In some, like Britain, privatisation of state-owned industries and services became a major thrust in the late 1980s, together with severe cutting of government services, such as health and education. Labour market reforms that reduced the power of trade unions and made wages and working conditions more flexible also became prominent in a number of OECD member countries in the 1980s. Deregulation of controls on competition between firms in various industries (for example, aviation) was also vigorously pursued in some cases. Generally, economic reform was most intense in the United States and Britain, and slower in some of the Western European countries, but its impact, especially in financial systems, could be seen everywhere (Kindleberger 1985).

At the beginning of the 1990s, the industrial countries slipped once more into a prolonged recession, the third since 1974. Unemployment levels were about twice those prevailing at the beginning of the 1970s, but inflation rates were below those of the last years of the Long Boom. This implied that stagflation was no longer a phenomenon in the industrial countries, but that high levels of unemployment and low levels of economic growth were likely to be the main features of the next economic cycle. The international economy had been fundamentally changed by the collapse of the Bretton Woods monetary system, financial and other economic deregulation and reform, and by the intensification of trade tensions and protectionism. It was against this backdrop, and the impact of the 1990–92 recession, that the Cold War came to an end, raising the prospect of the emergence of a new world order in the last decade of the millennium. How globalisation developed in the 1990s is discussed in more detail in Chapters 12 and 13.

**SUMMARY BOX**

The oil price rise in the early 1970s created new flows of international capital that were recycled through the international banking system. These banks were well placed to undertake this task as they had played a major role in the development of the Eurodollar market in the late 1960s. 'Petrodollars' were lent to the governments of developing countries during the 1970s, creating a problem of 'Third World debt' by the beginning of the 1980s. This crisis revived the global prominence of the International Monetary Fund that put together various 'rescue packages' for the indebted nations. Meanwhile, the international banks were again flush with funds following the 1979 'second price shock'. After the early 1980s recessions ended, these funds were channelled into loans to corporations looking for funds to expand and finance take-overs, and into the world's booming share markets and other asset markets. Financial deregulation undertaken by many countries in the early 1980s and generally expansionary monetary conditions further stimulated such capital flows. Eventually, the world's major asset markets overheated and in the correction that followed, the industrial economies entered their third recession in 15 years. Although not planned as a new international monetary system, the floating exchange rates that emerged in the early 1970s became permanent. Governments that tried to resist changes in their exchange rates discovered that the international financial system was far more powerful. In the mid-1980s, the US dollar fell against the Japanese yen, inaugurating the so-called 'high yen crisis' that led to massive capital flows from Japan to the United States. By the 1980s, the end of the Long Boom led many governments to adopt policies of far-reaching economic reform, of which financial deregulation was the most significant. Australia followed this international trend from 1984.

# Suggested further reading

Bergsten, C.F. & Cline, W.C. 1987, *The United States–Japan Problem*, Institute for International Economics, Washington DC.
Bleaney, M. 1985, *The Rise and Fall of Keynesian Economics*, Macmillan, London.
Burstein, D. 1989, *Yen! The Threat of Japan's Financial Empire*, Schwartz, New York.
Ito, M. 1990, *The World Economic Crisis and Japanese Capitalism*, St Martin's Press, New York.
Maddison, A. 1991, *Dynamic Forces in Capitalist Development, a Long Run Comparative View*, Oxford University Press, Oxford.
Murphy, R.T. 1996, *The Real Price of Japanese Money*, Weidenfeld & Nicolson, London.

Skidelsky, R. (ed.) 1977, *The End of the Keynesian Era: Essays on the Disintegration of Keynesian Political Economy*, Macmillan, London.

van Der Wee, H. 1986, *Prosperity and Upheaval: The World Economy 1945–1980*, Pelican, London.

## End note

1    The three original organisations – the European Coal and Steel Community (ECSC), the European Economic Community (EEC) and the European Atomic Energy Community (EAEC) – were brought together as the European Community in 1965. In 1973, membership was expanded by the addition of the United Kingdom, the Republic of Ireland and Denmark. Greece joined in 1981, and Spain and Portugal in 1986. The process of closer integration began in 1985 with the signing of the Single European Act, and continued through the Maastricht Treaty on European Union in 1992.

# 11

# Stagflation and economic reform: Australia in the global economy, 1974–1989

Economic conditions were more turbulent and uncertain as Australia passed from the conditions of the Long Boom to those of the era of **stagflation** and rising **unemployment**. At the beginning of this period it was not clear where Australia was heading. Rising **inflation** created an illusion of economic activity that masked the real deterioration of the economy. Australian workers received the largest money wage rises they had ever seen and although unemployment increased, it did so gradually. The crisis of the 1970s was not as sudden or cataclysmic as earlier crises; for example, that of 1930. It took perhaps as much as a decade for the realisation to sink in that a return to the conditions of the Long Boom was not an immediate possibility. Only then could attention be focused positively on economic reform and restructuring, the two themes that dominated economic policy-making in the 1980s. This chapter examines the transition from high growth, **full employment** and rising living standards to the era of stagflation and economic failure. It considers the main elements in the economic reform agenda of the 1980s that 'globalised' the Australian economy and which carried on through into the final decade of the century.

## Economic performance: signs of deterioration

### The Long Boom ends in Australia

The Long Boom ended in Australia in 1974 at the same time and for the same reasons as it ended in all the developed economies. Just as the **boom** was internationally transmitted, so was its demise. The Australian economy could not hope to escape the impact of a concerted downturn in the **economic growth** of the industrial countries in 1974 any more than it had been able to do in 1930, though the impact was less ferocious (Norton 1982). As happened in other developed

243

**Table 11.1**    Economic growth, unemployment and inflation in Australia, 1973–74 to 1989–90

| Year | Real economic growth (percentage change from previous year) | Unemployment (percentage of labour force, August) | Inflation (percentage change in consumer price index, annual average) |
|---|---|---|---|
| 1973–74 | 4.6 | 1.8 | 12.9 |
| 1974–75 | 1.9 | 2.4 | 16.7 |
| 1975–76 | 2.9 | 4.6 | 13.0 |
| 1976–77 | 2.9 | 4.7 | 13.8 |
| 1977–78 | 1.0 | 5.7 | 9.5 |
| 1978–79 | 5.6 | 6.2 | 8.2 |
| 1979–80 | 2.1 | 5.9 | 10.2 |
| 1980–81 | 3.5 | 5.9 | 9.4 |
| 1981–82 | 2.3 | 5.6 | 10.4 |
| 1982–83 | −1.7 | 6.7 | 11.5 |
| 1983–84 | 6.1 | 9.9 | 6.9 |
| 1984–85 | 5.1 | 8.5 | 4.3 |
| 1985–86 | 3.9 | 7.9 | 8.4 |
| 1986–87 | 2.6 | 8.0 | 9.3 |
| 1987–88 | 5.2 | 7.8 | 7.3 |
| 1988–89 | 4.3 | 6.8 | 7.3 |
| 1989–90 | 3.1 | 5.7 | 8.0 |

Source: Based on RBA 1996, pp. 225, 180, 243.

economies, inflation rates increased sharply in the early 1970s in Australia. In the first half of the 1960s the average annual rate was 1.9 per cent. In the second half it averaged 3.1 per cent. However, in 1970–71, the rate lifted to 4.9 per cent and in the following financial year, to 6.8 per cent (see Table 11.1). The new Labor Government that came into office in December 1972 took some palliative measures to slow down inflationary forces and the rate for 1972–73 declined a little to 5.9 per cent. However, the apparently booming economy encouraged the Whitlam government in its policies for social reform, larger welfare expenditure, a higher social wage and greater economic equity. Government outlays, which had been steady over the previous decade at 23 per cent of **GDP**, suddenly increased to 28 per cent in one fiscal year (1974–75) and the Commonwealth **Budget** deficit rose from 0.5 per cent of GDP in 1973–74 to 3.8 per cent the following year.

This expansion in government spending and rise in the Budget deficit was strongly inflationary in an economy where inflationary forces were already strong. As a result, the inflation rate hit a 20-year high of 13.1 per cent in 1973–74 and accelerated to 16.7 per cent in the year ending June 1975. Wage rises and strong consumer **demand**, both fuelled by the acceleration in the value of world trade and rapid **capital** inflow, were further stimulants to rising price levels. Wages increased because the **labour** market was tight and unions were in a strong bargaining position. However, that had been the case throughout the 1960s. The significant new factors were first, the decision to cut immigration levels and second, the decision to

**Figure 11.1**    Australia's terms of trade, 1971–72 to 1989–90

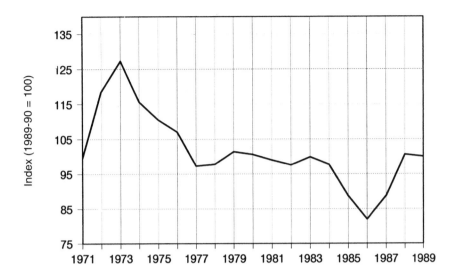

Source: Based on RBA 1996, p. 30.

increase award wages. Net immigration declined from 114 000 in 1971 to just 67 000 in 1972 and 62 000 in the following year. As the annual average for the five years to 1971 had been 129 000, this reduction represented a fall of over 50 per cent. In the past, Australian governments had cut immigration in response to a weaker domestic economy and rising unemployment. On this occasion, the intake was cut in response to community fears that Australia, with a population of just less than 13 million, was becoming overcrowded.[1] The fall in net migration impacted on those industries most reliant on immigrant labour. In steel and vehicle building, wage rises were acceded to that were well above the existing norms and these quickly flowed on to other workers. A wages explosion resulted (Hughes 1980, pp. 67–75). This was exacerbated by the introduction of long overdue equal pay provisions by the new government. These raised award wages for female workers by as much as 40 per cent in 1973–74.

**Commodity** prices increased rapidly in the early 1970s, particularly oil prices in 1972 and 1973. This source of inflation was transmitted to Australia through its **international trade**. By 1972, Australia was undergoing an export boom that raised its **trade balance** to a surplus of over $2 million, in 1972–73, compared to less than $1 million the year before, and pushed the **current account** balance into surplus for the first time in two decades. As commodity prices soared, the **terms of trade**, previously in gentle decline, now turned sharply in Australia's favour (see Figure 11.1). Wool prices, for example, jumped 150 per cent in 1972–73 and cereal prices rose 80 per cent in the next year.

To counter these various inflationary forces, the government **revalued** the currency, at first in December 1971 by 6.3 per cent against the US dollar. This did little to discourage inflows of foreign capital, which fell only slightly in 1971–72 by 9 per cent. The dollar was revalued again in December 1972 and had appreciated against the floating US dollar by 19 per cent by June 1973. Further revaluation brought it to a high point of $US1.49 in June 1974, an overall appreciation of the Australian currency against the American of 34 per cent since the US dollar left the **gold standard** in September 1971. These **exchange rate** rises, together with the passing of the *Foreign Companies (Takeovers) Act* in November 1972, stemmed the inflow of foreign funds. In 1972–73, capital inflow fell by 68 per cent, to its lowest level since 1963–64 (new **direct foreign investment** was at its lowest since 1958–59), and remained low in 1973–74. The Whitlam government raised the Treasury rediscount rate from 5.7 per cent to 12 per cent and in July 1973 cut **tariffs** by 25 per cent across the board as further anti-inflationary measures. The anti-inflationary actions were unsuccessful at stemming the rise of the price level, and between them discouraged firms from further **investment**. By June 1973, the **money supply** had risen 25 per cent in one year, an unprecedented increase. The Australian economy was awash with money and price inflation continued.

The inflationary forces in play in the Australian economy in 1972 and 1973 might not, of themselves, have caused an economic **recession**. But in early 1974, the impact of the economic downturn in the industrial nations began to hit Australia. The terms of trade now moved against Australia and the current account deficit increased. To combat a looming **balance of payments** crisis, the Australian government followed policies that were by now becoming familiar around the members of the OECD. The government imposed a severe **credit squeeze** in the middle of 1974. In August, the Australian dollar was **devalued** by 12 per cent and in December tariff rates were raised. This caused economic growth to slow and unemployment rose sharply. Inflation continued, now pushed along by the lower dollar and higher **import duties**. Public expenditure rose sharply in 1974–75 as the Labor government honoured election pledges to improve the social **infrastructure** and raise living standards through increased **transfer payments**. Real economic growth in 1974–75 fell to 1.3 per cent, half the level of the previous year. This was low by Long Boom standards, but no worse than the dip in trend growth that occurred in 1961–62. However, in that year inflation was 0.4 per cent, but by 1974–75, inflation was over 16 per cent and unemployment had doubled to 4.6 per cent. Stagflation had now arrived in Australia.

## SUMMARY BOX

The Long Boom ended in Australia in 1974 through a combination of inflation and world recession. Some of Australia's inflation was domestically generated through Commonwealth Government Budget deficits and a wages explosion, and part resulted from the boom in the international economy in 1972 and 1973 that produced record export earnings and large capital inflows. Unlike some of the major OECD countries, Australia did not experience negative growth, but growth was negligible and unemployment increased to unprecedented post-war levels. Inflation continued to soar. When combined with the stagnant economic conditions, it produced the ongoing problem of 'stagflation'.

# Stagflation

It took well over a decade to squeeze stagflation out of the Australian economy (see Table 11.1). Between 1974–75 and 1982–83, real economic growth averaged barely 2 per cent a year, while the annual inflation rate ran at 12 per cent. In the mid-1980s, growth picked up to around 4 per cent and inflation came down to 8 per cent. Only in the 1990s was there a return to low inflation and medium-level growth (see Chapter 13), but even so, unemployment did not fall to its Long Boom levels. Unemployment averaged over 7 per cent during the mid-1980s, rising sharply at the end of the decade. During the Long Boom it had rarely exceeded 2.5 per cent. In short, from 1974, Australia experienced weak growth and high inflation (and rising unemployment) for as long a period as it had experienced the opposite conditions in the 1950s and 1960s.

It took some time for the extent of the crisis following the end of the Long Boom in 1974 to be realised and a further period of time elapsed before governments took significant action. The Australian economy continued to deteriorate between 1975 and 1978. Inflation increased to 14 per cent, unemployment reached a post-war high of 400 000 persons (representing 6.2 per cent of the **labour force**) and economic growth was virtually stagnant. The new government's economic policy was only mildly restrictionist and some specific measures, such as the devaluation of the Australian currency by 12.5 per cent in December 1976, fuelled the inflation rate. The balance of payments worsened as exports were sluggish and the cost of servicing the **foreign debt** trebled in the space of four years (1974–75 to 1978–79). The current account deficit peaked in 1978–79 at 3.4 per cent of GDP, its highest level since 1968–69 (see Table 11.2).

There was a brief upswing in the world economy at the end of the 1970s as the industrial countries expanded output (see Table 10.1). Demand for **primary products** recovered and Australia's terms of trade improved. But the oil price rise in late 1979 slowed growth in the industrial countries and Australia's terms of trade again moved down in 1980–81 and 1981–82 (see Figure 11.1). Exports were static but imports continued to grow causing a merchandise trade deficit to emerge that in turn fed into a current account deficit that was the largest since the Korean War. Economic policy was directed to reducing the trade deficit by slowing demand in the Australian economy. When the industrial countries went into economic recession in 1981 and 1982, Australia's export earnings were cut, further slowing economic growth and for the first time in peacetime for over 50 years, the Australian economy recorded an annual contraction in 1982–83 (Table 11.1). At this point, inflation ran at 11.5 per cent and unemployment touched 10 per cent. Stagflation persisted.

Recovery in the industrial countries, the end of a severe drought in eastern Australia and a change of government in 1983 produced a dramatic turnaround. From a contraction of 2.5 per cent, the Australian economy grew at 5.5 per cent in 1983–84. This set in train the 'boom' of the mid-1980s, faltering only in 1986–87. From 1983–84 to 1989–90, real growth averaged 4.2 per cent and unemployment fell from 10 per cent to less than 6 per cent. Inflation was lower than in the worst years of stagflation, 1981–82 and 1982–83, but at around 7 per cent was still high and heading upwards at the end of the decade. Lending and credit creation by

**Table 11.2**   Australia's balance of payments, current account, 1973–74 to 1989–90

| Year | Exports | Imports | Trade balance (exports minus imports) | Balance of transport services | Balance of travel services | Balance of other services | Balance of income account | Net transfers | Balance of services, income & transfers | Current account balance | Current account balance as a % of GDP |
|---|---|---|---|---|---|---|---|---|---|---|---|
| 1973–74 | 6 754 | 5 767 | 987 | -500 | -280 | -210 | -738 | -180 | -1 908 | -921 | -1.7 |
| 1974–75 | 8 512 | 7 665 | 847 | -521 | -428 | -170 | -723 | -200 | -2 042 | -1 195 | -1.8 |
| 1975–76 | 9 476 | 7 930 | 1 546 | -558 | -560 | -132 | -1 393 | -326 | -2 969 | -1 423 | -1.9 |
| 1976–77 | 11 446 | 10 350 | 1 096 | -744 | -599 | -285 | -1 605 | -298 | -3 531 | -2 435 | -2.8 |
| 1977–78 | 12 006 | 11 149 | 857 | -806 | -649 | -345 | -1 770 | -257 | -3 827 | -2 970 | -3.1 |
| 1978–79 | 14 072 | 13 385 | 687 | -920 | -741 | -138 | -2 179 | -340 | -4 291 | -3 604 | -3.3 |
| 1979–80 | 18 589 | 15 831 | 2 758 | -1 118 | -651 | -101 | -2 727 | -135 | -4 732 | -1 974 | -1.6 |
| 1980–81 | 18 718 | 19 177 | -459 | -1 322 | -547 | -208 | -2 759 | -140 | -4 976 | -5 435 | -3.9 |
| 1981–82 | 19 376 | 22 389 | -3 013 | -1 620 | -617 | -172 | -3 208 | -192 | -5 779 | -8 792 | -5.5 |
| 1982–83 | 20 930 | 21 725 | -795 | -1 451 | -688 | -588 | -2 788 | -195 | -5 710 | -6 505 | -3.8 |
| 1983–84 | 23 661 | 23 475 | 186 | -1 651 | -725 | -341 | -4 883 | 115 | -7 485 | -7 299 | -3.7 |
| 1984–85 | 29 730 | 30 080 | -350 | -2 190 | -969 | -575 | -6 792 | 198 | -10 328 | -10 678 | -4.9 |
| 1985–86 | 32 148 | 35 691 | -3 543 | -2 342 | -634 | -820 | -7 940 | 683 | -11 053 | -14 596 | -6.1 |
| 1986–87 | 36 038 | 37 152 | -1 114 | -1 962 | -240 | -795 | -8 747 | 1 183 | -10 558 | -11 672 | -4.4 |
| 1987–88 | 41 515 | 40 386 | 1 129 | -2 044 | 271 | -679 | -10 527 | 1 633 | -11 346 | -10 217 | -3.4 |
| 1988–89 | 43 894 | 47 012 | -3 118 | -2 670 | 518 | -526 | -13 562 | 2 173 | -14 067 | -17 185 | -5.1 |
| 1989–90 | 48 564 | 50 992 | -2 428 | -3 182 | -160 | -801 | -17 188 | 2 290 | -19 041 | -21 469 | -5.8 |

Note: A minus sign indicates that the value of payments made by Australian residents to foreigners exceeded the value of payments made by foreigners to Australian residents.

Source: Based on RBA 1996, pp. 3–19.

banks and other financial institutions grew at an accelerating rate during the second half of the decade, fuelling massive asset price appreciation in residential housing, the stock market and commercial property. The balance of payments current account remained high and the net foreign debt soared from $30 billion to $131 billion in seven years.

The government attempted to control the rate of inflation and rein in the current account by slowing down the rate of economic growth. Three tactics were employed. Wage restraint was achieved under agreements between the Labor Government and the ACTU known as the Accord. These agreements kept real wage rises to low levels and real unit labour costs declined. Real earnings fell by 4.2 per cent in the four years from 1983–84 to 1987–88. Thereafter, real earnings slowly rose, but remained below their 1983–84 level. Second, fiscal consolidation was achieved by a series of declining federal government budget deficits, from 1983–84 to 1986–87 followed by surpluses in the next three years. This outcome was largely the result of cuts to government spending. In real terms, the rate of growth of federal government expenditure slowed from 8.7 per cent in 1983–84 to 2.3 per cent two years later. Real expenditure then fell by an average of 1.9 per cent per annum over the next four years. Finally, monetary growth was restricted by a policy of high **interest** rates: bank housing loan rates, for example, increased from 11.5 per cent in 1983–84 to 17 per cent in 1988–89, the highest rate ever recorded in Australia in the twentieth century.

These measures were intended to give the Australian economy a 'soft landing'. Growth would be slowed but not eliminated. Then, as the inflation rate fell and the current account deficit declined, growth could be resumed. This was a scenario that

**SUMMARY BOX**

High inflation rates persisted in Australia from the early 1970s to the beginning of the 1990s. During that period, economic growth was on average below the levels of the previous two decades and there were recurrent bouts of economic stagnation. The full employment conditions of the post-war period were gradually eroded, with double-digit **unemployment rates** being reached at the beginning of the 1980s and the 1990s. Australia's **external balance** deteriorated, causing a balance of payments crisis by the early 1980s. Attempts were made to curb inflation and reduce the external deficit by slowing economic growth but the recession in the industrial countries pushed Australia into an economic contraction in 1982–83. Despite recovery and higher growth in the mid-1980s, the balance of payments continued to be weak and Australia's foreign debt soared. By the end of the decade, the economy had a foreign debt crisis and an over-heated domestic economy that necessitated government action to slow down the rate of growth. While a soft landing from this procedure had been hoped for, a slowdown in the OECD at the same time precipitated Australia into another recession in 1990–91.

had been played out numerous times in the Long Boom period when inflation and current account problems had emerged (Whitwell 1986). Unfortunately, in this instance, similar forces in the rest of the OECD had led to similar policy decisions, and all of the industrialised economies began to slow in 1989. The 'soft landing' proved, therefore, to be rather harder than had been anticipated, as detailed in Chapter 13.

Australia experienced two economic cycles of growth after the end of the Long Boom in 1974–75, punctuated by recessions in 1981–83 and 1990–92. In each cycle, real economic growth was lower than in the Long Boom years and both inflation and unemployment were higher. In the mid-1970s cycle, 1975–76 to 1980–81, real economic growth averaged only 2.8 per cent per year and inflation averaged 10.7 per cent per year with only a slight downward trend. These were the worst years of stagflation. In the 1980s cycle, 1983–84 to 1989–90, average real economic growth was higher at 4.2 per cent and inflation was lower, averaging 6.8 per cent. This was not full-blown stagflation perhaps, but nor was it a return to the economic performance of the Long Boom. By the end of the 1980s such a return seemed less and less likely.

## Balance of payments problems and foreign debt

Slower growth of world trade from the mid-1970s revealed the structural weaknesses of Australia's export sector. International demand was weak for those commodities (unprocessed primary products) in which Australia was competitive. In other exports, particularly manufactures, Australian firms were generally less competitive. Australia's terms of trade were adversely affected by stagflation in the industrial economies. Their sluggish economic growth reduced demand for imports of food and raw materials, while their high inflation rates pushed up the price of manufactures that Australia imported. The impact on Australia of the worsening conditions in the international economy was masked by the oil price rises in 1973 and 1979 (discussed in Chapter 10). These increased the price and value of Australia's energy exports so that overall the merchandise trade account was in surplus. However, the second oil price rise also caused a second wave of recessions in the industrial countries at the beginning of the 1980s, cutting international demand for Australia's exports.

Unstable and declining exchange rates were both a reflection of and a contributor to Australia's weak external position following the end of the Long Boom (see Figure 11.2). The Australian currency was at its strongest both against the US dollar and the Trade weighted index (TWI) in 1973–74, when it was 33 per cent above its Bretton Woods rate. It fell steadily to 1978–79, when it was 17 per cent below its 1970–71 level as measured by the index, though about the same as the Bretton Woods rate against the US dollar. It rose over the next three financial years by almost 10 per cent (TWI) as the market responded to Australia's prospects as a net energy exporter and the possibilities of a new resources boom. When this failed to materialise, however, the Australian dollar fell again.

Imports continued to flow into the Australian economy and from 1980–81, Australia experienced a series of balance of trade deficits, something that had not

**Figure 11.2**    Australian dollar: exchange rates, 1973–74 to 1989–90

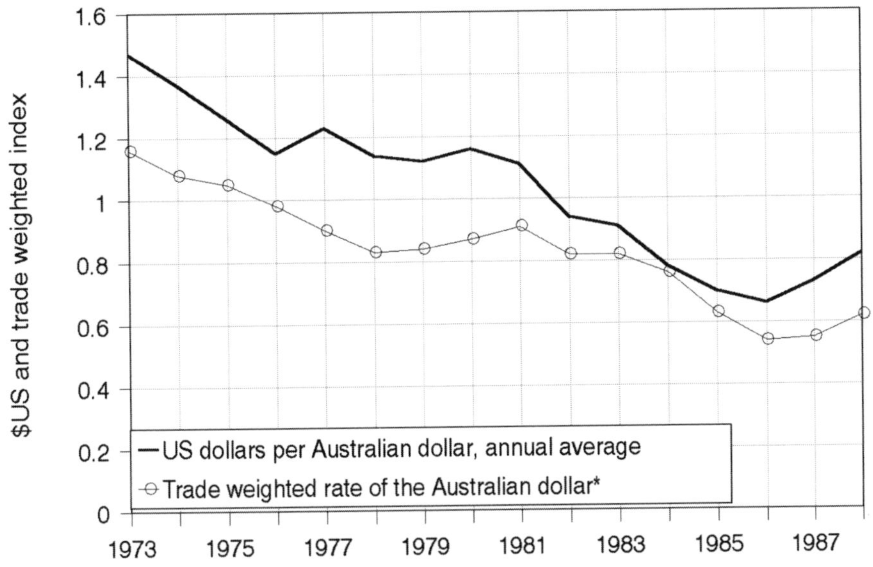

* Trade weighted index of value of the Australian dollar vis-à-vis currencies of Australia's
trading partners (May 1970 = 1.00), annual average.
Source: Based on RBA 1996, p. 44.

occurred during the Long Boom (see Table 11.2). Previous **trade surpluses**, particularly the very large one in the second oil price surge of 1979–80, had kept the overall
current account deficit below 4 per cent of GDP. Now the deficits on the merchandise trade balance, **net services**, **income** and **transfers**, combined to produce a series
of the largest current account deficits in Australia's post-war economic history.

Cumulative deficits caused the foreign debt to rise sharply (see Figure 11.3).
Servicing the debt contributed to continuing high current account deficits. By the
end of the 1980s, Australia was caught in a foreign debt crisis. The gross foreign
debt increased from 11 per cent of GDP to 50 per cent between 1981 and 1992. At
the beginning of this period, the Australian government owed almost one-third of
the external debt, but this proportion declined during the decade to less than one-
quarter. The external debt of publicly owned enterprises, however, increased
rapidly, from 13 per cent of the total to 18.5 per cent. Private firms also increased
their share, from 55 per cent to 58 per cent. Of more significance than its absolute
size was the cost of servicing this debt. Interest and repayments were equivalent to
12 per cent of Australia's **foreign exchange** earnings from exports of goods and
services in 1981, but almost 28 per cent 10 years later. The increase in this outflow
made it more difficult to reduce the current account deficit and thus lessen the
constraint that the balance of payments placed on Australia's economic growth.
Altogether, this marked the worst balance of payments crisis in Australia since the
Great Depression 60 years before.

**Figure 11.3**   Australia's external debt, 1976 to 1990

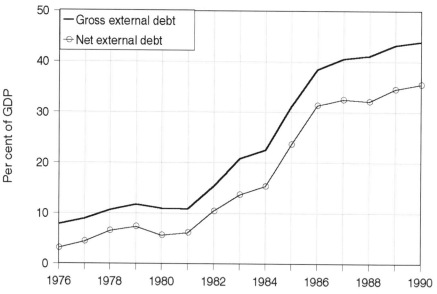

Source: Based on RBA 1996, pp. 60–1.

Continued weak terms of trade, together with rising import volumes, left the merchandise trade balance in deficit and the current account posting higher and higher deficits. The poor results in merchandise exports were only slightly offset by improvements in the balance on services, mainly resulting from a boom in inbound tourism from the late 1980s onwards. The transfer account also improved as the funds brought into Australia by migrants began to exceed the funds sent out by migrants after 1983–84. The **income account**, on the other hand, moved more heavily into deficit as Australia's foreign debt soared. Loss of confidence by the foreign financial markets led to a fall in the value of the Australian dollar against the US dollar (see Figure 11.2). From November 1981 to July 1986, it declined by 48 per cent, notably between the beginning of 1984 and mid-1986, a 30-month period when the Australian dollar's value declined by 37 per cent. The Australian currency remained low. Its highest point after the low point of 1987 was at the end of 1989–90 when it was up by 9 per cent (TWI).

The effect of the declining exchange rate was to provide protection to those sectors of the Australian economy competing against imports and to make Australian exports cheaper in world markets (as long as their price was denominated in Australian dollars). This effect should have improved the balance on goods and services and perhaps in certain sectors it did. Had the exchange rate remained at its earlier higher levels, the trade deficits may have been even larger. However, whatever favourable impact exchange depreciation did have was not sufficient to produce the trade surpluses that would have shored up Australia's balance of payments in these years. Demand for Australia's major exports depended more on the state of economic activity in the industrial countries that consumed them than on their price. While the industrial nations remained gripped by stagflation, and wedded to policies of agricultural **protectionism**, demand for primary commodities was weak, as shown by Australia's declining terms of trade. Exchange depreciation was also inflationary as it added to the cost of imports. This raised the cost of production in Australia of both exports and import competing goods, making both less competitive, and raised the cost of investment in new imported plant and equipment.

Exports performed better in 1983–84 and 1984–85 as the industrial countries staged a hesitant recovery from the 1981–82 recession, but petered out as they slowed again in 1986. Over the next two years, export earnings improved and import growth slowed, partly as a result of the lower exchange rate. The current account deficit fell back to 3.4 per cent of GDP in 1987–88, the lowest level in the 1980s. In the following two financial years, however, stronger economic growth in Australia pulled in imports faster than exports were able to expand and the trade balance moved back into heavy deficits, producing historically high current account deficits again in 1988–89 and 1989–90 (see Table 11.2). The causes of the 1980s trade crisis lay in the inability of Australian manufacturers to compete with imports (despite the advantage to Australian firms of the falling exchange rate) combined with weak international demand for Australia's commodity exports, especially following the collapse of international oil prices in 1986.

## SUMMARY BOX

Australia avoided balance of payments difficulties in the 1970s because high prices for energy exports masked the effect of economic stagnation in the industrial OECD countries. In the 1980s, however, this effect diminished and the stronger growth in Australia from 1983–84 pulled in imports. The result was a series of trade deficits that produced unusually high current account deficits. Foreign borrowing, made easier by financial deregulation, financed these. As the foreign debt increased, so did the outflow of funds needed to service it. This outflow made the current account deficit higher and Australia entered a spiralling foreign debt crisis in the late 1980s. The fundamental cause of Australia's balance of payments crisis in the 1980s, however, was not foreign borrowing as such, but the lack of international competitiveness by Australian manufacturing industry combined with weak global demand for Australia's exports of primary products – including energy exports after 1986.

## International trade

The declining terms of trade throughout the post-Long Boom period highlighted the structural disadvantages of Australia's export mix (see Table 11.3). The main structural change was the relative decline of foodstuffs and raw materials and the relative increase in fuels. The share of foodstuffs in total merchandise exports rose to a peak in the food price boom of 1972 and then fell slowly to 1981–82. The effect of the severe drought in eastern Australia between 1981 and 1983 reduced the volume of food exports and their share in the total fell sharply. In the mid-1980s, Australian output recovered and expanded, but the world market for food-stuffs, especially grains, was over-supplied, partly due to measures taken by the European Community and the United States to raise foodstuffs production levels. Consequently, world prices for foodstuffs weakened.

Exports of raw materials, dominated by wool and iron ore, declined in impor-tance largely because of the slower growth experienced by the industrial nations after 1974. The decline was stemmed to some extent by the expansion of non-ferrous metal exports after 1977 as Australia's giant bauxite-alumina export indus-try developed, but by the end of the 1980s, the share of raw materials had fallen from around 33 per cent to about 27 per cent. Energy exports were unimportant in the Long Boom. Exports of fuels (coal and petroleum products) accounted for only 5 per cent of Australia's exports in 1969–70, reflecting the slight development of Australia's oil resources and the relatively low world prices of fuels in the 1960s. By 1975–76, however, the share of fuels in Australia's exports rose to 13 per cent and after the second oil price rise in 1979, to over 20 per cent. The peak point was reached in 1984–85 when fuels contributed one-quarter of Australia's merchandise export earnings. After that, world oil prices declined and the share of fuels fell back to less than 20 per cent by the end of the decade. The increasing share of fuels reflected both price rises and considerable increases in production. When prices fell, producers continued to expand production to maintain revenues, but the increases in volumes could not fully compensate for the decline in price.

The price boom in oil and other energy resources between 1972 and 1980 represented an aberration in the long-term decline in international commodity prices relative to those of manufactures. From 1986, oil prices weakened consider-ably to below the levels reached in the second oil crisis. The energy price boom did not, therefore, lead to a permanent shift in Australia's terms of trade. Although the Australian economy benefited from being a net energy exporter at a time in the history of the world economy when the price of internationally traded energy resources passed through two unprecedented explosions, the structural changes that took place simply emphasised one group of unprocessed primary exports (fuels) over another (foodstuffs and raw materials). The Australian trade balance remained as dependent on primary exports as ever. Indeed, unprocessed commodities made up 48 per cent of merchandise exports in 1973–74, but 54 per cent in 1986–87, largely due to greater exports of coal, wool and wheat in the 1980s. The share of manufactures in Australia's exports declined in the 1970s and 1980s, from their high point of 27.4 per cent in 1974–75 to a low point of 18.7 per cent in 1984–85 and 1985–86 (see Table 11.3). The share of simply transformed manufactures (STMs, for example, non-ferrous metals, chemicals) tended to fall rather more quickly than that of elaborately transformed ones (**ETMs**, such as vehicles, machinery and equipment) but for both groups the trend was away from the potential evident in the late 1960s and early 1970s (see Chapter 9).

Manufactures exports were particularly sensitive to changes in the interna-tional competitiveness of Australian industry. Competitiveness was affected by

**Table 11.3**   Australia's exports by commodity group, 1973–74 to 1989–90 (percentage of total merchandise exports)

| Year | Foodstuffs, raw materials and fuels | Manufactures | Other |
|---|---|---|---|
| 1973–74 | 72.9 | 25.9 | 1.2 |
| 1974–75 | 71.0 | 27.4 | 1.6 |
| 1975–76 | 74.3 | 23.8 | 1.9 |
| 1976–77 | 74.2 | 23.9 | 1.9 |
| 1977–78 | 72.3 | 24.6 | 3.1 |
| 1978–79 | 76.3 | 21.4 | 2.3 |
| 1979–80 | 75.9 | 21.1 | 3.0 |
| 1980–81 | 76.7 | 20.4 | 2.9 |
| 1981–82 | 77.4 | 20.1 | 2.5 |
| 1982–83 | 76.6 | 20.4 | 3.0 |
| 1983–84 | 76.1 | 20.7 | 3.5 |
| 1984–85 | 78.1 | 18.7 | 3.2 |
| 1985–86 | 77.2 | 18.7 | 4.1 |
| 1986–87 | 71.2 | 22.3 | 6.5 |
| 1987–88 | 67.9 | 23.4 | 8.7 |
| 1988–89 | 67.0 | 24.5 | 8.5 |
| 1989–90 | 66.0 | 25.1 | 8.9 |

Source: Based on ABS, *Foreign Trade Australia*, various years.

changes in the exchange value of the Australian dollar, relative inflation rates and wage rate trends. In periods following **currency depreciation**, for example, 1973–74, 1976–77 and 1985–86, manufactures exports (particularly the higher value-added ETMs) surged, but improved competitiveness from exchange depreciation was not sustained over time. When the dollar appreciated, as happened for example in the first half of 1988, some exporters of manufactures lost their previous gains. Although real wages were held down in Australia under the Accord from 1983, wage rates in Australia's highly protected manufacturing sectors remained well above those paid by their international competitors and increased more quickly. For example, average wages in Australia increased 222.4 per cent between 1975 and 1988, whereas in Japan the increase was 97.1 per cent, and in the United States, 127.3 per cent.[2] Inflation in Australia was also higher during the 1970s and 1980s than the OECD average (see Table 12.2). Over half of Australia's exports of manufactures were concentrated in four markets: Japan, New Zealand, the United States and the European Community, each of which became more protectionist during the 1980s towards imports of manufactured goods. For these reasons, Australian manufacturing firms lost ground both in export markets and the domestic market in the years following the end of the Long Boom (Pinkstone 1992, pp. 217–26).

These structural shifts, such as they were, in the mix of Australia's exports, did not result in any major change in the principal markets for Australia's goods. Asia remained the principal region, a position it had reached in the 1960s. It took

**Table 11.4**   Australia's exports by country group, 1977–1990 (percentage of total merchandise exports)

| Year | North Asia | South & South-East Asia | Middle East & Africa | Europe | America | New Zealand & Pacific |
|---|---|---|---|---|---|---|
| 1977 | 41.8 | 8.4 | 7.1 | 21.9 | 12.8 | 9.6 |
| 1978 | 41.0 | 9.0 | 7.2 | 20.1 | 14.4 | 8.4 |
| 1979 | 39.0 | 9.9 | 7.5 | 20.1 | 14.9 | 8.6 |
| 1980 | 36.6 | 9.7 | 9.1 | 21.1 | 14.9 | 8.5 |
| 1981 | 39.1 | 10.5 | 9.3 | 17.5 | 14.3 | 9.3 |
| 1982 | 38.1 | 10.8 | 9.5 | 18.5 | 12.9 | 10.2 |
| 1983 | 39.1 | 9.9 | 7.6 | 19.0 | 12.6 | 11.8 |
| 1984 | 39.6 | 9.0 | 9.1 | 17.9 | 13.4 | 11.0 |
| 1985 | 41.5 | 9.7 | 8.4 | 18.1 | 12.9 | 9.4 |
| 1986 | 41.5 | 8.4 | 7.3 | 20.2 | 13.4 | 9.2 |
| 1987 | 40.1 | 8.3 | 5.6 | 21.1 | 13.9 | 10.9 |
| 1988 | 43.2 | 10.0 | 4.8 | 19.1 | 13.4 | 9.5 |
| 1989 | 41.4 | 11.6 | 5.3 | 18.9 | 13.4 | 9.4 |
| 1990 | 41.0 | 13.3 | 5.3 | 17.4 | 14.0 | 9.0 |

Source: Based on DFAT 1998a.

42.5 per cent of Australia's merchandise exports in the last five years of the Long Boom, a proportion that rose gradually to 50 per cent by the end of the 1980s (see Table 11.4). The share going to Japan declined somewhat, from over 30 per cent in the mid-1970s to around 26 per cent at the end of the 1980s. The rest of Asia generally took a rising share, especially China, Korea and South-East Asia. These results reflected the slowing down of the Japanese economy (and price falls in energy resources in the later 1980s) and the speeding up of industrialisation in ASEAN (Association of South-East Asian Nations),[3] the Republic of Korea, Taiwan and the People's Republic of China. The shares going to North America and Western Europe remained largely unchanged. The United Kingdom diminished as a market: by the end of the 1980s it bought less than 4 per cent of Australia's exports, but this was a trend that had started 30 years earlier (Pinkstone 1992, pp. 228, 289).

Changes to import sources in the 1970s and 1980s followed a similar pattern to export markets. The decline of the United Kingdom as a supplier continued while the share from Asia and the Pacific continued to grow, particularly from Japan, Hong Kong, ASEAN, Korea and Taiwan. The types of product imported changed little. **Consumer goods** continued to make up a little under one-fifth of imports by value, industrial supplies (raw materials for industry) almost 30 per cent, capital equipment about one-quarter and transport equipment (mainly motor vehicles) 15 per cent. Fuels increased their share of Australia's imports by value in the 1970s because of the oil price rises, but declined to 6 per cent in the 1980s, about the same share as they held at the end of the Long Boom. For both imports and exports, then, there was a remarkable stability of structure and direction during two decades when the international economy underwent such dramatic upheavals. The world economy changed, but Australian merchandise trade remained stuck in the patterns developed in the earlier post-war decades.

Services exports, however, did change in at least one unexpected way, with the development of inbound tourism (Pinkstone 1992, pp. 282–6; Garnaut 1989). Receipts from tourism increased as a share of all services exports from less than 10 per cent in the early 1960s to 15 per cent by the end of the Long Boom. By 1976–77, its share had risen to over 20 per cent and to 25 per cent three years later. Its rise continued and reached 30 per cent by 1985–86. At this point, tourism earned as much foreign exchange as iron ore exports. A peak was reached in 1988–89, reflecting overseas visitor interest in Australia's bicentennial. At this time, tourism accounted for 41 per cent of all services exports, 8 per cent of all exports of goods and services, and was almost as valuable an earner of foreign exchange as coal. In 1987–88 and 1988–89, tourism became a net export industry; that is, the value of inbound tourism exceeded the cost to the balance of payments of Australian tourism abroad for the first time. The growth of the tourism industry, and to a lesser extent the export of education services following the decision in 1986 to allow full fee-paying foreign students to enter Australian universities, reduced somewhat the burden of the deficit on services in the balance of payments. At the end of the 1980s, for example, the services deficit contributed only 18 per cent of the current account deficit, compared to over 60 per cent at the end of the previous decade.

**SUMMARY BOX**

International demand for Australia's traditional exports of foodstuffs and raw materials was weak in the 1970s and 1980s because of the slower growth in the major industrial countries, leading to a downward trend in Australia's terms of trade. In the 1970s, energy exports boomed in response to both increased Australian output of oil and coal and the international oil price 'shocks'. In the 1980s, however, oil prices fell, especially from 1986, and the importance of energy exports for Australia declined. Exports of foodstuffs continued to be hampered by the protectionist policies towards food imports by the United States, the **EEC**, and Japan. Manufactures exports in the 1970s and 1980s did not fulfil the potential shown in the 1960s and declined in importance. Thus, as far as goods exports was concerned, Australia remained heavily dependent on primary products. The trend towards greater reliance on Asia for international trade continued. One novel development in the 1980s was the rise of inbound tourism as a significant earner of foreign exchange. This eased Australia's traditional deficit in its international trade in services. Overall, however, the long-established patterns in Australia's international trade persisted during the 1970s and 1980s.

## International capital flows

Fluctuations in Australia's current account balance as the Long Boom came to an end led governments to try to manage the inflows and outflows of capital. Having taken measures to restrict inflows in 1972 and 1973, measures were taken in 1974, 1975 and 1976 to encourage capital inflow. The variable deposit requirement, introduced in December 1972 to discourage Australian firms from raising funds abroad, was reduced and then suspended during 1974. An embargo that had been placed in 1972 on Australian firms borrowing short-term funds overseas was relaxed at the end of 1974. And having revalued the Australian currency four times in the 21 months between December 1971 and September 1973, the dollar was devalued in September 1974 and again in November 1976. Capital inflow increased by 60 per cent in 1974–75 to something like the levels of the early 1970s. It declined in the following year, but surged again and early in 1977 the government reacted by tightening restrictions. The variable deposition requirement was reintroduced and the restrictions on Australian firms seeking **short-term** foreign capital extended.

Later in 1977, however, it became clear that world energy prices were beginning to rise again, in response to economic recovery in the industrial economies. The Australian government launched a strategy to lift Australian production of energy resources in order to take advantage of the expected boom. It was apparent that if Australia were to participate in a world energy boom, more investment, including foreign investment, would be required in the energy resources sector. The adoption of the 'resources boom' strategy prompted a relaxation of curbs to capital inflow and special encouragement was given to foreign investment in natural resources, especially the natural gas of the North-West Shelf. In particular, firms with less than the required 50 per cent Australian **equity** could 'phase-in' the additional Australian ownership over a number of years. In 1978, regulations were further relaxed. The rule that Australian equity in new uranium mining projects must be at least 75 per cent was reduced to 50 per cent in the following year. State governments were exhorted to seek foreign and domestic investment for projects in the energy resources sector and to give concessions to such investors.

Foreign capital surged into Australia at unprecedented levels. The average annual inflow in the two years 1976–1978 was $1.6 billion. But over the next two years the inflow averaged $2.7 billion and over the following two years, $7.7 billion. Direct foreign investment slowed in 1981–82 and fell by 61 per cent in 1982–83 as the energy resources boom began to wane. This was caused by the onset of recession in the industrial countries that was itself a reaction to the earlier rise in energy prices. Capital continued to flow into Australia, however, as the current account deficit was increasingly financed by **portfolio** and loan investment rather than by direct investment. Direct foreign investment had for a long period accounted for about 60 per cent of total foreign investment in Australia, but in 1982–83 it declined to less than 10 per cent and remained at about one-quarter for the rest of the decade. Thus by the early 1980s, a structural change was occurring in foreign investment in Australia as debt became more significant than equity investment.

For most of the 1970s it was the services sector of the Australian economy rather than manufacturing or mining that received the most attention from foreign

**Figure 11.4**   Capital inflow to Australia, 1969–70 to 1989–90

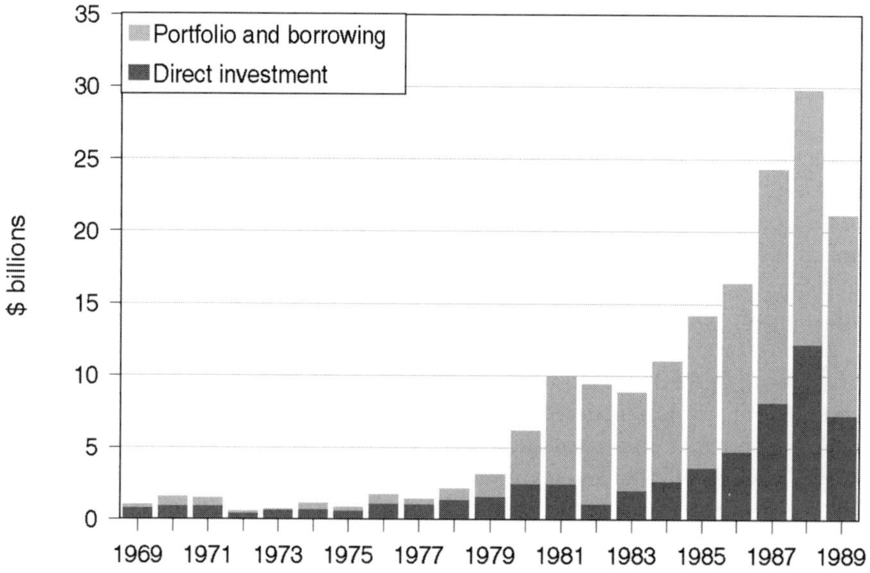

Source: Based on RBA 1996, p. 38.

investors. The slower rates of economic growth, rising levels of unemployment and uncertainty about the future made manufacturing less attractive than it had been in the Long Boom. The mining sector was more affected by the various restrictions and provisions for minimum levels of Australian ownership enacted during the first half of the decade. In the energy resources boom in the late 1970s and early 1980s, foreign investment in mining grew faster than the other two sectors, but when the energy boom faded, it was again the services sector that received a growing share of foreign capital. Services with significant foreign investment included wholesale and retail trade, commerce, oil distribution, insurance, banking, finance and property. The deregulation of the financial sector from 1984 and removal of restrictions on foreign investment in property and non-bank finance greatly stimulated foreign investment in finance, property and business services. The collapse of world oil prices in 1985 diminished new foreign interest in energy resources in Australia and again accelerated the shift towards the services sector.

The rise in the debt–equity ratio in total foreign investment was one of the most striking aspects of foreign investment in Australian during the 1980s (see Figure 11.4). The share of debt in total foreign investment doubled from one-third to two-thirds in the first six years of the decade. In the early 1980s it was the private sector that set the pace in foreign borrowing, particularly the financial services sector. In the second half of the decade, governments (mainly at state level) raised their share of the gross external debt and the share of public enterprises became more prominent. As a result, the share owed by the private sector fell back from two-thirds to about half of the total.

Why did the debt–equity ratio behave in this way during the 1980s? To some extent it was part of the worldwide phenomenon towards debt that occurred in most of the world's major economies. As the world's financial markets became more integrated through improved electronic communications and data processing, access to foreign borrowing by Australian enterprises and governments became easier. In the international climate of economic uncertainty in the 1980s, foreign investors were more inclined to lend than to acquire equity, especially where interest rates were high, as was the case in Australia. There were also tax advantages in raising capital by borrowing as interest payments were tax deductible. In some years, the Australian government preferred to borrow rather than to reduce expenditure or raise taxation, and foreign borrowing was usually cheaper than domestic borrowing.

The overall result of this period of heavy international borrowing was the emergence of a 'foreign debt crisis' by the end of the 1980s. Once again, the government took action to slow down and stabilise the inflow of foreign capital. The administrative controls used in the 1970s were no longer available because of financial deregulation. Instead, monetary and **fiscal policy** was tightened, as Chapter 13 details, and this led Australia into another bout of economic recession.

> **SUMMARY BOX**
>
> Australia retained its status as a capital-importing country during the 1970s, though the flows became more unstable. Except during the short-lived resources boom, most direct foreign investment in the 1970s and 1980s was in the services sector rather than mining or manufacturing. Attempts to manage Australia's international capital flows through administrative controls in the 1970s produced further short-term oscillations. At the end of the decade, a 'resources boom' led to a large surge in foreign investment in Australia. Although the resources boom collapsed in the early 1980s, foreign capital continued to flow in during the 1980s to finance Australia's growing current account deficits. Financial deregulation in Australia and 'globalisation' of the world's financial markets led to a marked shift away from equity and towards debt in foreign investment in Australia. By the end of the decade, the high levels of foreign borrowing were regarded as unsustainable, again requiring policy action to stabilise them.

## Immigration

With the end of the Long Boom and the demise of the White Australia Policy occurring at around the same time, the role of immigration in Australian society entered a state of flux from 1974. Should immigration levels be lowered in tune with the slower rates of economic growth and higher unemployment? Or would a return to the immigration patterns of the Long Boom restore the economic condi-

**Figure 11.5**   Australian immigration, 1970–71 to 1989–90 (excess of arrivals over departures)

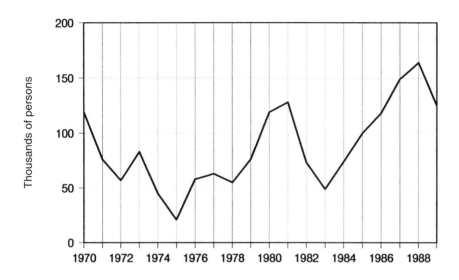

Source: Based on RBA 1996, p. 177.

tions that prevailed in the 1960s? If race was no longer to be used to discriminate among potential immigrants, what criteria should replace it? Did the end of the White Australia Policy, with its ingrained pro-British bias, signal a new era in Australian immigration in which migrants would be selected for their '**human capital**'? Or would non-economic considerations prevail? And with the restrictions on Asian immigration gone, would Australia in fact receive large numbers of Asian migrants? The actual outcomes in the 1970s and 1980s were not what many expected at the beginning of the period.

## Immigration levels

The immediate effect of the crisis in the world economy in 1974, swiftly followed by a recession in Australia, was to reinforce the earlier move towards permanently lower levels of settler intake, as shown in Figure 11.5. The role of immigration in an economy beset by stagflation and rising unemployment might not be the same as in earlier decades. The economic rationale for immigration had been that immigration eased constraints on economic growth caused by labour shortages and filled various niches in the labour market – such niches in the Long Boom being significantly different for non–English-speaking immigrants than for English-speaking ones. Immigration had also been justified on population and defence grounds in the 1950s and early 1960s, but neither of these criteria was seen as very important in the 1970s (Borrie 1988, pp. 111–18). Indeed, the effect of immigration on population growth was now viewed with alarm.

Immigration policy in the Long Boom had been selective, but had discriminated more on race than on skill or educational attainment. Nevertheless, the proportion of immigrants in the skilled and semi-skilled categories during the Long Boom was higher than the proportions in those categories within the Australian labour force as a whole (Centre for International Economics 1988). The economic crisis in the mid-1970s suggested an immigration policy that was based on a smaller overall net intake, reflecting the rising levels of unemployment and concerns about over-population, and one that selected migrants on skill and non-economic criteria (such as family reunion) rather than on race. As a result, it was not expected that Australia would receive such large numbers of immigrants as in the past. Nor was it anticipated that the abolition of the White Australia Policy would result in large numbers coming from Asia. If Asian immigration was to expand, it was thought that growth would continue the previous pattern of an intake of highly qualified persons from the English-speaking countries of Asia.

Economic conditions continued to exert considerable influence over short-term changes to immigration policy. The number of migrant settlers arriving in Australia fell dramatically once the extent of the 1974 economic crisis was evident. Arrivals in 1975 were only 45 per cent of the previous year's level and net immigration reached its lowest level – 25 000 – since 1947. A 'points system' was introduced in 1973 to discriminate between migrant applicants. This made skills, educational attainments and qualifications, sponsorship by an employer and family reunion the major criteria for selection.

However, with such low numbers, immigration looked likely to play a smaller role in the Australian economy than until that point. Net immigration in 1975, for example, contributed only 15 per cent of Australia's population increase in that year, compared to over 30 per cent in earlier years. Although the immigration intake was reduced in 1974 and 1975 in response to the end of the Long Boom, the numbers entering did not remain low. Settler arrivals increased over the next four years and were one-third higher in 1979 than in 1975. Since rather fewer people left Australia permanently, the net migration rate was almost twice its 1975 level by 1979. This trend continued, as settler arrivals increased at a more rapid rate in 1980 and 1981, peaking at two-thirds above the 1979 point. Once again, the numbers leaving Australia for good (or at least for more than one year) declined, so that the net immigration rate rose faster, reaching almost four times its 1975 level by 1981 (see Figure 11.5). This rise in immigration in the six years following 1976 seemed hardly justified by the rate of economic growth in these years and contrary to the higher level of unemployment. The intake level remained high in 1982, but the number of settler arrivals was reduced again in 1983 in a lagged response to the worsening economic climate, and numbers fell again slightly in 1984. The level in the latter two years averaged 75 750 per annum, which was two-thirds of the peak reached in 1981 and 1982.

The decline in immigration that was a response to the 1980–82 economic downturn was short-lived. As the economy grew strongly and unemployment declined, net immigration rose by 25 per cent in 1985 and by 33 per cent in the following year. Expansion was continued in 1987 when net immigration jumped by 28 per cent. A peak was reached in 1988 when the net intake was 131 000, compared to 50 000 four years before. This expansion followed the economic cyclical upswing and represented a return to the average immigration level of the late 1960s, but greater emphasis was now placed on family reunion as a criterion for settlement. Family reunion was seen as providing Australia with a more stable immigration intake in contrast to one based on 'guest workers', who would add little to **aggregate demand** and who would remit the bulk of their earnings to their families back home (Borrie 1988, pp. 114–15). It was argued that family reunion would encourage family formation, which had long been regarded as a major element promoting social stability in Australia. Immigrants who formed families in Australia would have a higher propensity to spend and any **saving** they made would be put into building up the household.

Family reunion was expanded as a category and extended by the inclusion of siblings. At the previous peak in immigration, in 1981 and 1982, family reunion accounted for 18 per cent of the total intake. Refugees represented a similar proportion and the remaining two-thirds came in under various skilled migrant programs. In the early 1980s, however, family reunion increased to over 60 per cent and remained above 50 per cent until 1989. The proportion of settlers arriving as refugees declined to less than 10 per cent, while the share of those entering as skilled migrants rose steadily to 40 per cent by the end of the decade. Of course, family reunion migrants might have useful skills and become part of the workforce, but that was not the criterion on which they entered and the reality was that many were dependants who did not enter paid employment.

## Asian immigration

Although recovery from the 1974–75 recession was partly responsible for the rise in immigrant intake, the main factor that drove Australian immigration to its peak in 1981 and 1982 was the sudden inflow of refugees from Indo-China. The end of the Vietnam war in 1975 created a refugee crisis that led to an exodus of ethnic Vietnamese and ethnic Chinese from the region that continued until the mid-1980s. Most came from the former South Vietnam, though there were refugees fleeing Laos and Cambodia as well (Viviani 1984; Coughlan & McNamara 1997). The refugee crisis presented a test for Australia's new non-racial immigration policy, as well as for its policy of positive engagement with the Asia region. As the most developed economy in the region and one with a well-established (though anti-Asian for much of its history) immigration program, Australia was in a position to take action to tackle the refugee crisis. As a former belligerent in the Vietnam War, Australia also carried some moral responsibility for the impact of the war on the inhabitants of the region.

There were barely a thousand Vietnamese living in Australia at the time of the fall of Saigon in May 1975. The Labor government was reluctant to allow the intake from Vietnam to increase, but the change of government in December 1975 marked a change in policy. The new minister for immigration, Michael Mackellar, announced that Australia would take increased numbers of refugees from Vietnam through the United Nations refugee agencies. Australia also allowed refugees who arrived as 'boat people' from the end of 1976 to settle. In 1982, in an attempt to

**Table 11.5**    Immigration: settler arrivals by region of birth, 1972–1990
(percentage of total settler arrivals)

| Year | Europe | Asia | America | Africa & Middle East | New Zealand & Pacific |
|------|--------|------|---------|----------------------|------------------------|
| 1972 | 69.8 | 7.3 | 9.4 | 9.1 | 4.4 |
| 1973 | 66.3 | 7.8 | 9.4 | 10.3 | 6.2 |
| 1974 | 64.8 | 7.9 | 12.8 | 9.2 | 5.3 |
| 1975 | 51.3 | 14.5 | 12.3 | 14.1 | 7.9 |
| 1976 | 44.8 | 15.0 | 9.9 | 21.0 | 9.2 |
| 1977 | 42.7 | 18.3 | 7.2 | 20.4 | 11.4 |
| 1978 | 39.5 | 28.7 | 6.0 | 10.6 | 15.3 |
| 1979 | 32.5 | 32.0 | 5.6 | 8.9 | 20.4 |
| 1980 | 43.9 | 27.1 | 4.0 | 7.6 | 17.3 |
| 1981 | 50.1 | 23.8 | 3.6 | 7.4 | 15.2 |
| 1982 | 54.5 | 23.3 | 4.2 | 6.8 | 11.3 |
| 1983 | 42.6 | 35.3 | 5.1 | 8.2 | 8.9 |
| 1984 | 28.8 | 41.6 | 7.6 | 10.4 | 11.5 |
| 1985 | 28.8 | 36.9 | 7.7 | 10.2 | 16.3 |
| 1986 | 31.8 | 33.2 | 6.4 | 12.4 | 16.2 |
| 1987 | 30.8 | 35.8 | 5.8 | 12.6 | 15.2 |
| 1988 | 29.4 | 35.9 | 5.1 | 10.0 | 19.5 |
| 1989 | 31.6 | 36.7 | 6.0 | 8.6 | 17.1 |
| 1990 | 30.6 | 43.4 | 5.8 | 9.0 | 11.2 |

Source: Based on ABS, *Arrivals and Departures* (Cat. no. 3404.0).

reduce the outflow of illegal refugees from Vietnam, Australia signed an orderly departure program with the Vietnamese government. Over the next three years, over 4000 people emigrated legally from Vietnam directly to Australia. They consisted of both ethnic Vietnamese and ethnic Chinese, and were all close relatives of people from Vietnam already in Australia.

Over the decade of the crisis, 1976–1985, almost 73 000 persons for whom Vietnam was their country of birth settled in Australia. This influx represented 8.8 per cent of total settler intake in these years. The peak years were 1979 to 1981 when 37 600 arrived, accounting for 13.2 per cent of the total settler intake of that period. The year when these migrants represented their highest proportion of the total inflow was 1979 when they were 17.7 per cent of the total. In addition to refugees from Vietnam, about 13 200 arrived from Cambodia over the ten years 1976–1985, representing 1.6 per cent of Australia's total settlers.

The refugee crisis in Indo-China after the end of the Vietnam War was not the only cause of increased immigration from Asia to Australia following the end of the White Australia Policy. Settlers also came in significant numbers from The Philippines, Malaysia, Hong Kong and China. Chinese immigration from Malaysia, Singapore, Hong Kong, Taiwan, Indonesia and the People's Republic of China added to the Chinese refugees from Vietnam, Laos and Cambodia. Most of the non-refugee Chinese migrants were in the skilled, professional and business categories, and some of the Chinese refugees from Indo-China were also from a business or merchant background. In the early 1980s, about half of those entering Australia as business migrants were ethnic Chinese who invested their capital and enterprise in hotels, restaurants, property development, shopping malls and food processing. Overall, the proportion of immigration from Asia rose from less than 10 per cent in the early 1970s to over 40 per cent in 1984 (see Table 11.5). Put another way, Asia supplied less than 5 per cent of Australia's settlers in the 1960s, 12 per cent in the 1970s and 33 per cent in the 1980s.

## The immigration debate and the Fitzgerald Report

By the mid-1980s, immigration policy was under attack from several quarters. The greater importance given to family reunion and refugee intake was criticised by those who argued that whatever the social desirability of family reunion immigration and fulfilment of Australia's humanitarian responsibilities, the new policy undermined the economic rationale that government immigration policy professed. Others questioned the wisdom of large immigration intakes at all in the economic climate of high unemployment. Some objected to the higher proportion of immigrants coming from Asia and wanted a return to the White Australia Policy (Blainey 1984). And those who had warned of the demographic dangers in high immigration in the early 1970s now complained that population growth was again being fuelled by excessive levels of immigration (Birrell, Hill & Nevill 1984). In response to these expressions of concern, the government established a committee of inquiry that reported in 1988 (Australia 1988, pp. 1–22).

The Committee canvassed the arguments surrounding Australian immigration policy and practice. Immigration raised the rate of population growth and expanded the size of the labour force. If immigrants were predominantly of working age, they would increase the size of the labour force by a greater proportion than they raised the size of the population. All else being equal, this should increase the output of the economy faster than the population grew and thus raise the rate of GDP growth per head. However, this argument assumed that the rate of growth of output was dependent only on the size and expansion of the labour force. It was also argued that by adding to the growth of aggregate demand, immigration stimulated investment in production and enhanced the rate of technological change. Moreover, if the domestic market were larger, Australian manufacturers would obtain economies of scale. These effects were difficult to quantify and the arguments foundered on the problem of demonstrating that immigration raised not only the rate of GDP growth but also the rate of growth of GDP per capita. Other economic advantages claimed for a return to the high net immigration rates of the Long Boom years included the bringing of additional skills and know-how, business acumen and **entrepreneurship**, and the benefits from migrants creating a more mobile and flexible workforce. These claims also were impossible to quantify, though there was anecdotal evidence of migrants as enterprising business people and entrepreneurs.

Much of the force of these type of arguments depended on the government being able to select migrants with the type of skills, attributes, business experience and capital, and so forth that was desired. A greater proportion of immigrants had been in the skilled and semi-skilled categories than the average for the resident workforce in the 1960s and 1970s, but in the 1980s this differential declined as a result of the growing proportion of immigrants entering under the family reunion program. Perhaps this could be rectified by changes to the immigration policy, but other critics pointed out that skilled immigration itself could have disadvantages. The easy availability of skilled workers from overseas tended to retard expenditure on appropriate training for Australian-born workers.

Similarly, the alleged economic benefits of high immigration on Australia's population growth were countered by considerations about the costs associated with faster rates of population increase. Immigration in the mid-1980s accounted for 40 per cent of Australia's population growth. Faster population growth put additional strain on the building of infrastructure, urban development (migrants disproportionately settled in cities), health, education and welfare services (Hugo 1986). With net immigration set at 125 000, it was estimated, Australia's population would reach 26.1 million by 2030, whereas with a zero rate of immigration it would be only 18.9 million (Centre for International Economics 1988, p. 34). The higher rate of population growth would cause more overcrowding in Australia's cities and raise the cost of preventing pollution and environmental damage.

The report (known as the Fitzgerald Report) recommended that settler intake should be maintained at about 150 000 persons, a similar level to that reached in 1987 and 1988. It placed great emphasis on the economic benefits of high immigration and argued that immigration needed to be brought into the mainstream of economic strategy. Most migrants should be selected on the basis of their age, existing skills, their aptitude for multi-skilling and potential as entrepreneurs. Family reunion and refugee categories together should not exceed one-third of the net intake, so that two-thirds (100 000 persons per year) would enter under various skills programs.

The report argued that the economic benefits to Australia were largely on the supply side. Immigration overcame specific job shortages, brought skills to Australia at small or no cost, stimulated investment and the use of new technology. Migrants generally, it was suggested, had more drive, energy and enterprise than the resident population.

The significance of the Fitzgerald Report was that it was the first attempt to examine comprehensively the rationale behind Australia's immigration policy in the era of lower economic growth and higher unemployment and after the end of the White Australia Policy. It aimed to integrate immigration policy with other policies that together worked towards the restructuring of the Australian economy. By recommending a large net intake of migrants, it was able to argue for a large increase in skilled and business migration without reducing Australia's commitment to humanitarian and family reunion programs. Above all, it tried to look forward to Australia's needs in a changing economic environment rather than looking back to an earlier era when different criteria for immigration had prevailed.

**Figure 11.6**   Settler arrivals by eligibility category, 1984–85 to 1990–91

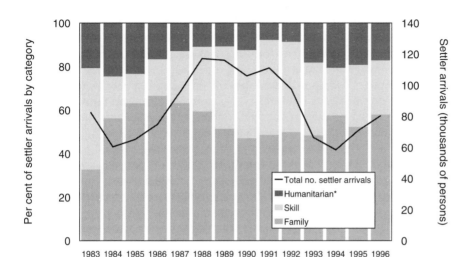

\* Humanitarian, refugees, special assistance and others with visas. Figures exclude immigrants without visas.
Source: Based on Bureau of Immigration, *Australian Immigration Consolidated Statistics* no. 18, p. 25.

But the report was not able to show that large economic benefits would flow from high immigration. Indeed, most economic effects it examined were negligible even if on the beneficial side. Many of its specific recommendations, such as reducing the number of categories under which migrants could enter Australia and overhauling the points system, were not acted on. Neither did the net intake remain at the high levels of 1987 and 1988. From a peak in 1988–89 of 136 000, the gross settler intake declined slowly to 109 000 in 1991–92 and fell sharply to 78 300 in 1992–93 in response to the 1990–92 recession. Persistently high levels of unemployment made it difficult politically to return to the high immigration rates of the late 1980s. Family reunions remained at around 55 per cent of settler intake and refugee and humanitarian categories accounted for about 10 per cent. This produced a share of a smaller net intake for skilled immigration of around 35 per cent, compared to the share of 65 per cent recommended in the Fitzgerald Report (see Figure 11.6).

Thus the Fitzgerald inquiry sparked a great deal of debate about the economic impact of immigration, but the results of the subsequent studies tended to dampen the hopes that a return to the high immigration levels of the Long Boom would be accompanied by a return also to that period's strong economic growth and full employment. If immigration policy could not be seen as an important element in economic outcomes, in future its social and cultural aspects were likely to be viewed as the more significant (Wooden, Holton, Hugo & Sloan 1990; Foster & Baker 1991).

**SUMMARY BOX**

The end of the White Australia Policy in 1973 indicated that racial origin would not be used to discriminate between potential migrants in future. However, the economic crisis from 1974 also suggested there would be a smaller immigration intake than during the Long Boom. In the short term, immigration levels responded as expected, with fewer numbers entering in the mid-1970s and again in the early 1980s. But numbers did not stay permanently low in this period. By the second half of the 1980s they were back to 1960s levels. The changed conditions after 1973 provided an opportunity for immigration policy to place greater emphasis on selecting migrants with skills, capital and enterprise. In fact, the two major forces that shaped patterns of immigration to Australia during the 1970s and 1980s were the refugee crisis in Vietnam and family reunion. Public debate about immigration led to an inquiry that reported in 1988. It came down firmly on the side of high immigration intakes and emphasised the economic benefits of immigration. Its recommendations, however, were largely ignored and from the late 1980s immigration policy tended to be placed in a social, humanitarian and cultural context rather than an economic one.

# Economic reform

From 1983, Australia entered into its most intense period of economic reform since the late 1940s. Many of the regulations that governed the behaviour of the Australian economy were questioned and a great number were swept away or radically altered. Economic policy shifted towards a greater role for market forces and a disengagement from the economy by the State. This led to the privatisation or corporatisation of many public enterprises, at both the Commonwealth and State level. Microeconomic reform was seen by many as the force that would end the economic slide Australia appeared to have been travelling on since the early 1970s. To others, sometimes harking back to the Vernon Report of 1965, these reforms were long overdue changes that had their intellectual origins in the Long Boom itself, but which had been delayed by political complacency and conservatism. However viewed, reform came to permeate every aspect of Australian commercial life in the 1980s, building a momentum that continued into the next decade.

Three areas of reform stood out and interacted: financial deregulation, tariff reform and microeconomic reform.

## Financial deregulation

An early priority in the reform movement was deregulation of the financial sector and removal or relaxation of controls over international capital flows. Foreign exchange controls were abolished in December 1983 allowing the Australian dollar to float. 'Floating the dollar' meant that the Reserve Bank of Australia (RBA) was no longer obliged to intervene in the **foreign exchange market** to maintain any partic- ular exchange value of the Australian currency, a practice that it had been following, in various ways, since 1972. Thus 12 years after the US dollar left the gold standard and the era of 'floating currencies' began, Australia took the final step of adopting a completely flexible exchange rate. From this point on, the international financial markets would determine the foreign exchange value of the Australian dollar, and although the Reserve Bank could intervene in the exchange market by buying or selling the Australian currency, its influence would be minimal.

The abolition of exchange controls meant that Australian businesses, banks and residents no longer required RBA permission to borrow funds overseas or to invest their funds outside of Australia. This removed the direct control over capital inflows that the **central bank** had operated since the Second World War. Aboli- tion of administrative controls over capital outflows meant that Australian firms could now extend their operations outside of Australia as much as they liked, including 'going offshore' completely if they wished. This was a freedom that had been denied them since the imposition of controls during the Second World War.

Deregulation in this area reduced significantly the power of the RBA to influ- ence changes in Australia's balance of payments and money supply. In the past these controls had been used to counteract the inflationary effects of sudden rises in export earnings caused by commodity price rises or, when the current account deficit was rising, to prevent Australia's external debt from rising faster than was thought appropriate. Judgements in these matters were now taken from the offi- cials of the RBA and the Treasury, and placed in the hands of the international financial markets.

These developments were followed by a major liberalisation of the controls on foreign investment. In September 1984, restrictions on foreign ownership of merchant banks were lifted. In February 1985, 16 foreign banks were permitted to enter the Australian banking industry. In October of the same year, the practice of requiring the demonstration of specific opportunities for Australians to purchase assets available for sale was abolished. At the same time, the threshold at which the permission of the Foreign Investment Review Board was required was raised in a number of categories and restrictions on foreign ownership in the remainder of the non-bank financial institutions sector were mostly removed. In July 1986, the neces- sity to show that Australia would receive a net economic benefit from a particular foreign investment proposal was replaced by the requirement merely to show that it was not against the national interest. This new rule applied to all sectors except civil aviation, electronic and print media, uranium mining and developed real estate. The rule that there must be a minimum Australian ownership of 50 per cent in stockbroking, real estate (other than developed commercial real estate) and tourism was abolished. Foreign ownership that had previously been prohibited in developed commercial real estate was now permitted up to 50 per cent.

As a result of these reforms, by 1987 there were no restrictions on direct foreign investment in manufacturing, services, resources processing, non-bank financial institutions, insurance, stockbroking, tourism, rural properties and primary industry (except mining). Sectors where foreign investment still faced some barriers were banking, civil aviation, media, developed commercial and residential real estate, and mining. In the latter there were no restrictions on foreign investment in exploration but there had to be at least 50 per cent Australian ownership and voting rights in all new projects worth $10 million or more. This requirement would be waived if it could be demonstrated that Australian capital could not be found on reasonable terms. There were no restrictions on foreign investment in uranium exploration, but no new uranium mining or processing ventures were permitted whether involving foreign capital or not.

Reforms to exchange rate practice and foreign investment controls were designed to integrate the Australian economy more fully into the world economy at a time when the world's financial and securities markets were themselves becoming more globally integrated. These changes intensified the impact that the international economy had on the Australian economy and were seen as an essential basis in the process of restructuring the economy and making Australian firms more competitive. Removing the heavy hand of bureaucratic control would, it was argued, free Australian business to raise capital, make investments and acquire assets as commercial opportunities arose, and to compete with the other players in the global economy (Indecs Economics 1992, pp. 89–93; Wanna 1994, p. 235).

In practice, the performance of Australian businesses over the first decade of financial deregulation was disappointing (Lewis, Morkel & Hubbard 1993, Chapters 17–22; Hilmer 1985). Many firms reacted to the uncertainty of the 1970s and early 1980s by becoming more reckless, particularly with regards to their newly enlarged capacity to raise foreign loans and to make foreign investments. As long-established rules and regulations were abandoned in the deregulation process, there was a tendency to test the limits of business behaviour from both a legal and an ethical perspective (Bosch 1990, Chapter 4; Grace & Cohen 1995). At the height of the late 1980s boom in asset prices, there was an ethos of 'anything goes' among some sections of the Australian business community. Many firms ran into debt problems and a large number recorded losses or folded. The difficulties of operating successfully in the unfamiliar deregulated global financial market led to mistakes and over zealousness among some well-established firms (for example, Westpac and Fairfax), as well as by the 'bold riders' like Alan Bond and Laurie Connell (Sykes 1994).

At the same time as the financial markets were becoming deregulated, there were a number of significant reforms introduced to the corporate taxation system, which both increased and decreased the taxation burden on firms. On the one hand, in 1985 a capital gains tax was introduced and the tax deductibility of entertainment expenses abolished. In 1986, a fringe benefits tax was brought in. On the other hand, in 1987, the practice of double taxation of dividends was ended and in 1988 the company tax rate was reduced from 49 cents to 39 cents and depreciation allowances altered. The corporate tax system thus appeared to be in a state of flux, heightening uncertainty as to exactly where the new boundaries of compliance ran. The Australian Taxation Office attempted to improve corporate compliance in paying tax by new methods of enforcement to reduce tax evasion and new rules to inhibit tax avoidance (including measures directed against 'bottom of the harbour' schemes). These attempts raised public awareness of the lengths many corporations were prepared to go to test the new taxation regime. Thus, by the end of the decade the behaviour and performance of many of Australia's firms led to widespread questioning of whether the deregulated environment was one in which greater efficiency and **productivity** would be stimulated. The longer term impact of 'globalisation' is examined in Chapter 13.

---

**SUMMARY BOX**

The chief elements in financial deregulation in Australia from 1983 were the floating of the dollar and abolition of exchange controls. Restrictions on Australians borrowing and investing abroad were ended and the regulations governing foreign investment in Australia were considerably relaxed. The government's strategy in pursuing financial deregulation was to 'globalise' Australian capitalism and to make it more efficient. The behaviour of many Australian firms in the new financially deregulated environment at the end of the decade, however, brought into question the wisdom of this strategy.

---

## Tariff reform

Financial deregulation was supported by a second set of reform initiatives designed to reduce barriers to international trade. Imports had long been subject to an array of controls consisting mainly of import duties (tariffs), but augmented in the 1970s and 1980s by global quotas, tariff quotas, production bounties, export incentives, local content schemes, government purchasing preferences and discriminatory domestic pricing arrangements. All of these measures were designed to protect Australian industry from import competition. Quotas were particularly powerful as they placed a limit on the physical quantity of a product that could be imported in any year. Tariff protection began to be reduced in 1973 when tariffs were cut by 25 per cent across the board. Rising inflation and the emergence of a strong **current account surplus** prompted this decision. The world recession of 1974–75, however, led to a return to a more cautious policy and the reduction in assistance continued more slowly.

Over the next 10 years, average effective rates of assistance to manufacturing as a whole declined from 27 per cent to 22 per cent. However, two sectors – textiles, clothing and footwear, and motor vehicles and parts – received more protection thanks to increased tariffs and the imposition of quotas. In 1974, a passenger motor vehicles plan was adopted that gave the industry quotas limiting imports to 20 per cent of the domestic market and required Australian car makers to achieve an average local content of 85 per cent. The average effective rate of assistance to motor vehicle manufacturers increased from 38 per cent in 1973–74 to 137 per cent in 1984–85. Textiles, clothing and footwear manufacturers also received quotas and increased tariffs that together raised the effective rate of protection for the sector from 64 per cent in 1973–74 to more than 250 per cent by 1984–85.

Reductions in **import protection** were pursued more vigorously from 1985. A new car plan in that year replaced quotas with tariff quotas and anticipated the removal of all **import quotas** by 1992. In 1988, this timetable was moved forward to the following year. New arrangements for the textile, clothing and footwear industry, adopted in 1987, reduced protection and envisaged an end to import quotas by 1996. Both of these sectors would, however, continue to receive more protection from imports than manufacturing in general. Moreover, several other sectors also remained more protected, including radio and television receivers, audio equipment, electronic equipment, batteries, household appliances and rubber and leather goods. As a result, these measures increased the divergence between these sectors (especially those subject to quota arrangements) that became more heavily protected and the rest of the manufacturing sector that became less so. However, because these sectors were so sheltered from import competition, they declined in importance within the manufacturing sector as a whole. As a result, their impact on average rates of protection became less.

A second round of across-the-board cuts in tariffs was implemented from 1988. These cut nominal tariff rates above 15 per cent to 15 per cent and those between 10 and 15 per cent to 10 per cent. By 1989–90, the average rate of protection for manufacturing had fallen to 10 per cent, the lowest level (for most sectors) since the 1920s. Motor vehicles and textiles, clothing and footwear products were excluded from these cuts, although their level of assistance was to be reduced in the future, albeit more gradually.

This was the second occasion when across-the-board cuts had occurred, and both were in reaction to economic crises. In 1973, a balance of payments current account surplus and rising inflation triggered the cuts. By contrast, in 1988, the cuts were in response to a balance of payments deficit and inspired by a desire to improve import substitution and raise the level of exports of manufactured goods. The momentum of the 1973 tariff cuts did not survive the end of the Long Boom and rising unemployment in 1974, but by the end of the 1980s the need for economic reform was more palpable and a greater determination to force tariffs into a long-term decline was shown. Unemployment in 1973 was less than 2 per cent and resistance to tariff reductions on the grounds that the cuts would cause unemployment was muted. In 1988, public concern about the employment implications of reductions to import protection was greater, but unemployment was declining (to less than 6 per cent, its lowest point of the decade). This drop allayed public concern to some extent. In any case, by the mid-1980s public opinion was more supportive of economic reform in general as a result of the experience of a decade of stagflation. The cuts announced in May 1988 were not reversed and tariffs continued to fall, until by the mid-1990s all of manufacturing, except the motor vehicle and textiles, clothing and footwear sectors, had only negligible tariff protection.

These reductions in import protection impacted on a manufacturing sector that was already in relative decline. Its share of output, employment, exports and domestic consumption fell from the mid-1960s or early 1970s. The share of manufacturing in Australia's gross domestic product fell from 26 per cent in 1965–66 to 21 per cent 10 years later, and 17 per cent by the end of the 1980s. As a source of employment, it accounted for only 15 per cent of the labour force in 1990 compared with 22 per cent in 1975 and 26 per cent in 1966. Manufactured goods represented about one-quarter of Australia's merchandise exports in 1973, but less than one-fifth in the first half of the 1980s.

The parlous state of Australian manufacturing was the subject of a number of official inquiries in the 1970s, notably the Jackson Committee in 1975 and the Crawford Inquiry in 1979. Both of these recommended gradual reductions in tariff protection and various incentives to boost exports of manufactures (Australia 1975b; 1979). Reduced levels of import protection, it was argued, would force Australian manufacturing to become internationally competitive. By expanding export sales, Australian manufacturers would achieve greater economies of scale and productivity growth. As significant tariff protection did not occur until the second half of the 1980s, there was little opportunity to see if these arguments were correct before the end of the decade. However, the share of manufactures exports in total merchandise exports jumped sharply in 1986–87 and continued in an upward trend into the 1990s (see Tables 11.3 and 13.6).

Unlike the late 1970s, when a small increase in the share of manufactures was associated with exchange depreciation, at the end of the 1980s the foreign exchange value of the Australian dollar rose sharply, a movement that was not helpful to manufactured exports. The rise in the share of manufactures in total exports from 1986–87 suggested, therefore, that Australian manufacturing firms had responded to the more internationally challenging environment by becoming more competitive and seeking out export opportunities, many of which lay in Asia.

## SUMMARY BOX

Although high import barriers on manufactured goods were criticised from the 1960s and tariff cuts began in 1973, completion of the task of reducing tariffs to negligible levels was long drawn-out. Meanwhile, the Australian manufacturing sector continued its relative decline that had started towards the end of the Long Boom. In the second half of the 1980s there was a more determined attitude towards tariff reduction shown by the federal government. Although the impact of tariff reductions on the manufacturing sector was not a simple one, there were signs at the end of the 1980s that increased competitiveness was being reflected in a rising share of manufactures in Australia's exports.

## Microeconomic reform and restructuring

The economic reforms of the 1980s reflected an ideology of 'economic rationalism' that was in the ascendant in a number of developed countries at this time, particularly in the United States and the United Kingdom. These reforms implied a retreat in the control of the economy by the State. Less protection from imports for Australian producers, easier access to foreign capital and enterprise and less direct control over the Australian financial and monetary system were the key planks.

A program of privatisation and pubic expenditure cuts reduced the size of the public sector, both absolutely and relatively. The government sold off long-held public assets such as the Commonwealth Bank, Qantas Airlines, Australian Airlines and the Australian National Line, and transferred the provision of various government services to the private sector. The national monopoly on telecommunications was broken by the introduction of private competitors to Telecom and by deregulation of the telecommunications market. State governments followed suit, divesting themselves of assets and activities across a wide range. Industrial relations and the centralisation of wage fixing were reformed with enterprise bargaining and more flexible wage structures being pursued.

The balance of payments and foreign debt crisis of the 1980s led the federal government to urge Australian firms to become more export-oriented, though it acknowledged that increasing protectionism (especially against primary products), as well as slower economic growth in many of the industrial countries, made it difficult to raise the rate of growth of Australia's exports.

In preparation for the eighth round of **multilateral** trade negotiations under the GATT in 1986, the Australian government initiated the establishment of the Fair Traders in Agriculture Group (known as the Cairns Group) to press for agricultural protection to be included in negotiations. Inaugural members of the Cairns Group comprised: Argentina, Australia, Brazil, Canada, Chile, Colombia, Fiji, Hungary, Indonesia, Malaysia, New Zealand, The Philippines, Thailand and Uruguay. This was a successful initiative, though the Uruguay Round itself took almost 10 years to complete.

In the mid-1980s the government adopted a more active policy towards export promotion. It established the Australian Trade Commission in 1986 and inaugurated a system of targeting foreign markets, especially in the Asia–Pacific region, aimed at raising Australia's share of their imports (Department of Trade 1985; National Export Marketing Strategy Panel 1985; Austrade 1988, pp. 6–46; 1989, pp. 38–44). A global marketing plan was developed that identified products likely to have export potential, including vehicle components and accessories, processed food, industrial and scientific equipment, computer software and education services. Mineral processing was also expected to become a larger export industry than before, so that more of the value added by processing took place within Australia. Closer economic integration of Australia and the Asia–Pacific region were also encouraged by Australia's involvement in the Pacific Economic Co-operation Conference established in 1980 and the South Pacific Forum Secretariat in 1988.[4] Closer ties with New Zealand followed the signing of the Australia–New Zealand Closer Economic Relations Trade Agreement in 1983.

Much was made at this time of the need for Australian society in general and Australian business in particular to develop an 'export culture', drawing from, perhaps, Australia's long history as a successful exporting nation (Garnaut 1989). Measures that it was claimed would move Australia in this direction included the adoption of an import protection policy that achieved zero tariffs by the end of the century, a commitment to deregulation of financial flows and a greater emphasis on microeconomic reforms. These latter reforms should embrace transport and communications, including reform of the waterfront, new rail links (such as the

Very Fast Train Project), airport development and deregulation of telecommunications, as well as reforms to produce a more flexible labour market. Politically there seemed to be a wide consensus on the need for microeconomic reform, with both sides of politics supporting the reform process. The government found, therefore, that the Opposition parties, which often argued that reform did not proceed far or fast enough, generally supported its reform agenda. Elite opinion in the late 1980s, emanating from the media and universities, also tended to support the move towards economic reform on a broad front.

Proponents of reduced import protection, financial deregulation and microeconomic reforms argued that the Australian economy required restructuring. The aim was to shift resources from low value-added to high value-added activity. Primary production was to move towards export of processed or semi-processed products rather than unprocessed raw materials and foodstuffs. Manufacturing industry was to become more capital intensive, include new 'high technology' sectors and seek out the productivity gains possible through investment in new technology. Australia had to become the 'clever country' in the 1980s and 1990s instead of relying on being the 'lucky country' of the Long Boom years. The services sector of the economy would become even more prominent, more internationally competitive and more export oriented. Service activities such as consultancy, design, project management, marketing, accounting, information technology, education, and medical and scientific research were regarded as important growth areas for Australia in the future, alongside the most successful of Australia's new service exports, tourism.

One particularly ambitious project was to support new high-technology industries, not through subsidies to particular firms or groups of firms, but by greater investment in education, science and technology research. The concept of the Multifunction Polis (MFP) was developed to act as a catalyst for the development of these kinds of industries. Originally the MFP was intended to bring together Japanese and Australian firms in joint research and development projects. However, as the idea grew it was envisaged that the MFP should be expanded to include other foreign countries and a wide range of high-tech activities taking place in an interactive way in an Australian 'techno-city' to be built on a greenfields site, preferably near the sea.

The MFP was not intended to be simply an export-processing zone, an isolated 'special economic zone' with separate laws and regulations and cheap labour as many newly industrialising countries had established. Rather it was projected as a place where 'knowledge industries' would be developed, providing the Australian economy with high-tech research and highly trained workers necessary for new, growing sectors of manufacturing and services (Inkster 1991). The MFP would be one way in which the Australian economy would be made more open to foreign capital, goods and ideas, leading Australian capitalism to become more mature and thus able to offset the long-term decline in the terms of trade of primary-producing economies.

The MFP was always stronger as a concept than as a practical solution to Australia's economic problems and it did not survive the downturn at the end of the 1980s. Nevertheless, it symbolised the vision and excitement about economic reform in the late 1980s that was one of the driving forces behind the changes that were accomplished. The Very Fast Train Project was a similar example of this momentum, though again, not in fact constructed.

The economic reforms begun in the 1980s had collectively a profound effect on the Australian economy, and facilitated the most significant period of structural change since the industrialisation of the 1940s and 1950s. Reform was resisted in the 1970s because it took some time for the fact that the Long Boom had ended to be accepted. At the end of the decade, Australian governments and business still believed it was possible that a commodity price boom would allow Australia to return to the conditions of the Long Boom without any need for restructuring. The economic recession of 1981 to 1983, however, convinced governments, employer groups and trade unions that there would not be a painless return to prosperity and that reform and restructuring were necessary and unavoidable (Edwards 1996; Carew 1992; Kelly 1992).

**SUMMARY BOX**

An economic reform movement developed force in the 1980s in the wake of the recent economic recession and the disappointments and failures of the Australian economy in the 1970s. Reform was pursued on a broad front with the aim of fostering a restructuring of the Australian economy that would make it more resilient to the vagaries of the international economy. By the 1980s it was recognised that the world economy of the Long Boom period had changed, and that Australia needed to respond to this. Economic reform was influenced by prevailing notions of economic rationalism and implied a retreat in economic intervention by the State. Visions of a new future for Australia were given expression through such concepts as the Multifunction Polis, though reform itself was a more down-to-earth process. Less was achieved by the end of the 1980s than some had expected and the rhetoric of reform had suggested, but nevertheless the movement represented a major change of direction for Australia and had sufficient momentum to continue into the next decade.

# Suggested further reading

Bell, S. 1993, *Australian Manufacturing and the State: the Politics of Industry Policy in the Post-war Era*, Cambridge University Press, Cambridge.

Capling, A. & Galligan, B. 1992, *Beyond the Protective State*, Cambridge University Press, Cambridge.

Carroll, J. & Manne, R. (eds) 1992, *Shutdown: the Failure of Economic Rationalism and How to Rescue Australia*, Text Publishing Company, Melbourne.

Catley, B. 1996, *Globalising Australian Capitalism*, Cambridge University Press, Cambridge.

Hughes, B. 1980, *Exit Full Employment: Economic Policy in the Stone Age*, Angus & Robertson, Sydney.

Pinkstone, B. 1992, *Global Connections: A History of Exports and the Australian Economy*, Australian Government Publishing Service, Canberra.

Quiggin, J. 1996, *Great Expectations: Microeconomic Reform and Australia*, Allen & Unwin, Sydney.

Stewart, R.G. (ed.) 1994, *Government and Business Relations in Australia*, Allen & Unwin, Sydney.

Whitlam, G. 1985, *The Whitlam Government 1972–1975*, Penguin, Melbourne.

Whitwell, G. 1986, *The Treasury Line*, Allen & Unwin, Sydney.

# End notes

[1]   A national population inquiry was established in 1970, see: Australian Institute of Political Science 1971; Australia 1975a.

[2]   The annual rates of increase over this period were: Australia 17.1 per cent, Japan 7.5 per cent and the United States 9.8 per cent. Reserve Bank of Australia 1991, pp. 272–3.

[3]   ASEAN was founded in 1967 with a membership of Indonesia, Malaysia, The Philippines, Singapore and Thailand. Brunei joined in 1984.

[4]   The Pacific Economic Co-operation Conference was the forerunner of the Asian Pacific Economic Co-operation group (APEC), formed in 1989. The South Pacific Forum Secretariat was previously the South Pacific Bureau for Economic Co-operation, formed in 1973. The South Pacific Forum itself was established in 1971.

# PART V

THE 1990s

# 12

## International economic impacts on Australia in the 1990s

Australia's position in the international economy deteriorated at the beginning of the 1990s because the developed industrial countries entered economic **recessions** that were followed by only hesitant recovery. World trade slowed but did not contract, largely due to the continued growth of China, east and South-East Asia. **International trade** relations were advanced by the delayed completion of the Uruguay Round of GATT and the creation of the World Trade Organisation. However, structural trade imbalances between the United States and Japan continued, and **protectionism** remained a serious threat to Australia and other small economies that looked to freer world trade. The world's financial markets were increasingly destabilised by speculative flows of '**hot money**' and the actions of **hedge funds**. A series of financial crises occurred as a result, the third of which, in Asia in 1997, caused a major world slowdown. The recession and recovery cycle, the continuing problems of world trade and the financial shocks are the main themes of this chapter.

Conditions in the international economy in the early 1990s had adverse effects on Australia, mainly through reduced **demand** for its exports. A number of the developed industrial economies that made up the Organisation for Economic Co-operation and Development (the OECD) entered recessions in 1990 and 1991, and recovered only very slowly during the first half of the decade.[1] The industrial-ising Asian 'tiger' economies (Korea, Taiwan, Singapore, Hong Kong, Malaysia, Indonesia, Thailand and The Philippines) experienced a slowdown in what had been very high rates of growth, though they still grew rapidly by world standards. Dramatic political upheavals in eastern Europe, the collapse and formal dissolution of the Soviet Union in 1991 and the Gulf War in the same year added to economic uncertainty and volatile, but generally depressed, **commodity** prices. The end of the Cold War produced neither a 'peace dividend' nor a stimulus to **economic growth**. Cuts in armaments expenditure cost jobs and reduced **investment** in both the former Soviet empire and (to a lesser extent) the United States and Western Europe. The former Soviet Union and its satellites entered a period of economic contraction that lasted most of the decade and further depressed the Western economies. At the end of the decade, Russia's financial problems came to have global ramifications.

There were serious consequences for the rest of the world economy of the slow growth policies followed by the industrialised group. If the old industrial countries could no longer be relied on to be the engines of growth in the international economy, the world economy would become more dependent on the growth areas of industrialising Asia, which might prove insufficient to stimulate growth throughout the world economy. Certainly Australia had, by the 1990s, come to rely heavily on the continuation of the Asian economic miracle.

# Recession and recovery in the OECD countries

## Onset of recession

Although the dramatic political events of 1990 and 1991 played their part, the economic slowdown in the OECD group was mainly a reaction to the high growth and inflationary conditions of the late 1980s (see Tables 12.1 and 12.2). As financial authorities tightened **monetary policy** in 1990, the major economies were pushed into recession. In the United States, the economy was virtually stagnant by mid-1990: business sentiment was negative and the financial sector was still affected by the wave of bankruptcies and losses following the 1987 stock market **crash**. The Gulf crisis pushed the US economy into recession in the last quarter: rising **inflation** due to higher oil prices prevented the government from loosening monetary policy

**Table 12.1**   Real economic growth in the OECD area, 1988–1998 (percentage change from previous year)

| Year | Australia | G7 | OECD |
|---|---|---|---|
| 1988 | 3.8 | 4.4 | 4.4 |
| 1989 | 4.2 | 3.6 | 3.6 |
| 1990 | 1.2 | 2.5 | 2.9 |
| 1991 | −1.3 | 0.7 | 1.1 |
| 1992 | 2.6 | 1.8 | 1.9 |
| 1993 | 4.0 | 1.1 | 1.2 |
| 1994 | 5.3 | 2.8 | 2.9 |
| 1995 | 4.1 | 2.1 | 2.3 |
| 1996 | 3.7 | 2.8 | 3.0 |
| 1997 | 2.8 | 2.8 | 3.2 |
| 1998 | 3.6 | 2.1 | 2.2 |

Note: G7 = the USA, Japan, Germany, France, Italy, the UK and Canada.
Source: Based on OECD 1998.

**Table 12.2**   Inflation in the OECD area, 1988–1997 (consumer prices, per cent changes from previous period)

| Year | Australia | G7 | OECD |
|------|-----------|-----|------|
| 1988 | 7.3 | 3.3 | 9.0 |
| 1989 | 7.5 | 4.4 | 6.4 |
| 1990 | 7.3 | 4.9 | 7.1 |
| 1991 | 3.2 | 4.3 | 6.4 |
| 1992 | 1.0 | 3.1 | 5.1 |
| 1993 | 1.8 | 2.7 | 4.4 |
| 1994 | 1.9 | 2.2 | 5.0 |
| 1995 | 4.6 | 2.4 | 5.8 |
| 1996 | 2.6 | 2.2 | 5.3 |
| 1997 | 0.3 | 2.1 | 4.7 |

Source: See Table 12.1.

and the crisis finished off business and consumer confidence. In Europe, the members of the Exchange Rate Mechanism (ERM) followed the **interest** rate lead of the Bundesbank as Germany was the strongest economy. Germany's **central bank** responded to the unification of Germany and the Gulf crisis by tightening monetary policy and raising interest rates in January 1991. The others were obliged to follow this tightening if they wanted to remain in the ERM. In Japan, the monetary authorities raised the discount rate from 2.5 per cent to 6 per cent between May 1989 and December 1990 to combat an overheated economy.

The impact of a tighter **money supply** was to reverse the trend of asset inflation, leading to stock market and property market downturns. This, however, raised concerns about the fragility of financial institutions that had lent on overinflated asset prices. In the United States, widespread bankruptcies in the **saving** and loan sector exacerbated this downturn. In the United Kingdom, monetary tightening began to bite in 1990. In the third quarter of that year, the United Kingdom went into recession (output fell by 5 per cent on an annual basis), and inflation remained at 10 per cent, thus bringing about a return to **stagflation**. By the end of 1990, the United Kingdom had high inflation, high interest rates and declining output. **Unemployment** increased. A similar pattern emerged in other countries. For example, in Canada, interest rates rose to 13 per cent in 1990 and output fell by 1 per cent in the second quarter of 1990.

Recovery was difficult to achieve because of the high levels of debt being carried by government, corporations and households. This debt was based on assets that were subject to considerable price inflation in the 1980s. As asset prices declined, strain was placed on banks, more bankruptcies occurred and debt crises followed. Banks were restrained in making new loans, making it difficult for investment to underpin a sustained upward growth path. Governments were unable to stimulate recovery for fear of reigniting inflation. So long as they could wear the political impact of high real interest rates and higher unemployment, they moved very slowly to take measures to stimulate demand and investment, and thus recovery, or at least a very vigorous recovery, was delayed. It became clear as the 1990s went on that macroeconomic policy was dominated by monetary considerations and that inflation was the major target, regardless of what happened to **incomes**, unemployment or growth. **Fiscal policy** was not employed effectively to end the 1990s recession because it was thought that fiscal stimulation would be inflationary. In any case, fiscal stimulus was less effective if consumers and firms were trying to pay off debt rather than looking to increase spending.

The international recession worsened in 1991, world output increasing by less than 1 per cent (see Figure 12.1). Continued stagnation in the developed economies together with the steep decline in output in the former Soviet and Eastern Bloc countries were the major causes of the deepening crisis. Economic policy in the developed industrial countries remained passive or worse. Indeed, further cuts to government **budgets** and public expenditure only made the recession deeper. Moreover, the financial deregulation undertaken in the 1980s now meant that the markets for **foreign exchange** and short-term funds dominated the world financial system. Governments might try to attract funds and/or retain funds, but in practice, they abandoned most of their interventionist instruments. The international financial system itself was biased towards recession since the financial markets would punish any country they regarded as following 'inflationary' policies – into which category policies for stimulating growth as followed in earlier periods of recession inevitably fell. Governments that wanted to win and retain the approval of the markets in this recession learned to keep a tight rein on inflation through restrictive monetary, fiscal and wages policies. Thus, governments continued to be reluctant to increase public spending – except when an overriding politi-

**Figure 12.1**    World output and world trade, 1983–1998

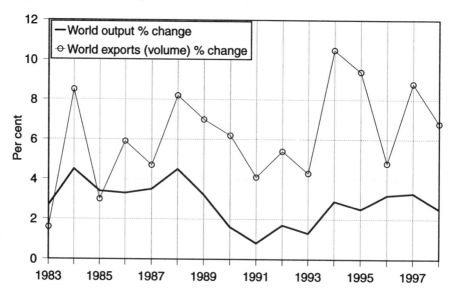

Source: Based on UN *World Economic and Social Survey* 1986, p. 12; 1988, p. 5; 1990, p. 1; 1998, p. 2.

**Table 12.3**    Unemployment in the OECD area, 1988–1998 (per cent of total labour force)

| Year | Australia | G7 | OECD |
|------|-----------|-----|------|
| 1988 | 7.1 | 6.2 | 6.5 |
| 1989 | 6.1 | 5.7 | 6.0 |
| 1990 | 7.0 | 5.6 | 5.9 |
| 1991 | 9.5 | 6.5 | 6.6 |
| 1992 | 10.7 | 7.2 | 7.3 |
| 1993 | 10.9 | 7.3 | 8.0 |
| 1994 | 9.7 | 7.2 | 7.9 |
| 1995 | 8.6 | 6.9 | 7.6 |
| 1996 | 8.5 | 7.0 | 7.5 |
| 1997 | 8.6 | 6.8 | 7.2 |
| 1998 | 8.2 | 6.7 | 7.1 |

Source: See Table 12.1.

cal concern arose, such as the Gulf War, bailing out ailing financial institutions (as in the case of the US saving and loans crisis) or reconstruction of the former German Democratic Republic in the case of Germany. Rising unemployment did not attract the same political imperative.

During 1991, five of the world's seven largest economies were in recession as Japan and Germany joined the United Kingdom, the United States and Canada. As a whole, the developed market economies grew by barely 1 per cent, the lowest growth since 1982. Unemployment rose sharply, though remaining lower in Japan and Germany (see Table 12.3). In 1992 and 1993, the crisis in the industrial countries worsened, except in the United States. Economic growth in the European Union slowed to 1 per cent in 1992 and became negative in 1993.[2] Japan's rate of growth declined from almost 4 per cent to around 1 per cent in 1992 and ground to a halt in 1993. During the period from 1991 to 1993, nearly every member of the OECD experienced at least one year of below 1.5 per cent growth and 15 OECD countries (including six of the seven largest) suffered at least one year of negative growth.[3]

Thus, caution and uncertainty prevailed throughout the developed economies in the early 1990s – a reaction to the past as well as an assessment of the future. If the **boom** of the 1980s was finance-led, the recovery too was hampered by financial constraints. The recession brought about a prolonged banking crisis. Banks were left in an awkward position: the fall in asset prices left them with bad loans; the fall in share prices reduced their own **reserves**, part of which were held in securities. If they sold their shares to cover their bad loans it would push down asset prices even more. Recovery in Japan depended on tackling the insolvency crisis of the banks, but this proved to be a long drawn out affair.

## Recovery

Recovery from the early 1990s' recession was seen in economies that had gone into recession first: the United States, Canada, the United Kingdom, Australia and

New Zealand. By 1994, the United States was growing at 3.5 per cent again, a similar rate to 1988 and 1989. Unemployment declined to just above 6 per cent from its high point in 1992 of 7.5 per cent. Inflation also fell: to under 3 per cent in 1994, the lowest level in the United States since 1986. Economic growth in Canada and the United Kingdom in 1994 was over 4 per cent, and in Australia and New Zealand over 5 per cent (in both cases higher than any year in the 1980s except 1984). As in the United States, unemployment in Canada, the United Kingdom, Australia and New Zealand declined, though remaining well above 1980s levels, and inflation was lower in Canada, Australia and New Zealand. It seemed to be a characteristic of the recovery from this recession that unemployment responded sluggishly to the faster rates of economic growth.

In other developed countries, 1993 was a year of recession; recovery in 1994 was only modest. Germany, France and Italy experienced negative growth in 1993 followed by rates of around 2.5 per cent in 1994, and **unemployment rates** in these three remained at record levels in 1994. In Japan, fiscal stimulation was used on several occasions, and public works programs were brought forward, but these initiatives failed to restore consumer spending or business confidence, and growth was virtually stagnant at around 0.5 per cent.

By 1995, recovery was evident in all of the developed economies, but unlike the recovery from the 1980–82 recession, growth rates remained subdued, and generally below those of the 1980s 'boom' (see Table 12.1). For example, growth

## SUMMARY BOX

The recessions in the OECD countries at the beginning of the decade were largely the result of domestic measures taken in response to the asset price inflation and increasing debt problems of the late 1980s. Political upheavals in Eastern Europe, the collapse of the Soviet Union and the Gulf War exacerbated world economic problems. Recovery was slow and economic growth in the 1990s was generally below the average for the 1980s, because governments did not want inflation to re-emerge. Additionally, the globalisation of financial markets made governments wary of following policies that would be interpreted by these markets as inflationary. Financial and banking crises in the United States, the European Union and Japan were further factors in the onset of recession and slow recovery. With slower economic growth, fiscal consolidation and a 'fight inflation first' mentality prevailing throughout the OECD, unemployment rates remained high. Australia was adversely affected by the recessions, particularly because of weakening international commodity prices. Australia was subject to similar domestic forces to other OECD members that led it into recession as well. The continued economic expansion of the newly industrialising countries of east and South-East Asia and China, however, provided Australia with an alternative source of international demand as it integrated further into the region.

rates in the United States, Germany, France, Italy, the United Kingdom and Canada were lower in 1995 and 1996 than in 1994. This was true of the European Union as a whole as well. Japan seemed finally to recover in 1996: after four years of virtual economic stagnation it recorded a rate of growth of output in 1996 of 3.5 per cent, still well below its average at the end of the 1980s of over 5 per cent, but nevertheless signalling an upward trend. But in 1997, recovery collapsed as the Japanese economy stagnated again and output contracted in the last quarter of 1997 and the first half of 1998. For the developed economies other than Japan, the slowdown in growth in 1995 and 1996 might have been simply a 'mid-cycle dip' (such as occurred in 1986) but stronger growth in 1997 was short-lived as the East Asian economic crisis (discussed below) impacted on the developed economies in 1998. Thus the recovery in the mid-1990s from the recession continued to be characterised by relatively low growth rates and, as a consequence, high levels of unemployment.

# World trade in the 1990s

## Strong growth: east and South-East Asia

The impact of the recessions in the OECD countries on world trade was not as severe as it had been in earlier recessions. In the 1990–93 recession, world trade slowed but, in contrast to the 1982 recession, did not contract. In the recovery period after 1993, world trade grew more rapidly than world output, with the gap widening during the mid-1990s as economic growth in the developed countries remained subdued, and Japan's economic recovery faltered. In 1994, for example, world output grew by only 2.9 per cent, but world trade by 10.5 per cent (see Figure 12.1). This represented a higher rate of growth of world trade than the peaks of the 1980s (1984 and 1988), and the gap between world output and world trade growth was certainly much wider in 1994 than in these earlier peak years (see Figure 12.1).

The major reason for the relative buoyancy of world trade from the late 1980s through the recession of the early 1990s was the dynamism of the economies of east and South-East Asia and China. These economies had the fastest rates of economic growth and it was also this region where external trade grew most rapidly – and where the growth of external trade outstripped the growth of output. Thus, an underlying feature of world trade in this period was the exceptionally strong economic performance by these Asian economies. And it was these economies that underpinned international demand for much of Australia's exports.

China and east and South-East Asian trade continued to be the major growth region for the world economy in the 1990s (see Table 12.4). Although exports to Japan slowed, intra-regional trade remained a strong growth factor. China's external trade growth was outstanding, helped by various trade liberalisation reforms. China rose from 27th place among world exporters in 1980 to 11th place in 1992. Moreover, the area of southern China, Hong Kong and Taiwan itself emerged as a significant growth region within the East Asia region. The share of manufactured

**Table 12.4**   Shares of world exports, major countries/regions, 1985, 1990, 1995 (per cent of total world exports by value)

| Country/region | 1985 | 1990 | 1995 |
|---|---|---|---|
| USA | 17.4 | 14.5 | 14.8 |
| European Union | 34.1 | 40.0 | 34.5 |
| Japan | 5.9 | 6.1 | 5.9 |
| East & South-East Asia (inc. China) | 8.7 | 11.3 | 15.6 |

Source: Based on UN *World Economic and Social Survey*, 1998, p. 2.

items in China's exports increased significantly, reflecting its industrialisation. In 1980, less than half of China's exports were manufactures, by 1991 over three-quarters were. China's industrialisation and trade liberalisation opened up opportunities for other economies to supply **capital** and intermediate goods.

Because of industrialisation in Asia and its export orientation, manufactured goods continued to increase their share of world merchandise trade, increasing from 56 per cent in 1980 to 73 per cent in 1992. This was largely due to the growth of manufactures exports from Asia where they accounted for 82 per cent of total merchandise exports. In fact, by the early 1990s, Asia had the highest proportion of manufactures in exports in the world. The strongest performing sector in manufacturing exports was machinery and transport equipment, and within that sector, office equipment (including computers) and telecommunications equipment (including mobile phones). In the 1990s, as the share of the Asian industrialising countries of these fast-growing items increased, the share of the 'old' industrial countries declined. This shift in importance in world trade from Europe and America to Asia was highly significant for Australia's growing integration with the Asia–Pacific region in the 1990s.

Regional trade emerged as a highly dynamic element in Asia. Regional diversity in east and South-East Asia intensified as the 'first generation' of Asia's newly industrialising countries (ANICs) (Korea, Taiwan, Hong Kong and Singapore) moved up to more sophisticated exports and the 'second generation' of ANICs (Thailand, Indonesia, Malaysia and The Philippines) moved up behind them. This resulted in considerable intra-regional investment and trade. The appreciation of the yen also brought more Japanese firms to the region to relocate production. China was a significant market for many countries in the region: as China's domestic market boomed, imports surged and China turned a **trade surplus** into a trade deficit, despite its impressive expansion of exports.

As economic growth slowed in 1996 and 1997, so did world trade – from a growth rate of over 10 per cent, it declined in 1996 to less than 5 per cent (see Figure 12.1). This dip in world trade growth affected Asia the most – Japan, China, east and South East Asia in particular. In the case of east and South-East Asia, the growth of exports fell below the growth of output, thus reversing the usual 'export-led' growth of previous years. The main cause was weaker demand for imports by the industrialised countries, especially Japan, whose falling value of the yen was the main factor in slowing import growth (just as the rise of the yen in 1994 and 1995 had led to strong growth in Japanese imports). This slowdown was also marked by a sharp drop in world demand for semi-conductors and information-technology equipment and products, including office equipment and telecommunications equipment. Of course, the countries most affected by this slowdown were the newly industrialising countries of east and South-East Asia, where a significant part of intra-regional trade was in electronic goods and components. Apart from the impact of demand for computer chips and the like, East Asian trade was also adversely affected by the appreciation of the US dollar, to which many of the region's major exporters linked their **exchange rates**. The appreciation of their currencies made their exports less competitive in the Japanese and European markets. This slow-down in what had been the world economy's most dynamic region brought into question whether the 'Asian economic miracle' would continue.

## Protectionism and regionalism in world trade

World trade in the 1990s remained dogged by protectionism, affecting both agricul-tural commodities and manufactured goods. Most of the developed nations resorted to increased protectionism during the 1990s. Like protectionism, regional trading arrangements continued to develop in the 1990s, and while the Uruguay Round of GATT (General Agreement on Tariffs and Trade) remained in stalemate, the growth of regional blocs represented an obstacle to achieving **multilateral** liberalisa-tion (see Chapter 10 for the origins of the Uruguay Round). The Uruguay Round covered sectors of world trade neglected in previous rounds, particularly trade in agricultural goods and clothing and textiles, as well as addressing new issues such as trade-related investment measures and trade-related aspects of intellectual prop-erty. The Uruguay Round was scheduled to be completed in four years, by end of 1990, but negotiations stalled in 1990 and 1991. The main problem was one that was of vital interest to Australia, namely, export **subsidies** in trade in agricultural products. However, agriculture was not the only area that remained unresolved – it also proved difficult to reach agreement on trade in services and intellectual prop-erty between the developed countries and the newly industrialising nations of Asia and China.

Impatience with the Uruguay Round led some countries to embark on unilat-eral measures designed to improve their international trade. The United States, for example, introduced legislation to protect its trade with Japan and a number of other countries that it regarded as 'unfair traders' (see Chapter 10). The 1990–92 recession and rising unemployment in US manufacturing industries only intensi-fied the pressure on the American government to use these measures. Countries that ran a trade surplus with the United States were targeted, principally Japan, China and east and South-East Asia.

## The new trend: regional trade blocs

Attention from multilateral trade agreements was also diverted in the 1990s by a continuation of the trend towards regional trading blocs. Western European economic integration was enhanced by the signing of the Maastricht Treaty in

1991, which led to the creation of a single market in 1992 and set the European Union on course for full monetary union by 1999. In addition, in 1991, the 12 members of the European Community and the seven members of EFTA reached an agreement to form the European Economic Area from the start of 1993. This created a **free trade** area of 380 million people and one that accounted for 40 per cent of world trade. Largely in reaction to these changes in Europe, the United States and Canada embarked on the creation of a free trade bloc by negotiating the North American Free Trade Agreement, NAFTA, which also included Mexico.

NAFTA signalled that the world economy might be breaking up into rival trading blocs (as it did in the 1930s). Obviously, Australia would be damaged by this. At the same time, Australia was instrumental in getting APEC together. Whether an Asia–Pacific bloc was likely to emerge, and if it did what Australia's position would be remained (and still remains).

The enthusiasm in the 1990s for joining regional groups was advanced as evidence that regionalism was not protectionist but rather spawned further trade liberalisation and increased regional trade and investment flows. Regional blocs, it was suggested, conferred economic and political benefits on members without disadvantaging non-members. On the economic side, intra-bloc trade was expected to rise, allowing smaller countries to expand markets and obtain economies of scale. Political benefits came if the bloc gained a stronger negotiating advantage against non-member countries or other blocs. They might also help to promote regional political co-operation and stability. On the other hand, blocs might be trade diverting rather than trade creating, they might provoke counter-productive trade retaliation and beggar-thy-neighbour effects and they might lead to more aggressive trade policies being followed generally. A country joining a trade bloc thus might obtain economic benefits through closer ties with fellow members – but might also lose trade and investment advantages with the wider world economy. Non-members might be disadvantaged by the creation or extension of a trade bloc – indeed, if world trade was static, the creation of a bloc would inevitably hurt non-members. Nevertheless, creating a bloc might raise incomes and stimulate imports, including those from non-members.

The countries that gained most from a strong, multilateral trading system in the 1980s and 1990s were the small, open, export-orientated countries, especially the developing economies of east and South-East Asia. These were precisely the ones with potentially the most to lose if the rest of the world became dominated by a number of powerful trading blocs. As Australia became more open and export-orientated, it too expressed a strong interest in keeping world trade free from restrictions and continued to voice its long-established criticisms of subsidies and trade barriers in agricultural products. The deepening and widening of the European Union together with the creation of NAFTA and other blocs led to a response from east and South-East Asia. At the beginning of 1992, members of the Association of South-East Asian Nations (ASEAN) agreed to take the first steps towards becoming a regional common market within 15 years by the establishment of an ASEAN Free Trade Area (AFTA). This represented a considerable step for ASEAN, which had previously shunned economic integration.[4] Was this the beginning of an East Asian trade bloc?

As these countries became heavily reliant on open global markets, they became very active within GATT and highly critical of protectionism. As most of the developed economies grew slowly and became less open to imports from East Asia and China, a split in the global economy into spheres of influence that excluded East Asia would be of great concern to the region. The United States continued to be East Asia's largest market, but East Asian regional trade grew rapidly, as did regional investment flows. As this happened without any formal bloc being created it could be concluded that a formal arrangement was superfluous. But two considerations worked against this view: other blocs might become more exclusionist, in which case an East Asian bloc could be seen as a sensible retaliation. Second, a Pacific Rim bloc might be beneficial to its members in any case by liberalising trade between them. Maybe this would not be as good an outcome as global free trade, but since that was not possible, it might be better than the status quo.

Apart from moves towards the commercialisation of ASEAN, greater East Asian regional integration was foreshadowed in 1990 when Malaysia proposed the establishment of an East Asian Economic Grouping to include all countries in east and South-East Asia.[5] It was envisaged that this group would follow policies of preferential trading and was widely regarded as a reaction to the protectionism of the West. In 1992, the proposal was watered down to an East Asia Economic Caucus, but potentially it could have become a trading bloc. A wider group, Asia–Pacific Economic Co-operation (APEC), was established as an official consultative forum in 1989 and included Australia, New Zealand, Canada and the United States, in addition to East Asian countries.[6] In 1995, APEC committed its 18 members to achieve free trade by 2010 for the industrialised countries and 2020 for **developing countries**. They pledged themselves to complete free trade in all industrial goods, and to making APEC trade concessions ultimately available to the rest of the world. By the end of the decade, however, the achievement of this timetable appeared less likely.

## World trade and the Uruguay Round

At the end of 1993, the Uruguay Round was finally completed, three years behind schedule. The main outcomes of the Round were reduced tariff barriers in developed economies, including on imports of textiles from developing countries and on agricultural goods imports. In addition, there was to be a considerable reduction or phasing out of non-tariff barriers, including most of such barriers in trade in agriculture, as well as the elimination of safeguarding and anti-dumping restrictions, and voluntary export restraint. Non-tariff restrictions in agricultural products were to be eliminated (although these could be replaced by **tariffs**, they had to be at lower levels). Domestic support for farming was to be significantly reduced: by 20 per cent for developed countries and 13 per cent for developing. Significant cuts were also to be made in export subsidies on agricultural products. Trade in services was to be made subject to 'most favoured nation' provisions (though with exemptions that could last up to 10 years). Computer programs were to be treated as literary works in an attempt to protect them and sound recordings from bootlegging. Trade-related investment measures (such as 'local content' rules) were outlawed if they violated GATT regulations. So-called 'safeguarding' measures where a country imposed illegal restrictions in order to 'safeguard' itself from unfair import competition were to be subject to 'sunset clauses'. 'Anti-dumping measures' were also brought under GATT rules. Export subsidies for agricultural and other goods were to be eliminated.

The Uruguay Round also led to an historic agreement to establish a World Trade Organisation (WTO), a body that had been agreed to at the Bretton Woods conference almost half a century earlier (see Chapter 7). The WTO encompassed the GATT and had as its main function the facilitation and implementation of multilateral trade agreements. It took over GATT's negotiating functions, its dispute settlement mechanisms and its policy review facilities.

Completion of the Uruguay Round was seen as strengthening multilateralism in the face of growing protectionism and 'managed' trade practices. It was anticipated that world trade would grow faster as a result of the liberalisation fostered by the agreement, with the largest gains being made in trade in agricultural produce and in textiles and clothing. It was also expected that it would enhance the growth of world trade in services. Countries signing the Uruguay Round agreements hailed it as a great achievement, but in the end, its success depended on how well the spirit of the agreement was upheld by its members. As the 1990s progressed,

**SUMMARY BOX**

The growth of world trade in the 1990s was very much dependent on the strength of the international trade of east and South-East Asia and China. These countries' external trade grew rapidly and was dominated by manufactures and intermediate goods. There were strong intra-regional trade and capital flows. However, Japan's continuing poor economic performance undermined the region's strong trade expansion. Protectionism in world trade by the developed economies continued to rise, affecting international trade in agricultural commodities, especially foodstuffs, and the types of manufactured goods exported by developing economies (textiles, footwear and electronic components). The conclusion of the Uruguay Round of GATT in 1993 signalled a reduction in protectionism in the future and was particularly welcomed by Australia because of its provisions on free trade in agricultural products. The creation of the World Trade Organisation also provided a stronger forum for pursuing arguments against protectionism. However, in reality, there was little sign of a major breakdown in protectionist attitudes as the century came to an end. Regional trade arrangements became more prominent, partly in response to frustration with the way in which protectionism was undermining global free trade. As Western Europe and North America strengthened regional trade ties, the appropriate response of the Asia–Pacific region was frequently discussed. However, a formal Asia–Pacific trade bloc was not forthcoming and Australia's position if such a bloc should emerge remained unclear.

there was not much evidence that the attitude of the most powerful countries towards managed trade and taking unilateral action to force changes on weaker partners was diminished. Arguments for protectionism based on low-cost import competition continued to be heard and the rising tide of disputes taken before the World Trade Organisation indicated that protectionism in world trade was far from over as the twentieth century drew to a close. Little real progress was made in reducing subsidies to agricultural production and protectionism in agricultural trade by the end of the decade.

There were also a number of issues that the Uruguay Round did not touch on and that remained to be tackled by the WTO, principally **labour** standards, and in particular the use of child labour in developing and developed countries, and violation of human rights generally. Although often viewed in the past as internal matters, such issues seemed likely to be brought into international trade negotiations to a much greater extent. Similarly, a wide range of environmental concerns were linked to rising world trade, especially concepts of 'sustainable development'. By the late 1990s, world trade was still plagued by protectionism. The question remained whether international agreements – regional or global – and the creation of the WTO provided some ground for optimism that protectionism could be effectively reversed in the new century.

# International capital flows and financial crises

International capital flows grew stronger in the 1990s once the recessions in the industrial countries were over. Japan's position as leading creditor nation was enhanced as Germany's capital exports declined. Capital flows between the developed countries were dominated by the US **current account** deficit (driven by its growing trade deficit) and Japan's **current account surplus**. Slow recovery and low growth in the 1990s in Japan left more of Japan's investible funds available for **foreign investment**. As a result, the world economy became highly dependent on Japanese foreign investment, particularly its continued financing of the US current account deficit. Flows to developing countries went chiefly to Latin America and east and South East Asia. Financial crises occurred in both these regions in the mid-1990s, eventually causing the collapse of the Asian 'economic miracles' of the 1980s and 1990s.

## Latin American financial crisis

The crisis in Latin America began with a Mexican currency crisis at the beginning of 1995. Mexico's economic growth was fairly weak during the 1990s and domestic investment was low. Domestic savings fell as a share of **GDP** (in contrast to the Asian 'miracle' economies). Pegging the peso to the US dollar kept its exchange rate up but it caused the peso to be over-valued in terms of Mexico's trading performance. The over-valued peso led to a rise in imports and made Mexico's exports less competitive. Trade liberalisation led to rising imports more than it stimulated exports. By 1994, the current account deficit reached 8 per cent of GDP and the Mexican government was forced to devalue the peso. Capital took flight from Mexico and the international money market sold off the Mexican currency in reaction. By the end of January 1995, the peso had fallen by 40 per cent against the US dollar and the central bank reserves were exhausted. To prevent the Mexican government from defaulting on its **short-term** foreign loans, the International Monetary Fund (IMF), the Bank of International Settlements, the United States government and various other central banks put together a $53 billion 'rescue package.' The loan from the IMF of $18 billion was the largest it had ever made to a member country and arranged in record time by the personal initiative of the Fund's managing director.

As a result of the crisis, the Mexican government made drastic cuts to public expenditure, which slowed economic growth and tightened monetary policy. This raised interest rates and caused difficulties for many businesses in Mexico. The depreciation of the peso made imports more expensive, which raised domestic prices. New foreign capital inflows ceased, leading to further cuts in expenditure and investment. In sum, the crisis led to a fall in GDP of about 10 per cent, increased unemployment, and reduced real consumption and wages.

The Mexican currency crisis caused reverberations throughout Latin America and in Argentina in particular. Argentina had also pegged its currency to the US dollar, but the 1994–95 Mexican crisis caused a reduction of foreign capital inflow to Argentina and a **balance of payments** crisis. Its fixed exchange rate (a '**currency board** system') meant that the fall in central bank reserves caused by the balance of payments deficit led to a shrinking of the domestic money supply, thus causing a severe contraction of the domestic economy. To try to increase capital inflow, the Argentine government adopted tighter fiscal and monetary policies, which drove the economy further into contraction. The central bank's reserves continued to fall in 1995, but the exchange rate was not altered. All of the adjustment costs fell on the domestic economy in terms of economic stagnation, rising unemployment and reduced living standards. This brought to an end the rather fragile economic recovery of Argentina from the crises of the 1980s.

The Mexico currency crisis was short-lived as far as the international money markets were concerned. Within a year, foreign investment returned to Mexico, albeit more cautiously than before. The lower peso boosted Mexico's exports and lower costs (including real wages) led to some return of investor confidence. What the crisis showed, however, was two things: first, how severely the global money market could react to a country that had a fixed exchange rate which its international position no longer supported. And second, how easily other countries in the region could be adversely affected by contagion and how long these effects could persist. Although not recognised at the time as a lesson for the newly industrialising countries of east and South-East Asia, as the East Asia currency crisis of 1997 unfolded, the Mexico crisis of 1995 was viewed in retrospect as a significant harbinger.

## Asian economic crisis

The economic crisis in east and South-East Asia that developed in 1997 was more serious for the world economy than the earlier Latin American crisis. One of the striking features of the 1997–98 crisis in East Asia was that it was so unexpected.

The countries that became embroiled in it did not appear likely candidates for such a catastrophe before it started in mid-1997.[7] The economies of the region had been growing strongly for a decade or more. They were outstanding export performers in a range of manufactured goods, rather than primary commodities, and, indeed, they had for some time been the only real bright spots in the expansion of world trade. Their economic progress over the previous twenty years was seen (with considerable justification) as an 'Asian economic miracle'. With their export-led growth and attractiveness to international direct investment, they were outward- not inward-looking. They had external debts, but the ratio of these to GDP was not particularly high. Unlike Mexico, their external debts were largely private, not 'sovereign' government debt. Internally, these economies did not appear to resemble 'banana republics': they had high **savings rates**, high investment rates and low public debt ratios. Their governments ran budget surpluses most of the time. Their 'fundamentals' seemed to be in better order than many other countries of similar size at the time, including Australia. However, a number of factors combined in 1997 to throw them into crisis.

From 1996, economic growth in east and South-East Asia slowed, reversing an acceleration that had begun in 1992. The cause of this slowdown was the emergence of the twin by-products of sustained rapid growth – inflation and balance of payments deficits – in the region's top growth performers: South Korea, Singapore, Indonesia, Malaysia and Thailand, all of which tightened monetary policy and raised interest rates. Investment activity also slowed somewhat, although foreign investment remained strong. The balance of payments deficits were financed by rising volumes of 'hot money' – short-term capital that flowed into these economies in response to higher interest rates. These flows were inherently unstable and they also put pressure on the local currencies to appreciate, despite the relatively poorer export prospects of these countries in the face of continued slow growth in Europe and Japan, and the slowdown in China. Other regional economies also slowed in 1996: Taiwan and Hong Kong were affected by political uncertainties and by a longer term restructuring away from manufacturing and towards services that led to a slowdown in investment. World trade slowed in the second half of 1996, exacerbating the problems of these highly export-orientated economies, particularly as world demand for semiconductors and information technology products entered a cyclical downturn at this time. During the year, it became clear that the 'high yen/low dollar' relationship between the currencies of the world's two largest economies was being reversed. The dollar appreciated against the yen (reflecting the booming US economy in contrast to the stagnant and financially troubled Japanese economy) and this had the further effect of increasing the yen exchange value of a number of the currencies of east and South-East Asia that were pegged to (or tracked) the US dollar. This made their exports to Japan and Europe less competitive, just at a time when the industrial countries seemed overstocked with computer chips and associated products.

Moreover, by the beginning of 1997 it was apparent that several of these countries – South Korea and Thailand in particular – were developing internal financial crises. Credit creation by banks and other financial institutions during the 1990s had led to asset price rises, especially real estate and equities. The problem was not only the extent of the credit creation (expanding considerably faster than economic growth) but also the source of loans and the uses to which they were put. Many of the loans were short-term foreign currency loans (predominantly from Japanese banks), making them vulnerable to an exchange rate fall. And although much of the foreign capital was used for investment rather than consumption, a large proportion of it flowed into speculative activity in the property and **equity** markets and to other risky ventures (including a number of industries that were suffering from over-production and into building **infrastructure** likely to exhibit low rates of return). A high level of bad debts and bankruptcies in the financial and industrial sectors, combined with weak and opaque financial supervisory and regulatory structures, led to a loss of investor confidence in these economies. Perhaps if there had been more financial transparency, better corporate governance and greater central bank or government supervision, the bubble would not have been allowed to get so big before it burst.

The crisis began in mid-1997 when the international financial markets finally began to show concern at the slowdown in the major export trades of the region. The country that was most vulnerable, Thailand, was affected first, with a severe drop in equity prices. The other markets in the region followed this fall. A decline in the **foreign exchange markets** followed immediately, but as the Thai baht collapsed in July 1997, the international money markets panicked and over-reacted. Currency collapse spread throughout the region by contagion as international investors reassessed each of the regional economies and sold off their currencies. Once the crisis was under way, the **credit ratings** agencies, Moody's and Standard and Poor, rather belatedly began downgrading the credit ratings of the East Asian economies, thus spreading the contagion further. During the six months from July 1997 to January 1998, the main currencies of the region tumbled: Indonesia's rupiah to one-fifth of its pre-crisis US dollar rate (measured in dollars per unit of foreign currency), Thailand's baht to just above two-fifths, South Korea's won to two-fifths, Malaysia's ringgit to one half, The Philippines' peso to three-fifths, and the Singapore and Taiwanese dollars to four-fifths. (The Hong Kong dollar main-tained its parity with the US dollar, but only at the cost of very high interest rates that brought Hong Kong's property and share market boom to a shuddering halt.) Slower economic growth turned into severe contraction, imports were greatly reduced, unemployment and social distress greatly increased. There were wide-spread bankruptcies and the loss of corporate and personal wealth. The crisis toppled three heads of government (in Thailand, South Korea and Indonesia).

With the Mexican currency crisis of three years earlier now recalled, the IMF, World Bank and the Asia Development Bank, together with several G7 govern-ments, acted quickly to arrange 'rescue' packages for Indonesia, Thailand and South Korea. A total of $110 billion was committed, just over half by the three international institutions and the remainder from Japan ($19 billion), the United States ($8 billion), the European Union ($6.3 billion) and a dozen other countries. By comparison, in 1995, Mexico alone had received rescue loans of $52 billion ($30 billion from the IMF, BIS, World Bank and Inter-American Development Bank and $20 billion from its neighbour, the United States).[8] Moreover, the loans to Mexico had been relatively free: those to the East Asian economies were condi-tional on recipient governments implementing wide reforms of their economies. These included improving prudential supervision of the financial sector, privatisa-tion of state-owned enterprises, elimination of various government monopolies and **cartels**, legislation to make corporate governance stronger and more transparent, the abolition of various structures deemed by the IMF to be obstructive to competition, and more public scrutiny and accountability of the relations between business and government.

## The Asian crisis and the world economy

The ramifications of the crisis spread throughout the region and then throughout the world economy. A number of other countries, including Russia, China and Brazil, were considered candidates for contagion, and these were economies that did not have such strong track records as those of east and South-East Asia. In 1998, Russia repudiated payment on its foreign loans and devalued the rouble, spreading the financial crisis to the European and US banks that had lent to Russia. Additional pressure was placed on these banks by the losses now made by hedge funds that had borrowed from the banks in order to speculate in loans to Russia and other emerging markets. Brazil was provided with IMF and US loans to help it to avoid **devaluation**, not that IMF intervention had prevented this in Russia's case. But above all, the crisis of the Asian NICs embroiled the world's second-largest economy, Japan, and once that became apparent, in mid-1998, the regional crisis took on much more serious implications.

Japan's involvement was twofold. On the one hand, its economy was deeply integrated in the regional economy through trade, investment and financial flows that had been stimulated during the 'high yen' decade. Japan was a major market for the East Asian economies whose exports became more competitive as the yen rose against the US dollar. Japan was the major source of **direct foreign investment** as Japanese firms had gone 'off-shore' during the decade of the high yen. And Japanese banks were the principal suppliers of the short-term yen loans that had financed the region's expansion. When the US dollar appreciated against the yen and the 'high yen' period came to an end, these conditions were reversed: exports to Japan were less competitive and Japanese capital flows to the region declined. On the other hand, Japan was experiencing its own internal crisis during the 1990s. Its period of rapid credit expansion and over-investment in equity markets and property speculation had burst in 1990. As the other industrial countries slipped into recessions in the early 1990s, Japan followed, but unlike most of its fellow OECD members, it could not recover. By the first half of 1998, Japan was in economic recession. Moreover, the bad loans that accumulated in the Japanese banking system following the bursting of the 1980s bubble were not exorcised. By 1998, these non-performing loans were estimated at 77 trillion yen, equivalent to about 17 per cent of Japan's GDP. This prevented a return of either business or consumer confidence.

It was, of course, serious enough that the world's second-largest economy should be in recession at a time when no industrial country (apart from the United States) had been able to return to the growth levels of the 1980s, as this threatened a worldwide slowdown. But the structural imbalances of the 1980s and 1990s between Japan and the United States had left the former the world's largest creditor nation and the latter the world's largest debtor. Much of the United States' external debt was owed to Japanese banks and other financial institutions, including large amounts of short-term Treasury bills. The danger lay in the possibility that Japanese funds would be repatriated to help Japan to recover from its recession and rebuild its financial sector, causing the United States to suffer a balance of payment crisis that would push it into a recession. Such a series of events could lead to a worldwide **depression**.

The East Asian currency crisis of 1997 was the third major monetary upheaval in five years (the first was the ERM crisis in Europe in 1992) and the one with the greatest global impact.[9] It inevitably raised questions about the global financial markets and their instability (Sorros 1998; Goldstein & Hawkins 1998; Delhaise 1997). In particular, the role of 'hedge funds' was widely criticised, especially after the collapse of a prominent New York hedge fund in 1998. For example, in September of that year, Long-Term Capital Management, a hedge fund that was run by people that many regarded as the best and brightest of the US financial industry, announced it had lost virtually all its capital (RBA 1998, p. 5).

Whatever the extent of 'vulnerability' and lax supervision of the financial industry, the East Asian economies – and the millions of people who lived and worked in them – did not need an 'external shock' of this magnitude to correct or adjust their economies (RBA 1998, p. 18). Neither should the world economy slip into recession because of a regional slowdown. The world economy in 1998 was supposed to be infinitely stronger and better organised than that of 1928, but the way in which unstable financial flows undermined economic growth and investment in the 1990s made comparisons with that earlier world economic disaster seem ever more pertinent.

**SUMMARY BOX**

The structural imbalance in capital flows between Japan and the United States, which emerged in the 1980s, continued to be evident in the 1990s. World capital markets were subjected to three major crises in the 1990s, each of which involved the unrestricted operations of currency speculators and hedge funds on a gigantic scale, in Western Europe, Latin America and East Asia. The crises in Europe of 1992, and in Mexico and Argentina in 1995, showed how countries with **fixed exchange rates** could become embroiled in massive speculative currency movements if their currency was regarded as **overvalued**. The third crisis, in east and South-East Asia, quickly had a major global impact, involving the repudiation of **foreign debt** by Russia and upheavals on Wall Street, as well as a slowing of the world economy. The prominent position of these economies in the world economy, together with the involvement of Japan (which had its own domestic financial difficulties), made the crisis highly contagious. The nature of this crisis brought into question the integration of Australia in the Asia–Pacific region over the previous decade. Would Australia's currency follow the others down? Would the contraction in Asian markets cause a balance of payments crisis in Australia? If the world economy slowed or went into recession, Australia was unlikely to escape the impact.

# Suggested further reading

Bello, W. & Rosenfeld, S. 1992, *Dragons in Distress: Asia's Miracle Economies in Crisis*, Penguin, London.

Delhaise, P.F. 1997, *Asia in Crisis: The Implosion of the Banking and Financial Systems*, John Wiley, Singapore.

Dicken, P. 1998, *Global Shift: The Internationalization of Economic Activity*, Chapman, 3rd edn, London.

Garnaut, R. & Drysdale, P. (eds) 1994, *Asia Pacific Regionalism*, Harper Educational, London.

Griesgraber, J. M. & Gunter, B.G. (eds.) 1996, *The World's Monetary System: Toward Stability and Sustainability in the Twenty-first Century*, Pluto Press, London.

Hirst, P. & Thompson, G. 1996, *Globalization in Question: the International Economy and the Possibilities of Governance*, Blackwell, Oxford.

Ito, T. & Krueger, A.O. (eds) 1996, *Financial Deregulation and Integration in East Asia*, Chicago University Press, Chicago.

Kapstein, E.B. 1994, *Governing the Global Economy: International Finance and the State*, Harvard University Press, Cambridge, Massachusetts.

Krugman, P. 1994, 'The myth of Asia's miracle', *Foreign Affairs*, 73 (6), pp. 62–78.

World Bank 1993, *The East Asian Miracle – Economic Growth and Public Policy*, Oxford University Press, Oxford.

# End notes

[1] The OECD was founded in 1961. Its membership in 1998 was: Australia, Belgium, Canada, the Czech Republic, Denmark, Finland, France, Germany, Greece, Hungary, Iceland, Ireland, Italy, Japan, Korea (Republic of), Luxembourg, Mexico, The Netherlands, New Zealand, Norway, Poland, Portugal, Spain, Sweden, Switzerland, Turkey, the United Kingdom and the United States of America.

[2] The European Union's original members were Belgium, France, Germany, Italy, Luxembourg and The Netherlands. This was enlarged in the 1970s by the accession of the United Kingdom, Denmark and Ireland; in the 1980s by that of Greece, Spain and Portugal; and in the 1990s by that of Austria, Finland and Sweden. Countries likely to join by the beginning of the twenty-first century include Bulgaria, Cyprus, the Czech Republic, Estonia, Hungary, Latvia, Liechtenstein, Lithuania, Malta, Poland, Romania, Slovakia, Slovenia, Switzerland and Turkey.

[3] Four member countries did not experience such a severe slowdown: Luxembourg, Norway, Mexico and Korea.

[4] The membership of ASEAN was expanded in the 1990s with the addition of Vietnam in 1995 and Laos and Myanmar (Burma) in 1997, with Cambodia and Papua New Guinea having observer status.

[5] Australia was excluded from this proposal.

[6] Its members in 1998 were: Australia, Brunei, Canada, Chile, China, Hong Kong, Indonesia, Japan, Korea (Republic of), Malaysia, Mexico, New Zealand, Papua New Guinea, Peru, The Philippines, Singapore, Taiwan, Thailand, and the United States of America.

[7] One of the few economists to question the 'Asian economic miracle', Paul Krugman, commented in 1998, 'Speculative attacks on currencies are nothing new, and some of us even warned a couple of years ago that South-East Asian countries might be at risk. But the scale and depth of this crisis have surprised everyone; this disaster has demonstrated that there are financial dangers undreamt of in our previous philosophy.' See: P. Krugman 1994, pp. 62–78; 1998, p. 21; RBA 1998, April, pp. 9–20.

8    In Mexico's case, the fact that the foreign debt was largely government debt led to a greater response by the IMF and the United States. In the Asian case, most of the foreign debt was private.

9    The Exchange Rate Mechanism operated to tie Western European currencies to the deutschmark. When the Bundesbank raised its interest rates to record post-war levels in 1992 (in response to the reunification of Germany), the financial markets became convinced that other European currencies would have to devalue against the mark. In August 1992, speculators and hedge funds sold off the British pound, which eventually was forced to leave the ERM. Other currencies were also sold off, so that by the beginning of 1993, Italy had also left the ERM and Spain, Portugal, Ireland, Sweden and Norway had devalued. Government attempts, either to reassure the financial markets or to intervene in markets directly, proved hopeless. The 1992–93 European currency crisis not only delayed economic recovery, but was reminiscent of the currency chaos of the 1970s. It illustrated the destabilising power of the globalised money markets, where the currency speculators and the hedge funds operated in a pattern that was to be repeated a number of times during the 1990s.

# 13

## The globalisation of Australia in the 1990s

Nearly all the OECD group of countries started the last decade of the twentieth century with a period of economic decline and rising **unemployment** as the late 1980s **'boom'** gave way to 'bust'. Australia was no exception, though its **recession** was shallower than the previous one, eight years earlier. Recovery was slower this time and unemployment levels remained stubbornly high. A burst of faster growth in 1994 was followed by a mid-decade slowdown. A further growth spurt was undermined by the onset of the Asian economic crisis in 1997. Meanwhile, the globalisation of the Australian economy that had begun in the early 1980s continued. The later 1990s provided a convenient vantage point to assess the impact of globalisation over the previous 15 years. The performance of the Australian economy in the 1990s and a perspective on globalisation form the two themes of this chapter.

## The Australian economy in the 1990s

### The early 1990s recession

Australia entered the worldwide recession in the middle of 1990, earlier than most OECD countries, and the economy continued to contract until reaching its lowest point in mid-1991. Apart from negative growth, the main effects were higher unemployment and lower **inflation** and inflationary expectations (see Table 13.1). Australia's inflation performance was in stark contrast to the recession in 1982–83. Although all the developed economies experienced a similar decline in inflation in the recession, in Australia the inflation rate fell to 2 percentage points below the OECD average, an unusual outcome in its recent economic history (see Figure 13.1). Unemployment rose sharply, also reaching unusually high levels by post–Second World War standards.

301

**Table 13.1**   Economic growth, unemployment and inflation in Australia,
1988–89 to 1997–98

| Year | Real economic growth (percentage change from previous year) | Unemployment (percentage of labour force, August) | Inflation (percentage change in consumer price index, June quarters) |
|------|------|------|------|
| 1988–89 | 4.3 | 6.8 | 7.3 |
| 1989–90 | 3.1 | 5.7 | 8.0 |
| 1990–91 | −1.2 | 8.2 | 3.4 |
| 1991–92 | 0.4 | 9.7 | 1.2 |
| 1992–93 | 3.4 | 10.0 | 1.9 |
| 1993–94 | 5.0 | 10.0 | 1.7 |
| 1994–95 | 4.7 | 8.7 | 4.5 |
| 1995–96 | 4.0 | 8.0 | 3.1 |
| 1996–97 | 3.0 | 8.4 | 0.3 |
| 1997–98 | 3.8 | 8.0 | 0.7 |

Sources: Based on RBA 1996, pp. 180, 224; Dec. 1998, pp. 115, 119, 122; ABS 1998, pp. 11, 60, 74.

The causes of the recession in Australia were the lagged effects of tight **monetary policy**, the **investment** cycle and the **terms of trade**. In the late 1980s, the Australian economy overheated because excessive **demand** growth built up, fuelled by rising terms of trade. High profits and the increasing share of profits over wages boosted business investment. Business and consumer confidence was high as the boom accelerated, stimulated by the decision of the Reserve Bank to ease monetary policy in the wake of the October 1987 Stock Market Crash. This surge in demand spilled over into imports and diverted domestic production from exports to domestic consumption, causing a **balance of payments** crisis. In response, monetary policy was tightened from April 1988, but it took at least a year to be felt despite short-term **interest** rates of 18 per cent by mid-1989. Monetary tightening was slow to have an effect because employment was still growing; this boosted demand. The terms of trade continued to rise, financial market liberalisation reduced the effectiveness of domestic interest rate increases and the asset price boom and rapid expansion of corporate borrowing was so strong it took time to slow down, particularly in the area of the prices of commercial property.

By the middle of 1990, however, a reversal was apparent. Business investment ceased growing as firms tried to cut costs. Commercial property prices began to fall and this, combined with high interest rates and high corporate debt, led some firms to fail to service their debt, causing problems for themselves and the banks that had lent to them. The impact of the international economy also reversed as the recession in the industrial economies caused **commodity** prices to weaken. Demand for Australia's commodity exports declined and Australia's terms of trade fell, reducing **national income** and consumption. Firms ran down stocks in anticipation of slower demand and thus placed fewer new orders. They also shed **labour** in an attempt to cut costs, causing a swift and sudden rise in Australia's **unemployment** rate: from being under 6 per cent in 1989, it was over 10 per cent by

**Figure 13.1**    Australian inflation, 1953–54 to 1997–98 (index of consumer prices)

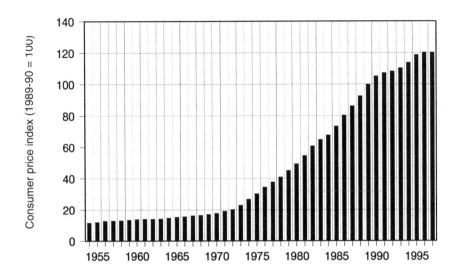

Sources: Based on RBA 1996, p. 244; ABS 1998, p. 60.

1991. Business confidence that had been riding high in the boom now became negative. Consumers, too, lost confidence in the face of an uncertain future and high interest rates. Demand for **consumer durables** shrank noticeably.

As the domestic economy contracted, imports fell and more domestic output was diverted to exports. Thus total domestic demand fell much more (four times more) than **GDP**. Farm **incomes** fell and farm output was affected by severe drought in eastern Australia. Those sectors that had escaped the 1982–83 recession were engulfed by this one; these included real estate services, financial services and the retail sector. Corporatisation of government business enterprises during the 1980s had the effect of making them more sensitive to market forces, and this sector contracted as well. Indeed, the only sectors that continued to increase output were some parts of the services sector; namely, community services, communications, electricity, gas and water. Regional variations were greater in this recession than 1982–83: manufacturing was now much more vulnerable owing to the reductions in **tariffs** from the mid-1980s. Australia's most industrial State, Victoria, alone accounted for two-thirds of the decline in national output.

One sector that in the past had been 'recession proof' was services, but this time services took a hammering – especially financial services, property services, business services and public administration. Only those services connected with the tourism boom continued to grow. Many service enterprises, including government-owned ones, shed labour and slashed costs. State governments cut expenditure in response to lower receipts and in order to reduce debt levels, adding to unemployment.

## The effects on employment

Unemployment started to rise in the first half of 1991. The period from 1983 to 1990 had been one of strong jobs growth, better than the average for OECD members, and unemployment fell from 1983 to a low of 5.7 per cent in late 1989 (see Table 11.1). At this point, unemployment reached 4.5 per cent in Victoria, the State with the tightest labour market. But by April 1991, the national rate was 10 per cent and rising. The average duration of unemployment rose from 11 to 23 weeks (for all groups). Male full-time blue-collar workers were hit hardest. The severity with which unemployment rose took observers by surprise because unlike 1982–83, in the late 1980s real wages had been held tightly in check. There was no 'wages explosion' to explain the sudden rise in unemployment. Rather, the cause of the sharp increase was the combination of slowing demand with ongoing structural adjustments caused by globalisation. The supply of labour slowed somewhat as immigration inflows fell noticeably (see Figure 13.2). Falling employment affected both full-time and part-time workers. In the 1980s and 1990s, Australia experienced a marked shift to part-time work. In the early 1990s' recession, official unemployment rates underestimated the real impact of the recession on the labour market because the **participation rate** fell, reflecting a rise in 'discouraged workers'. There was also a rise in the number and proportion of part-time workers who wanted to work longer hours. The number of registered unemployed was also artificially reduced by a rise in the number of workers on sickness and invalidity benefits.

**Figure 13.2**   Net immigration to Australia, 1981–82 to 1997–98 (excess of arrivals over departures)

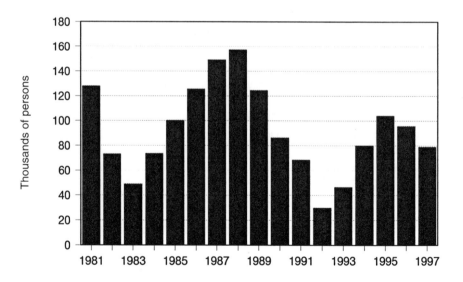

Source: ABS *Migration 1996–1997*, p. 44.

The degree to which price inflation declined was also surprising and, of course, much greater than in 1982–83 when Australia experienced severe 'stagflation'. **Disinflation** was largely the result of the absence of any kind of wages explosion. Not only had the Accord effectively held down real wages, but in April 1991 the Industrial Relations Commission limited wage increases to 2.5 per cent, a decision that many workers refused to accept. As a result, wages hardly rose at all in most sectors in 1990–91. Subsequent decisions of the Commission, for example, an $8 per week pay rise for those on minimum award rates in 1993, continued to keep the lid on wage-push inflation.

## Trade

Australia's balance of payments improved in the recession (see Table 13.2). The trade deficit turned into a surplus in 1990–91 as exports increased and imports declined. This produced the first **trade surplus** since 1986–87. Export volumes increased considerably, especially of energy and manufactures. Energy exports increased in volume in reaction to the sharp price rise in oil during the Gulf crisis. Manufactures exports had been rising strongly since the mid-1980s and continued to do so during the recession, mainly because the growth was centred on export to the Asia–Pacific region and reflected the continued strong growth of these economies. For this reason, Australia's manufactures exports were less vulnerable to the recession in the industrial economies of Europe and North America than they had been in the past.

**Figure 13.3**   Australia's terms of trade, 1981–82 to 1997–98

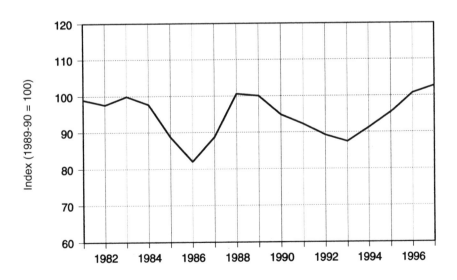

Sources: Based on RBA 1996, p. 30; ABS 1998, p. 70.

**Table 13.2**  Australia's balance of payments, current account, 1988–89 to 1997–98 ($ million)

| Year ended 30 June | Exports | Imports | Trade balance (exports minus imports) | Balance of transport services | Balance of travel services | Balance of other services | Balance of income account | Net transfers | Balance of services, income & transfers | Current account balance | Current account balance as a % of GDP |
|---|---|---|---|---|---|---|---|---|---|---|---|
| 1989 | 43 894 | 47 012 | -3 118 | -2 670 | 518 | -526 | -13 562 | 2 173 | -14 067 | -17 185 | -5.1 |
| 1990 | 48 564 | 50 992 | -2 428 | -3 182 | -160 | -801 | -17 188 | 2 290 | -19 041 | -21 469 | -5.8 |
| 1991 | 52 568 | 49 681 | 2 887 | -941 | 494 | -2 928 | -17 423 | 222 | -20 576 | -17 689 | -4.7 |
| 1992 | 55 427 | 51 469 | 3 958 | -1 122 | 1 163 | -2 978 | -14 264 | -134 | -17 335 | -13 377 | -2.9 |
| 1993 | 60 634 | 59 934 | 700 | -1 051 | 1 589 | -3 296 | -12 802 | -350 | -15 910 | -15 210 | -3.8 |
| 1994 | 64 419 | 64 863 | -444 | -951 | 2 659 | -3 498 | -13 843 | -339 | -15 972 | -16 416 | -3.8 |
| 1995 | 67 101 | 75 317 | -8 216 | -2 274 | 3 684 | -3 092 | -18 423 | -528 | -20 633 | -28 849 | -6.3 |
| 1996 | 76 146 | 77 729 | -1 583 | -1 962 | 4 264 | -2 660 | -19 907 | -26 | -20 265 | -21 848 | -4.4 |
| 1997 | 80 934 | 79 438 | 1 496 | -1 791 | 4 157 | -2 077 | -18 983 | 126 | -18 568 | -17 072 | -3.3 |
| 1998 | 88 484 | 92 093 | -3 654 | -2 319 | 3 534 | -1 889 | -19 567 | 44 | -20 197 | -23 851 | -4.4 |

Source: Based on ABS 1998, p. 20.

**Figure 13.4**   Australian dollar: exchange rates, 1985–1998 (indices of units of foreign currency per $Aus)

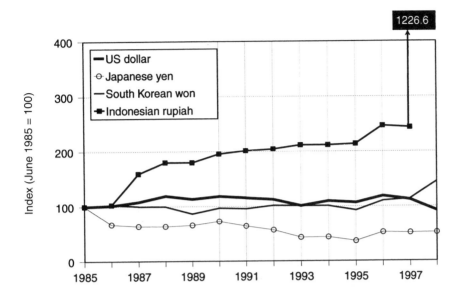

Source: Based on RBA 1998, pp. 105–6.

The expansion in manufactures exports was in contrast to very weak prices for Australia's traditional rural exports, especially agricultural commodities. These were weak because international trade **protectionism** and **subsidies** led to over-supply and because the industrial economies were in recession. The terms of trade declined sharply in 1990–91 in response to the falling commodity prices, setting off a fall in the **exchange rate** of the Australian dollar (see Figures 13.3 and 13.4). The recession eased Australia's **foreign debt** problem. **Foreign debt servicing** costs fell as world interest rates declined, lower corporate profits reduced foreign borrowing and firms took measures to reduce their overseas debt. However, debt servicing costs were still high at around 20 per cent of exports of goods and services, and net dividends added a further outflow of 6 per cent. The **net services** deficit declined as inbound tourism continued the boom it had entered in the late 1980s. As the Australian dollar weakened somewhat on **foreign exchanges**, inbound tourism was further stimulated, while overseas travel cost Australians more.

The overall effect of a trade surplus, a smaller net services deficit and an easing in the foreign debt burden, was to lower the **current account** deficit to 2.9 per cent of GDP, its lowest level for 12 years. Even with this lower current account deficit, however, Australia still had the third-highest deficit among OECD nations and its net external debt continued to rise (see Table 13.3). However, the recession did signal a structural change in Australia's external liability and a reversion to the pattern of the 1970s. In the 1980s, foreign debt rose much more rapidly than net

**Table 13.3**  Australia's net foreign liabilities, 1989–1998

| Year (June) | Australia's net foreign liabilities | | | | Service payments on net foreign liabilities | | | Debt service ratios | |
|---|---|---|---|---|---|---|---|---|---|
| | Net debt $ billions | Net equity $ billions | Total net foreign liabilities $ billions | Total net foreign liabilities as a % of GDP | Net interest payments $ billions | Net income payments $ billions | Total payments on net foreign liabilities $ billions | Net interest payments to exports % | Net income payments to exports % |
| 1989 | 117.2 | 35.9 | 153.1 | 45.0 | 9.4 | 2.8 | 12.2 | 65.2 | 81.7 |
| 1990 | 130.6 | 41.2 | 171.8 | 46.2 | 11.9 | 3.3 | 15.2 | 73.0 | 93.7 |
| 1991 | 142.1 | 48.8 | 190.9 | 50.1 | 12.9 | 4.3 | 17.2 | 79.2 | 103.8 |
| 1992 | 159.7 | 45.4 | 205.1 | 52.7 | 10.7 | 3.3 | 14.0 | 67.9 | 90.1 |
| 1993 | 176.1 | 49.0 | 225.1 | 55.1 | 9.4 | 3.3 | 12.7 | 53.2 | 73.0 |
| 1994 | 167.9 | 74.4 | 242.3 | 56.0 | 9.2 | 4.5 | 13.7 | 44.1 | 62.2 |
| 1995 | 186.3 | 76.9 | 263.2 | 57.2 | 11.0 | 7.4 | 18.4 | 49.1 | 82.9 |
| 1996 | 194.7 | 93.2 | 287.9 | 58.5 | 11.6 | 8.2 | 19.8 | 47.5 | 81.6 |
| 1997 | 213.5 | 98.1 | 311.6 | 60.3 | 11.6 | 7.4 | 19.0 | 45.8 | 76.7 |
| 1998 | 220.4 | 105.7 | 326.1 | 59.9 | 11.5 | 7.6 | 19.1 | 41.6 | 68.4 |

Total merchandise exports included re-exports.
Source: Based on RBA 1998, pp. 137–9.

foreign liabilities, so that, whereas in 1980 net external debt represented 25 per cent of net foreign liabilities, by 1991 they represented 75 per cent. Indeed, foreign **equity** holdings in Australia declined as a share of GDP over the decade. This was a complete turnaround in the pattern established in the 1960s and 1970s. In the 1990s, the pattern returned once more to that obtained before 1980. In 1990–91, net equity flows accounted for 70 per cent of net **capital** transactions as lenders took equity when borrowers were unable to service their loans. In addition, Australian firms sold off **foreign investments** and used the proceeds to reduce domestic debt and many Australian firms were not in a good position to seek more foreign borrowing.

## Policy response

The very high interest rates employed to slow down the late 1980s' boom combined with widespread debt problems across Australian business to produce a 'hard' rather than a 'soft' landing. Declining terms of trade from mid-1989 also made the landing harder by reducing Australia's purchasing power and spending. Monetary policy was eased at the beginning of 1990 in response to falling levels of inflation (both actual and anticipated). Inflationary expectations were lower than at any time since the 1960s, an outcome unique to this recession. The overnight cash rate fell from 18 per cent to 7.5 per cent over the 24 months to January 1992. The exchange rate, however, remained firmer than expected, considering the decline in the terms of trade and the easing of monetary policy. A major factor here was the oil price 'shock' caused by the Gulf War in 1990 and the fact that Australia still had relatively high real interest rates by international standards.

The recession brought to an end the fiscal consolidation of the later 1980s as the Commonwealth **budget** moved from a small surplus (0.5 per cent of GDP) in 1990–91 to a deficit of 1.2 per cent in 1991–92. This change was caused by increased expenditure, especially on unemployment benefits, together with weaker tax revenues. Tax receipts fell because of rising unemployment, lower nominal wage increases (less bracket creep), and personal tax cuts that came into effect in January 1991. Reforms to the wholesale tax structure to exempt business inputs also reduced receipts from indirect tax, while lower tariffs produced less from customs duties. State governments also moved into deficit as the recession reduced their tax intake. A number of them had to increase expenditure to bail out insolvent State banks and other financial institutions, themselves the victims of financial deregulation.

## Recovery and expansion in the mid-1990s

Most sectors of the economy grew in 1992–93 after contracting in 1991–92, but recovery from the recession in Australia was weak and slow, as it was in most of the OECD. The main difficulty in achieving faster growth was insufficient private business investment, chiefly because firms were still reeling from their debts of the late 1980s. Private consumption kept up well during the recession compared to some other countries, but the growth of disposable income was so flat that much of

**SUMMARY BOX**

Australia entered the international recession in 1990 slightly earlier than other OECD countries. Unemployment rose sharply as it had done in the previous recession, but unlike 1982–83, inflation in this recession declined to very low levels. The recession was caused by the bursting of the assets price boom and a tightening of monetary policy, together with reduced demand for Australia's commodity exports from the industrial countries. Disinflation was largely the result of wage restraint. The recession improved Australia's balance of payments by reducing domestic demand, which reduced imports and diverted a greater proportion of production to exports. The continued growth of the newly industrialising countries of east and South-East Asia assisted export growth, especially of manufactures. The recession eased Australia's foreign debt burden, though the foreign debt remained high. The current account deficit was further reduced by a fall in the net services deficit, largely due to the continued influx of foreign tourists. The current account deficit was financed more by foreign equity investment than by fresh foreign borrowing. The recession also caused the Commonwealth budget to move back into deficit.

this consumption had to be financed by higher household debt, now easier to obtain because of deregulation of the financial system. Private investment in residential dwellings increased and this boosted spending on consumer durables (though not motor vehicles). Household **saving** ratios fell to a 15-year low, indicating that households were spending more of their stagnant **disposable income** (chiefly on housing and consumer durables) and getting further into debt. Thus the recovery was consumer-led – but at a moderate pace.

## Jobless growth

Business investment, by contrast, remained very low. It peaked in mid-1989, but then declined by one-third over the next four years. Indeed, non-dwelling construction as a share of GDP declined by 50 per cent between 1989 and 1992, falling to a 40-year low. Businesses in Australia were more concerned to cut costs and reduce the size of their workforce than they were to make new investments. By the early 1990s, there was a great deal of excess capacity in the Australian economy and therefore output could increase without much new investment.

As the unemployment rate exceeded 11 per cent and showed little sign of a speedy fall, there was much debate during the recovery period on the question of 'jobless growth'; that is, over the relative roles of **economic growth** and structural change in causing changes in employment. Was unemployment high because **productivity** had improved so that fewer jobs were created for any given level of output growth (that is, **structural unemployment**)? Or was unemployment high simply because growth was weak (cyclical unemployment)? These were not, of course, mutually exclusive, but it seemed that in Australia's case there had been a structural shift so that fewer jobs were created for any given level of output growth. Cyclical unemployment could become structural if unemployed persons lost skills and became out of touch with the labour market. The rise in unemployment and the perception that it was less responsive to an upturn in economic growth than in the past persuaded governments to introduce training schemes of various sorts for those who had been out of work for some time. However, in the face of such weak recovery, the number of long-term unemployed continued to rise.

## Balance of payments

Recovery from the recession brought renewed pressure on Australia's balance of payments. The surplus on merchandise trade peaked in 1991–92 (see Table 13.2) as imports remained subdued by the recession and exports grew. But in 1993, the **trade balance** again went into deficit as imports grew strongly (exports grew too but not by as much). Part of this was due to adverse terms of trade caused by weak commodity prices, reflecting the impact of the recession in the world's major industrial nations. Australia's terms of trade fell continuously for five years to 1993–94, to 13 per cent below its 1988–89 peak (see Figure 13.3).

Despite weak commodity prices and world protectionism in agricultural commodities, Australia's export performance was not as bad as it might have been. Much of this was due to the growth of exports of manufactured goods, mainly to the still expanding markets of east and South-East Asia. Between 1985 and 1993, manufactures exports increased as a share of total merchandise exports from 17 per cent to 30 per cent, and elaborately transformed manufactures exports increased even faster. Moreover, although Australia remained heavily in deficit in its **international trade** in manufactured goods, the gap between exports and imports of manufactures narrowed in the 1990s (see Table 13.4).

Four factors accounted for this development. First, wage restraint lowered the costs of production of manufactured goods and made Australian manufactures more competitive in world markets. Second, tariff cuts and microeconomic reforms had the effect of lowering input costs to firms and heightening manufacturing firms' orientation to the international economy. An export culture was emerging among Australian manufacturers, especially among small- and medium-sized firms. Third, an export culture was emerging among Australian manufacturers, especially among small and medium-sized firms. Exports of manufactures were no longer driven simply by insufficient domestic demand. This was especially noticeable in high value-added manufactures (**ETMs**) and exports of sophisticated services (McKinsey & Co. 1993). Finally, the industrialisation boom going on in east and South-East Asia provided Australian manufacturers with opportunities to export what was not available (or that they were less aware of) in earlier years. By the 1990s, Asia was clearly Australia's major market for exports of manufactures (Table 13.5).

Services exports also boomed, particularly inbound tourism, helped by the additional spending money tourists gained from the depreciation of the Australian dollar. The structural change in the services account that first appeared

**Table 13.4** Australia's exports of manufactures, 1983–1997

| Year | Exports of manufactures as a % of total merchandise exports | Exports of elaborately transformed manufactures (ETMs) as a % of exports of total manufactures | Exports of simply transformed manufactures (STMs) as a % of exports of total manufactures | Exports of ETMs as a % of imports of ETMs | Exports of STMs as a % of imports of STMs | Exports of total manufactures as a % of imports of manufactures |
|------|------|------|------|------|------|------|
| 1983 | 19.0 | 63.0 | 37.0 | 20.2 | 82.6 | 29.1 |
| 1984 | 18.0 | 58.1 | 41.9 | 17.1 | 72.9 | 25.2 |
| 1985 | 17.1 | 57.0 | 43.0 | 14.7 | 71.6 | 22.3 |
| 1986 | 19.1 | 60.6 | 39.4 | 16.2 | 68.2 | 23.2 |
| 1987 | 22.3 | 60.5 | 39.4 | 19.7 | 74.8 | 28.1 |
| 1988 | 23.9 | 56.3 | 43.7 | 19.0 | 85.4 | 29.1 |
| 1989 | 24.6 | 57.3 | 42.7 | 17.6 | 86.1 | 27.2 |
| 1990 | 25.1 | 60.5 | 39.5 | 21.3 | 95.3 | 31.2 |
| 1991 | 26.3 | 64.3 | 35.7 | 25.1 | 94.0 | 34.5 |
| 1992 | 27.8 | 66.8 | 33.2 | 26.8 | 89.9 | 35.3 |
| 1993 | 29.8 | 69.3 | 30.7 | 28.2 | 88.6 | 36.0 |
| 1994 | 31.5 | 69.3 | 30.7 | 27.7 | 89.6 | 35.4 |
| 1995 | 33.5 | 70.3 | 29.7 | 29.0 | 91.2 | 36.9 |
| 1996 | 32.2 | 73.0 | 27.0 | 31.0 | 86.8 | 38.0 |
| 1997 | 31.9 | 72.9 | 27.1 | 31.8 | 92.0 | 39.1 |

Note: Elaborately transformed manufactures (ETMs) are products with unique features that can be identified as differentiated products on world markets; that is, 'finished products'. Over half of Australia's exports of ETMs are classified as 'engineering products', such as machinery, office equipment, telecommunications equipment, motor vehicles and transport equipment. Simply transformed manufactures (STMs) consist mainly of basic metal manufactures.

| Region/country group | 1987 | 1988 | 1989 | 1990 | 1991 | 1992 | 1993 | 1994 | 1995 | 1996 | 1997 |
|---|---|---|---|---|---|---|---|---|---|---|---|
| **Total exports of merchandise** | | | | | | | | | | | |
| East Asia | 47.4 | 51.2 | 51.0 | 52.3 | 56.9 | 57.4 | 58.0 | 59.4 | 60.3 | 57.8 | 56.7 |
| Europe | 20.5 | 18.9 | 18.8 | 17.1 | 15.1 | 14.7 | 13.1 | 12.2 | 12.5 | 12.0 | 11.5 |
| NAFTA | 13.1 | 12.6 | 12.5 | 13.3 | 11.7 | 10.6 | 10.3 | 9.2 | 8.3 | 8.3 | 9.0 |
| Pacific | 8.2 | 7.6 | 7.7 | 7.2 | 7.3 | 7.5 | 8.3 | 9.2 | 9.6 | 10.0 | 9.6 |
| Middle East | 4.7 | 4.1 | 4.7 | 4.7 | 3.1 | 3.0 | 3.2 | 3.0 | 2.5 | 3.7 | 4.3 |
| Rest of world | 6.1 | 5.6 | 5.3 | 5.4 | 5.9 | 6.8 | 7.1 | 7.0 | 6.8 | 8.2 | 8.9 |
| OECD | 66.4 | 65.8 | 65.5 | 66.4 | 64.4 | 61.7 | 60.7 | 59.5 | 59.2 | 57.1 | 55.5 |
| APEC | 68.2 | 70.7 | 70.6 | 72.2 | 75.2 | 74.8 | 75.8 | 77.1 | 77.4 | 75.3 | 74.6 |
| **Exports of primary products** | | | | | | | | | | | |
| East Asia | 44.2 | 43.8 | 46.0 | 48.1 | 53.7 | 53.1 | 52.6 | 51.6 | 51.3 | 48.9 | 47.8 |
| Europe | 20.0 | 20.5 | 18.2 | 13.9 | 13.4 | 12.9 | 10.2 | 10.7 | 10.3 | 9.3 | 9.9 |
| NAFTA | 10.2 | 9.3 | 7.2 | 8.0 | 6.7 | 6.5 | 6.1 | 5.2 | 3.9 | 4.3 | 4.4 |
| Pacific | 1.8 | 1.7 | 1.7 | 1.6 | 1.7 | 1.8 | 2.1 | 2.3 | 2.6 | 2.7 | 2.7 |
| Middle East | 5.8 | 5.1 | 5.6 | 5.1 | 3.0 | 1.7 | 1.9 | 1.7 | 1.8 | 1.9 | 1.6 |
| Rest of world | 18.0 | 19.6 | 21.3 | 23.3 | 21.5 | 24.0 | 27.1 | 28.5 | 30.1 | 32.9 | 33.6 |
| OECD | 58.5 | 59.0 | 56.3 | 55.8 | 58.2 | 57.3 | 54.2 | 52.7 | 48.5 | 44.9 | 43.6 |
| APEC | 56.7 | 55.3 | 55.4 | 58.1 | 62.6 | 61.8 | 61.2 | 59.4 | 57.9 | 56.4 | 55.2 |
| **Exports of manufactures** | | | | | | | | | | | |
| East Asia | 40.3 | 47.3 | 46.1 | 45.5 | 47.6 | 46.0 | 48.8 | 48.7 | 49.5 | 46.4 | 46.0 |
| Europe | 15.0 | 13.4 | 13.4 | 14.1 | 12.7 | 14.0 | 11.7 | 10.9 | 11.6 | 11.6 | 9.8 |
| NAFTA | 12.6 | 11.5 | 11.7 | 13.5 | 13.4 | 12.3 | 12.2 | 11.0 | 9.3 | 10.6 | 12.1 |
| Pacific | 23.1 | 20.6 | 20.4 | 19.0 | 17.9 | 18.5 | 18.8 | 19.8 | 19.7 | 20.7 | 20.2 |
| Middle East | 1.5 | 1.5 | 1.3 | 1.9 | 1.6 | 1.8 | 1.7 | 1.3 | 1.1 | 1.5 | 2.3 |
| Rest of world | 7.5 | 5.7 | 7.1 | 6.0 | 6.8 | 7.4 | 6.8 | 8.3 | 8.8 | 9.2 | 9.6 |
| OECD | 64.5 | 64.3 | 63.2 | 63.2 | 59.1 | 55.9 | 53.7 | 53.8 | 52.6 | 52.0 | 52.1 |
| APEC | 74.8 | 77.9 | 77.1 | 76.8 | 77.7 | 75.4 | 78.2 | 78.3 | 77.6 | 76.3 | 77.0 |

East Asia: Brunei, China, Hong Kong, Indonesia, Japan, Korea Republic, Malaysia, The Philippines, Singapore, Taiwan, Thailand.
Europe: Albania, Austria, Belgium, Bulgaria, the Czech Republic, Denmark, Finland, France, Germany, Greece, Hungary, Iceland, Ireland, Italy, Luxembourg, The Netherlands, Norway, Poland, Portugal, Romania, Slovak Republic, Soviet Union (former), Spain, Sweden, Switzerland, the United Kingdom, Yugoslavia (former).
NAFTA: Canada, Mexico, Puerto Rico, the United States, Virgin Islands.
Pacific: Cook Island, Micronesia, Fiji, Kiribati, Marshall Islands, Nauru, New Zealand, Niue, Papua New Guinea, Palau, Samoa, Solomon Islands, Tonga, Tuvalu, Vanuatu.
Middle East: Bahrain, Cyprus, Egypt, Iran, Iraq, Israel, Jordan, Kuwait, Lebanon, Oman, Qatar, Saudi Arabia, Syria, United Arab Emirates, Yemen.
OECD: Australia, Austria, Belgium, Canada, the Czech Republic, Denmark, Finland, France, Germany, Greece, Hungary, Iceland, Ireland, Italy, Japan, Korea Republic, Luxembourg, Mexico, The Netherlands, New Zealand, Norway, Poland, Portugal, Spain, Sweden, Switzerland, Turkey, the United Kingdom, the United States.
APEC: Australia, Brunei, Canada, Chile, China, Hong Kong, Indonesia, Japan, Korea Republic, Malaysia, Mexico, New Zealand, Papua New Guinea, The Philippines, Singapore, Taiwan, Thailand, the United States.
Primary products consist of foodstuffs, fuels (petroleum, coal and gas), minerals (including metal ores) and textile fibres (wool and cotton).
Source: Based on DFAT 1997, pp. 78–89.

in the recession was confirmed during the recovery period as Australia's net deficit on services became negligible and then turned into a surplus, the first time this had happened in peacetime in the twentieth century (see Table 13.2). Another product of the recession that continued into the recovery phase was the stabilisation of Australia's foreign debt and the easing of the foreign debt burden. Net external debt reached a peak of almost 45 per cent of GDP in 1991–92, but declined thereafter to settle at just under 40 per cent. The foreign debt burden subsided dramatically in response to lower international interest rates and relatively buoyant export earnings from goods and services. From almost 21 per cent in 1989–90, the foreign debt burden was down to 12 per cent by 1992–93 and then hovered around 10 to 11 per cent (see Table 13.3). These reversals in the trend of foreign debt compared to the previous decade helped to strengthen Australia's resilience to international economic fluctuations: as long as this trend continued, the Australian economy in the 1990s became less, not more, vulnerable to sudden changes in the global economy.

## Expansion

Following a drawn-out recovery phase, the Australian economy picked up in 1994 and 1995, returning to pre-recession growth rates of between 4 and 5 per cent per year (see Table 13.1). Inflation remained low and unemployment fell, but the external balance worsened. The main contribution to this domestic expansion came from the household sector where disposable incomes increased as unemployment levels eased and personal **income tax** cuts boosted consumption. With consumer **credit** cheaper than it had been for 20 years, households restocked on consumer durables and motor vehicles. There was also greater demand for and investment in housing. Mortgage rates were low, demand for housing had been pent-up during the recession and the **crash** in commercial construction had kept building costs down. Australian households became more indebted, but remained less so than the business sector (and than the household sector in some other OECD countries). The business sector, by contrast, did not play such a strong role in the mid-decade expansion, with the exception of public investment, boosted by government initiatives to build **infrastructure** under its One Nation package announced in 1993. Despite a return to profitability, firms did not significantly increase their investment as many were still trying to reduce past debt and there was much spare capacity in the economy. Not surprisingly, where firms did make fresh investments they preferred to finance these from ploughed back earnings and new equity rather than add to their already onerous burden of debt.

The domestic expansion had some impact on the unemployment rate, with a fall in the rate in 1994 for the first time for four years, but a return to the pre-recession levels proved impossible, underlining concerns about 'jobless growth'. Employment expanded in all sectors except public administration, defence (because of government cutbacks), agriculture, forestry, fishing and mining (agriculture was hit by a drought and mineral prices remained very subdued). The trend towards part-time work continued, with part-time employment growing faster than full-time. Partly this was caused by young people being unable to find full-time work and partly by households requiring a second income to cope with rising household expenditure and debt. The number and the share of long-term unemployed declined, but structural unemployment remained high so that the faster economic growth could not get unemployment rates down to the low points of the 1980s.

Wages growth remained subdued during the domestic expansion thanks to the Accord, now in its seventh stage. With no wages explosion in sight and relatively tight monetary settings, inflation continued to be held down, producing smaller rises in the **consumer price index** than had been experienced since the early 1960s. Import prices fell as the Australian dollar appreciated by about 10 per cent in **real terms**. However, inflation did pick up as the expansion continued into 1995, reaching an annual rate of 3.2 per cent in that year and over 4 per cent the next. This was still well below the inflation rates of the previous 25 years, but by the standards of the 1990s, 4 per cent was above the rate acceptable to the Reserve Bank, with a tightening of monetary policy the inevitable response.

Australia's balance of payments worsened in the expansion. Export earnings continued to grow, but at a slower rate (see Table 13.2). Exports of manufactures to Asia remained the most buoyant sector, although overall the terms of trade declined in 1993–94. Earlier declines in the exchange value of the Australian dollar were now reversed, again hitting export earnings. On the other hand, the expansion in the domestic economy spilled over into import growth, stimulated by the appreciation in the dollar. The trade balance in 1993 moved back into a small deficit that widened considerably in 1994–95, producing the largest trade deficit for 13 years. Tourism helped keep the net services deficit down, but other parts of the balance of payments worsened, so that most of the worsening trade balance was translated into a higher current account deficit in 1994–95, the biggest since 1985–86. Despite this balance of payments 'blow-out', the net external debt rose only slightly because of the appreciation of the dollar and because Australian firms were using foreign equity rather than borrowing to finance expansion. Low world interest rates and continued export growth also kept the foreign debt burden stable.

## SUMMARY BOX

After a shallow recession, the Australian economy entered a period of recovery and modest growth in the first half of the 1990s. Private business investment remained subdued because confidence was low and many firms were still coping with high debt levels. Household expenditure helped the recovery and expansion, but at a cost of a fall in the household **saving rate**. Unemployment levels declined, but not to the average level of the previous decade. Inflation gradually increased in the recovery process leading to a tightening of monetary policy. The balance of payments deteriorated as imports grew strongly. Export growth was weak but it was helped by continued growth in exports of manufactures to Asia and receipts from tourism. Although the current account deficit suffered a 'blow-out' in 1994–95, Australia's external debt remained stable and the foreign debt burden fell.

## Slowdown and the impact of the Asian crisis

Tighter monetary policy at the end of 1994 imposed in order to rein in inflation had the effect of slowing economic growth in 1995. As before, the household sector continued to underpin domestic demand, but business investment and sentiment declined. The early part of 1996 saw some recovery, but in the second half of the year the economy slowed again, producing a rate of growth in 1996–97 two-thirds of its previous level (see Table 13.1). The main cause of the slowdown was the deterioration in the foreign balance as imports surged, stimulated by domestic demand, and exports slowed in response to the appreciation of the dollar.

## Unemployment

Employment growth was stagnant in the first half of 1996 even before the slowdown in the second half. There was a temporary improvement in late 1996, but employment growth slowed again throughout 1997. In the first six years of the 1990s, employment grew at only half the rate of the first six years of the 1980s' upswing. The chief cause was firms substituting capital for labour in response to rising real unit labour costs (the result of wage increases minus productivity gains). In the 1980s cycle (1982–83 to 1989–90), real unit labour costs declined by 10 per cent, but in the 1990s cycle (1992–93 to 1997–98), they rose by 1 per cent (RBA 1996, p. 207; ABS 1998, p. 89). The slowdown in economic growth in the second half of 1996 led to further slowing of employment in the first half of 1997. Employment was flat or contracting in construction, retailing, public sector and manufacturing (though it did improve in manufacturing in the second half of 1996). However, employment growth was strong in the private sector service industries, which typically had a much higher proportion of part-time workers, and this explained why part-time employment growth was faster than full-time. Nearly one-quarter of part-time workers (and 40 per cent of male part-time workers) were involuntary in the sense that they would have liked to have worked more hours. Full-time employment actually fell in the first half of 1997, while part-time employment was growing at an annual rate of 6 per cent.

In the recovery phase, unemployment had come down rapidly to reach 8.5 per cent by mid-1995, but with the mid-decade slowdown the unemployment rate stopped falling and remained at around the same level thereafter (see Table 13.1). Wages increased quite rapidly in the second half of 1995, reaching an annualised rate of 6 per cent. But the rate of increase then declined in 1996 and 1997 because of rising unemployment. Thus Australia returned to wage moderation after a brief period of faster growth. Wage rises under enterprise bargaining were much higher than those granted to workers under the award system. In real terms, award wages fell in 1996 and the first half of 1997, whereas enterprise bargaining wages increased by almost 5 per cent and executive salaries by almost 6 per cent in the 12 months to June 1997. Lower award wage outcomes kept the average down to be within the inflation targets set by the Reserve Bank. Indeed, the inflation rate declined: the underlying rate fell from 3.3 per cent in the first quarter of 1996 to 1.5 per cent in the third quarter of 1997. This brought Australia's inflation rate down to levels below the average for the OECD, an outcome due mainly to the slowdown in wages and cheaper imports because of the appreciation of the dollar.

## Balance of payments

The current account deficit peaked in the first half of 1995 at 6 per cent, a dangerously high level as far as the financial markets were concerned. Rural export volumes fell steeply in 1995 because of the drought, but with the coming of good rain, rural exports recovered sharply in 1996 and 1997. Manufactures exports were strong and, to a lesser extent, so were services exports, despite the appreciation of the dollar. On the import side, there was a reduction in the growth of volumes of **capital goods** and intermediate products. The terms of trade improved as reflected in the appreciation of the exchange rate. The trade deficit narrowed and then became a small surplus. This brought the current account deficit down towards 3 per cent, which was considered to be the long-term sustainable level for Australia. Despite this reduction, however, net foreign liabilities rose again, to 60.2 per cent of GDP (up from 58.6 per cent). Both net foreign debt and net foreign equity increased, though equity rose more strongly. Net foreign debt (39.6 per cent) remained high but below the peak of 42.7 per cent reached in the third quarter of 1993. This fall in the foreign debt was caused by stronger economic growth in the early 1990s, the rise in the value of the dollar and the rise in the share of equity in foreign investment inflows.

## East Asia crisis

When the East Asian currency crisis began in mid-1997, the Australian economy was exhibiting low inflation, modest but steady growth and an easing of its balance of payments position, though still with a high foreign debt. The domestic economy rebounded from the slowdown in 1996–97 and accelerated in the second half of 1997. The rate slackened a little in the first half of 1998, but economic growth for 1997–98 came out at 4 per cent, compared with 2.8 in the previous fiscal year. Lower demand for Australian exports as a result of the crisis in Asia was offset to a considerable extent by a depreciation of the dollar and the ability of exporters to divert trade to other destinations (including North America and Europe), as yet less affected by the Asian downturn. The United States, in particular, provided a growing market for imports from the rest of the world. Although Australia's export mix was more diversified than in the past (see Table 13.6), over half of this mix still contained rural and resource-based commodities that could be sold to many different countries, although at somewhat reduced prices. Since many of the commodities Australia exported were denominated in US dollars, the fall in their world price was offset in Australian dollar terms by the depreciation of the exchange rate.

Diversification to other export markets in the face of a temporary or permanent shift in demand from 'traditional' customers was not especially novel in Australia's export history (Pinkstone 1992). The growth in the share of Australia's exports going to Japan and the decline in the share going to the United Kingdom in the 1960s is a well-known example. And in the early 1990s, Australian exporters had

**Table 13.6** Commodity structure of Australian trade, 1983–1997

| Year | Exports (% of total merchandise exports) | | | | | Imports (% of total merchandise imports) | | |
|---|---|---|---|---|---|---|---|---|
| | Unprocessed primary products | Processed primary products | Total primary products | Manufactures | Other | Total primary products | Manufactures | Other |
| 1983 | 47.9 | 19.4 | 67.3 | 19.0 | 13.7 | 19.8 | 77.7 | 2.5 |
| 1984 | 54.3 | 15.3 | 69.6 | 18.0 | 12.4 | 17.9 | 78.9 | 3.2 |
| 1985 | 56.8 | 12.0 | 68.9 | 17.1 | 14.0 | 15.0 | 81.0 | 4.0 |
| 1986 | 54.1 | 12.2 | 66.3 | 19.1 | 14.6 | 13.0 | 82.4 | 4.6 |
| 1987 | 48.9 | 12.7 | 61.6 | 22.3 | 16.1 | 13.4 | 81.2 | 5.3 |
| 1988 | 45.0 | 12.6 | 57.6 | 23.9 | 18.5 | 12.6 | 84.3 | 3.1 |
| 1989 | 42.8 | 12.7 | 55.5 | 24.6 | 20.0 | 12.8 | 85.1 | 2.1 |
| 1990 | 39.5 | 13.8 | 53.4 | 25.1 | 21.5 | 13.3 | 84.4 | 2.3 |
| 1991 | 38.5 | 15.3 | 53.8 | 26.3 | 20.0 | 13.4 | 84.4 | 2.2 |
| 1992 | 35.8 | 15.5 | 51.4 | 27.8 | 20.9 | 13.3 | 84.4 | 2.3 |
| 1993 | 32.3 | 15.9 | 48.2 | 29.8 | 22.0 | 13.4 | 84.7 | 1.9 |
| 1994 | 29.9 | 15.8 | 45.8 | 31.5 | 22.7 | 12.0 | 86.5 | 1.5 |
| 1995 | 28.7 | 14.4 | 43.1 | 33.5 | 23.3 | 12.0 | 86.6 | 1.4 |
| 1996 | 28.7 | 14.7 | 43.4 | 32.2 | 24.4 | 12.9 | 85.9 | 1.2 |
| 1997 | 29.9 | 13.8 | 43.7 | 31.9 | 24.4 | 12.7 | 86.0 | 1.3 |

Note: Primary products consist of foodstuffs, fuels (petroleum, coal and gas), minerals (including metal ores) and textile fibres (wool and cotton).
Sources: Based on DFAT 1997, pp. 96–108; 1998b, pp. 22–3.

already substituted other markets (some of them in Asia) in response to faltering Japanese demand. In the mid-1990s, there was considerable growth in Australian exports to a variety of destinations: India, the Middle East, Russia, South America, New Zealand as well as to Europe, the United States and Canada. The export diversification at the end of the twentieth century was likely to be as significant as that at the beginning (Chapter 3) and in the 1960s (Chapter 9). Moreover, much of Australia's exports to Asia consisted of raw materials and intermediate manufactured inputs that were used by Japan, Korea and others to produce exports. To the extent that these economies were able to trade their way out of their financial and economic crises, their demand for Australian goods would expand.

The one export sector that was hit hard by the Asian crisis and unlikely to recover was inbound Asian tourism to Australia. The number of tourists from Asia to Australia fell swiftly in the second half of 1997 and stabilised in 1998 at about half the pre-crisis level. Not only did this reduce international earnings from tourism, but it also undermined projections that had been made of continued expansion of tourism through the late 1990s and into the early years of the next century. The solution was to diversify tourism by tapping other sources of potential international visitors, but although the cheaper Australian dollar did lead to some increase in tourism from Europe and North America, it was insufficient to offset the decline in tourists from Asia. Tourism from Asia was also adversely affected by the publicity given to the political campaigns of the One Nation party in Australia at this time.

Domestic demand in Australia remained strong, offsetting the impact of economic contraction in Asia, and domestic demand, rather than foreign demand, was the main contributor to economic growth. Once again, household spending was the key factor. Australian households responded to stronger employment growth and a decline in the unemployment rate together with lower interest rates (and rising household wealth, which provided more collateral) by increasing their consumption (of services, consumer durables and motor vehicles), investing more in housing and getting further into debt. In contrast to the rise in public saving as a result of fiscal consolidation, the household saving ratio continued its decline. Private business investment was also strong in the second half of 1997, though fell away somewhat as business confidence fell in the first half of 1998.

Externally, the Australian dollar depreciated against the US dollar and the European currencies, but rose against those of its major trading partners in Asia (see Figure 13.4). The depreciation against the US dollar helped cushion the decline in international commodity prices (denominated in US dollars), particularly for minerals. The main impact of the crisis fell on Australia's exports of manufactures and services, most of which went to Asian customers. The volume of ETM exports, for example, fell to half the average for the previous decade. Overall, however, the depreciation of the Australian dollar and ability to divert goods to other markets led to growth in export earnings that was in line with that of recent years (see Table 13.2). On the other hand, stronger domestic demand also pulled in an increased volume of imports and, whereas export earnings of goods and services rose by 8.4 per cent, imports increased by 14.5 per cent. The trade balance moved from a surplus to a deficit, producing a current account deficit of 4.4 per cent of GDP, the second highest of the 1990s cycle and the highest for three years (Commonwealth Treasury of Australia 1998; ABS 1998).

## Escaping the crisis?

The lesson drawn from the response of the Australian economy over the first 18 months of the Asian economic crisis was that globalisation of the Australian economy over the previous 15 years had made Australia less vulnerable to major international downturns than it was in the past (Commonwealth Treasury of Australia 1998, p. 29). The dollar depreciated against the US dollar, but was fairly stable in terms of the trade weighted index. One of the main problems faced by the East Asian economies was that their exchange rates were inflexible and became **overvalued**. Australia's, by contrast, was freely floating and if anything **undervalued**. The international financial markets appeared to make a clear distinction between the Asian currencies that were tumbling in value and the Australian dollar so that 'contagion' was largely avoided (see Chapter 12).

Australia's record of low inflation and fiscal consolidation enhanced foreign investor confidence in Australia so that a 'sell-off' of the Australian dollar was less likely. Australia's economic growth record in the 1990s was better than most OECD countries and domestic demand remained fairly buoyant, further underlining that there was no need for an Asian-style financial crisis. Another factor in the Asian problem was a credit-driven asset price boom such as Australia (and many other developed countries) experienced in the late 1980s. However, in the 1990s there was not a repeat performance in Australia of the excesses of the previous decade, again reducing vulnerability to financial turbulence. Similarly, the Australian banking system in Australia appeared to have overcome its bad loans problems of the recession and perhaps had learned valuable lessons from this experience. The banking sectors in **developing countries** like Thailand and Korea as well as in Japan, by contrast, were viewed by the financial markets as having far too much non-performing debt for which adequate provision had not been made.

On the other hand, international financial markets could be expected to show concern at Australia's rising current account deficit and the level of its foreign debt. Although the trade balance was better in the 1990s than the 1980s, the impact of servicing the foreign debt meant that current account deficits were about the same on average in the two periods. The fact that it did not deteriorate in the 1990s (even if it did not improve) led financial markets to be less concerned about Australia's external position than they might have been if the unstable domestic conditions of the 1980s had continued. High inflation and runaway domestic demand were not features of the 1990s Australian economy. Economic growth was slower, but steadier. Similarly, although the net foreign debt was high by international standards (fourth highest in the OECD), the gross foreign debt (the measure most relevant to the confidence of the financial markets) was not (thirteenth highest). Moreover, the external debt (gross or net) did not continue to increase as a share of GDP in the 1990s and the proportion of export earnings required to service it declined by almost half (RBA April 1998, pp. 1–8).

Thus, foreign investor confidence, the collapse of which in past crises proved disastrous, was maintained by keeping inflation low and moving the Commonwealth budget into surplus. The floating exchange rate allowed the dollar to decline, thus cushioning the impact of lower demand in some Asian markets. A more flexible and competitive domestic market meant Australian producers could react to the overseas crisis by quickly diverting production from export to domestic consumption. And the depreciation in the Australian dollar against the United States and European currencies allowed Australian exporters to divert trade away from Asia. In the end, however, the impact of the East Asian crisis on Australia depended on the resilience (and continued economic growth) of North America and Europe. If the Asian crisis led to a world economic **slump**, then diverting exports to other markets would no longer be an option, and foreign investor confidence might well be eroded in view of Australia's worsening balance of payments and high foreign debt. Moreover, by making imports more expensive, a depreciation in the foreign exchange value of the Australian dollar could lead to higher inflation. If so, this would force the monetary authorities to take disinflationary measures that might well reduce the level of economic activity.

## SUMMARY BOX

In the middle of the decade, the Australian economy slowed somewhat, bringing to an end the fall in unemployment that had occurred during the recovery period. The balance of payments position improved as a result of the slowdown as import growth slowed and rural exports recovered from drought. Australia's external debt remained high, however. The domestic economy rebounded from the mid-decade slowdown in the second half of 1997 and continued to expand into 1998, producing relatively high economic growth rates of 4 to 5 per cent. This occurred at the same time as the Asian economic crisis unfolded from July 1997 onwards. The impact of the Asian crisis on Australia was, therefore, to some extent masked or delayed (or mitigated) by the upward domestic **trade cycle**.

The main immediate impact of the Asian economic crisis on Australia was reduced exports to East Asia. Less certain were the indirect effects of the spread of the crisis to the rest of the global economy. Exports to Thailand, Indonesia, Korea, Malaysia and The Philippines fell to about two-thirds of their pre-crisis trend level. Exports to Hong Kong, China, Taiwan and Singapore also fell, though by a smaller proportion. Resources exports were least affected as they could be diverted to non-Asian markets. Australian exports of manufactures and services, however, were hit harder. Inbound tourism was particularly badly affected, though the fall in the Australian dollar against European currencies and the US dollar, together with the impetus given to tourism by the Sydney Olympics, provided some cause for optimism. The domestic economy continued to grow strongly in 1998 as household expenditure remained high. In the end, the impact on Australia would depend on the extent to which the regional crisis became a global one.

# Impact of globalisation on Australia

In view of Australia's long history of involvement with the world economy, 'globalisation' was in some respects an ambiguous term. There were, however, three ways in which it had relevance to Australian economic history in the 1990s. First, it related to the way in which the domestic economy was integrated with the international economy. Second, it was to do with the removal or reduction of barriers between the Australian economy and the international economy. Third, it included the many related microeconomic reforms that were implemented in response to the reduction of international barriers.

## The nature of late twentieth-century Australian globalisation

Although comments were sometimes made about Australia 'joining the world economy', there was nothing new about Australia being integrated in the international community. 'Integration' could have several meanings. The one most associated with globalisation was integration in the international economy. Australia had a long history of this type of integration. Since European invasion it had been importing capital goods and equipment and **consumer goods**, attracting inflows of capital in the forms of foreign investment and foreign loans, and directing an influx of people as permanent settlers. To pay for imports and capital inflows, ever-rising volumes of exports of **primary products** and manufactured goods flowed out of Australia to world markets. There was also integration at another level, which may be termed political integration. In relation to its size, Australia in the twentieth century played a disproportionately important role in world affairs – through its membership of the British Empire–Commonwealth in the first half of the century and of the United Nations and other international bodies, such as APEC, in the second half. Finally, there was intellectual integration through the international flows of ideas and new knowledge, with Australia being both an importer and exporter in this regard. Most economic and social policies implemented in Australia during the twentieth century had an international context as well as an Australian one. The economic policies adopted in the 1980s in Australia that impacted on globalisation were themselves part of an international movement towards a more laissez faire economic philosophy. In view of these international linkages and their long-term importance, it would be misleading to depict Australia as 'isolated' or 'inward looking' during the twentieth century in any absolute sense.

However, the degree of integration did change over time and there is no doubt that in the last quarter of the century – and particularly the last one and a half decades – barriers that had been erected in former times were removed or reduced. Highly significant changes to the way in which immigrants were selected for entry to Australia were made in the early 1970s, though that reform did not make Australia's immigration program any less restrictive in terms of overall numbers. And at the same time, attempts were made to begin the process of reducing import barriers, though the momentum was lost in the late 1970s and early 1980s. In the early 1980s, however, there were three important structural changes that 'globalised' Australia: the floating of the dollar in 1983, financial deregulation in 1984 and reductions in **import protection**, particularly those announced in 1988.

These three changes can be seen as the driving force behind the many other changes that were started in the 1980s and continued in the 1990s under the general heading of 'microeconomic reform' (discussed in Chapter 11). Once begun, the process of economic reform was continuous as changes in one part of the economy produced ripple effects (or indeed, 'cascade effects') elsewhere. The pace and timing of change, of course, remained highly political, and the significance and extent of reform was at some times emphasised more than at others. But the underlying process of economic reform ran in one direction – away from restriction and administrative regulation and towards deregulation and the freer play of market forces. In following this direction, Australia was hardly alone, or for that matter, in the vanguard. Globalisation in the late twentieth century was, as the term implied, a world-wide phenomenon, and not simply a set of policy shifts that Australia happened to decide to implement. The signal for the world economy to change direction towards financial deregulation and global integration was the decision to take the US dollar off the **gold standard** in August 1971. Similarly, the decision to float the Australian dollar in December 1983 was the shot from the starting gun in Australia's move to 'globalisation'.

Technological changes, particularly the use of computers and the creation of new global communications networks, were significant in bringing about a more closely knit international economy in a short period of time. But globalisation was driven by policy changes implemented by governments, rather than by advances in communications and data-processing techniques. In the end, therefore, the drive towards globalisation at the end of the twentieth century was a matter of choices made by governments, and in many cases by democratically elected ones. It reversed many of the choices made by the same governments 40 years earlier, during and immediately after the Second World War. Like that earlier set of reforms, taken with the immediate past perspective of the 1930s Great Depression, globalisation was pursued in reaction to the perceived failures of the previous regime. In neither case were these policy shifts mindless, irrational or inevitable, even if their ramifications were not always anticipated or welcomed.

By the late 1990s, internationalisation of the Australian economy had been going on for about a decade and a half, and it was therefore pertinent to ask about its impact. Internationalisation was itself part of a wider commitment to economic reform in Australia from the early 1980s. Part of what was meant by 'globalisation' referred to microeconomic reforms that were domestic in nature but inspired by a desire to improve Australia's international competitiveness, however that rather nebulous concept was defined at various times.

Of the three main structural changes involved in globalisation, floating the dollar had the most dramatic impact, partly because the tariff cuts were introduced quite gradually (stretching into the next century in the case of the most protected sectors of manufacturing). Financial deregulation as it applied to international transactions allowed Australian businesses to build up foreign debt, which they enthusiastically set about doing. But although debt was preferred over equity in foreign investment and current account deficits became much larger in the late 1980s, this situation was not as novel as it might have seemed. Australia had had higher foreign debt levels in the past and historically had always been a capital-importing economy. The switch to a floating exchange rate, by contrast, was unprecedented and by its nature such a transformation could not be a gradual one.

The impact of these changes was complex and they were, of course, interrelated. Reducing import protection, for example, meant that more and more prices in the Australian economy were influenced by import prices; and an important influence on import prices were movements in the exchange rate, now freed from administrative control. Similarly, deregulating capital flows and floating the currency heightened the influence that world financial markets had on Australian government economic policy.

---

**SUMMARY BOX**

The integration of the Australian economy in the international economy, the reduction of barriers to that integration and the range of related microeconomic reforms that followed from this process were the main features of the 'globalisation' of Australia. The three main structural changes that 'globalised' Australia in the 1980s and 1990s were the adoption of a floating exchange rate in 1983, the introduction of far-reaching financial deregulation in 1984 and an ongoing program of tariff reduction and elimination. Of these, floating the dollar was the most potent reform. Similar measures were introduced in many countries in the 1970s and 1980s, and they were enhanced by various technological advances in international communications in the 1980s that made global transactions speedier and more flexible. The impact of globalisation was diffused and not easily isolated or quantified.

---

# Globalisation: judging the impacts

Globalisation by its nature had widespread effects that were not easily isolated or quantified. Impacts in one area caused changes in others so that the origin of the change was often obscured. Among the many ways in which globalisation had an impact in the late twentieth century, five are worth examining more closely, though the interrelatedness of each of these needs to be stressed: domestic prices; balance of payments; openness, structural changes and investment flows; the labour market; and globalisation and productivity.

## Domestic prices

Reducing tariffs was disinflationary: it made imported goods cheaper. As some of these were inputs to production in Australia, there was a lowering of production costs which, in an increasingly competitive domestic market, were passed on in lower prices. Furthermore, the more intense pressure from import competition induced Australian producers to keep other costs down; that is, to improve **productivity** of labour and capital and to resist wage increases.

Movements in the exchange rate certainly affected domestic prices, but as these movements could be in either direction, in principle floating the dollar was neither inflationary nor disinflationary. However, the move to a floating rate did alter the way in which the terms of trade impacted on Australian prices. Under a **fixed exchange rate** regime, falls in the terms of trade were disinflationary because they reduced Australia's national income by reducing export earnings (as happened, for example, in the early 1930s; see Chapter 6). Similarly, rises in the terms of trade were inflationary (compare the early 1970s; see Chapter 7).

Under a floating exchange rate, however, a fall in the terms of trade led to a depreciation in the foreign exchange value of the Australian dollar, thus making imports more expensive and, given the greater influence of import prices generally, this had an inflationary effect. If the depreciation was large enough to offset the fall in export earnings by stimulating foreign demand (which ultimately depended on the **elasticity of demand** for Australia's exports), the fall in the terms of trade could have an overall inflationary impact. As it happened, Australia's terms of trade tended to fall in the 1980s and 1990s (see Figure 13.3), but the move to a floating exchange rate prevented this from having such a disinflationary effect as it would have done under a fixed regime, and may even have been inflationary. The decline in inflation in the second half of 1996, for example, was attributed almost entirely to the rise in the exchange value of the dollar (OECD 1997a, p. 29).

Perhaps of more significance, internationalisation increased the power of global financial markets over domestic macroeconomic policy and, since the markets reacted negatively to what they perceived to be inflationary tendencies, this imposed a strong incentive on governments to follow disinflationary fiscal and monetary policies. Once inflation and inflationary expectations were reduced to very low levels in the early 1990s recession, government policy was directed towards keeping low inflation 'locked-in'. As can be seen from Figure 13.1, the rate of inflation in Australia levelled off in the 1990s, the first time it had done so since the 1950s and 1960s. Globalisation was only one factor in producing this result: the 1990–91 recession and slower economic growth in the 1990s on the one hand, and disinflationary macroeconomic policies on the other, were also important in the explanation. So were lower inflation rates among Australia's trading partners. Disentangling the relative significance of these various disinflationary forces would be a prodigious task.

## SUMMARY BOX

The impact on domestic prices of tariff reductions was disinflationary both by directly reducing the cost of imported goods and through competition effects. Floating the dollar altered the way in which the terms of trade impacted on Australian domestic price levels, with falling terms of trade now being inflationary, in contrast to past experience. The greater power of international markets over Australian domestic economic policy was an important source of pressure for the maintenance of a low inflation regime. Lower inflation in the 1990s, however, was the result of a number of factors, of which globalisation was only one.

## Balance of payments

Internationalisation allowed Australia to run much larger current account deficits in the 1980s and 1990s (see Table 13.2). These deficits were persistent. They did not come down when the exchange rate fell in the mid-1980s, nor when the Commonwealth budget moved into surplus in the four years 1987–88 to 1990–91. Even in the recession in the early 1990s, the deficit did not decline by much and in the 1990s its average was almost as high as in the 1980s. In the late 1990s, the current account again reached high levels, despite fiscal consolidation by the Commonwealth. Since these deficits were financed in the 1980s by borrowing rather than foreign equity investment, Australia's external debt soared (see Figure 11.3). In the past, the danger of such debt was that Australia's **creditors** lost confidence and declined to continue financing the current account deficit. This happened in 1890 and 1930 with highly damaging consequences for the Australian economy (see Chapters 3 and 6 for details). However, in the globalised financial markets of the late twentieth century, a loss of confidence by foreign lenders in the Australian economy was more likely to be manifested in increased costs of borrowing and a depreciation in the exchange value of the Australian dollar than by a cutting off of funding altogether. Nevertheless, foreign confidence was more fragile in relation to an economy with a large external debt than if the debt was smaller, and thus the stabilisation of the foreign debt in the early 1990s was greeted generally as a positive development by the global markets.

In the past, Australia's foreign debt crises were related mainly to high public borrowing and the failure of such borrowing to be devoted to investment that would increase export earnings needed to service the loans. In the 1950s to 1970s, this problem was avoided by the current account deficits being financed by direct private foreign investment. In the era of globalisation, foreign borrowing outweighed foreign direct investment, but the borrowing was to a large extent by

---

**SUMMARY BOX**

Removal of international financial regulations allowed Australia's current account deficit to be much larger in the late 1980s and 1990s than at any other time since the 1930s. As a consequence of the way these deficits were financed, Australia's foreign debt soared to a peak in the early 1990s and then stabilised. The persistence of high foreign debt was not as dangerous as in the past, but nevertheless it did make international financial markets more sensitive to Australia's economic position. The return to foreign equity investment in the 1990s, therefore, was welcomed by the markets as a sign that Australia's external liabilities were more sustainable. Whether the higher levels of foreign ownership that this implied would lead to a political backlash in Australia (as occurred in the 1960s) remained to be seen. Either way, this aspect of globalisation focused more attention on Australia's low domestic savings rate and possible ways to increase it.

the private sector. In principle it might have been expected that such private borrowing would not suffer from the same problems that had plagued public foreign borrowing in, say, the 1920s. In practice, the private foreign debt of the late 1980s was arguably less productively invested than the public foreign debt of earlier generations. The reversion to the dominance of equity in Australia's inward capital flows in the 1990s was a sign that foreign capital investment was more sustainable, but, as occurred in the 1960s and 1970s, it was also likely to exacerbate nationalistic feelings of antagonism towards higher levels of foreign ownership. In spite of increases in Australian outward foreign investment, some of which was also dramatically loss-making in the late 1980s, Australia's net capital flows remained heavily in deficit: Australia had been a net capital importer since the eighteenth century, and it was likely to remain one well into the twenty-first.

## Openness, structural changes and investment flows

The Australian economy became more open as a result of reductions in import barriers and financial deregulation. The effective rate of assistance to Australian manufacturing fell from the mid-1980s, but by international standards Australia was quite slow to adopt tariff reform (Productivity Commission 1998, p. 58). Tariffs declined slowly from the mid-1970s to the mid-1980s and then rather more quickly into the 1990s (see Table 13.7). By the beginning of the twenty-first century it was expected that Australia's average tariff would still be above 3 per cent, a level that most of the OECD reached in 1985. Much higher tariffs on passenger motor vehicles and textiles, clothing and footwear accounted for the relatively high averages.

Measuring the impact of tariff changes on the economy was complicated. On the one hand, the costs of lower tariffs were obvious, immediate and concentrated – job losses, bankruptcies, disinvestment and regional crisis. On the other hand, the benefits were diffused and long term. Moreover, the greatest gains from tariff reforms came from their interaction with other microeconomic reforms, so a 'balance sheet' approach was methodologically difficult. By removing distortions in the economy, tariff reform could be expected to raise productivity. In addition, a more open, internationally orientated economy would be one in which firms were subjected to stronger international competitive forces, leading, it was hoped, to better management and higher quality and innovative production. This was particularly important in a small economy like Australia's where high levels of concentration in manufacturing often muted domestic competition. However, the full benefits from the tariff reductions undertaken in the late 1980s and 1990s might not be realised until the second decade of the twenty-first century (EPAC 1995).

One of the effects of lowering tariff barriers that did emerge fairly quickly was a rise in Australia's trade ratio; that is, the share of imports and exports in GDP. This ratio returned to levels not attained since the early 1950s (see Figure 1.2 in Chapter 1). A higher import ratio implied greater competition in the Australian market for Australian producers. A higher **export ratio** implied that Australian manufacturing firms were exporting a greater share of their output. Manufacturing, and to some extent services, therefore became more export orientated and

**Table 13.7**  Average effective rates of assistance to manufacturing industries, 1968–69 to 2000–01 (per cent, selected years)

| Code | Industry | 1968–69 | 1972–73 | 1976–77 | 1980–81 | 1984–85 | 1988–89 | 1992–93 | 1996–97 | 2001–01* |
|---|---|---|---|---|---|---|---|---|---|---|
| 21 | Food, drink and tobacco | 16 | 19 | 16 | 10 | 6 | 3 | 4 | 2 | 2 |
| 23 | Textiles | 43 | 45 | 51 | 55 | 74 | 72 | 41 | 25 | 17 |
| 24 | Clothing and footwear | 97 | 88 | 141 | 140 | 250+ | 171 | 73 | 52 | 34 |
| 25 | Wood, wood products and furniture | 26 | 23 | 18 | 15 | 17 | 17 | 10 | 4 | 4 |
| 26 | Paper, paper products and publishing | 52 | 51 | 30 | 25 | 16 | 12 | 7 | 2 | 2 |
| 27 | Chemical, petroleum and coal products | 31 | 32 | 21 | 15 | 12 | 12 | 7 | 3 | 3 |
| 28 | Non-metallic mineral products | 15 | 14 | 7 | 4 | 3 | 3 | 3 | 2 | 2 |
| 29 | Basic metal products | 31 | 29 | 14 | 10 | 10 | 9 | 6 | 4 | 4 |
| 31 | Fabricated metal products | 61 | 56 | 34 | 31 | 22 | 20 | 15 | 4 | 4 |
| 32 | Transport equipment | 50 | 51 | 54 | 63 | 66 | 39 | 29 | 19 | 13 |
| 33 | Other machinery and equipment | 43 | 39 | 22 | 20 | 23 | 19 | 14 | 5 | 5 |
| 34 | Miscellaneous manufacturing | 34 | 31 | 25 | 28 | 24 | 24 | 17 | 7 | 7 |
| 21–34 | Total manufacturing | 36 | 35 | 27 | 23 | 22 | 17 | 12 | 6 | 5 |

*Commission estimates.

Note: The 'effective rate of assistance' shows the percentage by which an industry's value-added per unit of production is greater than it would have been in the absence of assistance.

Miscellaneous exports include confidential items (about 20 per cent) and gold (about 75 per cent).

Sources: Based on IAC *Annual Reports* various years; 1987, p. 64; Productivity Commission 1998, p. 58.

subject to greater pressure from imports. Both developments implied that successful firms would have to raise productivity, but there was little evidence of a general
rise in productivity in the Australian economy in the 1990s. Indeed, productivity
growth in manufacturing seemed to be occurring at about the same pace as in the
1970s, when the manufacturing sector was larger and more protected from international competition (see below). A further noticeable effect on manufacturing
firms of globalisation was cheaper imported capital goods that gave them more
access to imported technology.

Meanwhile, the size of the Australian manufacturing sector continued to
decline. At its height in the early 1960s, manufacturing accounted for 27 per cent
of the **labour force** and 22 per cent of GDP, but by the mid-1990s this had declined
to 14 per cent and 15 per cent respectively. By the end of the century, manufacturing was about the same size as it was in 1913 (see Table 13.8). Globalisation might
have been pushing Australian manufacturing towards being more efficient and
more export orientated, but it also speeded up the shrinking of the manufacturing
sector as a whole, reversing the trend of the first six decades of the century.

Manufactures increased their share of both exports and imports, so the trade
deficit in manufactures continued, though declining somewhat (see Tables 13.4
and 13.6). Manufactures exports that did well were specialised products that found

**Table 13.8**   Structural change in the Australian economy, twentieth century

| Year ended 30 June | Distribution of real GDP by sector (% of total) | | | |
|---|---|---|---|---|
| | Agriculture | Mining | Manufacturing | Services |
| 1901 | 18.6 | 9.7 | 12.4 | 59.3 |
| 1920 | 19.2 | 3.5 | 13.3 | 64.0 |
| 1939 | 22.6 | 2.4 | 16.3 | 58.7 |
| 1963 | 10.1 | 1.8 | 27.6 | 60.5 |
| 1973 | 6.1 | 6.2 | 20.7 | 67.0 |
| 1980 | 4.7 | 3.6 | 18.3 | 73.4 |
| 1990 | 4.0 | 4.3 | 15.2 | 76.5 |
| 1998 | 3.7 | 4.3 | 13.2 | 78.8 |
| | Distribution of employment by sector (% of total) | | | |
| 1901 | 25.4 | 7.6 | 14.7 | 52.3 |
| 1920 | 23.1 | 2.9 | 19.4 | 54.6 |
| 1939 | 20.3 | 2.4 | 23.9 | 53.4 |
| 1950 | 14.9 | 1.7 | 28.4 | 55.0 |
| 1961 | 11.3 | 1.3 | 28.2 | 59.2 |
| 1973* | 7.4 | 1.2 | 23.9 | 67.5 |
| 1980* | 6.5 | 1.3 | 19.7 | 72.5 |
| 1990* | 5.5 | 1.2 | 14.9 | 78.4 |
| 1998 | 5.2 | 1.0 | 13.2 | 80.6 |

*August of year stated.
Sources: Based on Butlin 1962, p. 60; Butlin & Dowie 1969, p. 153; RBA 1986, p. 194; ABS
1998, pp. 13, 79.

niche markets, especially in Asia and the Pacific, and also those associated with intra-industry trade. Manufactures exports were the most dynamic element in merchandise exports (and grew faster than GDP), but it was not only the high-tech end that was the driving force, as sectors like basic metal products, mineral processing, wool scouring, and food, drink and tobacco also increased their exports. The rise of manufactures exports reduced the share of commodities in Australia's export mix, which reduced the volatility of Australia's terms of trade since international commodity prices fluctuated more than those of manufactures. Unprocessed primary products accounted for almost half of Australia's exports in 1983, but less than 30 per cent in 1997 (see Table 13.6).

Australia also became more open to international trade in services. These grew rapidly in both scale and variety, stimulated by globalisation, technological advances, trade liberalisation and the deregulation of the services sector in many countries in the 1980s and 1990s. As part of the Uruguay Round of GATT, the world's first binding **multilateral** agreement on trade in services came into force in 1995. The General Agreement on Trade in Services (GATS) was the first step towards freeing this fast-growing sector of world trade from a wide array of national barriers, including various restrictions on international investment in services. This agreement was of particular significance for Australia in view of the important role services played in its economy. By the 1990s, over 70 per cent of Australia's GDP and total employment was generated by the services sector. This put Australia at or near the top among developed economies in terms of share of services in the national economy. Not only were services important in output and employment, but many services were inputs into the production of goods in Australia. Moreover, services provided much of the infrastructure necessary for investment and economic growth, which meant that the efficiency of the services available was significant for overall productivity.

Services represented an important part of the Australian economy throughout the twentieth century, accounting for a greater share of GDP than either primary industry or manufacturing. In the last third of the century their share increased (particularly as manufacturing contracted) and for the first time international trade in services became significant. Until the 1960s, nearly all services consumed in Australia were produced domestically. Since then, deregulation and technological advances made international services trade possible. It became much easier and cheaper for people to move and communicate across international borders. The expansion of civil aviation produced a global boom in tourism and travel in the 1980s and 1990s that Australia was able to participate in. As a result, an important change in the structure of Australia's balance of payments occurred in the 1990s. Up to the mid-1980s, Australia's imports of services grew at about the same rate as its exports of services and since the value of services imports was larger, Australia had a large net deficit in services trade. From the mid-1980s, however, the export of services grew more rapidly than imports, so that by 1994 for the first time in its history, net services became a positive item in Australia's balance of payments. In reflection of this trend, services exports increased as a share of total exports from 17 per cent in the mid-1980s to 23 per cent 10 years later.

The major driving force in the export of services was tourism, increasing as a share of total services exports from 20 per cent in 1976 to 50 per cent in 1996.

Although world tourism was booming, the numbers of visitors to Australia in the 1980s and 1990s grew even faster, chiefly because Australia was able to participate strongly in the fastest growing sector of world travel: outbound tourism from Asia. One-quarter of tourists to Australia came from Asia (mainly Japan) in 1984, but by 1995 Asian visitors represented 50 per cent of the total. Australia's proximity to Asia combined with a depreciating Australian dollar to produce this phenomenon. Moreover, outbound Asian tourism was strongly linked to **per capita incomes** in Asia, and as these rose through the 1980s and 1990s (until the Asian economic crisis occurred) so too did outward tourism. Apart from tourism, other services exports that helped to push the services account into the black were financial services, health and education, each of which were subject to deregulation and microeconomic reform in the 1980s and 1990s. The trade balance on financial services, for example, became positive in 1987–88 and by the mid-1990s produced a net surplus of around $125 million (Commonwealth of Australia 1997, p. 619). Transportation services, although a net deficit item, also moved towards surplus in response to reform and deregulation.

Internationalisation also affected capital flows, although, there was nothing new as such about inward capital flows to Australia. The main structural change was the rise in outward Australian foreign direct investment, which increased in the 1980s in reaction to the lifting of restrictions, global financial deregulation and the greater access to foreign borrowing available to Australian business (Australia 1997, p. 619). Outward investment peaked in 1988, although it remained high by historical standards in the 1990s. It was directed mainly to the same countries that inward foreign investment to Australia came from: North America and Western Europe with relatively little going to Asia, despite Australia's closer trade ties with the region. Australian manufacturing firms that went off-shore generally did so in a search for cheap labour and included the more labour-intensive sectors such as clothing, footwear and textiles, paper and machinery and equipment. One exception were firms in the beverage and food industry that went abroad to find markets similar to Australia rather than low-cost labour.

Inward foreign direct investment also increased in the 1980s in response to deregulation, particularly of the financial sector (banking and insurance). Although expanding rapidly in services, inward investment was also directed to most sectors of Australian manufacturing, indicating that foreign investors did not completely desert manufacturing when it lost its high import protection. Indeed, foreign-owned manufacturing firms spearheaded the restructuring of manufacturing in the 1990s, in both export-orientated sectors and those with a strong domestic market like food, drink and tobacco. Weak world mineral prices did dampen foreign interest in Australian mining, however. As foreign investment increased and became more important for the Australia economy, greater emphasis was placed on the domestic conditions that made Australia attractive. Like the foreign financial markets, foreign direct investors influenced the economic policies adopted by the Australian government. These included the taxation regime, the efficiency of infrastructure, the competitive environment, the quality of **human capital** and industrial relations – the gamut, in fact, of microeconomic reform.

The growth of services was also evident in foreign investment, both into Australia and from Australia to the rest of the world. For a number of services, such as advertising, banking, insurance and data processing, foreign direct investment was the main way in which foreign customers were supplied. Services were the fastest growing sector in international investment in the late twentieth century, reaching 50 per cent of the stock of foreign investment worldwide by the 1990s, and accounting for about two-thirds of the flows. This was another trend of globalisation that Australia was caught up in. More than half of incoming investment was in services, principally in the finance and insurance industries following deregulation and the admission of foreign banks in the early 1980s. Indeed, by the end of the century, virtually all of Australia's merchant banks were foreign owned. Other services sectors that received substantial amounts of inward foreign direct investment in Australia were property services such as property operators, developers and real estate agents; and business services, such as computer services, legal and accounting services and marketing and business management services. Wholesale trade was also an important recipient of inward investment.

As with inward investment, services featured prominently in Australian investment abroad, accounting for about one half of the total with financial and insurance services dominant. Manufacturing made up much of the rest as mining and agriculture declined in importance. The types of manufacturing Australians invested in overseas were printing, publishing and recorded media on the one hand, and primary resources processing on the other – both areas where Australian firms could claim some global advantages. In the 1980s, Australian investment in foreign brewing operations was popular, but this activity diminished in the 1990s following some spectacular losses. Going off-shore in search of cheaper labour remained an important motive in the last decade of the century and this had some impact on the growing trend towards Australian foreign investment flowing to the Asia–Pacific

## SUMMARY BOX

Reducing import barriers increased Australia's openness and speeded up structural changes in the economy. The negative impacts of tariff reductions were more immediate, visible and concentrated than the positive effects. To a large extent, the full benefits of tariff reductions could only be gained through further microeconomic reforms that intensified competition in the domestic economy. This made their impact both long-term and complex. An early effect of the tariff reductions was a rise in Australia's trade ratio. A major structural change was the continued decline in size of the manufacturing sector. At the same time, manufacturing became more export orientated. A further structural change was the greater role of international trade in services. Here Australia was able to participate in the worldwide boom in tourism. This, together with some other services exports, pushed the services account into surplus for the first time in Australia's peacetime history. Services also featured prominently in capital flows, both inward and outward foreign direct investment.

region in the 1990s. The bulk of the flows, however, remained between Australia and its 'traditional' investment partners: the United States, the United Kingdom, Japan and New Zealand.

## Impact on the labour market

One of the major aspects of the globalisation process was reduction and virtual elimination of import barriers. As discussed throughout this book, these barriers had been put in place for a variety of reasons, but their employment implications were always important. Tariff protection of the manufacturing industry, it was argued from the 1920s onwards, was necessary to provide employment for both the Australian-born worker and the immigrant. In the twentieth century, the expansion of manufacturing offered far more scope for employment than agriculture, providing a source of protected employment in addition to the already protected services sector. Other arguments for maintaining import protection fell away in the last quarter of the twentieth century, as the real costs of protection began to be widely appreciated. But the employment arguments continued to hold limited sway, as the case of the very extended transition period to freer trade for textiles and motor vehicles suggested.

In view of the role that employment creation had played in the erection and maintenance of a high tariff regime in Australia in the twentieth century, it was not surprising that a great deal of the structural adjustment that followed the dismantling of that regime fell on the labour market. Nearly all sectors of manufacturing lost labour during the 1980s, and overall manufacturing employment contracted by almost one-quarter. In the most protected sector – clothing, footwear and textiles – the labour force was reduced directly by competition from cheaper imports, and this sector also exhibited an alarming tendency to resort to sweated labour through outwork. Apart from this industry, however, the sectors with the greatest labour losses were those with the highest productivity gains and generally were ones not especially affected by direct import competition, particularly from low-wage economies. This suggested a direct and an indirect effect on employment in the setting of lower tariffs: a direct effect from increased competition from low-cost suppliers and an indirect effect as firms invested in cost-saving technology to compete against imports, and in so doing they shed labour. Thus, reducing tariffs cost jobs in manufacturing through two mechanisms and the indirect mechanism appeared to be both stronger and more widespread. It was also the case that the most successful exporters of ETMs were those firms that shed the most labour, as they raised productivity through investment in new technology.

Eventually internationalisation caused some productivity gains in all sectors of the economy, not only in manufacturing, with corresponding job losses. Even **'non-tradeable'** sectors like public utilities, telecommunications and transport were subjected to competitive pressure arising from internationalisation to raise productivity, and in order to do so, these sectors reduced the size of their labour force.[1]

The implication for many less skilled workers was that they faced a 'diabolical trade-off' between lower relative real wages and higher unemployment. The only viable alternative appeared to be obtaining more skills so as to move out of the less skilled category. In a fully internationalised economy, there would be no protected sectors where unskilled labour could be paid artificially higher wages or where artificially higher levels of employment could be maintained – indeed, that was the whole point of internationalisation as it was viewed at the end of the century. In practice, complete internationalisation of the Australian economy was unlikely and progress towards the ideal was very uneven. Nevertheless, internationalisation, like all structural changes, produced winners and losers and therefore posed the question of how public policy should and could be directed to moving losers into the winners' camp. Or at least, adequately compensating the losers (and the region where they lived).

This raised some large issues that remained to be tackled as the third millennium approached. Investment in education and training to increase the supply of skilled workers relative to unskilled and to stimulate the establishment and expansion of new knowledge-based industries was clearly required, but what sort of training, how it was to be delivered and who was to pay for it remained undecided. Indeed, in the later part of the 1990s, job programs to help the long-term unemployed (about one-third of the total) were virtually eliminated altogether. Regional development policy also remained inadequate. Even if it was true that productivity-induced job losses would occur throughout the Australian economy, it was likely that they would occur less in the services sector. This suggested that public policy should be directed to expanding the services sector (for example, by investing in health and education and other community services, as well as facilitating business services) so as to expand employment.

The extent to which the job losses in manufacturing translated into higher aggregate levels of unemployment depended on whether the services sector was stimulated by the productivity gains in manufacturing to expand (and/or was expanding anyway) and how well the labour market worked in moving labour displaced from manufacturing into services. There was, therefore, considerable

**SUMMARY BOX**

Globalisation impacted on employment by increasing competition from imports derived from low wages and by inducing firms to invest in labour-saving technology in order to meet the challenge of heightened foreign competition. This added significantly to the decline in employment in the manufacturing industry and highlighted the structural shift in the labour market towards the services sector. However, in the end nearly all sectors of the domestic economy were subject to greater international competition by globalisation, with attendant impact on employment. Low-wage, low-skill workers were those most affected, often facing declining real relative wages or unemployment. More investment in human capital in Australia was urgently needed, but not forthcoming. Ultimately, reducing the level of unemployment required faster sustained economic growth than occurred in the 1990s.

debate on how the labour market could be made more flexible without losing the equity qualities of the centralised wage fixing system. Reform of the Australian industrial relations system tended to lag behind the other microeconomic reforms during the 1980s. Wage rises were increasingly tied to productivity gains and, from the end of the decade, moves toward enterprise bargaining began. Further reforms followed in the 1990s, but the question of reducing structural unemployment through changes to the labour market institutions remained unresolved. Whether structural unemployment would have been less had the reforms to the labour market preceded or accompanied the process of internationalisation was a moot point. Ultimately, the achievement of lower unemployment levels required higher economic growth, but economic growth depended on how well **factors of production** were used, as well as on how many of them there were. Thus, faster economic growth was itself partly a matter of solving the structural problems thrown up by globalisation.

## Globalisation and productivity

Raising productivity was one of the benefits that globalisation was expected to bring. Indeed, the diffusion of reform and structural change throughout the economy was supposed to make all Australians 'work smarter' (though not necessarily harder). In the past, it was alleged, too much of Australia's economic growth had been the result of simply increasing volume of the factors of production (more **land**, more labour, increased investment), and not enough had flowed from the quality of these factors and combining them in ways that led to ever-rising levels of efficiency. Globalisation, therefore, was anticipated to have a major impact on productivity.

## Australia's productivity record

Australia's track record in productivity growth was not particularly inspiring over the twentieth century and although it was better in the third quarter it still lagged behind other developed economies and its own potential. Productivity gains by both labour and capital were highest during the Long Boom when strong economic growth combined with **full employment** and (for most of the period) low inflation. However, even during this period more of the economic growth was due to increases in the supply of labour and capital than to improvements in the efficiency with which they were used in production.

In the 1970s, productivity growth slowed in response to stagflation and the macroeconomic policies taken to tackle it. Wages explosions more than offset the now lower rates of productivity growth. The conditions of high growth and full employment during the Long Boom had created (or entrenched) social and organisational rigidities (for example, inflexible work practices) that were now more conspicuous. In the 1980s, productivity slowed down even more as the Accord drove down real wages. Together with high domestic interest rates, lower labour costs reduced the incentive for firms to replace labour with capital and to invest in new technology.

A turning point came at the end of the 1980s, with a gradual climb in the rate of productivity growth through the 1990s and a return to the levels of the 1970s.

Some of the improvement in the 1990s was due to the recovery from the recession at the beginning of the decade. On the other hand, productivity continued to strengthen into the second half of the decade when the recovery period had been completed. This suggested, perhaps, that globalisation and associated microeconomic reforms were having a positive impact (Productivity Commission 1996). Businesses in Australia now faced a more competitive climate and therefore had more incentive to make organisational changes to improve efficiency. Reforms removed some restrictive work practices and reduced the possibility of **rent-seeking behaviour** by both labour and management. Nevertheless, investment in new technology, often embedded in new plant and equipment, remained an important source of productivity growth, especially within the manufacturing sector (Industry Commission 1997, p. 13).[2]

## The impact of productivity on employment

Did raising productivity always cost jobs? Historically there seemed to be little correlation between productivity growth and employment. Some firms experiencing high productivity growth shed labour, while others took on more workers as they expanded output. Similarly, firms with declining productivity reduced their labour force as they contracted. Whether a firm was in a high or low productivity sector did not predict whether it would be a larger or smaller employer. Different industries have had different experiences with productivity and employment patterns at different times in their history, with no clear pattern being discernible. Sometimes productivity and employment trends moved together, sometimes in opposite directions and sometimes independently of each other. Internationally, industries with similar productivity changes might have quite different employment patterns.

What was clear from the past development of the Australian economy was that productivity growth and employment growth could co-exist for long periods, as happened in the 1950s and 1960s. Over the twentieth century, productivity in Australia increased about threefold, but the size of the labour force increased four and half times (from around 2 million to 9 million). Indeed, if there was a correlation it was between high productivity growth and high employment growth, rather than between high productivity growth and rising unemployment. This was because productivity growth was an important (though not the major) source of economic growth and rising unemployment was partly a result of slower economic growth rates. Historically, new technologies increased incomes more than they displaced labour, though not necessarily at the same pace. Not only did new technology result in higher output and productivity, but also in the medium term an expansion of employment. Thus, Australia's problem during the period of rising unemployment from 1974 onwards was not that there was too much productivity growth, but rather that there was not enough to produce a higher rate of economic growth. For this reason, reducing real wages so as to slow productivity growth and make production more labour intensive, as happened in Australia in the 1980s, in the longer run was counter-productive because firms that did not keep up with the productivity gains of their competitors eventually went under. Similarly, attempting to improve the competitiveness of Australian business by following a strategy of cheap labour was a recipe for disaster.

This was true at the aggregate level. But at the firm or industry level, productivity gains through new technology or new work practices did cause job losses. Since the Industrial Revolution, technological change had led to both deskilling and upskilling, but not always in the same industry nor at the same speed. The impact of productivity gains on employment in particular firms and sectors raised concerns about the future employment prospects for low-wage and low-skill workers, and how well short-run adjustment problems would be tackled. Productivity changes were not the only influences on the demand for unskilled and skilled labour, but they could have huge negative effects in the short term on certain groups and regions. Jobs lost in one industry might take time to be offset by jobs growth elsewhere, especially if the overall rate of economic growth was low. There might be mismatches, where demand for labour of certain types was not matched by supply. Workers needed to retrain, but this took time and money. Adequate compensation needed to be paid. In the 1990s, some of these issued were being tackled, and there was evidence from higher school retention rates and the proportion in post-secondary education that a more educated, higher skilled and more adaptable workforce might develop in the early part of the twenty-first century. It remained the case, however, that Australian policy-makers and governments seemed rather more efficient at bringing in micro-economic reforms and more competitive arrangements than they were at devising adequate means to deal with the subsequent adjustment upheavals.

## Productivity and future living standards

Raising productivity remained the key to future economic growth and rising living standards in Australia at the end of the twentieth century. The strong growth in the Long Boom had rested largely on the high growth of inputs (labour and capital). Since the 1960s, about half of Australia's economic growth came from more inputs and about half from productivity gains. But in the future, economic growth would be more dependent on productivity. Inputs of labour were likely to be constrained. Population growth would be slower and immigration levels lower (with a smaller proportion of immigrants entering the labour force). The labour participation rate (previously driven by the rising female participation rate) was likely to slow. The length of the working year was falling and unemployment was higher. Capital investment was influenced by globalisation: as it became more mobile, capital investment could not be taken for granted. If capital was used more efficiently, less of it would be required to achieve any particular rate of growth of output. This might be significant given the persistence of Australia's current account deficits and its high foreign debt.

Moreover, mature industrial economies like Australia had less scope for rapid productivity gains in manufacturing than newly industrialising nations. Mature economies had a larger services sector with lower productivity levels and productivity growth potential. Services increased from 61 per cent of Australia's GDP in 1962–63 to 79 per cent in 1997–98, and accounted for four-fifths of employment (see Table 13.8). It was uncertain how new technology and microeconomic reform would impact on services. There might be large productivity gains from computerisation and advances in information technology (for example, **e-commerce**) to be reaped. The historical evidence over the twentieth century was that the services sector grew strongly as new technologies created new services, producing a more and more diverse sector. A whole raft of new services emerged as a result of new technologies, as well as a result of changing lifestyles, employment patterns, leisure time and use, and so on. On the other hand, consumers of services could be expected to demand higher quality over time and this would imply more labour intensity in some service sectors, such as health, child-care, education, hospitality and community services.

Australia's productivity trend rate was high at the end of the 1990s, indeed it was the second highest on record according to the Productivity Commission (Industry Commission 1997, p. xix). Moreover, there was evidence that firms in the 1990s were spending far more on research and development (R&D) than they had done in the 1980s, and that the increased productivity rates were occurring across a broad range of industry sectors. In the past, much of the gain from productivity increases had been captured by capital and labour, with the exact share between these two varying over time in accordance to their relative bargaining strengths. However, in the more competitive, low inflation environment of the late 1990s, more of the productivity increases in the market sector manifested itself in the form of lower prices, which lowered costs of production elsewhere in the economy and stimulated consumption. In this way, productivity gains were likely to be more effective in stimulating economic growth than they had been in the past. And there was plenty of scope for further gains, from manufacturing, utilities and services: Australia's mediocre productivity performance in the past ensured that there were great gaps remaining to be filled.

The role of public policy was to recognise the need to invest in public sector services – to raise their productivity and, through investment in education, training and health, raise the productivity of all sectors. Gains in productivity here were vital, although less visible in the statistical account. Continued growth in productivity held out the prospect that in future Australians could work less hard, but more intelligently and productively, and that Australia might (at last) make the transition from the 'lucky country' of the 1960s to the 'clever country' of the next millennium.

## SUMMARY BOX

Globalisation was expected to have a major impact on raising productivity in the Australian economy. A rise in productivity in the 1990s led to guarded optimism that this was in fact occurring. By the late 1990s, productivity was back to the level of the 1970s, though still behind that of the 1960s. Productivity gains were sometimes seen to be obtained at the expense of employment, but the historical record suggested that Australia's problem was too little productivity gain rather than too much. In the future, economic growth would depend more on productivity gains than in the past. Therefore, raising productivity should increase the pace of economic growth with a beneficial impact on employment. And there seemed to be much scope for further productivity rises as the century drew to a close. Certainly, improving productivity remained the key to increasing living standards in Australia in the future.

# Suggested further reading

Bell, S. & Head, B. (eds) 1994, *State, Economy and Public Policy in Australia*, Oxford University Press, Melbourne.

Capling, A. & Galligan, B. 1992, *Beyond the Protective State*, Cambridge University Press, Cambridge.

Catley, B. 1996, *Globalising Australian Capitalism*, Cambridge University Press, Cambridge.

Economic Planning Advisory Commission 1995, *Globalisation: Issues for Australia, Commission Paper No. 5*, Australian Government Publishing Service, Canberra.

Fagan, R. & Webber, M. 1994, *Global Restructuring: The Australian Experience*, Oxford University Press, Melbourne.

Fitzgerald, V.W. 1993, *National Saving: A Report to the Treasurer*, Australian Government Publishing Service, Canberra.

King, S. & Lloyd, P. (eds) 1993, *Economic Rationalism: Dead End or Way Forward?*, Allen & Unwin, Sydney.

Quiggin, J. 1996, *Great Expectations: Microeconomic Reform and Australia*, Allen & Unwin, Sydney.

Reserve Bank of Australia 1994, *International Integration of the Australian Economy: Proceedings of a Conference*, Sydney.

Wiseman, J. 1998, *Global Nation?: Australia and the Politics of Globalisation*, Cambridge University Press, Melbourne.

# End notes

[1]  The non-tradeables sector comprises: electricity, gas and water; construction; wholesale trade; retail trade; accommodation, cafes and restaurants; transport and storage; communication services; finance and insurance; property and business services; government administration and defence; education, health and community services; cultural and recreational services; and personal and other services.

[2]  There are well-known problems encountered in measuring productivity and it is far from being an exact science. In particular, it is difficult to measure productivity changes in the non-tradeables or services sectors. Changes in quality are taken into account when measuring productivity in the tradeables sector, but not in the non-tradeables. Moreover, as productivity is measured as a residual (that part of economic growth left over after taking increases in factors of production into account) it is not possible to separate the contribution of the various causes of productivity growth. In addition, the way in which inputs of factors of production are measured obscures the role of new technology embodied in capital goods and human skills embodied in labour. Finally, productivity is easier to measure at the firm level, rather than at the sector or industry level. The more aggregated the productivity measure is, the less accurate it becomes.

# BIBLIOGRAPHY

Albert, B. & Graves, A. (eds) 1988, *The World Sugar Economy in War and Depression, 1914–40*, Routledge, London.

Aldcroft, D.H. 1977, *From Versailles to Wall Street, 1919–1939*, Allen Lane, London.

—— 1993, *The European Economy 1914–1990*, Routledge, London.

Alford, B.W.E. 1996, *Britain in the World Economy since 1880*, Longman, London.

Alford, K. 1986, 'Colonial Women's Employment as seen by Nineteenth Century Statisticians and Twentieth Century Economic Historians', *Labour History*, 51, pp. 1–10.

Anderson, D.L. 1983, *Foreign Investment Control in the Mining Sector: Comparisons of Australian and Canadian Experience*, Australian National University Press, Canberra.

Anderson, K. & Garnaut, R. 1986, 'Australia: Political Economy of Manufacturing Protection', in C. Findlay & R. Garnaut (eds), *The Political Economy of Manufacturing Protection: Experiences of ASEAN and Australia*, Allen & Unwin, Sydney, pp. 158–9.

Armstrong, C. & Nelles, H.V. 1985, 'The State and the Provision of Electricity in Canada and Australia, 1880–1965', in D.C.M. Platt & G. di Tella (eds), *Argentina, Australia and Canada: Studies in Comparative Development*, Macmillan, London, pp. 207–30.

Armstrong, P., Glyn, A. & Harrison, J. 1991, *Capitalism since 1945*, Blackwell, Oxford.

Arndt, H.W. 1948, *The Economic Lessons of the 1930s*, Oxford University Press, Oxford.

—— 1968 'The Vernon Report', in H.W. Arndt, *A Small Rich Industrial Country: Studies in Australian Development, Aid and Trade*, Cheshire, Melbourne.

Arndt, H.W. & Sherk, D.R. 1959, 'Export Franchises of Australian Companies with Overseas Affiliation', *Economic Record*, 35, pp. 239–42.

Atkin, J.M. 1977, *British Overseas Investment 1918–1931*, Arno Press, New York.

Atkinson, A. 1988, 'Taking possession: Sydney's first householders', in G. Aplin, *A Difficult Infant: Sydney Before Macquarie*, NSWU Press, Sydney, pp. 72–90.

Austrade 1988, *Annual Report 1987–88*, Australian Government Publishing Service, Canberra.

—— 1989, *Annual Report 1988–89*, Australian Government Publishing Service, Canberra.

Australia 1954, *Yearbook of the Commonwealth of Australia*, Commonwealth Government Printer, Canberra.

— 1965, Committee of Economic Enquiry, Report of the Committee of Economic Enquiry, Government Printer, vol. 1, Canberra.

— 1975a, *Population and Australia: A Demographic Analysis and Projection: First Report of the National Population Inquiry*, 2 vols, Australian Government Publishing Service, Canberra.

— 1975b, Committee to Advise on Policies for Manufacturing Industry, *Policies for Development of Manufacturing Industry*, Australian Government Publishing Service, Canberra [The Jackson Report].

— *Official Yearbook of the Commonwealth of Australia, 1901* and subsequent issues, Australian Government Publishing Service, Melbourne and Canberra.

— 1979, *Study Group on Structural Adjustment*, Report of the Study Group on Structural Adjustment, Australian Government Publishing Service, Canberra, 2 vols [The Crawford Report].

— 1988, *Immigration: A Commitment to Australia. The Report of the Committee to Advise on Australia's Immigration Policies*, Australian Government Publishing Service, Canberra, pp. 1–22 [Fitzgerald Report].

Australian Bureau of Statistics (ABS) 1976, *Foreign Ownership and Control in Manufacturing Industry 1972–73*, Cat. no. 5321.0, Canberra.

— *Migration 1996–1997*, Canberra.

— 1998, *Australian Economic Indicators* (Cat. no. 1350.0), Canberra, November.

— *Overseas Arrivals and Departures* (Cat. no. 3404.0), annual publication, Canberra.

— *Foreign Trade Australia* (Cat. no. 5410.0), Canberra.

Australian Institute of Political Science 1971, *How Many Australians? Immigration and Growth: Proceedings of the 37th Summer School Canberra*, Angus & Robertson, Sydney.

Bambrick, S. 1968, Australian Price Indices, unpublished PhD Thesis, Australian National University, Table VIII/1.

— 1970, 'Australia's Long-run Terms of Trade', *Economic Development and Cultural Change*, 19, 1, p. 5.

— 1993, *Australian Minerals and Energy Policy*, Australian National University Press, Canberra.

Barnard, A. (ed.) 1962, *The Simple Fleece: Studies in the Australian Wool Industry*, Melbourne University Press, Melbourne.

— 1971, 'Wool Brokers and the Marketing Pattern, 1914–1920', *Australian Economic History Review*, 11, pp. 1–20.

— 1987, 'Government Finance', in W. Vamplew (ed.), *Australians: Historical Statistics*, Fairfax, Syme & Weldon, Sydney.

Barnard, A., Butlin, N.G. & Pincus, J.J. 1977, 'Public and Private Sector Employment in Australia, 1901–1974', *Australian Economic Review*, 1st Quarter, pp. 43–52.

Beaumont, J. (ed.) 1995, *Australia's War, 1914–1918*, Allen & Unwin, Sydney.

— 1996, *Australia's War, 1934–1945*, Allen & Unwin, Sydney.

Bell, S. 1993, *Australian Manufacturing and the State: the Politics of Industry Policy in the Post-war Era*, Cambridge University Press, Cambridge.

Bell, S. & Head, B. (eds) 1994, *State, Economy and Public Policy in Australia*, Oxford University Press, Melbourne.

Bello, W. & Rosenfeld, S. 1992, *Dragons in Distress: Asia's Miracle Economies in Crisis*, Penguin, London.

Bennett, S. (ed.) 1975, *Federation*, Cassell, Melbourne.

Bergsten, C.F. & Cline, W.C. 1987, *The United States–Japan Problem*, Institute for International Economics, Washington DC.

Birrell, R. 1988, 'Employment and the Occupational System since the Second World War', in J. Jupp (ed.), *The Australian People: An Encyclopedia of the Nation, its People and their Origins*, Angus & Robertson, Sydney.

Birrell, R., Hill, D. & Nevill, J. (eds) 1984, *Populate and Perish? The Stresses of Population Growth in Australia*, Fontana, Sydney.

Black, S.W. 1985, *Learning from Adversity: Policy Responses to Two Oil Shocks*, Princeton University Press, Princeton.

Bleaney, M. 1985, *The Rise and Fall of Keynesian Economics*, Macmillan, London.

Blainey, G. 1969, *The Rush That Never Ended: A History of Australian Mining*, 2nd edn, Melbourne University Press, Melbourne.

— 1984, *All for Australia*, Methuen Haynes, N. Ryde.

Block, F.L. 1977, *The Origins of International Economic Disorder: a Study of United States International Monetary Policy from World War II to the Present*, University of California Press, Berkeley.

Boehm, E.A. 1971, *Prosperity and Depression in Australia, 1887–1897*, Clarendon Press, Oxford.

— 1993, *Twentieth Century Economic Development in Australia*, 3rd edn, Longman Cheshire, Melbourne.

Borrie, W.D. 1988, 'Changes in Immigration Patterns since 1972', in J. Jupp (ed.) *The Australian People: An Encyclopedia of the Nation, its People and their Origins*, Angus & Robertson, Sydney.

Bosch, H. 1990, *The Workings of a Watchdog*, Heinemann, Melbourne.

Brash, D.T. 1966, *American Investment in Australian Industry*, Australian National University Press, Canberra.

— 1988, *Migrant Hands in a Distant Land: Australia's Post-war Immigration*, Pluto Press, Sydney.

Brawley, S. 1995, *The White Peril: Foreign Relations and Asian Immigration to Australasia and North America, 1919–1978*, UNSW Press, Sydney.

Broomhill, R. 1979, *Unemployed Workers: A Social History of the Great Depression in Adelaide*, Queensland University Press, Brisbane.

Brown, P.M. 1996, *The Merchant Princes of Fremantle*, University of Western Australia Press, Perth.

Brown, P. & Hughes, H. 1970, 'The Market Structure of Australian Manufacturing Industry, 1914 to 1963–64', in C. Forster (ed.), *Australian Economic Development in the Twentieth Century*, Allen & Unwin, London.

Brown, W.A. 1940, *The International Gold Standard Re-interpreted 1914–1934*, National Bureau of Economic Research, New York.

Brownlee, W. E. 1979, *Dynamics of Ascent: A History of the American Economy*, Knopf, 2nd edn, New York.

Buckley, K. & Wheelwright, T. 1988, *No Paradise for Workers: Capitalism and the Common People in Australia, 1788–1914*, Oxford University Press, Melbourne.

Bureau of Agricultural Economics 1973, *Statistical Handbook of the Sheep and Wool Industry*, 4th edn, Canberra.

Bureau of Immigration, *Multicultural and Population Research 1984–1995*, *Australian Immigration, Consolidated Statistics*, nos 13–18, Australian Government Publishing Service, Canberra.

Burley, K.H. 1961, 'The organisation of the overseas trade in New South Wales coal, 1860–1914', *Economic Record*, 37, pp. 371–81.

Burnett, J. 1994, *Idle Hands: The Experience of Unemployment 1790–1990*, Routledge, London.

Burnley, I.H. 1982, *Population, Society and Environment in Australia*, Shillington House, Melbourne.

Burstein, D. 1989, *Yen! The Threat of Japan's Financial Empire*, Schwartz, New York.

Butlin, M.W. 1977, 'A preliminary annual database 1900/01 to 1973/74', Reserve Bank of Australia Research Discussion Paper 7701, May, Sydney.

Butlin, N.G. 1959, 'Some Structural Features of Australian Capital Formation, 1861 to 1938/39', *Economic Record*, 72, December, pp. 390–5.

— 1962, *Australian Domestic Product, Investment and Foreign Borrowing 1861–1938/39*, Cambridge University Press, Cambridge.

— 1964, *Investment in Australian Economic Development, 1861–1900*, Cambridge University Press, Cambridge.

— 1983, 'Trends in Public/Private Relations, 1901–75', in B.W. Head (ed.), *State and Economy in Australia*, Oxford University Press, Melbourne.

— 1986, 'Contours of the Australian Economy, 1788–1860', *Australian Economic History Review*, 26, no. 2, September, pp. 101–4.

— 1993, *Economics and the Dreamtime: A Hypothetical History*, Cambridge University Press, Melbourne.

Butlin, N.G., Barnard, A. & Pincus, J.J. 1982, *Government and Capitalism: Public and Private Choice in Twentieth Century Australia*, Allen & Unwin, Sydney.

Butlin, N.G. & Dowie, J.A. 1969, 'Estimates of Australian Workforce and Employment, 1861–1961', *Australian Economic History Review*, 9, pp. 138–55.

Butlin, S.J. 1955, *War Economy, 1939–1942*, Australian War Memorial, Canberra.

Butlin, S.J. & Schedvin, C.B. 1977, *War Economy, 1942–1945*, Australian War Memorial, Canberra.

Cain, N. 1973, 'Political Economy and the Tariff: Australia in the 1920s', *Australian Economic Papers*, 12, pp. 1–20.

Camm, J.C.R. & McQuilton, J. 1987, *Australians: A Historical Atlas*, Fairfax, Syme & Weldon Associates, Sydney.

Cannon, M. 1971, *The Land Boomers*, Melbourne University Press, Melbourne.

Capling, A. & Galligan, B. 1992, *Beyond the Protective State*, Cambridge University Press, Cambridge.

Carew, E. 1992, *Paul Keating, Prime Minister*, Allen & Unwin, Sydney.
— 1997, *Westpac:The Bank that Broke the Bank*, Allen & Unwin, Sydney.
— 1998, *Fast Money – 4*, Allen & Unwin, Sydney.
Carmody, A.T. 1952, 'The Level of the Australian Tariff: A Study in Method', *Yorkshire Bulletin of Economic and Social Research*, 4, 1, pp. 51–65.
Carroll, J. & Manne, R. (eds) 1992, *Shutdown: the Failure of Economic Rationalism and How to Rescue Australia*, Text Publishing Company, Melbourne.
Catley, B. 1996, *Globalising Australian Capitalism*, Cambridge University Press, Cambridge.
Catley, R. & McFarlane, B. 1983, *Australian Capitalism in Boom and Depression*, Penguin, Melbourne.
Centre for International Economics 1988, *The Relationship between Immigration and Economic Performance*, Australian Government Publishing Service, Canberra.
Chandler, A.D. 1977, *The Visible Hand: The Managerial Revolution in American Business*, Belknap, Cambridge, Mass.
Cipolla, C.M. (ed.) 1973, *The Fontana Economic History of Europe Volume 4: The Emergence of Industrial Societies*, Collins, Glasgow.
Coghlan, T.A. 1886, *The Wealth and Progress of New South Wales*, Government Printer, Sydney.
— 1890, *A Statistical Account of Australasia*, Government Printer, Sydney.
Collins, J. 1975, 'The Political Economy of Post-war Immigration', in E.L. Wheelwright & K. Buckley (eds), *Essays in the Political Economy of Australian Capitalism*, Vol. I, A&NZ Book Co., Sydney, pp. 105–29.
— 1988, *Migrants' Hands in a Distant Land*, Pluto Press, Sydney.
Commonwealth Bureau of Census and Statistics (CBCS) 1914, *Trade, Customs and Excise Revenue of the Commonwealth of Australia, 1913*, Melbourne.
— *Overseas Trade*, various issues, Melbourne and Canberra.
— 1952, *The Australian Balance of Payments 1928–29 to 1949–50*, Commonwealth Government Printer, Canberra.
Commonwealth of Australia 1965, *Report of the Committee of Economic Enquiry*, Government Printer, Canberra.
— 1997, *Financial System Inquiry Final Report*, Australian Government Publishing Service, Canberra.
Commonwealth Treasury of Australia 1998, *Economic Roundup*, Australian Government Publishing Service, Canberra, Spring.
Conlon, R.M. & Perkins, J.A. 1997, 'Political Economy of Assistance to the Automotive Industry in Australia: Have We Seen It All Before?', *Economic Papers*, vol. 16, no. 2, June, pp. 76–91.
Coombs, H.C. 1944, 'The Economic Aftermath of War', in D.A.S. Campbell (ed.), *Post-war Reconstruction in Australia*, Australasian Publishing Company, Sydney.
— 1971, *Other People's Money: Economic Essays*, Australian National University Press, Canberra.
Cooper, R.N. & Lawrence, R.Z. 1975, 'The 1972–75 Commodity Boom', *Brookings Institute on Economic Activity*, 3, pp. 671–723.
Copland, D. (ed.) 1960, *Giblin: The Scholar and the Man*, Cheshire, Melbourne.

Corden, W.M. 1957, 'The Calculation of the Cost of Protection', *The Economic Record*, 33, pp. 29–51.

—— 1962, 'The Logic of Australian Tariff Policy, *Economic Papers*, 15, 38–46, reprinted in Corden 1997.

—— 1966, 'The Vernon Report: Protection', *The Economic Record*, 42, pp. 129–48, reprinted in Corden 1997.

—— 1974, *Trade Policy and Economic Welfare*, Clarendon Press, Oxford.

—— 1997, *The Road to Reform: Essays on Australian Economic Policy*, Addison Wesley Longman, Melbourne.

Coughlan, J.E. & McNamara, D.J. (eds) 1997, *Asians in Australia: Patterns of Migration and Settlement*, Macmillan, Melbourne.

Costa, M. & Easson, M. (eds) 1991, *Australian Industry: What Policy?*, Pluto Press, Sydney.

Crawford, J.G. 1968, *Australian Trade Policy 1942–1966: a Documentary History*, Australian National University Press, Canberra.

Curzon, G. 1965, *Multilateral Commercial Diplomacy*, Michael Joseph, London.

Darian-Smith, K. 1996, 'War and Australian Society', in J. Beaumont, *Australia's War, 1939–45*, Allen & Unwin, Sydney.

Davidson, B.R. 1982, 'A Benefit Cost Analysis of the New South Wales Railway System', *Australian Economic History Review*, 22, pp. 127–50.

Davidson, F.G. 1962, 'Agriculture', in W. Vamplew (ed.) 1987, *Australians: Historical Statistics*, Fairfax, Syme & Weldon, Sydney.

—— 1969, *The Industrialization of Australia*, 4th edn, Melbourne University Press, 1969, Melbourne.

Davidson, F.G. & Stewardson, B.R. 1974, *Economics and Australian Industry*, Longman, Melbourne.

Davies, M. 1985, 'Blainey Re-visited: Mineral Discoveries and the Business Cycle in South Australia', *Australian Economic History Review*, 25, pp. 112–28.

Davison, G. 1970, 'Public Utilities and the Expansion of Melbourne in the 1880s', *Australian Economic History Review*, 10, pp. 168–89.

Delhaise, P.F. 1997, *Asia in Crisis: The Implosion of the Banking and Financial Systems*, John Wiley, Singapore.

Denning, W. 1937, *Caucus Crisis: The Rise and Fall of the Scullin Government*, Cumberland Argus, Parramatta.

Denoon, D. 1983, *Settler Capitalism: The Dynamics of Dependent Development in the Southern Hemisphere*, Clarendon Press, Oxford.

Department of Foreign Affairs and Trade (DFAT) 1997, *Exports of Primary and Manufactured Products*, Australian Government Publishing Service, Canberra.

—— 1998a, *Direction of Trade Time Series 1977–1997*, Australian Government Publishing Service, Canberra.

—— 1998b, *Exports of Major Commodities 1980–97*, Australian Government Publishing Service, Canberra.

Department of Trade 1985, *Annual Report 1984–85*, Australian Government Publishing Service, Canberra.

Dicken, P. 1998, *Global Shift: The Internationalization of Economic Activity*, Chapman, 3rd edn, London.

Dingle, T. 1988, *Aboriginal Economy: Patterns of Experience*, McPhee Gribble, Melbourne.

Drummond, I.M. 1964, *Imperial Economic Policy, 1917–1939: Studies in Expansion and Protection*, Allen & Unwin, London.

— 1981, *The Floating Pound and the Sterling Area, 1931–39*, Cambridge University Press, Cambridge.

— 1987, *The Gold Standard and the International Monetary System 1900–1939*, Macmillan, Basingstoke.

Dunsdorfs, E. 1956, *The Australian Wheat Growing Industry, 1788–1948*, Melbourne University Press, Melbourne.

Dyster, B. & Meredith, D. 1990, *Australia in the International Economy in the Twentieth Century*, Cambridge University Press, Cambridge.

Eastwood, J.J. & Smith F.B. (eds) 1964, *Historical Studies, Australia and New Zealand: Selected Articles*, Melbourne University Press, Melbourne.

Economic Planning Advisory Commission 1995, *Globalisation: Issues for Australia, Commission Paper No. 5*, Australian Government Publishing Service, Canberra.

— 1995, *Tariff reform and economic growth*, Commission Paper No. 10, Australian Government Publishing Service, Canberra.

*The Economist* 1979, 'The OPEC Decade', 29 Dec., London, pp. 39–60.

Edelstein, M. 1982, *Overseas Investment in the Age of High Imperialism, the United Kingdom, 1850–1914*, Columbia, New York.

Edwards, J. 1996, *Keating: The Inside Story*, Viking, Melbourne.

Eichengreen, B. 1992, *Golden Fetters: the Gold Standard and the Great Depression 1919–1939*, Oxford University Press, New York.

— 1996, *Globalizing Capital: A History of the International Monetary System*, Princeton University Press, Princeton.

Encarnation, D. 1992, *Rivals Beyond Trade: America Versus Japan in Global Competition*, Cornell University Press, Ithica NY.

Fagan, R. & Webber, M. 1994, *Global Restructuring: The Australian Experience*, Oxford University Press, Melbourne.

Falkus, M.E. 1971, 'United States Economic Policy and the "Dollar Gap" of the 1920s', *Economic History Review*, 2nd ser., 34, pp. 599–623.

Fitzgerald, R. 1994, *Red Ted; the Life of E.G. Theodore*, University of Queensland Press, Brisbane.

Fitzgerald, T.M. 1974, *The Contribution of the Mineral Industry to Australian Welfare*, Australian Government Publishing Service, Canberra.

Fitzgerald, V.W. 1993, *National Saving: A Report to the Treasurer*, Australian Government Publishing Service, Canberra.

Fitzpatrick, B. & Wheelwright, E.L. 1965, *The Highest Bidder: A Citizen's Guide to Foreign Investment in Australia*, Landsdowne Press, Melbourne.

Foreman Peck, J. 1983, *A History of the World Economy: International Economic Relations Since 1850*, Wheatsheaf, Brighton.

Forster, C. 1964, *Industrial Development in Australia, 1920–1930*, Australian National University Press, Canberra.

— 1977, 'Federation and the Tariff', *Australian Economic History Review*, 17, pp. 95–116.

—— 1988, 'Unemployment and the Australian Economic Recovery of the 1930s', in R.G. Gregory & N.G. Butlin (eds), *Recovery from the Depression: Australia and the World Economy in the 1930s*, Cambridge University Press, Melbourne.

—— 1989, 'The Economy, Wages and the Establishment of Arbitration', in S. Macintyre & R. Mitchell (eds), *Foundations of Arbitration: The Origins and Effects of State Compulsory Arbitration, 1890–1914*, Oxford University Press, Melbourne, pp. 203–24.

Forsyth, P. (ed.) 1992, *Microeconomic Reform in Australia*, Allen & Unwin, Sydney.

Foster, W. & Baker, L. 1991, *Immigration and the Australian Economy*, Australian Government Publishing Service, Canberra.

Fox, C. 1991, *Working Australia*, Allen & Unwin, Sydney.

Frances, R. 1993, *The Politics of Work; Gender and Labour in Victoria, 1880–1939*, Cambridge University Press, Melbourne.

Frost, L. 1990, *Australian Cities in Comparative View*, McPhee Gribble, Melbourne.

Fry, K. 1985, 'Soldier Settlement and the Australian Agrarian Myth after the First World War', *Labour History*, 48, pp. 29–43.

Gammage, B. 1990, 'Who gained, and who was meant to gain, from land selection in New South Wales', *Australian Historical Studies*, no. 94, April, pp. 104–22.

Gardner, R.N. 1956, *Sterling–Dollar Diplomacy*, Clarendon Press, Oxford.

Garnaut, R. 1989, *Australia and the Northeast Asian Ascendancy*, Australian Government Publishing Service, Canberra.

Garnaut, R. & Drysdale, P. (eds) 1994, *Asia Pacific Regionalism*, Harper Educational, London.

Garton, S. 1996, *The Cost of War: Australians Return*, Oxford University Press, Melbourne.

Gelber, H.G. 1966, *Australia, Britain and the EEC, 1961 to 1963*, Oxford University Press, Melbourne, pp. 23–43.

George, S. 1990, *A Fate Worse than Debt*, Penguin, London.

Giblin, L.F. 1951, *The Growth of a Central Bank: The Development of the Commonwealth Bank of Australia, 1924–1945*, Melbourne University Press, Melbourne.

Gilbert, R.S. 1973, *The Australian Loan Council in Federal Fiscal Arrangements, 1890–1965*, Australian National University Press, Canberra.

Glezer, L. 1982, *Tariff Politics: Australian Policy-making 1960–1980*, Melbourne University Press, Melbourne.

—— 1988, 'Business and Commerce', in J. Jupp (ed.), *The Australian People: An Encyclopedia of the Nation, its People and their Origins*, Angus & Robertson, Sydney, pp. 860–4.

Glynn, S. 1975, *Government Policy and Agricultural Development: A Study of the Role of Government in the Development of the Western Australian Wheat Belt, 1900–1930*, University of Western Australia Press, Perth.

Goldstein, M. & Hawkins, J. 1998, *The Origin of the Asian Financial Turmoil*, Research Discussion Paper 9805, Reserve Bank of Australia, Sydney, May.

Gollan, R. 1968, *The Commonwealth Bank of Australia: Origins and Early History*, Australian National University Press, Canberra.

Goodall, H. 1996, *Invasion to Embassy: Land in Aboriginal Politics in New South Wales, 1770–1972*, Allen & Unwin, Sydney.

— 1997, *Bringing Them Home: Report of the National Inquiry into the Separation of Aboriginal and Torres Strait Islander Children from their Families*, Human Rights and Equal Opportunity Commission, Sydney.

Grace, D. & Cohen, S. 1995, *Business Ethics*, Oxford University Press, Melbourne.

Graham, M. 1995, *A.B. Piddington: The Last Radical Liberal*, UNSW Press, Sydney.

Graves, A. 1988, 'Crisis and Change in the Australian Sugar Industry, 1914–1939', in B. Albert & A. Graves (eds), *The World Sugar Economy in War and Depression, 1914–40*, Routledge, Sydney.

— 1993, *Cane and Labour: The Political Economy of the Queensland Sugar Industry*, Edinburgh University Press, Edinburgh.

Great Britain, Department of Trade and Industry 1984, *British Business*, 2, March, p. 423.

Gregory, R.G. & Butlin, N.G. 1988, *Recovery from the Depression: Australia and the World Economy in the 1930s*, Cambridge University Press, Cambridge.

Gregory, R.G., Ho, V. & McDermott, L. 1988, 'Sharing the Burden: The Australian Labour Market during the 1930s', in R.G. Gregory & N.G. Butlin (eds), *Recovery from the Depression: Australia and the World Economy in the 1930s*, Cambridge University Press, Melbourne.

Gregory, R.G. & Pincus, J.J. 1982, 'Industry Assistance', in L.R. Webb & R.H. Allen (eds), *Industrial Economics: Australian Studies*, Allen & Unwin, Sydney.

Griesgraber, J. M. & Gunter, B.G. (eds) 1996, *The World's Monetary System: Toward Stability and Sustainability in the Twenty-first Century*, Pluto Press, London.

Groenwegen, P.D. 1983, 'The Political Economy of Federalism, 1901–1981', in B.W. Head (ed.), *State and Economy in Australia*, Oxford University Press, Melbourne.

Groenewegen, P. & McFarlane, B. 1990, *A History of Australian Economic Thought*, Routledge, London.

Grosser, A. 1980, *The Western Alliance: European–American Relations since 1945*, Macmillan, London.

Haig-Muir, M. & Hay, R. 1996, 'The Economy at War', in J. Beaumont (ed.), *Australian War, 1939–45*, Allen & Unwin, Sydney.

Hall, A.R. 1963, *The London Capital Market and Australia, 1870–1914*, Australian National University Press, Canberra.

Hancock, W.K. 1940, *Survey of British Commonwealth Affairs: Problems of Economic Policy, 1918–1939*, part I, vol. II, Oxford University Press, London.

Havinden, M. & Meredith, D. 1993, *Colonialism and Development: Britain and its Tropical Colonies*, Routledge, London.

Head, B. & Patience, A. (eds) 1989, *From Fraser to Hawke*, Longman Cheshire, Melbourne.

Heathcote, R.L. 1965, *Back of Bourke: A Study in Land Appraisal and Settlement in Semi-arid Australia*, Melbourne University Press, Melbourne.

Hilmer, F. 1985, *When the Luck Runs Out*, Harper & Row, Sydney.

Hirst, P. & Thompson, G. 1996, *Globalization in Question: the International Economy and the Possibilities of Governance*, Blackwell, Oxford.

Hoffman, R.J.S. 1933, *Great Britain and the German Trade Rivalry, 1875–1914*, University of Pennsylvania Press, Philadelphia, reprinted in New York by Russell & Russell in 1964.

Hogan, M.J. 1987, *The Marshall Plan: America, Britain and the Reconstruction of Western Europe 1947–52*, Cambridge University Press, Cambridge.

Holstein, W.J. 1990, *The Japanese Power Game: What it Means for America*, Macmillan, New York.

Hudson, P. 1992, *The Industrial Revolution*, Arnold, London.

Hughes, B. 1980, *Exit Full Employment: Economic Policy in the Stone Age*, Angus & Robertson, Sydney.

Hughes, H. 1964, *The Australian Iron and Steel Industry, 1848–1962*, Melbourne University Press, Melbourne.

Hugo, G. 1986, *Australia's Changing Population: Trends and Implications*, Oxford University Press, Melbourne.

Hunter, A. (ed.) 1963, *The Economics of Australian Industry: Studies in Environment and Structure*, Melbourne University Press, Melbourne.

Indecs Economics 1982–90, *State of Play 2, 3, 4, 5 and 6*, Allen & Unwin, Sydney.

Industries Assistance Commission (IAC) *Annual Reports*, various years, Australian Government Publishing Service, Canberra.

—— 1987, *Assistance to Manufacturing Industries*, Australian Government Publishing Service, Canberra.

Industry Commission 1997, *Assessing Australia's Productivity Performance*, Research Paper, Australian Government Publishing Service, Canberra.

Inkster, I. 1991, *The Clever City: Japan, Australia and the Multifunction Polis*, Sydney University Press, Sydney.

International Labour Office (ILO) 1946, *Yearbook of Labour Statistics 1945–46*, Geneva.

International Monetary Fund (IMF), *Yearbook of International Financial Statistics*, Washington DC.

Ito, M. 1990, *The World Economic Crisis and Japanese Capitalism*, St Martin's Press, New York.

Ito, T. & Krueger, A.O. (eds) 1996, *Financial Deregulation and Integration in East Asia*, Chicago University Press, Chicago.

Jeans, D.N. 1972, *An Historical Geography of New South Wales to 1901*, Reed Educational, Sydney.

Johnson, C. 1982, *MITI and the Japanese Miracle: the Growth of Industrial Policy 1925–1975*, University of California Press, Stanford.

Jones, C.A. 1987, *International Business in the Nineteenth Century: The Rise and Fall of a Cosmopolitan Bourgeoisie*, Wheetsheaf Books, Brighton.

Jordens, A.-M. 1995, *Redefining Australians: Immigration, Citizenship and National Identity*, Hale and Iremonger, Sydney.

Jupp, J. (ed.) 1988, *The Australian People: An Encyclopedia of the Nation, its People and their Origins*, Angus & Robertson, Sydney.

—— 1991, *Immigration*, Sydney University Press, Sydney.

Jupp, J. & Kabala, M. (eds) 1993, *The Politics of Australian Immigration*, Bureau of Immigration Research, Australian Government Publishing Service, Canberra.

Kapstein, E.B. 1994, *Governing the Global Economy: International Finance and the State*, Harvard University Press, Cambridge, Massachusetts.

Keating, M. 1973, *The Australian Workforce, 1910–11 to 1960–61*, Australian National University, Canberra.

Kelly, P. 1992, *The End of Certainty: the Story of the 1980s*, Allen & Unwin, Sydney.

Kemp, T. 1978, *Historical Patterns of Industrialization*, Longman, London.

Kennedy, M.J. 1992, *Hauling the Loads: A History of Australian Working Horses and Bullocks*, Melbourne University Press, Melbourne.

Kenwood, A.G. 1995, *Australian Economic Institutions since Federation: an Introduction*, Oxford University Press, Melbourne.

Kenwood, A.G. & Lougheed, A.L. 1983, *The Growth of the International Economy 1820–1980*, Allen & Unwin, London.

Kiernan, V.G. 1969, *The Lords of Human Kind: Black Man, Yellow Man and White Man in the Age of Empire*, Little Brown, Boston.

Kindleberger, C.P. 1973, *The World in Depression, 1929–1939*, University of California Press, Berkeley.

— 1984, *A Financial History of Western Europe*, Allen & Unwin, London.

— 1985, *Keynesianism versus Monetarism, and other Essays in Financial History*, Allen & Unwin, London.

King, S. & Lloyd, P. (eds) 1993, *Economic Rationalism: Dead End or Way Forward?*, Allen & Unwin, Sydney.

Knibbs, G.W. 1918, *The Private Wealth of Australia and its Growth as Ascertained by Various Methods*, Commonwealth Bureau of Census and Statistics, Melbourne.

Krugman, P. 1994, 'The myth of Asia's miracle', *Foreign Affairs*, 73 (6), pp. 62–78.

— 1998, 'Asia: what went wrong?', *Fortune*, 2 March, p. 21.

Kunz, E.F. 1988, 'Post-war Non-British Immigration', in J. Jupp (ed.), *The Australian People: An Encyclopedia of the Nation, its People and their Origins*, Angus & Robertson, Sydney.

La Nauze, J.A. 1972, *The Making of the Australian Constitution*, Melbourne University Press, Melbourne.

Landes, D.S. 1969, *The Unbound Prometheus: Technological Change and Industrial Development in Western Europe from 1750 to the Present*, Cambridge University Press, Cambridge.

League of Nations 1930, *Review of World Trade 1929*, Geneva.

— 1931, *The Course and Phases of the World Economic Depression*, Geneva.

— 1936, *Review of World Trade 1935*, Geneva.

— 1941, *Europe's Trade*, Geneva.

— 1942, *The Network of World Trade*, pp. 84–7, Geneva.

— 1944, *International Currency Experience: Lessons of the Inter-war Period*, Geneva.

— 1945a, *Economic Stability in the Post-war World: the Conditions of Prosperity after the Transition from War to Peace. Report of the Delegation on Economic Depression, Pt. II*, Geneva.

— 1945b, *Industrialisation and Foreign Trade*, League of Nations.

— 1946, *Raw Materials: Problems and Policies*, Geneva.

Lee, S.P. & Passell, P. 1979, *A New Economic View of American History*, Norton, New York.

Lever-Tracy, C. & Quinlan, M. 1988, *A Divided Working Class: Ethnic Segmentation and Industrial Conflict in Australia*, Routledge, London.

Lewis, A.W. 1949, *Economic Survey 1919–1939*, Allen & Unwin, London.

Lewis, C. 1938, *America's Stake in International Investment*, Arno Press, New York.

Lewis, G. 1973, *A History of the Ports of Queensland: A Study in Economic Nationalism*, University of Queensland Press, Brisbane.

Lewis, G., Morkel, A. & Hubbard, G. (eds) 1993, *Australian Strategic Management: Concepts, Context and Cases*, Prentice Hall Australia, Sydney.

Lewis, W.A. 1978, *Growth and Fluctuations, 1870–1913*, Allen & Unwin, Boston.

Lincoln, E.J. 1990, *Japan's Unequal Trade,* The Brookings Institute, Washington DC.

Lloyd, T.O. 1979, *Empire to Welfare State*, Oxford University Press, London.

Loveday, P. 1982, *Promoting Industry: Recent Australian Political Experience*, University of Queensland Press, St Lucia.

Lowndes, A.G. (ed.) 1956, *South Pacific Enterprise: the Colonial Sugar Refining Company Limited*, Angus & Robertson, Sydney.

Luard, E. 1983, *The Management of the World Economy*, Macmillan, London.

Macintyre, S. 1983, 'Labour, Capital and Arbitration, 1890–1979', in B.W. Head (ed.), *State and Economy in Australia*, Oxford University Press, Melbourne.

—— 1986, *The Oxford History of Australia, vol. 4, 1901–1942, The Succeeding Age*, Oxford University Press, Melbourne.

Macintyre, S. & Mitchell, R. (eds) 1989, *Foundations of Arbitration: The Origins and Effects of State Compulsory Arbitration, 1890–1914*, Oxford University Press, Melbourne.

Mackinolty, J. (ed.) 1981, *The Wasted Years? Australia's Great Depression*, Allen & Unwin, Sydney.

Madden, J.T., Nadler, M. & Sauvain, H.C. 1937, *America's Experience as a Creditor Nation*, Prentice Hall, New York.

Maddison, A. 1982, *Phases of Capitalist Development*, Oxford University Press, Oxford.

—— 1991, *Dynamic Forces in Capitalist Development, a Long Run Comparative View*, Oxford University Press, Oxford.

Maddock, R. & McLean, I. (eds) 1987, *The Australian Economy in the Long Run*, Cambridge University Press, Cambridge.

Mahony, G. (ed.) 1993, *The Australian Economy under Labor*, Allen & Unwin, Sydney.

Mandle, W.F. 1978, *Going it Alone: Australia's National Identity in the Twentieth Century*, Penguin, Melbourne.

Mansfield, B. 1965, *Australian Democrat: The Career of Edward William O'Sullivan, 1846–1910*, Sydney University Press, Sydney.

Markus, A. 1979, *Fear and Hatred: Purifying Australia and California, 1850–1901*, Hale & Iremonger, Sydney.

Martin, A.W. (ed.) 1969, *Essays in Australian Federation*, Melbourne University Press, Melbourne.

Martin, H.-P. 1997, *The Global Trap: Globalization and the Assault on Prosperity and Democracy*, Pluto Press, London.

Maxcy, G. 1963, 'The Motor Industry', in A. Hunter (ed.), *The Economics of Australian Industry: Studies in Environment and Sructure*, Melbourne University Press, Melbourne.

McAllister, I. & Kelley, J. 1984, '"Immigrants" Earnings, Status and Politics', in J. Jupp (ed.), *Ethnic Politics in Australia*, Allen & Unwin, pp. 53–68.

McEvedy, C. & Jones, R. 1978, *Atlas of World Population History*, Penguin, London.

McKern R.B. 1976, *Multinational Enterprise and Natural Resources*, McGraw Hill, Sydney, pp. 36–47.

McKernan, M. 1980, *The Australian People and the Great War*, Nelson, Melbourne.

McKinsey & Co. 1993, *Australia's High Value-added Manufacturing Exporters*, Australian Manufacturing Council, Melbourne.

McLean, I. 1989, 'Growth in a Small Open Economy: an Historical View', in B. Chapman (ed.), *Australian Economic Growth*, Macmillan, Melbourne.

Meinig, D.W. 1970, *On the Margins of the Good Earth: the South Australian Wheat Frontier, 1869–1884*, Rigby, Adelaide.

Meredith, D. 1987, 'Imperial Images: the Empire Marketing Board, 1926–1932', *History Today*, 37, pp. 30–6.

Mills, R.C. & Walker, E.R. 1935, *Money*, Angus & Robertson, Sydney (13th edn 1952).

Millward, A.S. 1984, *The Reconstruction of Western Europe, 1945–1951*, Methuen, London.

Millward, A.S. & Saul, S.B. 1977, *The Development of the Economies of Continental Europe 1850–1914*, Allen & Unwin, London.

Mitchell, B.W. 1992, *International Historical Statistics 1750–1988*, 3 vols, Macmillan, Basingstoke.

Mitchell, T.J. 1962, 'J.W. Wainwright: the Industrialisation of South Australia, 1935–1940', *Australian Journal of Politics and History*, VIII, pp. 27–40.

Moore, A. 1989, *The Secret Army and the Premier: Conservative Paramilitary Organisations in New South Wales, 1930–1932*, UNSW Press, Sydney.

Morgan, A. 1992, *Admission Impossible*, Film Australia, Lindfield, NSW.

Moulton, H.G. & Pasvolsky, L. 1932, *War Debts and World Prosperity*, The Brookings Institute, Washington.

Muir, L. 1987, 'Public Spending and Private Property: The Illawarra Line Cabal', in M. Kelly (ed.), *Sydney: City of Suburbs*, Sydney University Press, Sydney, pp. 30–52.

Murphy, R.T. 1996, *The Real Price of Japanese Money*, Weidenfeld & Nicolson, London.

Nairn, N.B. 1986, *The Big Fella: Jack Lang and the Australian Labor Party, 1891–1949*, Melbourne University Press, Melbourne.

National Export Marketing Strategy Panel 1985, *Lifting Australia's Performance as an Exporter of Manufactures and Services*, Australian Government Publishing Service, Canberra.

Nester, W.R. 1990, *Japan's Growing Power over East Asia and the World Economy*, Macmillan, Basingstoke.

Nicholas, S. (ed.) 1988, *Convict Workers*, Cambridge University Press, Melbourne.

Nieuwenhuysen, J.P. & Drake P.J. (eds) 1977, *Australian Economic Policy*, Melbourne University Press, Melbourne.

Norton, W.E. 1982, *The Deterioration in Economic Performance: A Study of the 1970s with Particular Reference to Australia*, Reserve Bank of Australia, Occasional Paper No. 9, Sydney.

Nurkse, R. 1954, 'International Investment Today in the Light of Nineteenth Century Experience', *The Economic Journal*, XLI, pp. 744–58.

OECD, 1980, 'The Impact of Oil in the World Economy', *Economic Outlook*, 27, Paris, pp. 114–31.

—— 1981, *International Investment and Multinational Enterprises*, Paris.

—— 1990, *Economic Outlook No. 48*, Paris.

—— 1997a, *Economic Outlook No. 62*, Paris.

—— 1997b, *Economic Survey – Australia 1996–97*, Paris.

—— 1998, *Economic Outlook No. 64*, Paris.

Olds, M. (ed.) 1993, *Australia Through Time*, Random House, Sydney.

Oliver, B. 1995, *War and Peace in Western Australia: The Social and Political Impact of the Great War, 1914–1926*, University of Western Australia Press, Perth.

Ostrow, R. 1987, *The New Boy Network: Taking Over Corporate Australia*, Heinemann, Melbourne.

Oxley, D. 1996, *Convict Maids*, Cambridge University Press, Melbourne.

Pagan, A. 1987, 'The End of the Long Boom', in R. Maddock & I. McLean (eds), *The Australian Economy in the Long Run*, Cambridge University Press, Cambridge.

Page, E. 1963, *Truant Surgeon: The Inside Story of Forty Years of Australian Political Life*, Angus & Robertson, Sydney.

Palfreeman, A.C. 1967, *The Administration of the White Australia Policy*, Melbourne University Press, Melbourne.

Patience, A. & Head, B. (eds) 1979, *From Whitlam to Fraser: Reform and Reaction in Australian Politics*, Oxford University Press, Melbourne.

Patterson, G.D. 1968, *The Tariff in the Australian Colonies, 1856–1900*, Cheshire, Melbourne.

Perkins, J.O.N. 1962, *Britain and Australia: Economic Relationships in the 1950s*, Melbourne University Press, Melbourne.

Pinkstone, B. 1992, *Global Connections: A History of Exports and the Australian Economy*, Australian Government Publishing Service, Canberra.

Polk, J. 1956, *Sterling: its Meaning in World Finance*, Harper, New York, pp. 71–102.

Pollard, S. 1970, *The Gold Standard and Employment Policies Between the Wars*, Methuen, London.

—— 1981, *The Integration of European Economies Since 1815*, Allen & Unwin, London.

Pope, D. 1987, 'Private Finance', in W. Vamplew (ed.), *Australians: Historical Statistics*, Fairfax, Syme & Weldon Associates, Sydney

—— 1994, 'Bank Deregulation in Historical Perspective', in M.R. Johnson, P. Kriesler & A.D. Owen (eds), *Issues in Australian Economics*, Allen & Unwin, Sydney.

Pope, D. & Alston, L.J. 1989, *Australia's Greatest Asset: Human Resources in the Nineteenth and Twentieth Centuries*, Federation Press, Sydney.

Pope, D. & Withers, G.A. 1992, *Do Migrants Rob Jobs? Lessons from Australian History, 1861–1991*, Department of Economics, La Trobe University.

Porter, B. 1975, *The Lion's Share: A Short History of British Imperialism 1850–1970*, Longman, London, Chapter 3.

Powell, J.M. 1981, 'The Debt of Honour: Soldier Settlement in the Dominions, 1915–1940', *Journal of Australian Studies*, 8, June, pp. 64–87.

—— 1988, *An Historical Geography of Modern Australia: The Restive Fringe*, Cambridge University Press, Cambridge.

— 1989, *Watering the Garden State: Water, Land and Community in Victoria, 1834–1988*, Allen & Unwin, Sydney, pp. 91–167.

Prebisch, R. 1981, 'Capitalism: the Second Crisis', *Third World Quarterly*, 3, pp. 433–40.

Price, C.A. 1974, *The Great White Walls are Built: Restrictive Immigration to North America and Australasia, 1836–1888*, Australian National University Press, Canberra.

Productivity Commission 1996, *Stocktake of Progress in Economic Reform*, Industry Commission, Canberra.

— 1998, *Trade & Assistance Review, 1997–98*, AusInfo, Canberra.

Pusey, M. 1991, *Economic Rationalism in Canberra*, Cambridge University Press, Cambridge.

Quiggin, J. 1996, *Great Expectations: Microeconomic Reform and Australia*, Allen & Unwin, Sydney.

Raby, G.W. 1996, *Making Rural Australia: An Economic History of Technical and Institutional Creativity, 1788–1860*, Oxford University Press, Melbourne.

Radi, R. & Spearritt, P. (eds) 1977, *Jack Lang*, Hale and Iremonger.

Rattigan, A. 1986, *Industry Assistance: the Inside Story*, Melbourne University Press, Melbourne.

Reitsma, A.J. 1960, *Trade Protection in Australia*, University of Queensland Press, Brisbane.

Reserve Bank of Australia (RBA) 1986, *Australian Economic Statistics, 1949–50 to 1984–85, Vol. 1*, Sydney.

— 1991, *Australian Economic Statistics 1949–50 to 1989–90*, Sydney.

— 1994, *International Integration of the Australian Economy: Proceedings of a Conference*, Sydney.

— 1996, *Australian Economic Statistics 1949–50 to 1994–95*, Sydney.

— 1998, *Bulletin*, Sydney, various months.

Reynolds, H. 1987, *The Law of the Land*, Penguin, Melbourne.

— 1990, *With the White People*, Penguin, Melbourne.

Richardson, P. 1987, 'The Origins and Development of the Collins House Group, 1915–1951', *Australian Economic History Review*, 27, pp. 3–29.

Rivett, K. (ed.) 1975, *Australia and the Non-White Migrant*, Melbourne University Press, Melbourne.

Rix, A. 1986, *Coming to Terms: the Politics of Australia's Trade with Japan 1945–1957*, Allen & Unwin, Sydney.

Roberts, J. 1995, *$1000 Billion a Day: Inside the Foreign Exchange Markets*, Harper-Collins, London.

Robinson, W.S. 1967, *If I Remember Rightly: The Memoirs of W.S. Robinson*, Cheshire, Melbourne.

Robson, L.L. 1990, *A History of Tasmania*, vol. II, Oxford University Press, Melbourne.

Roe, J. 1987, 'Chivalry and Social Policy in the Antipodes', *Historical Studies*, 88, April, pp. 395–410.

Roe, M. 1995, *Australia, Britain and Migration, 1915–1940: A Study of Desperate Hopes*, Cambridge University Press, Cambridge.

Rosenberg, N. & Birdzell, L.E. 1986, *How the West Grew Rich: The Economic Transformation of the Industrial World*, Tauris, London.

Rowe, J.W.F. 1965, *Primary Commodities in International Trade*, Cambridge University Press, Cambridge.

Rutland, S.D. 1988, 'Jewish Refugee and Post-war Immigration', in J. Jupp (ed.), *The Australian People: An Encyclopedia of the Nation, its People and their Origins*, Angus & Robertson, Sydney, pp. 647–52.

Sahlins, M. 1974, *Stone Age Economics*, Tavistock, London.

Saint-Etienne, C. 1984, *The Great Depression 1929–1938: Lessons for the 1980s*, Hoover Institution Press, Stanford, California.

Salter, A. 1951, *Foreign Investment*, Princeton University Press, Princeton, pp. 2–10.

Sampson, A. 1976, *The Seven Sisters: the Great Oil Companies and the World they Made*, Coronet, London.

Saul, S.B. 1954–55, 'Britain and World Trade, 1870–1914', *Economic History Review*, 2nd ser., VII, pp. 46–66.

— 1960, *Studies in British Overseas Trade*, Liverpool University Press, Liverpool.

Scammell, W.M. 1965, 'The working of the Gold Standard', *Yorkshire Bulletin of Economic and Social Research*, 17, pp. 32–45.

— 1975, *International Monetary Policy: Bretton Woods and After*, Macmillan, London.

— 1983, *The International Economy since 1945*, Macmillan, London.

Schedvin, B. 1971, 'E.G. Theodore and the London pastoral lobby', *Politics*, VI, pp. 26–41.

Schedvin, C.B. 1970, *Australia and the Great Depression: A Study of Economic Development and Policy in the 1920s and 1930s*, Sydney University Press, Sydney.

— 1992, *In Reserve: central banking in Australia 1945–1975*, Allen & Unwin, Sydney.

Schmitz, C. J. 1993, *The Growth of Big Business in the United States and Western Europe 1850–1939*, Cambridge University Press, Cambridge.

Serle, G. 1963, *The Golden Age*, Melbourne University Press, Melbourne.

Sexton, M. & Adamovich, A. 1981, *The Regulation of Foreign Investment in Australia*, CCH, Sydney.

Shann, E.O.G. & Copland, D.B. (eds) 1931a, *The Crisis in Australian Finance, 1929–1931: Documents on Budgetary and Economic Policy*, Angus & Robertson, Sydney.

— 1931b, *The Battle of the Plans: Documents Relating to the Premiers' Conference, May 25th to June 11th, 1931*, Angus and Robertson, Sydney.

Shergold, P. 1987, 'Prices and Consumption', in W. Vamplew (ed), *Australians: Historical Statistics*, Fairfax, Syme & Weldon Associates, Sydney.

Shergold, P.R. & Milne, F. (eds) 1984, *The Great Immigration Debate*, Federation of Ethnic Communities Councils of Australia, Sydney.

Sherington, G. 1980, *Australia's Immigrants, 1788–1978*, Allan & Unwin, Sydney.

Shlomowitz, R. 1979, 'The Search for Institutional Equilibrium in Queensland's sugar industry, 1884–1913', *Australian Economic History Review*, 19, pp. 91–122.

Simon, M. 1968, 'The pattern of new British portfolio foreign investment, 1865–1914', in A.R. Hall (ed.), *The Export of Capital from Britain, 1870–1914*, Methuen, London.

Sinclair, K. 1988, 'New Zealand', in J. Eddy & D. Schreuder (eds), *The Rise of Colonial Nationalism*, Allen & Unwin, Sydney, pp. 111–30.

Sinclair, W.A. 1970, 'Capital Formation', in C. Forster (ed.), *Australian Economic Development in the Twentieth Century*, Allen & Unwin, London.

Skidelsky, R. (ed.) 1977, *The End of the Keynesian Era: Essays on the Disintegration of Keynesian Political Economy*, Macmillan, London.

Skully, M.T. 1975, 'Australia's Immigration Programme: An Evaluation of its Effectiveness', *International Migration*, 15, pp. 21–34.

Smith, B. 1971, 'Immigration Policy: A Survey of the Issues', *The Australian Quarterly*, 43, pp. 8–15.

Smyth, P. 1994, *Australian Social Policy: The Keynesian Chapter*, UNSW Press, Sydney.

Snape, R.H. 1973, *International Trade and the Australian Economy*, 2nd edn, Longman Cheshire, Melbourne.

Snooks, G.D. 1988, 'Government Unemployment Relief in the 1930s: Aid or Hindrance to Recovery?', in R.G. Gregory & N.G. Butlin (eds), *Recovery from the Depression: Australia and the World Economy in the 1930s*, Cambridge University Press, Melbourne.

Solomon, D. 1992, *The Political Impact of the High Court*, Allen & Unwin, Sydney.

Sorros, G. 1998, *The Crisis of Global Capitalism*, Little, Brown & Co., New York.

Souter, G. 1988, *Acts of Parliament*, Melbourne University Press, Melbourne.

Spearritt, P. 1978, *Sydney Since the Twenties*, Hale & Iremonger, Sydney.

Stephenson, M.A. & Ratnapala, S. (eds) 1993, *Mabo: A Judicial Revolution*, University of Queensland Press, Brisbane.

Stewart, R.G. (ed.) 1994, *Government and Business Relations in Australia*, Allen & Unwin, Sydney.

Storer, D. & Hargreaves, K. 1976, 'Migrant Women in Industry', in S. Staats (ed.), *Social Policy and Problems of the Work Force*, ACTU Social Welfare Unit, Vol. 1, Melbourne, pp. 39–103.

Stretton, H. 1974, *Housing and Government*, Australian Broadcasting Commission, Sydney.

Swan, P.L. 1968, 'The Australian Balance of Payments and Capital Imports, 1914–15 to 1923–24', *Australian Economic Papers*, 7, pp. 91–103.

Sykes, T. 1994, *The Bold Riders: Behind Australia's Corporate Collapses*, Allen & Unwin, Sydney.

Thomas, B. 1967, 'The Historical Record of International Capital Movements to 1913', in J.H. Alder (ed.), *Capital Movements and Economic Development*, St. Martin's Press, London, pp. 3–32.

Thomas, M. 1988, 'Manufacturing and Economic Recovery in Australia, 1932–37', in R.G. Gregory & N.G. Butlin (eds), *Recovery from the Depression: Australia and the World Economy in the 1930s*, Cambridge University Press, Melbourne.

—— 1995, 'A Substantial Australian Superiority? Anglo-Australian Comparisons of Consumption and Income in the Late Nineteenth Century', *Australian Economic History Review*, 35, no. 2, September, pp. 10–38.

Todd, J. 1994, *Milk for the Metropolis: A Century of Co-operative Milk Supply in New South Wales*, Hale & Iremonger, Sydney.

Tsokhas, K. 1986, *Beyond Dependence: Companies, Labour Processes and Australian Mining*, Oxford University Press, Melbourne.
— 1990, *Markets, Money and Empire: The Political Economy of the Australian Wool Industry*, Melbourne University Press, Melbourne.
Tsuru, S. 1993, *Japan's Capitalism: Creative Defeat and Beyond*, Cambridge University Press, Cambridge.
Tweedie, S.M. 1994, *Trading Partners: Australia and Asia 1790–1993*, UNSW Press, Sydney.
United Nations, *Demographic Yearbook*, annual publication, New York.
— *Yearbook of International Trade Statistics*, various years.
— *World Economic and Social Survey*, various years.
United States, Bureau of the Census 1960, *Historical Statistics of the United States: Colonial Times to 1957*, Washington DC.
United States, Bureau of Commerce 1947, *Statistical Abstract of the United States*, US Government Printer, Washington DC.
— Bureau of Foreign and Domestic Commerce 1943, *The United States in the World Economy*, Washington DC.
— Department of Commerce 1974, *Survey of Current Business*, Aug. (part II).
Vamplew, W. (ed) 1987, *Australians: Historical Statistics*, Fairfax, Syme & Weldon Associates, Sydney.
van Cleveland, H. & Brittain, W.H.B. 1976, *The Great Inflation: a Monetarist View*, National Planning Association, Washington DC.
van Der Wee, H. 1986, *Prosperity and Upheaval: The World Economy 1945–1980*, Pelican, London.
Viviani, N. 1984, *The Long Journey: Vietnamese Migration and Settlement in Australia*, Melbourne University Press, Melbourne.
Wachtel, H.M. 1990, *The Money Mandarins: The Making of a Supranational Economic Order*, Pluto Press, rev. edn, London.
Wanna, J. 1994, 'Can the State "Manage" the Macroeconomy?', in S. Bell & B. Head (eds), *State, Economy and Public Policy in Australia*, Oxford University Press, Melbourne.
Weber, A.F. 1965, *The Growth of Cities in the Nineteenth Century: A Study in Statistics* [1899], reprinted Ithaca, NY, Cornell University Press.
Weidenbaum, M.L. 1988, *Rendezvous with Reality: The American Economy After Reagan*, Basic Books, New York.
Wheelwright, E.L. 1963, 'Overseas Investment in Australia', in A. Hunter, *The Economics of Australian Industry: Studies in Environment and Structure*, Melbourne University Press, Melbourne.
White, C. 1992, *Mastering Risk: Environment, Markets and Politics in Australian Economic History*, Oxford University Press, Melbourne.
Whitlam, G. 1985, *The Whitlam Government 1972–1975*, Penguin, Melbourne.
Whitwell, G. 1986, *The Treasury Line*, Allen & Unwin, Sydney.
Whitwell, G. & Sydenham, D. 1991, *A Shared Harvest: The Australian Wheat Industry, 1939–1989*, Melbourne University Press, Melbourne.
Willcox, W.F. 1929, *International Migrations*, National Bureau of Economic Research, New York.

Williamson, J.G. & Hatton, T.J. (eds.) 1994, *Migration and the International Labour Market, 1850–1939*, Routledge, London.

Wilson, Sir R. 1997, *Bringing Them Home: Report of the National Inquiry into the Separation of Aboriginal and Torres Strait Islander Children from their Families*, Sydney, Human Rights and Equal Opportunity Commission.

Wiseman, J. 1998, *Global Nation?: Australia and the Politics of Globalisation*, Cambridge University Press, Melbourne.

Withers, G., Endres, T. & Perry, L. 1985, Australian Historical Statistics: Labour Statistics, *Source Paper in Economic History*, no. 7, Australian National University.

—— 1987, 'Labour', in W. Vamplew (ed.) *Australians: Historical Statistics*, Fairfax, Syme & Weldon Associates, Sydney.

Wood, C. 1988, *Boom and Bust: the Rise and Fall of the World's Financial Markets*, Sidgwick & Jackson, London.

Wooden, M., Holton, R., Hugo, G. & Sloan, J. 1990, *Australian Immigration: A Survey of the Issues*, Australian Government Publishing Service, Canberra.

Woodruff, W. 1966, *The Impact of Western Man: A Study of Europe's Role in the World Economy, 1750–1960*, Macmillan, London.

World Bank 1993, *The East Asian Miracle – Economic Growth and Public Policy*, Oxford University Press, Oxford.

—— 1984a, *World Development Report*, Oxford University Press, Washington DC, pp. 11–50.

—— 1984b, *World Debt Tables, First Supplement*, Washington DC.

Yarwood, A.T. 1964, *Asian Immigration to Australia: The Background to Exclusion 1896–1923*, Melbourne University Press, Melbourne.

—— 1989, *Walers: Australian Horses Abroad*, Melbourne University Press, Melbourne.

Yarwood, A.T. & Knowling, M.J. 1982, *Race Relations in Australia: A History*, Methuen, Sydney.

Yates, P. L. 1943, *Commodity Control: A Study of Primary Products*, Jonathan Cape, London.

# GLOSSARY OF ECONOMIC TERMS

**Aggregate demand**  Total expenditure in an economy on goods and services, including expenditure on investment in capital goods and stocks, plus exports of goods and services minus imports of goods and services.

**Aggregate income**  See national income.

**Baby boomer (baby boom)**  Person born during the decade or so following the end of World War II when the birth rate rose considerably. This baby boom occurred in most OECD countries.

**Balance of payments**  A record of the financial transactions of one country with all other countries and international institutions over a stated period. Receipts and payments arising from merchandise trade, trade in services, income from investments and transfers together make up the current account of the balance of payments. Capital transactions (foreign investment and investment by foreigners) are shown in the capital account of the balance of payments. If receipts and payments from foreigners exceed those made to foreigners the account is in 'surplus'; if the opposite is the case, it is in 'deficit'.

**Bilateral**  Between two parties. A bilateral trade agreement is one between two countries that confers rights and privileges not extended to other countries.

**Boom**  An economic boom is a period (short or long) during which an economy exhibits sustained growth at a relatively rapid rate in real terms (say 5–10 per cent of GDP per year). A price boom occurs when the price of a commodity increases rapidly; for example, the oil-price boom of 1971–74. A stock market boom refers to a period when share prices rise strongly. Similarly, a period when international trade and capital flows grow rapidly may be referred to as a world economic boom.

**Budget**  A government's revenue and expenditure regime. A balanced budget is one where government revenue matches expenditure; a budget surplus refers to a situation where revenue exceeds expenditure; and a budget deficit is where expenditure exceeds revenue.

**Capital**  One of the four factors of production; in general, capital is any asset from which income is generated. The asset may be physical (or 'fixed capital'; for example, machinery) or financial (that is, money), but it has to have been produced at some time in the past. In this sense 'land' and 'labour' are considered to be separate from 'capital'.

**Capital goods**   Goods that assist in the production of other goods as opposed to consumer goods that are desired for their own sake. Also known as 'producer goods'. Depending on the use to which they are put, particular articles might be capital or consumer goods: it is the use rather than the nature of the goods that differentiates capital goods from consumer goods.

**Capital widening**   Capital widening takes place when the stock of capital is increased in such a way as to leave the proportions of the factors of production unchanged; when the stock of capital increases relative to the other factors of production (for example, labour employed) capital deepening is said to have occurred.

**Cartel**   A monopoly organised by a group of firms to control prices and output in a particular market and thereby eliminate free competition. Member firms remain independent but a central selling/buying agency is established that fixes prices and allocates market shares. Nations can form cartels in certain circumstances, as when the major oil-exporting nations formed the Organisation of Oil Exporting Countries (OPEC) in 1960.

**Central bank**   A nation's bank, often state-owned, that controls the credit policy of the commercial banks by acting as a 'lender of last resort'; that is, being willing to lend to the banking system at all times – but on its own terms. This allows the central bank to influence interest rates and the nation's money supply. The central bank also performs the function of banker to the government.

**Commodity**   In a general sense primary products: unprocessed raw materials, foodstuffs and minerals.

**Common Market (EEC)**   France, West Germany, Italy, The Netherlands, Belgium and Luxembourg established the European Economic Community in 1957. Other European nations joined later; for example, the United Kingdom, Republic of Ireland and Denmark joined in 1973; Greece in 1981 and Spain and Portugal in 1986. The EEC is a customs union with a common external tariff and its aim is to reduce or eliminate obstacles to the free movement of labour, capital and trade in goods and services between its member states.

**Comparative advantage**   A concept in international trade where the costs of production in different countries are compared. It suggests that a country benefits most by concentrating its productive resources (land, labour and capital) in those goods in which its comparative advantage is greatest; that is, in those goods it can produce more cheaply than other countries. If a country cannot achieve this, it should specialise in goods where its comparative disadvantage is least. The 'law of comparative advantage' forms the theoretical basis for the argument in support of free trade between nations.

**Consumer durable**   A good that yields benefits over an extended period (that is, a number of years); for example, household appliances.

**Consumer goods**   Goods purchased for their own sake and not to be used for further production. A consumer good may be a consumer durable or an article immediately consumed.

**Consumer price index (CPI)**   An index of the retail prices of goods and services in an economy weighted to reflect expenditure patterns. The CPI is the most commonly used measure of retail price changes in Australia.

**Convertibility**   A convertible currency is one that is freely exchangeable for another currency or gold. See also, exchange control.

**CPI**   See consumer price index.

**Crash**   A sudden and large fall in prices. Any market can crash, for example, a 'stock market crash' or a 'property market crash'.

**Credit**   Goods and services supplied without immediate payment are said to be 'on credit'. Extending or advancing credit to a customer means supplying them with goods or services without immediate payment, but usually with some agreement as to when and how the payment will be made in the future. Banks 'create credit' by making loans to customers.

**Credit-rating**   The assessment of the likelihood of a borrower meeting their obligation to pay interest and repayments of a loan.

**Credit squeeze**   A credit restriction policy imposed by a nation's monetary authorities; in practice, interest rates for loans are raised and access to commercial bank loans reduced.

**Creditors**   Persons, firms or institutions (including government) to whom money is owed.

**Creditor nations**   Nations where the value of all foreign investments (foreign assets) owned by their residents exceed the value of all investments held in them by foreigners (foreign liabilities). It may also refer to a nations that are currently investing more in foreign countries than foreign countries are investing in them; that is, a countries that have a current account balance of payments surplus. Debtor nations are the exact opposite.

**Currency appreciation/depreciation**   Currency appreciation (depreciation) occurs when one currency becomes more (less) valuable in terms of another currency, a basket of foreign currencies or gold.

**Currency board**   A method by which the foreign exchange value of a country's currency is fixed ('pegged') to another currency or basket of currencies. For example, a country might decide to fix its exchange rate to the US dollar. This would mean that its exchange value would rise and fall against other currencies exactly as the dollar rose and fell.

**Currency bloc (zone)**   A group of nations that agree to maintain convertibility and fixed exchange rates between their currencies even though their currencies may not be fixed or freely convertible to non-bloc currencies.

**Currency depreciation**   Occurs when a currency loses exchange value in terms of other currencies or (before the 1970s) gold.

**Current account**   Of the balance of payments records a national economy's foreign transactions in terms of merchandise trade, services, income receipts and payments, and transfers.

**Current account surplus**   Where the value of payments, receipts and income to a national economy from abroad is greater than the value of payments, expenditure and income paid to all foreign countries. A current account deficit is the opposite situation.

**Debt**   See foreign debt.

**Debtors**   Persons, firms or institutions (including government) who owe money to a creditor.

**Debtor countries**   See creditor nation.

**Deflation**   A situation where prices are falling. A deflationary policy is one that is aimed at reducing the level of prices. In economic statistics, 'deflation' refers to the adjustment of values to eliminate the effect of price changes, as, for example, in calculating real GDP.

**Demand**   See aggregate demand.

**Depression**   A period of heavy unemployment and stagnation of economic activity. The total output of the economy contracts.

**Devaluation/revaluation**   A reduction (increase) in the official value of a currency in relation to other currencies or gold under fixed exchange rate regimes such as the gold standard and the Bretton Woods system. Under a floating exchange rate regime a currency is said to 'depreciate' or 'appreciate' when its foreign exchange value changes.

**Developing countries**   See less developed countries.

**Direct foreign investment**   Foreign investment (loans or purchases of shares) by a firm that already owns a certain proportion (for example, 10 per cent) of the foreign firm being invested in. It differs from indirect (or 'portfolio') foreign investment in that the firm making the investment has some degree of ownership of the firm which is the object of the investment. The degree of ownership that is regarded as crucial in this respect varies from country to country and over time. The firm being invested in may be a wholly owned subsidiary or branch of a foreign firm.

**Disinflation**   Where the rate of increase in prices is declining. Disinflationary policies are those aimed at a reduction in the rate of price inflation. See also deflation.

**Disposable income**   The income of a household remaining after payment of income tax and any other compulsory payments (for example, where national superannuation schemes operate).

**Distribution of income**   See income distribution.

**Domestic income**   See national income.

**Double-income household**   A household where there are two or more members receiving income from paid employment.

**E-commerce**   Electronic commerce: economic transactions that are made through the Internet.

**Economic development**   Growth in national income per head of population. Economic development is used in a general way to refer to structural changes occurring in an economy, typically a decline in the relative importance of agriculture and a rise in manufacturing industry and services.

**Economic growth**   Growth of national income or total output of a country. National income may be measured in money or real terms.

**Economies of scale**   Economies of scale are effected when the average cost of production falls as total output increases. The concept thus refers to the benefits to be gained by a larger scale of production.

**EEC**   See European Economic Community.

**Elasticity of demand/supply**   The degree of responsiveness of demand or supply to a change of price. Demand or supply is said to be elastic if a small change in price causes a large change in demand or inelastic if a large change in price calls forth only a small response in demand or supply. Elasticities may be measured by dividing the percentage change in quantity demanded or supplied by the percentage change in price.

**Entrepreneur** A person who organises factors of production (land, labour and capital) to produce goods and services. In doing so an entrepreneur undertakes risk and is rewarded with profit. In a modern business corporation the entrepreneur's function is split between the shareholders (who collectively carry the risk) and the board of directors (who manage the firm). Entrepreneurship is recognised by many economists as a fourth factor of production.

**Equilibrium** A condition where economic variables are in perfect balance. In equilibrium, economic forces have no tendency to change from the state they are in. In a country's balance of payments, equilibrium is reached when all receipts from foreigners equal all payments made to foreigners.

**Equity capital** The capital in a company or corporation owned by the shareholders, as opposed to loan capital, that is owed to creditors such as banks. Shareholders are theoretically regarded as the 'true owners' of a business since they bear the ultimate risk.

**ETMs** Elaborately transformed manufactures. These consist mainly of goods that are 'finished products' such as machinery and equipment.

**European Common Market** See Common Market.

**European Economic Community (EEC)** See Common Market.

**Exchange control** Regulations imposed by the government on resident individuals and firms to restrict their ability to remit funds abroad and to convert domestic currency into foreign currency. A currency that cannot be freely converted into a particular foreign currency because of exchange controls is said to be partly to wholly non-convertible to that foreign currency. For example, the United Kingdom's currency, sterling, was non-convertible to US dollars for a period after the World War II.

**Exchange rate** The price at which one currency may be exchanged for another.

**Export income** Total receipts from sale of exports.

**Export ratio** Value of exports (of merchandise only or of goods and services) as a proportion of GDP.

**Export surpluses** A situation where merchandise exports exceed merchandise imports in value over a given period of time.

**External balance** The current account balance of the balance of payments.

**External deficit** A current account deficit in the balance of payments; that is, where payments for goods and services to foreigners exceed receipts for goods and services from foreigners, including payments made and receipts received on account of foreign investment.

**Factors of production** Resources used in the process of production; four categories are usually recognised: land, labour, capital and entrepreneurship.

**Fiscal policy/fiscal management** One of the two chief economic tools of government (the other is monetary policy). Fiscal policy refers to the state of the government's budget: the level and nature of taxation, the level and nature of government expenditure, and the difference between these levels.

A relaxation or easing of fiscal policy involves lower taxation or greater expenditure, or both, and a move in the budget towards deficit. Tighter fiscal policy involves the opposite.

**Fixed capital**   Assets of a permanent nature such as buildings, plant, machinery and equipment.

**Fixed exchange rates**   Under the pre-1914 gold standard, exchange rates were fixed in the sense that each currency on the gold standard was freely convertible into a stated quantity of gold. Under the Bretton Woods system, 1944–71, exchange rates were fixed so that each country announced a par value for its currency in terms of US dollars (the only currency remaining on the gold standard). In practice, most currencies were not fully convertible to the US dollar until the late 1950s. The rules of the International Monetary Fund allowed for exchange rate fluctuations of up to 1 per cent on either side of the par value and, in certain circumstances, for par values to be changed (that is, a revaluation or a devaluation). Since 1971, various methods have been used by certain countries to fix the exchange value of their currency, often by tying it to another currency such as the US dollar (see also currency board).

**Floating exchange rates**   An exchange rate system in which rates are determined by market forces rather than by government control or intervention. If some degree of control or intervention by the government does occur it may be termed a 'managed float' or a 'dirty float'.

**Foreign debt**   The value of all liabilities owed by residents of a country to non-residents. If the value of assets owned abroad by residents of the country are deducted, the result is termed the net foreign debt.

**Foreign debt servicing**   The outflow of funds in the balance of payments arising from the payment of interest on borrowing from foreigners.

**Foreign exchange**   The system in which one currency is converted into another; the term may also be used as a synonym for 'foreign currency'.

**Foreign exchange market**   The market in which transactions involving the conversion of one currency to another takes place. Nowadays the various foreign exchange markets are linked electronically and operate on a global basis.

**Foreign income**   The value of total receipts from abroad.

**Foreign investment**   See international investment.

**Free trade**   Completely unrestricted international trade. A situation where a nation does not impose any import duties, quotas or export subsidies (and like measures) in its foreign trade. A group of countries that do not impose restrictions on trade with each other constitute a free trade area or bloc.

**Full employment**   See unemployment.

**GDP**   See gross domestic product.

**Gold and foreign exchange reserves**   The financial reserves of a central bank consisting of gold (coin or bullion), foreign currency and interest-bearing securities issued by a foreign government.

**Gold backing (of currency)**   Gold kept by a central bank as a guarantee of the value of the nation's currency. In most cases of gold-backed currencies there was a statutory requirement that the value of the gold retained for this purpose had to bear a fixed relationship to the value of the currency in circulation. A currency that was fully backed by gold was one where the value of currency in circulation was no greater than the value of gold reserves of the central bank.

**Gold-based currency** A nation's currency, which consists at least partly of gold coins the face value of which is determined by the weight of the gold content of the coin and the official price of gold. Gold-based currencies operated widely in the nineteenth century, in a limited way in the inter-war period and not at all after World War II.

**Gold exchange standard** A currency system in which part or all of the central bank's reserves are kept in a foreign currency that is convertible on demand to gold at a fixed official price. Holders of the nation's currency may exchange it for the foreign gold-standard currency, but not for gold itself.

**Gold standard** A currency system in which the currency is convertible on demand for a specified amount of gold. (For many countries on the gold standard in the nineteenth century, gold coins formed a part of the currency, but this was not an essential condition for being on the gold standard).

**Gold reserves** See gold and foreign exchange reserves.

**Gold stocks** See gold and foreign exchange reserves.

**Gross domestic product (GDP)** The value of all production of goods and services within a country excluding net income from abroad. Valuation may be at market prices or – by deducting indirect taxes and adding subsidies – at 'factor cost' (to be equivalent to the value of incomes paid to the factors of production).

**Gross national product (GNP)** Gross domestic product plus net income from abroad.

**Hedge fund** An investment fund that uses its members' money plus borrowed funds to speculate internationally in financial markets. They originated in Wall St in the 1950s, but became more prominent in the 1980s and 1990s following global financial deregulation. They have a reputation for secrecy and the ability to manipulate markets by the sheer size of their investments.

**Hot money** Short-terms funds that move rapidly between financial centres to seek high interest rates or profits from foreign exchange movements.

**Human capital** The stock of human capital of a nation consists of the number of people it contains and their attributes; for example, age, gender, skills, experience and health. Investment in human capital generally refers to expenditure on improving the educational attainments of the population together with improving their health and well-being.

**Hyperinflation** Price inflation of such a great extent that money loses all value and a new currency has to be issued.

**Import control** See import restrictions.

**Import duties** See tariffs.

**Import licence** See import restrictions.

**Import protection** A policy of using import restrictions to protect domestic producers from competition from imported goods and services.

**Import quotas**   See import restrictions.

**Import restrictions**   Measures taken by governments to limit imports. These include: import duties, quotas (that limit the physical quantity permitted to enter), import licences (whereby importers can only import if they have a licence to do so), restrictions on the access of importers to foreign exchange, direct prohibition, voluntary restraint by exporters, import deposits (whereby importers are obliged to deposit a proportion of the value of imports with the government) and temporary import surcharges.

**Import surplus**   A situation where the value of imports of merchandise exceeds the value of exports of merchandise.

**Income**   Money received in the form of wages, interest, rent, profit or transfers, by individuals, households, firms, government and, in aggregate, the nation.

**Income (balance of payments)**   See net income from abroad.

**Income account**   See net income.

**Income distribution**   The frequency distribution of incomes among a group; for example, the number of households classified according to levels of annual income.

**Income elasticity**   The degree of responsiveness of demand to a change in consumers' incomes. Demand is said to be income elastic if a small change in income causes a large change in demand and inelastic if a large change in income calls only a small response in demand. Elasticities may be measured by dividing the percentage change in quantity demanded by the percentage change in income.

**Income per head**   National income divided by the nation's total population.

**Income support**   See transfer payments.

**Income tax**   A tax imposed by the government on income. The tax may be levied at different rates for different levels of income.

**Index number**   A device for estimating the relative movement of a statistical variable (which might be price, value, output, and so on). Each year is compared to a standard or base year, the value of which is given as 100. Each subsequent (or previous) year's value is expressed as a percentage of the base year's value.

**Inflation**   A condition where there is a sustained increase in prices as a result of the volume of purchasing power persistently running ahead of the volume of output of goods and services available for purchase. As prices rise the value of money declines.

**Infrastructure**   Utilities and services such as roads, railways, water supply, power supply and telecommunications services. Social infrastructure includes education, health and housing.

**Interest**   The amount of money a borrower has to pay to a lender for the use of funds for a specified period of time.

**Interest rate**   The price of borrowing money determined by the supply of loanable funds and the demand to borrow in any particular market. The price is expressed as a proportion of the value of the loan.

**International capital flow**   See international investment.

**International currency**   A nation's currency that is used by foreign residents for the purposes of international trade and by foreign central banks (or government) for the purpose of reserves. The main examples are the pound sterling and the US dollar.

**International division of labour**   The specialisation of nations in various types of production, supposedly based on comparative advantage, and typically distinguishing 'primary producing' countries from 'industrial' countries.

**International investment**   The acquisition by residents (individuals or firms) or governments, or both, of one country of assets in a foreign country. Investment may be direct or portfolio. See also direct foreign investment.

**International liquidity**   The total amount of funds available for the finance of international trade, consisting of gold, international currencies and, since, 1968, Special Drawing Rights.

**International trade**   Exchange of goods and services between the residents of different countries; goods and services purchased from foreigners are imports; goods and services sold to foreigners are exports.

**Investment**   Real capital formation that will produce a stream of goods and services in the future. For example, a business invests when it builds factories, buys plant and machinery, or accumulates stocks of goods (inventories). A government invests when it builds such amenities as roads, hospitals or power stations. Households (including individuals) invest when they buy a newly built home (but not a second-hand one). Investment involves the sacrifice of current consumption.

**Invisible schedule**   See invisible trade.

**Invisible trade**   A term formerly used to describe international trade in services (for example, tourism, shipping, insurance and banking) together with payments/receipts of interest and dividends from foreign investment. That part of the balance of payments accounts that showed these transactions was known as the 'invisible schedule'.

**Labour**   All forms of human effort – except entrepreneurial – that contribute to the production of goods and services. Labour is one of the four factors of production.

**Labour force**   The number of people either gainfully employed or actively seeking paid employment.

**Labour productivity**   Value of output per unit input of labour.

**Land**   One of the four factors of production. Land includes all natural resources (including those in the sea, the atmosphere and outer space).

**Land of recent settlement**   A phrase formerly used to denote regions outside of Europe that were invaded and occupied by European settlers from the fifteenth century onwards.

**Land tax**   A tax imposed by the government on land. The tax may be at a 'flat rate' (so much per hectare) or be based on an assessment of the value of the land.

**Land tenure**   Form by which land is held; for example, land ownership or land tenancy.

**Lender of last resort**   See central bank.

**Less developed countries**   Also known as 'developing countries', these are nations that have not developed a significant industrial economy and where national income per head is relatively low.

**Merchandise surplus**   Where the value of exports of merchandise exceed the value of imports of merchandise.

**Monetary gold**   Gold in the form of coins.

**Monetary management**   See monetary policy.

**Monetary policy**   Measures taken by a national government to control the supply of money in the economy, the level of interest rates and (before the era of floating) the exchange rate. A relaxation of monetary policy implies an expansion of the money supply, lower interest rates and a lower exchange rate; a tightening of monetary policy implies the opposite. Monetary policy is one of the two main economic tools in the hands of government (the other is fiscal policy), which can be used to affect the level of economic activity and inflation.

**Monetary squeeze**   See credit squeeze.

**Money supply**   The total sum of cash (banknotes and coins) in circulation in a national economy, plus bank current accounts, bank deposit accounts, and other deposit or interest-bearing accounts in the economy.

**Most favoured nation**   A term used in international trade agreements whereby each party agrees to extend to the other any favourable trading terms it subsequently offers to third or further parties.

**Multilateral**   Between three or more parties. A multilateral trade agreement is one between three or more countries. Multilateral trade is trade between three or more countries. See also bilateral.

**National income**   The sum of all incomes received by residents in a national economy over a specified period of time after deductions have been made for replacing capital used up in the process of production (that is, for depreciation). National income is the same as net national product at factor cost. National income before deductions for depreciation is the same as gross national product.

**Net exports**   Value of exports minus imports; that is, the same as the balance of trade.

**Net income from abroad**   The differences between receipts and payments on account of foreign investment and investment by foreigners in the current account of the balance of payments.

**Net services**   The different between the value of exports of services and the value of imports of services in the balance of payments.

**Non-tradeable**   Goods and services that cannot be bought or sold on international markets. Non-tradeables are goods and services that are consumed entirely domestically and are not available for purchase by or from foreigners. Non-tradeables are often services, though some goods (for example, perishables) can also be non-tradeable. Tradeables are goods that are subject to international trade and competition. They consist of exports, imports, goods that are produced and consumed domestically but that could be exported, and goods that are produced domestically and that compete against imports. The impact of 'globalisation' at the end of the twentieth century tended to reduce the share of non-tradeables in the Australian economy.

**Oligopoly**   A market where a small number of producers account for all or most of production.

**Open economy**   An economy where foreign trade is a large proportion (say over 20 per cent) of gross domestic product. Such an economy will be affected by changes in international trade to a greater extent than a less open one. Openness can also refer to the share of tradeables in the economy – the higher the share the more open the economy.

**Overvalued currency**   See undervalued currency.

**Participation rate**   The proportion of the population of working age that is gainfully employed or actively seeking paid employment.

**Per capita income**   See income per head.

**Portfolio foreign investment**   The acquisition by residents in one country of assets such as stocks, shares and bonds in another country.

**Price freeze**   A policy aimed at combating inflation by preventing all price rises within the economy for a certain period.

**Primary commodities**   See primary products.

**Primary exports**   Exports of primary produce.

**Primary production**   Foodstuffs and raw materials (agricultural and mineral). A country that is described as being a 'primary producer' or 'primary producing country' is one that specialises in the production (and usually export) of primary produce.

**Producers' goods**   See capital goods.

**Productivity**   Productivity refers to the output of goods and services in relation to inputs of factors of production. See labour productivity.

**Protectionism**   A policy aimed at protecting domestic producers from competition from imports.

**Quantum index**   An index of international trade measured in constant prices; movements in the index reflect changes in the volume of international trade.

**Quotas**   See import restrictions.

**Real terms**   The money value of a variable after allowance has been made for price changes. The variables most commonly expressed in real terms include: production of goods and services (real GDP), incomes and wages, and interest rates. For example, the real interest rate is the nominal interest rate minus the expected (or actual) rate of inflation. The real wage is the money wage adjusted for the rate of inflation. Measuring in real terms is also referred to as measuring at constant prices.

**Recession**   A slow-down in the growth of real GDP to levels approaching or reaching zero. Although 'recession' is not a precise term, it is sometimes defined as occurring when real GDP falls in two successive quarters.

**Reflation**   A policy to stimulate economic activity (that is, to increase aggregate demand) leading to a rise in the general price level and a fall in the level of unemployment.

**Rent-seeking behaviour**   Where an individual or firm attempts to increase its share of output or income rather than to attempt to increase total output or income. In general usage it refers to selfish behaviour that seeks to improve one's own position at the expense of the position of others.

**Reserve currency**   See international currency.

**Reserve multiplier**   The cumulative effect within an economy of a fall in investment or expenditure in a substantial sector or activity.

**Reserves**   See gold and foreign exchange reserves.

**Revalue**   See devaluation.

**Saving**   Income that has not been spent on consumption. All income is either consumed or saved. If expenditure exceeds income it is called dissaving. In the public sector, saving occurs if the government collects more in tax revenues than it expends on goods and services, transfer payments and subsidies. Companies save when they do not distribute all of their profits to shareholders.

**Saving rate/ratio**   The proportion of income that is saved.

**Short term**   One year or less.

**Slump**   A severe and prolonged economic depression. There has only been one international slump in the twentieth century (1929–34), but Australia's experience in the early 1890s could be termed a slump. Colloquially, a recession might be called a slump.

**Specie**   Coin or bullion.

**Squeeze**   See credit squeeze.

**Stagflation**   The co-existence of high rates of unemployment, low or negative rates of real economic growth and high rates of inflation.

**Structural unemployment**   See unemployment.

**Subsidies**   Government payments to suppliers of goods and services, usually intended to keep the price of the good or service down, or to keep the income of the producer up, or to maintain the level of employment in a particular firm or industry, or all three.

**Surplus nation**   A nation whose balance of payments current account is in surplus.

**Tariffs**   Customs duties charged on imported goods. The level, incidence and nature of such charges make up tariff policy. Since these charges make imported goods more expensive to consumers, tariffs are a major form of import protection. However, customs duties may be designed to raise revenue rather than protect domestic producers by being set at a low level or imposed on goods that are not produced domestically, or both. Nonetheless, even these so-called 'revenue tariffs' have some protective effect.

**Terms of trade**   A measure of the relationship between the price of exports of merchandise and the price of imports of merchandise. The terms of trade are calculated by dividing the price index of exports by the price index of imports (using the same base year) and multiplying by 100. If the index rises the terms of trade are said to be improving or becoming more favourable; when the index falls, the terms of trade are said to be moving adversely or unfavourably. Favourable terms of trade imply that a country can purchase more imports with a given volume of exports; unfavourable terms of trade imply the opposite. Terms of trade in this sense are also known as the net barter terms of commodity trade.

**Tradeable**   See non-tradeable.

**Trade balance**   The difference between the value of exports and the value of imports.

**Trade cycle**   More or less regular fluctuations in economic activity in a national economy. When the trade cycle is moving from its peak to its trough, economic activity slows, unemployment rises and prices fall (or grow less quickly); when moving from its trough to its peak, economic activity increases, unemployment falls, wages and prices rise. In the nineteenth century the duration of the cycle (peak to peak) was about 7 to 8 years. Trade cycles became less easy to discern in the twentieth century, and after World War II government intervention in the economy was directed towards evening out peaks and troughs in order to obtain steadier economic growth.

**Trade schedule**   See trade balance.

**Trade surplus**   A situation where the value of exports exceeds the value of imports in a specified period. The opposite is a trade deficit.

**Traditional income**   The goods and services available within an Aboriginal economy before European contact.

**Transfer payments**   Payments made not in return for services rendered; for example, old-age pensions and unemployment benefits.

**Transfer problems**   The problems a debtor nation has in earning sufficient gold or foreign exchange through exporting goods and services in order to service its foreign debt; that is, to make payments to the creditor nation. If the creditor nation imposes restrictions on imports from its debtors – as did the United States in the 1930s – this will make the transfer problem more difficult.

**Transfers**   See unrequited transfers.

**Undervalued currency**   A currency whose official exchange rate is below its free market rate. Under the Bretton Woods system this would occur to currencies of countries where the rate of inflation was lower than that prevailing in its main trading partners. Undervaluation can be corrected by a revaluation of the official rate of exchange. An undervalued currency will tend to encourage exports and discourage imports, and contribute to a balance of payments surplus. An overvalued currency has the opposite effects.

**Unemployment**   The state of actively looking for but being unable to find paid employment. Unemployment is measured as the proportion of the labour force out of work and actively seeking gainful employment (the 'unemployment rate'). Structural unemployment arises when the structure of the economy changes causing some industries to decline permanently. Cyclical unemployment refers to unemployment caused by an inadequate level of aggregate demand to support full employment. Full employment is a situation where only voluntary (or 'frictional') unemployment exists; it implies that the economy is operating at full capacity, and is sometimes defined as occurring when the unemployment rate is less than 2.5 per cent.

**Unemployment rate**    See unemployment.

**Unrequited transfers**    Transfers of funds abroad for which there is no reciprocal inflow. Official transfers consist mainly of foreign aid payments by governments. Unofficial or residential overseas transfers are gifts of money between individuals; for example, immigrants may send money back to relatives in their country of origin.

**Visible trade**    Imports and exports of merchandise.

**Wage freeze**    A policy designed to prevent all wage increases in an economy during a specified period.

**Wages policy**    Measures adopted by a government to influence wage outcomes in the economy. These measures may be formal ('wage-fixing') or informal. They may involve the targeting of particular groups of wage-earners; for example, measures to raise the relative wages of female employees.

**Work force**    See labour force.

# INDEX